Company Valuation Under IFRS

Third edition

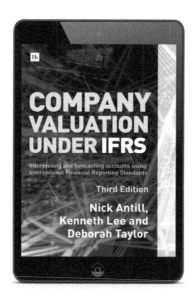

Company Valuation Under IFRS:
Interpreting and forecasting accounts using International Financial Reporting Standards

Third edition

Nick Antill, Kenneth Lee and Deborah Taylor

Hh

HARRIMAN HOUSE LTD
3 Viceroy Court
Bedford Road
Petersfield
Hampshire
GU32 3LJ
GREAT BRITAIN

Tel: +44 (0)1730 233870
Email: enquiries@harriman-house.com
Website: www.harriman-house.com

First published in Great Britain in 2005
This third edition published 2020
Copyright © Nick Antill, Kenneth Lee and Deborah Taylor

The right of Nick Antill, Kenneth Lee and Deborah Taylor to be identified as the authors has
been asserted in accordance with the Copyright, Design and Patents Act 1988.

Hardback ISBN: 978-0-85719-776-4
eBook ISBN: 978-0-85719-777-1

British Library Cataloguing in Publication Data

A CIP catalogue record for this book can be obtained from the British Library.

Contents

About the Authors

Nick Antill

After graduating in economics and politics, Nick began his career in the oil industry, working for BP and Saudi Aramco. He subsequently spent 16 years in the City of London as an equity investment analyst specialising in European energy companies, and finishing as head of Morgan Stanley's European oil and gas equity research team. Since 2000, he has been a director of an energy consultancy company, provided financial training mainly to investment bankers and has been retained as a consultant by the European equity research departments of two major investment banks. He has authored numerous articles, and a previous book (with Robert Arnott) entitled *Valuing Oil and Gas Companies* (Woodhead Publishing Ltd, 1994 and 2000).

Kenneth Lee

Kenneth's career has steadfastly remained centred around finance, research and education. Kenneth is an Associate Professorial Lecturer at the London School of Economics and Political Science, where he lectures on financial analysis and equity valuation, as well as being the programme director for the MSc Accounting and Finance and MSc Accounting, Organisations and Institutions.

Before academia Kenneth was a Managing Director and Head of European Equity Research at Barclays Capital, where he worked for eight years before leaving in August 2017 to take up a number of academic positions. Prior to this he was also a Managing Director and a ranked accounting and valuation analyst at Citi Investment Research in London. During this time Kenneth published extensively on accounting and valuation topics for investors and was ranked in the top three in the Institutional Investor Survey over more than a continuous ten-year period.

In the lead up to his investment banking career, Ken was a professional trainer for many years both in professional practice and financial markets. This love of training was behind his decision to leave his banking career for academia.

Kenneth graduated from Trinity College Dublin/Dublin Institute of Technology with a degree in Management Science. He is a Fellow of the Institute of Chartered Accountants, a member of the Institute of Taxation, a CFA Charterholder and a member of the Securities Institute. He holds a doctorate from Aston University on how sell-side analysts make stock recommendation decisions.

In addition to co-authoring *Company Valuation Under IFRS*, Ken has also co-authored an accounting book (with Deborah Taylor) entitled *Financial Statement Analysis Under IFRS* (Financial Edge, 2018).

Deborah Taylor

Deborah works as a professional trainer at Financial Edge, where she provides accounting, modelling and valuation training to investment banks.

Deborah's move into professional training was relatively recent, having worked at Barclays until May 2019, where she was a Director in Equity Research and co-head of Sustainable and Thematic Investing. Deborah spent eight years at Barclays, focussing on accounting and valuation research whilst working with her co-author Kenneth, and where they were one of the top ranked teams in their sector. In the later years, Deborah had broadened her remit to include research on corporate governance issues, including corporate taxation and regulation.

Deborah is a Chartered Accountant, having qualified at Deloitte where she worked in the Financial Services audit division. Prior to training as an accountant, she graduated from the Queen's College, Oxford University with a Master's degree in Physics. She is also co-author of the book *Financial Statement Analysis Under IFRS* (Financial Edge, 2018).

Preface to the Third Edition

Much as it pains the original authors to admit, it is over 15 years since the first edition of this book was published. In the preface to that edition we retold the infamous story of an analyst who had recommended an equity, in part on the basis of a discounted cash flow valuation. It subsequently transpired that capital expenditures had been mistakenly added to the stream of cash that was being discounted, rather than deducted. The firm responded promptly with a second piece of research on the same equity. It acknowledged the mistake in its previous research, which it had corrected in the second. The new research also contained a number of other adjustments to its forecasts for the company concerned. And the result? The 'target price' for the share concerned had increased, not decreased!

The purpose of recounting the story is to emphasise that the apparent sophistication of valuation methodologies is mostly illusory. In this case, despite a significant and basic error, other levers could be used to eliminate the valuation deficiency and restore the target price, despite the correction of the error. The truth is that at the heart of all but the simplest approaches to valuation are subjective judgements about a range of material inputs. The only way to ensure that valuation models are robust is to be as rigorous as possible with the underlying analysis. In this text we suggest that, along with proven, professional modelling methods, detailed financial statement analysis is key to this.

We consider accounting as the central information set for valuation. Over the years one of the most common, and depressing, statements we have heard is:

"It does not matter – it is only a non-cash item."

What matters is not just that this proposition is completely false, it is also that it is symptomatic of an approach to the analysis, and valuation, of companies that is entirely misguided. It is generally based on the idea that if it is true that the value of a company is the net present value of the discounted stream of cash flow that it will generate between now and infinity, why should we care about anything other than cash flows. This misses the point that, in order to capture these future streams of cash flows, we need to use financial statement information. Why? First, the information set we are presented with in a set of financial statements is hugely detailed, whereas there is very limited cash flow disclosure. Secondly, accrued benefits and costs are clearly relevant to these future cash streams and so we want to extract these from the financial statements. It turns out that forecasting earnings first, and subsequently converting this to free cash flow, is a much more effective valuation process than forecasting cash flows directly.

The authors believe that while cash flow is certainly a member of the royal family, it is profit that is the king!

This is not to deny that measures of profit during any particular period will be dependent on the accounting conventions used by the company, or even that they are malleable. Accounting under IFRS or US GAAP is complex and involves judgements. However, over recent years the closure of loopholes in accounting, coupled with increased levels of disclosure and international alignment of rules, provide users with a powerful suite of accounting tools.

Sophisticated interpretation of accounts is a critical skill to develop. This text seeks to link the practice and theory of valuation with the information that can be gleaned from accounting analysis. The two together present valuers with the best chance of success. Therefore, we firmly reject the idea that an appropriate response is to declare accounting profits irrelevant, and to revert to a simple reliance on cash flows as the central tool for valuation. Cash flow analysis has its place, but not through turning away from accounting information.

1. How the book is structured

The book is set out in eight chapters.

Chapter One

The first chapter states the main thesis, which is that it is in effect impossible to value a company without reference to profit and capital employed. Attempts to avoid this simply result in implicit assumptions, often foolish ones, replacing explicit assumptions irrespective of how flawed the latter may be. In addition, it argues that far from being unimportant, accruals represent key information about value, whether or not it is represented in the framework of a Discounted Cash Flow (DCF) model.

Chapter Two

Chapter two attempts to explode another myth, that the cost of capital for a company is an unambiguous figure, and that it is stable. Neither is the case. We show how the traditional Weighted Average Cost of Capital (WACC) can be reconciled with a more transparent approach based on Adjusted Present Value (APV), and argue that the traditional framework within which practitioners operate has at its core an assumption about the value of tax shelters. Our approach supports the view that there has been a systematic overvaluation of the benefits from leverage. In addition, there is an ambiguity at the heart of the treatment of debt in the standard Capital Asset Pricing Model (CAPM). Different interpretation of the risk premium on corporate debt results in very different estimates for WACC, and for the value of the enterprise.

In addition to creating tax shelters, leverage also creates option value for shareholders, and this is systematically missed in intrinsic value models of companies. It can only be captured systematically as a transfer of option value from the bond-holder to the shareholder. Chapter two closes with a discussion of the application of real options theory, relating a discussion of whether or not the risk premium on debt is market risk or specific risk to the correct use of these models as applied to capital arbitrage (the trading of alternative capital instruments issued by the same company).

Chapter Three

Economists talk about Net Present Value (NPV) and Internal Rate of Return (IRR). Investors talk about Returns on Capital Employed (ROCE). But a company's accounting return on capital employed is not the same as the internal rate of return that it earns on its assets. There are several ways of attempting to address this problem, none wholly satisfactory. What they tell us is that depreciation charges are not necessarily equivalent to impairment of value, and that the capitalisation and depreciation of fixed assets is a key component of the way in which accounts can influence perceptions of valuation. Chapter three explains the problem, and looks in some detail at one proposed panacea, Cash Flow Return On Investment (CFROI). This is shown to be a rearrangement of the standard discounted cash flow methodology, with potential advantages in the case of capital intensive companies with long asset lives.

Although relatively short, the first three chapters provide the theoretical framework for what follows, which comprises a discussion of accounting issues and then their applications to valuation models.

Chapter Four

Chapter four explores accounting issues and how they impact valuation. Instead of concentrating on accounting standards, it concentrates on what investors need to know, and the ways in which accounts do, or do not, provide them with the information that they need. In this, the longest section of the book, the authors address key accounting issues from two approaches: the latest changes in proposed accounting treatment, and the implications for market valuation of companies. These include topical areas such as leasing, revenue recognition, pension accounting, accounting for derivatives and off balance sheet finance.

Chapter Five

The fifth chapter begins by taking the theoretical and the accounting points discussed in the first four chapters and discussing their application to the forecasting and valuation of a company. It turns out that a large part of the problem relating to the latter task concerns treatment of the terminal value of the company, which relates to what happens after the explicit forecast period.

If an industry is exceptionally profitable, capital will flood it. If it is hopelessly unprofitable, retrenchment follows. And, in the long run, no company grows faster than nominal Gross Domestic Product (GDP), or, in the end, it takes over the world. So, we would expect company returns on capital to regress to their cost of capital, and their growth rates to ultimately fall to below nominal GDP growth rates. Does this happen? Well, yes and no. This debate takes us to the heart of definitions regarding what constitutes capital and what constitutes an operating cost. Chapter five demonstrates that one of the problems with valuing companies is a direct result of the fact that much of what would ideally be capitalised is not. If it were then the task of monitoring performance and deriving market values would be much easier.

After a full discussion of a stable, mature company, the chapter concludes with suggested treatment for companies that are expected to have a significant change to their balance sheet structure, are cyclical, are asset light, or are growth stocks. Each presents its own problems.

Chapter Six

Accounts were designed by bankers, and the system of double entry reflects this history. But most reports and accounts are prepared by industrial companies. Accounting conventions largely reflect the problem of reporting the performance of a business that utilises fixed assets to add value to raw materials, and which is mainly financed by a combination of debt and equity. But there are large parts of the equity market that do not fit this model well, for one reason or another. Chapter six addresses the techniques required to interpret the accounts of, and to value, companies in areas such as banking, insurance, mineral extraction, regulated utility and technology industries, where particular treatments are needed and where in some cases accounting rules are very specific to the industry.

Chapter Seven

In chapter seven we address the modelling and valuation of mergers and acquisitions. It includes consideration of the treatment of goodwill and how it might be interpreted as we explore the value added or subtracted by the merger.

Chapter Eight

The final section of the book is entitled 'Conclusions and continuations'. As mentioned in the preface one of the important conclusions is that far from cash, it is profit that is of prime importance to valuation and to understanding a company's value. It is profit and balance sheets that are required, not simple streams of cash. That there will always be disagreements about what to put into the income statement and balance sheets, for the past as well as for the future, is what the makes the subject of investment endlessly fascinating.

2. Supporting website

The website supporting this book and containing all of the more important models used in the text can be found at:

www.harriman-house.com/ifrs

3. Acknowledgement

Putting together a detailed technical text is a major undertaking. We could not have achieved this without the support of the excellent publication team at Harriman House. In particular our sincere thanks to Craig Pearce and Emma Tinker for their support, patience and advice throughout the process.

Chapter One

It's Not Just Cash; Accounts Matter

1. Introduction – Valuation refresher

The key valuation technology that underpins the views expressed in this text is based around the importance of financial statements as a foundation for sensible and accurate valuations. Before exploring this further let us refresh some core ideas about equity valuation.

Valuation language is based around financial ratios

Open any financial website or the financial section of a newspaper, and somewhere you will be confronted by tables of share prices, accompanied by at least two ratios: Price/Earnings (P/E) and dividend yield. P/E is a measure of the share price divided by the last year's earnings. Dividend yield is the dividend paid by the company during the past twelve months, divided by the share price. The first is a measure of payback period: how many years is it before I earn my money back? The second is a measure of income yield: what am I going to receive in income on a pound or euro invested?

There is a third ratio in the triumvirate which is rarely shown, though, ironically, academic testing shows that it has the highest explanatory value in predicting future share price movements. This is the ratio of Price/Book (P/B) which is the ratio of the share price divided by the per share value of shareholders' equity in the balance sheet. This tells me what premium I am paying over the amount that has been invested in the business in subscriptions to equity capital and in retained earnings.

The three ratios are clearly related. To the extent that companies retain earnings, rather than paying them out, they increase the book value of their equity. Moreover, the same considerations will determine whether I am prepared to buy a share on a high P/E ratio, a low dividend yield or a high P/B ratio. In each case I should be happier to pay more for a company that looks safe, is highly profitable, or grows faster than others.

True returns: the IRR and NPV rule

When companies make investment decisions, they go beyond simple calculations of payback. More sophisticated approaches include calculating the Internal Rate of Return (IRR) on the investment, or using a required discount rate to calculate a Present Value (PV), from which the investment cost can be deducted to derive a Net Present Value (NPV). If the latter is positive, invest: if not, do not invest.

The same consideration applies to shares. We can move beyond simple multiples to derive present values, and much of this book is concerned with interpreting accounts and building models that do this accurately. But it should not be forgotten that just as there is usually a relationship between payback periods and IRRs (fast payback usually goes with a high IRR) so there is usually a relationship between simple share price ratios, so long as they are sensibly interpreted, and the results of a more sophisticated valuation model.

Valuation models: sophistication versus simplicity

In extreme simplifying cases (where the stream of cash flow is flat, or grows steadily in perpetuity) the output of a sophisticated valuation model and the application of a simple ratio will both give the same answer. It is only when the cash flows are unstable that we benefit from a more detailed approach. This is as true for companies as it is for projects.

Enterprise value rather than equity

When valuing shares there are two basic approaches: value the equity directly or value the business (debt plus equity), and then deduct the debt component to leave the equity value. The key advantage of using the latter route is that it separates the valuation of a business from the issue of how it is financed. It also involves using cleaner accounting numbers. The ratios mentioned so far (P/E, P/B and dividend yield) relate purely to equity, but similar versions are often also constructed for Enterprise Valuations (e.g., EV/invested capital or EV/NOPAT [Net Operating Profit after Tax]). An EV approach is often more intuitive than attempting to value equity directly. For example, in valuing your house, the sensible approach would be to value it on the basis of the rental yield that it would generate, and then subtract the mortgage, rather than to think in terms of cash flows net of interest payments. In practice, nobody would do the latter for a house, so why do so for a company?

Economic profit differs from accounting profit

Accounting profit is determined by accounting rules and embraces fundamental accounting concepts such as accruals, which allocates expenses and income to the periods to which those items relate. Although we find concepts such as accruals appealing, accounting profit does omit one cost: a charge for equity capital. This is where economic profit plays a role. Economic profit starts with accounting profit and then subtracts a charge for equity capital. The remaining balance after this deduction is termed 'economic profit', 'residual income' or 'abnormal earnings'. We shall explore how useful this concept is later on in the text.

The problems of cash flow

A final point. Readers may have seen reference to another group of ratios. These relate not to book capital, or to earnings, or to income, but to cash flow from operations. One of the aims of this book will be to encourage readers to use these figures (cash earnings per share, EBITDA to enterprise value) with extreme caution. Firstly, they rarely measure a real cash number. Secondly, to the extent that they do, they do not represent a sustainable stream, as they precede the investments that a company must make to survive. In pure form, they can only help to provide liquidation values, not going concern values.

Reconciling multiples with present values

Much of the above will (we hope) be clearer by the end of this chapter. At first sight, the formulae that we shall be using may not seem to bear much resemblance to the familiar P/Es and yields from the daily newspaper. But we hope that our readers will be reassured, by the end of this chapter, that the resemblance is very close indeed, and that there are good reasons for proceeding with the slightly more sophisticated approaches.

Actually, we have taken the precaution of relegating all mathematical proofs to a Mathematical Appendix. Those who are interested will find all that they need to derive their valuations formally, but this is by no means essential. From the authors' experience, while most practitioners constantly use the ideas of this chapter, only a tiny proportion of them could explain why they work! Our aim is to provide all readers with the tools to model and value companies properly, and to make the supporting theory available to those who are interested.

2. Distributions, returns and growth

Many books on valuation have been written in order to propound the virtues of one mechanical approach as against another. So the devotees of DCF, EVA™ (a branded acronym for Economic Value Added), CFROI, dividend discounting and residual income all battle it out. We shall explain all of these variants on intrinsic valuation as the book progresses, but our concerns are a little different. We shall have something to say about which approaches we regard as more desirable in practice, to address specific types of company. However, one point should be made right at the start. Correctly handled, the main valuation methodologies should all generate the same result for any one company, whether or not it is cash or economic profit that is discounted, or whether the streams are to capital or to equity.

What matters far more than the mechanics of how to translate a forecast into a valuation is where the assumptions that feed the forecasts come from, and the interplay between interpretation of historical accounts and forecasting of prospective ones. These connections are, we believe, often systematically ignored or even misunderstood.

Let us begin by keeping the picture simple. Take a company that has no debt in its balance sheet. Every year, it generates (we hope) some profit. Profit is calculated after deductions not only for cash costs, such as Cost of Goods Sold (COGS), employment costs, taxation, and so on, but also after a provision for the deterioration of the fixed assets that will one day have to be replaced. This provision is known as depreciation. So, in our very simple example, cash flow into the company is the sum of net profit and depreciation. Cash out takes the form of capital expenditure, increase in working capital (inventory and receivables, less payables), and dividends to the shareholders.

Furthermore let us assume that the company is going to run with no debt and no cash in the balance sheet. So dividends each year must equal the cash flow after capital expenditure and change in working capital (free cash flow). Exhibit 1.1 illustrates the profit and loss account, cash flow statement, and balance sheets for Constant company over its first five forecast years.

Exhibit 1.1: Constant growth company accounts

Profit and loss account year	0	1	2	3	4	5
Profit and loss account						
Sales		1,000	1,050	1,103	1,158	1,216
Operating costs		(750)	(788)	(827)	(868)	(912)
Profit		250	263	276	289	304
Tax		(100)	(105)	(110)	(116)	(122)
Earnings		150	158	165	174	182
Balance sheet						
Year	0	1	2	3	4	5
Balance sheet						
Fixed assets	1,000	1,060	1,123	1,189	1,259	1,332
Working capital	500	515	531	547	565	583
Total assets	1,500	1,575	1,654	1,736	1,823	1,914
Equity	1,500	1,575	1,654	1,736	1,823	1,914
Cash flow						
Year	0	1	2	3	4	5
Cash flow						
Earnings		150	158	165	174	182
Depreciation		100	106	112	119	126
Cash flow from operations		250	264	278	293	308
Capital expenditure		(160)	(169)	(178)	(188)	(199)
Change in working capital		(15)	(16)	(17)	(17)	(18)
Dividend (=free cash flow)		(75)	(79)	(83)	(87)	(91)
Net cash flow		0	0	0	0	0

Now, suppose that we know what is an appropriate discount rate to apply to the dividend (free cash flow) stream that we expect to receive from our company. We can use the standard discounting formula to convert all the future cash flows into present values, as follows:

$$PV = CF_t / (1+k)^t$$

where PV is the present value of a cash flow in year t (CF_t) discounted at a cost of equity (k).

Companies are not generally expected to be wound up at any particular date in the future. So, unlike the situation with a bond, we are discounting a stream that continues to infinity. This is one of the particular problems of valuing equities, the other being that even the medium term cash flows are uncertain. So unless we want to use an infinitely large spreadsheet, somewhere we have to call a halt, and assume that from that point onward the company will grow at a constant speed. This could be negative, or zero, or positive, but is generally taken to be positive.

So how do we calculate a present value for a stream that is going to grow to infinity? Exhibit 1.2 illustrates the problem.

Exhibit 1.2: Nominal dividend projection

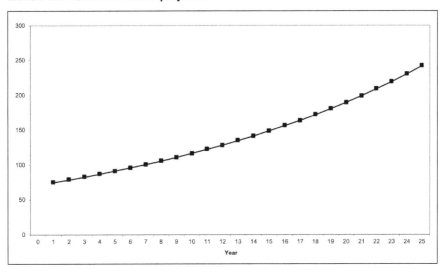

Our problem is that each of the forecast items is getting bigger. But there is solution. So long as our discount rate is larger than our growth rate, by the time that the stream of dividend has been discounted to present values, instead of expanding, it contracts. The same stream of dividend is illustrated in the form of present values in exhibit 1.3.

Exhibit 1.3: Discounted dividend projection

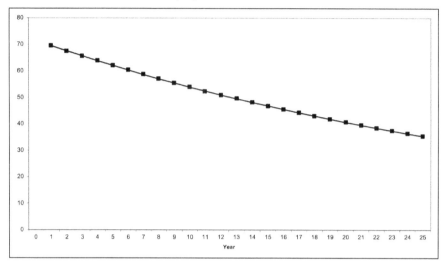

So now all the projections are getting smaller, and as we add them up, they become progressively less significant to the answer. It is now intuitively plausible that there should be a simple formula that would tell us what the sum of all these present values tends towards, as the stream of dividends gets longer and longer, and there is indeed such a formula. It is known as the Gordon Growth model, and it is as follows:

$$V = D*(1+g)/(k-g)$$

where V is the value now, D is last year's dividend, g is the growth rate, and k is the discount rate. Clearly, it will only yield a sensible result if the discount rate is bigger than the growth rate (k>g). (A proof of the Gordon Growth model is provided in the Appendix.) As the Gordon Growth model is a general formula for valuing perpetuities with a flat compound rate of growth, it applies equally whether we are valuing a stream of dividend or a stream of cash flow from operations.

So that is all that we need to do to value a company, then. We project our financial items for a few years, and then assume a constant growth rate at a sensible level, and convert our stream of dividends after the final explicit forecast into a so-called terminal value. If we add together the present value of the next few dividends and the present value of the terminal value (because it is a value at the end of the forecast period, and we want to bring it back to today's date), then we get the value, now, of the equity in the company. And that is it.

Exhibit 1.4 shows a valuation of Simple Co., which pays dividends that rise from 5.0 to 9.0 over the next five years (clearly not a constant compound rate) and then grow at 5% compound from a base level of 10.0 in year 6. Because year 6 is being used as a base to value all the dividends that include and follow it, it is often referred to as the 'terminus'. Along with the discount rate of 10%, if we apply the Gordon Growth model to it we arrive at a future value of the terminal value of 200.0. That is to say that a share in Simple Co. will be worth 200.0 in five years' time. We want a value now. So we need five factors by which to discount the individual dividends and the terminal value. The standard formula for discounting a value is:

$$PV = FV / (1+k)^n$$

where PV=present value, FV=future value, k=discount rate and n=number of years.

Notice that the terminus is discounted for five years, not six. This is despite the fact that it is based on a year 6 dividend. The reason is that the Gordon Growth model has as its first term the cash item that you expect to receive in one year's time. So a stream which begins in year 6 is capitalised as a value in year 5, and we then have to bring it back to now by discounting it back another five years.

Exhibit 1.4: Simple Co. dividend discount model

Simple Co. year	1	2	3	4	5	Terminus
Discount rate	10%					
Growth in terminus	5%					
Dividend	5.0	6.0	7.0	8.0	9.0	10.0
Discount factor	0.9091	0.8264	0.7513	0.6830	0.6209	0.6209
FV terminal value						200.0
Discounted dividend	4.5	5.0	5.3	5.5	5.6	124.2
Value per share	150.0					

Sadly, for the vast majority of valuation models currently in use in banks, investment institutions and companies, that is indeed it. Of course they are adjusted to permit companies to be financed both with debt and with equity (a point to which we shall return later) and they accommodate accounts which include goodwill, provisions and other items (often badly – that is another point to which we shall return). But in principle, this is how most of them work, and it is dangerously simplistic.

Let us return to Constant company and change the rate of growth in the terminal value calculation. The resulting effect on value is illustrated in exhibit 1.5.

Exhibit 1.5: Value versus growth

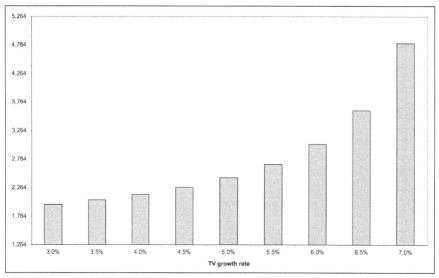

Well, that is impressive! Tiny changes in growth rate are having an increasingly enormous effect on our value. (The first 1,264 of value is coming from the 25 years of forecast dividend, so the columns are illustrating merely the impact of changes in the assumed growth rate after 25 years!) But is this realistic? To answer the question, let us think back to the components of the Gordon Growth model: dividend, growth rate, and discount rate. What we are doing is changing the growth rate and leaving the other two unchanged. Is this plausible? Can we grow at different speeds and still distribute exactly the same amount of dividend? Surely not. If we want to grow faster then we need to retain more of our profits within the company, and reinvest them to grow the business. An extreme case is what happens if we distribute all of our profit, and do not grow at all. So what our first calculation did was to assume that the choices look like those in exhibit 1.6. It assumed that we are free to imagine that the same company could plausibly grow at different growth rates without any change to the amount of its profit that it ploughs back into the business, which is ridiculous.

Exhibit 1.6: Possible cash flows (1)

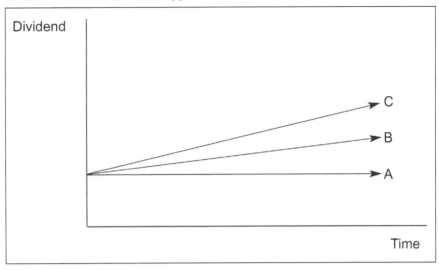

But the reality is that if a company wants to grow faster, it has to reinvest more of its profits. And if it chooses to pay out more of its profit, then the trade-off will be slower growth. So the real choices confronting investors actually look more like the streams of dividend illustrated in exhibit 1.7.

Exhibit 1.7: Possible cash flows (2)

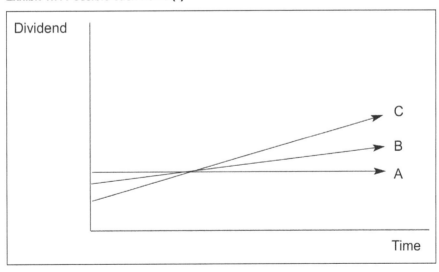

So, there is a trade-off. We can have more cash distributed to us now, but accept that the stream will grow more slowly, or we can take less out of the company now, let it reinvest more, and enjoy a higher rate of growth in our income. What sets the terms of the trade-off? The return that we make on the incremental equity that we are reinvesting.

There is a formula for this (with, again, a proof in the Appendix). This is it:

$$g = b*R$$

where g is growth, b is the proportion of profits that are reinvested in the business, and R is the return that we make on the new equity.

Notice, incidentally, that the return that we make on new equity does not have to be the same as the return that we are making on existing equity. Suppose that we had a wonderful niche business making fantastic returns, luxury shops on ideal sites, for example. It might be that they could continue to produce a very high return for us, on the existing investments. But if we were to invest some of the profits in new sites, perhaps less good ones, then our returns on new equity would be below that on the existing equity. It is the return on the incremental equity that generates the incremental profit.

Usually, we think about this relationship the other way round. Rather than setting the retention ratio and the return, it often makes more sense to set the growth rate and the return, and let the retention ratio be a result. Then:

$$b = g/R$$

The proportion of our profit that we pay out, which is the first item in the stream of cash that we are trying to discount, is (1-b) so our dividend in any one year will be:

$$D = Y*(1-g/R)$$

where Y is earnings.

Substituting this into the Gordon Growth model gives:

$$V = Y*(1-g/R)/(k-g)$$

where V is value, Y is earnings, g is the growth rate, R is return on incremental equity, and k is the discount rate.

Now we have a formula which will value for us streams of cash that look like our more realistic example, in exhibit 1.7. This begs an important question. What happens to our value if we assume that a company has a choice between different levels of reinvestment, and subsequently, of growth?

Let us take a concrete example. Exhibit 1.8 shows a table of resulting values per share based on a set of input assumptions, and then for what happens as we alter either the growth rate or the return on incremental equity. For the base case we shall use a return on equity of 10%, a growth rate of 5%, and a discount rate of 8%. Then we shall flex the input assumptions for the performance of the company. Let us look at the extremes first. If the company pays out all of its profits, and does not grow, then the return on incremental equity is irrelevant because there is none. The value will simply be earnings divided by the discount rate. Now, suppose that the company earns exactly the same return on new investments as the rate at which the market discounts them. Clearly, they can have no impact on its value, and the growth rate becomes irrelevant. New investments, and the earnings growth that results, only matters if the return that the company makes on them is above or below its cost of equity. Growth can be bad. Look at what happens if we push up the growth rate with R<k!

Exhibit 1.8: Company valuation sensitivities

Profit	100
ROE	10.0%
G	5.0%
K	8.0%
Value	**1,667**

		Growth rate				
		4.0%	4.5%	5.0%	5.5%	6.0%
ROE	11.0%	1,591	1,688	1,818	2,000	2,273
	10.0%	1,500	1,571	1,667	1,800	2,000
	9.0%	1,389	1,429	1,481	1,556	1,667
	8.0%	1,250	1,250	1,250	1,250	1,250
	7.0%	1,071	1,020	952	857	714

There are real examples of companies that have driven their share prices down to the point at which they are worth less than they would be if management promised never, ever, to make another incremental investment. Generally, they get taken over in the end. In these days of shareholder activism an alternative is the removal of the management by a group of institutional shareholders.

Let us take some time to review what we have discussed so far in this chapter. Of course the examples have been kept simple. We are looking at constant growth companies, with stable returns on incremental investment. We have kept debt out of the picture. Both of these assumptions can be relaxed. We shall do that in later sections of this book. But what we have already done makes it absolutely clear that it is impossible to value a company without taking views on profitability.

Think again about our simple extrapolation exercise from exhibit 1.6. Knowing what we do now, we can see that there must have been an implicit assumption about returns on equity for each rate of growth. If a company can grow faster while paying out the same amount of dividend and reinvesting the same amount of equity, then it must be making higher and higher returns on the incremental equity. As a small exercise, look at exhibit 1.9. Ask yourself, is it investing too much or too little to produce an assumed growth rate of 5%?

Exhibit 1.9: Growth rate = 5% annually

Profit	–	100
Depreciation	–	50
Cash flow	–	**150**
Capital expenditure	–	(60)
New working capital	–	(10)
Free cash flow	–	**80**

This company has profit of 100. It is reinvesting 20% of its profit and growing at a rate of 5% annually. So its return on incremental equity must be 25%! And the faster the assumed rate of growth, the higher the assumed return must be. No wonder exhibit 1.5 gave us such exciting valuations as we began to increase the assumed growth rate.

The conclusion is that you cannot have a pure cash flow model that does not (at least implicitly) make assumptions about profitability. Implicit assumptions are dangerous. Much better to make them explicit. But where, in the real world, are they going to come from? Clearly, they are likely to be heavily influenced by the company's real historical experiences, and those of its competitors, as represented in their reports and accounts. Which, in turn, means that the numbers in companies' financial statements do matter a lot.

Having committed the heresy of arguing that discounted cash flow models are ultimately dependent on accounts for their assumptions, we shall now go one step further, and argue that valuation should include lots of items that do not reflect cash flow at all, and should exclude lots of items that are real, measurable, cash flow into the company. Put like that it may sound complicated, so let us make it very clear. Accruals matter.

3. Cash, accruals and profits

Imagine a property company which earned a 5% annual rental yield on the market value of its property. In addition, the market value of its existing property portfolio goes up by 5% every year. Meanwhile, its administrative and financing costs also represent 5% of the market value of its portfolio each year.

This is a very simple company to understand. It has zero free cash flow prior to new investments in new properties, and to the extent that it does grow its cash flow is negative. Its value goes up each year to the extent of its new investments, and because of the 5% increase in value of the opening property portfolio.

Now imagine trying to build a discounted cash flow of the company. So long as it was growing, it would have negative cash flow. Once it stopped growing it would have zero cash flow. But the value of its portfolio would be rising at 5% compound, without any new investment. At any stage, it would be possible to turn this accrual into cash. Just liquidate the portfolio and realise the value. What we want is an approach to valuation that recognises the fact that the company has added 5% to the value of its opening portfolio, without this having to be reflected in its cash flows.

What we have in our property company is two forms of accretion of value. The first is a realised cash stream of rental payments. The second is an unrealised increase in property values. To be set against these are the administrative and financing costs, both of which are again streams of cash.

Now let us take a different example. Suppose that we were analysing a power generation company, all of whose plants are nuclear. These might be expected to generate substantial amounts of cash flow most of the time, since the operating cost of a nuclear plant is low. But its decommissioning costs are not. So the accounts of the nuclear power generator may be characterised by a profit that is net of a very large provision for the eventual decommissioning of its plant.

This is the opposite of our property company. Discounting a stream of cash flows growing to infinity on the basis of this company's accounts would give a ridiculously high value to the company, because it would implicitly assume that its power stations would never be decommissioned. So could we solve the problem by taking the provisions that it has built up in its balance sheet and subtracting them from our valuation, as if they were debt? No, because this would only deal with the cost associated with the decommissioning of this generation of power stations. What about the ones that they will build to replace these? After all, we are extrapolating the sales to infinity, so we should also be extrapolating these large, highly irregular, costs to infinity.

This is going to create pretty odd looking discounted cash flow models. In some cases we are going to find ourselves adding into our definition of 'cash flow' things that are not cash items at all, namely, unrealised benefits. Then, in other cases, we are going to subtract from our cash flows items that are also not cash items at all, namely, provisions that represent a real cost to the company.

Note: Now, there is no reason at all why companies cannot be modelled using the framework of a DCF, so long as such adjustments are made. In effect, we exclude cash flow that does not belong to us, and we add back accrued benefits that we have not realised but could in principle have realised.

---

4. The Economic Profit model

This is an appropriate point at which to introduce the main alternative to DCF: the economic profit model. Just as DCF can be applied either to equity (dividend discounting) or to capital (firm free cash flows), so the economic profit model can be applied either to equity (residual income) or to capital (often referred to as EVA™).

Instead of thinking about value as being created by a stream of future cash flows, the economic profit model thinks of value as being balance sheet book value (the depreciated value of an asset) plus or minus a correction for the fact that it earned more or less for us than we expected it to (i.e., a stream of residual income). We shall show you below that the two approaches yield the same result, whether we stick to our simple equity-only constant growth company, or move on to something that looks more like the real world. But the attraction of economic profit models is that because they start with balance sheets and profit they naturally accommodate accruals as having an impact on the valuation. If the value is calculated using profits that are net of a deduction for (say) decommissioning costs, then there is no risk of the valuer forgetting the adjustment for the accrual, as he or she might in the case of the DCF approach discussed above. That said, as we shall see in later chapters, we shall often want to include some accruals and exclude others, so the reality is that whichever valuation is used, thought and care have to go into the process of defining either what constitutes free cash flow or what consititutes profit.

Instead of expressing the Gordon Growth model in terms of income, let us instead express it in terms of shareholders' equity.

$$V = D_1/(k-g)$$

was where we started, where D1 is the prospective dividend.

$$D = B*R*(1-b)$$

where B is book value (shareholders' equity), R is return on equity and b is retention ratio, so the Gordon Growth model can be rewritten as:

$$V = B*R*(1-b)/(k-g)$$

Since, as we have seen, g = b*R,

$$V = B*(R-g)/(k-g)$$

Exhibit 1.10 shows what happens to the Price/Book value of the company as we alter the assumptions for growth rate and the return on equity, and it is similar to the earlier table calculated using the income-based formula. The same comments naturally apply about the relationships between profitability, growth and value. Why are the answers only the same for the row in which return on equity equals 10%? Because in exhibit 1.9 above, we had 1,000 of invested capital earning a 10% return to give a profit of 100, and we flexed the assumed returns on new capital. Here we are assuming that both new and old capital earn the same return. The distinction is crucial (though often ignored in valuation models) and we shall return to it in chapter five.

Exhibit 1.10: Price/book sensitivities

ROE	10.0%
g	5.0%
k	8.0%
Value	**1.67**

		Growth rate				
		4.0%	4.5%	5.0%	5.5%	6.0%
ROE	11.0%	1.75	1.86	2.00	2.20	2.50
	10.0%	1.50	1.57	1.67	1.80	2.00
	9.0%	1.25	1.29	1.33	1.40	1.50
	8.0%	1.00	1.00	1.00	1.00	1.00
	7.0%	0.75	0.71	0.67	0.60	0.50

An insight into this version of valuation can be gleaned by what happens if we set growth at zero. Then the ratio of value to book is simply the ratio of return on equity to cost of equity. So, if we always make a return on equity of 8% and we discount at 8% we shall always be worth our book value. If we make a return of 10% with a discount rate of 8% and do not grow, then our Price/Book value would be 10/8=1.25. Now look at the boxed value in the table for a 10% ROE and a 5% growth rate. The fair value Price/Book ratio is 1.67. This implies that the value that is added by the ability to make new investments which grow the company at 5% annually justifies the difference between a Price/Book ratio of 1.25 and a Price/Book ratio of 1.67.

We shall use both valuation methodologies in the examples given later in this book, but will have to be slightly more sophisticated in separating out the returns achieved by old capital and the returns expected from incremental capital, when we turn to real company examples. The point to grasp here is that there is fundamentally no difference between valuing a company in terms of a stream of dividend income or in terms of a series of earnings and book values.

5. The real world of specific forecasts

Of course, most companies do not conform to the assumption of constant growth. In practice, we are not going to be able to forecast specific numbers to infinity, so what ends up happening is a hybrid of specific forecasts and a so-called terminal value: the future value of the business at the point at which we give up with the specific forecasts and assume that the company becomes a constant growth company. This is conventionally taken to be when it is mature and at a mid-cycle level of margins and profitability. This was how we valued Simple Co. in exhibit 1.4.

We have claimed, but not shown, that our two methodologies will handle a stream of cash flows, or returns, that are different from one another every year. The discounted stream of cash flow to equity can be written as follows:

$$V = \sum D_t / (1+k)^t$$

where $\sum$ represents the sum of series from time t=0 to t=∞. The alternative valuation can be written as:

$$V = B_0 + \sum X_t / (1+k)^t$$

where B_0 is the book value now and X_t is the residual income that the company is expected to earn in year t. X can be written as:

$$X_t = Y_t - B_{t-1}{}^*k$$

which is to say that residual income is earnings (Y) minus a charge for the equity that we were employing in the business at the start of the year.

The challenge is to demonstrate that the two measures of value, the discounted stream of dividend and the opening book value plus the discounted stream of residual income, will always provide the same value, and we provide a proof of this in the Appendix. Intuitively, the connection is that a dividend in any year can be expressed as the earnings achieved minus the growth in book value during the year. Discounting dividends ascribes value to the dividend. Discounting residual income ascribes value to the earnings but then increases the future charges for equity for the extra equity ploughed back into the business. The two must equate to one another.

So it makes no difference whether we discount a stream of cash flow to equity in the form of a conventional dividend discount model, or whether we discount a stream of residual income (the difference between profit and a charge for equity) and then add it to the opening balance sheet equity.

One advantage of the latter is that there is no presumption, if one is thinking in terms of profits rather than dividends, that there is any particular cash flow attached to the calculation. Accrued benefits or charges are intuitively fine within the residual income framework. This is less true for discounted dividend or discounted cash flow models, since it seems highly counter-intuitive to start with a stream of cash and then to deduct part of it and add on unrealised gains. But that is what you have to do if the model is to produce a reasonable valuation. This is why many academics prefer residual income-type models.

6. Introducing debt

We started with a constant growth company which was only financed by equity, and discovered that even that could only be properly analysed with reference to accounting entities such as profits and balance sheets. We then made matters worse by accepting that whatever the form of our model, it would to have to take account of accruals. We then generalised it to relax the constant growth assumption, which made no difference to anything, except that it is not practicable to forecast individual years to infinity. But however far forward we project individual years, that represents no methodological problem, just a practical one.

Now we are going to relax the assumption of no debt (or cash) in the balance sheet. Intuitively, it should make no difference whether we discount cash flows to capital at a cost of capital or cash flows to equity at a cost of equity. Again, we leave the proof to the Appendix, but the point is that:

$$V_E = V_F - V_D$$

where the three values stand for equity, the total firm, and debt, respectively. What we need to know is that it makes no difference whether we value equity directly as:

$$V_E = D*(1+g)/(k-g)$$

or as:

$$V_E = FCF*(1+g)/(WACC-g) - V_D$$

where FCF is last year's free cash flow, and WACC is the weighted average cost of capital.

Free cash flow is calculated as being after a notional taxation rate, which is levied on operating profit, to derive a so-called Net Operating Profit After Taxation (NOPAT). Exhibit 1.11 shows the calculation of NOPAT and free cash flow for a constant growth company partially financed by debt. The same value will be derived, if the calculation is done correctly, whether the company is valued by discounting its free cash flows at the weighted average cost of capital and deducting the value of the debt, or whether its free cash flows to equity are discounted at a cost of equity (as we have done up to this point). (The relationship between the two discount rates will have to await the next chapter. Here it must be taken as read.)

Exhibit 1.11: NOPAT and free cash flow

EBIT	100	
- Notional tax @ 40%	(40)	
= **NOPAT**	**60**	
+ Depreciation	50	
- Capital expenditure	(60)	} Net Investment
- New working capital	(10)	
= **Free cash flow**	**40**	

There are two important points to note in this calculation. The first is that the taxation charge is a notional one, so that the free cash flows are calculated on the presumption that the company is fully equity financed. The cash flows are unleveraged. The second point is that the net of the three items, depreciation, capital expenditure and change in working capital, represents net investment. They are the proportion of NOPAT that is ploughed back into the business and the free cash flow is that which is paid out. For a really unleveraged company, NOPAT equals earnings and free cash flow equals dividend, which is what we assumed in our simplified discussions above.

So we now have four possible ways of valuing a company: using cash flow to equity (dividend discounting); cash flow to capital (DCF); using economic profit to equity (residual income) or economic profit to capital (EVA™). Just as equity can be valued either by discounting free cash or by adjusting its book value for its economic profit, so can capital. And they all give us the same answer, but they all depend on accounts for the forecasts, They must all be adjusted to take account of accruals. It is absolutely not true that discounting cash flows releases us from either obligation.

To spell this out, the only non-cash charge that is not included in the numerator of our valuation model is depreciation of tangible assets or amortisation of intangible ones. In a DCF model, cash flow is NOPAT (including accruals) less net investment (capital expenditure and change in working capital minus depreciation and amortisation). In an economic profit model, NOPAT again includes accruals. Capital, from which the charge for capital is derived, grows with capital expenditure and change in working capital and is reduced by depreciation. So all non-cash items other than depreciation should be reflected in the stream of cash flow, or profit, that is being discounted, or they will end up being ignored. The only difference between the two models is that in a DCF depreciation is a source of cash, and in an economic profit model it reduces future capital charges.

Chapter Two

WACC – Sixty Years On

Introduction to CAPM

1. What do risk and return mean in the financial sense?

2. How do investors trade them off against one another?

3. Are assets assessed individually, or as parts of portfolios, and why does this matter?

4. How can we quantify the appropriate discount rate to apply to the cash flows of an asset?

5. Companies are financed by a combination of debt and equity, so how does shifting the balance between them affect the discount rate that an efficient market will apply to its cash flows?

Miller and Modigliani addressed the fifth question. The answers to the first four questions lead us to the Capital Asset Pricing Model (CAPM). The development of this branch of investment theory is associated with Markowitz, Treyner, Sharpe, Mossin and Lintner.

1. Risk and return

Exhibit 2.1 describes the risk and return characteristics of three different assets: a government bond, a share in a large company, and a receipt for a bet placed on a horse-race. That the three assets represent risk-taking of increasing proportions is not hard to understand. What may be less clear is why the return promised by the third asset is negative, and not positive.

In financial terms, return is the mean (arithmetic average) expected return to be derived from an asset, taking into account all of the possible outcomes and weighting them by their probabilities. It is possible that a bet on an outsider to win will generate a high return to the gambler, but it is improbable. Bookies make money by setting the odds so that they are highly likely to pay out less in prizes than they take in stakes. In other terms, the expected return on a bet on a horse is negative, as will be familiar to most who have enjoyed an afternoon at the races.

Exhibit 2.1: Risks and returns

The Third Item is NOT Recommended

- Government Bond
- Large Cap Equity
- 2.20 at Kempton Park

- Low return, low risk
- Medium return, medium risk
- *Negative* return, high risk

If by return we imply the mean expected return from holding the asset, how can we quantify risk? It is generally taken to be defined in terms of the dispersion of the range of possible outcomes. If the outcome is known, or known within a very narrow range, then the investment is low risk. If the outcome is highly uncertain, then this means that the investment is high risk. The probability distribution of all the possible outcomes from two investments are illustrated in exhibit 2.2.

The continuous curve illustrates all of the possible outcomes for an investment with a mean expected return of 9%, with a standard deviation (measure of dispersion of outcomes) of 1%, and the dotted curve illustrates all the possible outcomes for an investment with a mean expected outcome of 11% and a standard deviation of 2%.

Exhibit 2.2: Probability distributions of returns

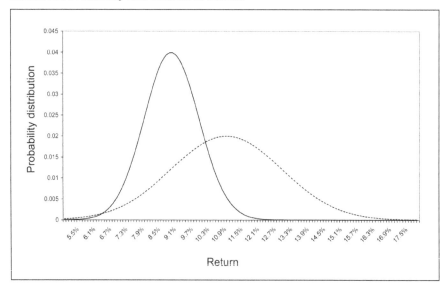

The curves have been drawn assuming that the appropriate probability distribution for the two assets is normal (a bell-shaped curve). This cannot necessarily be assumed to be the case. It is certainly not the case for the bet at the horse race, for which there are only two outcomes: a small probability of a high return if the horse wins, or a high probability of the loss of the stake (100% loss) if the horse does not win. The assumption that expected returns are normally distributed holds good for assets in which the returns are composed of compounding small positive or negative increments over a long series of periods, in each of which the probability of a gain or a loss is 50%. This is a reasonable model of what happens to share prices. They tend to rise and fall in small incremental movements, following a so-called random walk, which compound over time to generate annual returns. This pattern through time is illustrated in exhibit 2.3, in which the extent of the up and down movements is a function of the volatility of the share (measured by standard deviation), and the probability attaching to the possible final outcomes is clearly greater in the centre of the distribution and lower at the extremes. As the number of periods approaches infinity, the resulting distribution gets closer and closer to a normal distribution.

Exhibit 2.3: Binomial share price progression

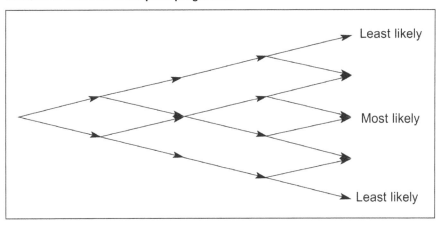

2. Diversification and portfolio effects

The bedrock of modern portfolio theory is that investors do not look at investments in isolation from one another. They think in terms of the risk and return characteristics of their overall asset portfolio. So far, we have assumed that we are examining a single investment in isolation. But investors do not hold only one asset in their portfolios. Private individuals, for instance, would typically own a house, some valuable personal effects, cash, be the beneficiaries of assets held on their behalf in a pension scheme, have taken out a life insurance policy, and possibly own equities, either directly or more commonly in pooled funds such as unit trusts or investment trusts.

Imagine owning shares in just two companies: British Airways (International Airlines Group) and British Petroleum. There are clearly a large number of factors that could increase or decrease the value of either share, but one item that they have in common is a very strong dependence on oil prices. An overall increase in the price of oil is good news for BP, as this will increase its revenues, but it is bad news for IAG, as it will increase its costs. (Aviation kerosene represents one of the larger operating costs for any airline.)

This implies two things. It implies that an investor who holds an appropriate combination of BP and IAG in his, or her, portfolio need not worry about movements in the oil price. And it implies that the share prices of BP and IAG will tend to move in opposite directions if there is a sharp change in the oil price. In this context, the oil price is known as a diversifiable risk, since holding more than one share allows it to be diversified away. The fact that the two shares will not always move together implies, in statistical terms, that they have a correlation of less than 1. Correlation can range from 1, for assets that move together systematically, to -1, for assets that move against one another systematically (as BP and IAG might, if the oil price was the only factor to change the value of their shares).

Exhibit 2.4 shows the range of possible portfolios that it is possible to create by holding a combination of two assets, A and B, where A has an expected return of 15% with a standard deviation of 4%, and B has an expected return of 9% and a standard deviation of 3.5%. If the expected returns to the two shares were perfectly correlated then the range of possible portfolios would be described by a straight line drawn from A to B.

Exhibit 2.4: Two-stock portfolio

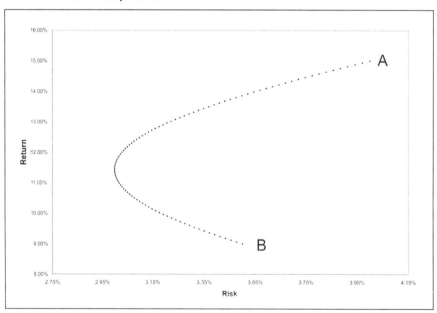

But this is not realistic because returns on shares are not perfectly correlated with one another, as we saw in our discussion of BP and IAG. There are times when they will move independently of one another, or even systematically in opposite directions. The curve representing possible investment portfolios constructed from the two shares in exhibit 2.4 is drawn using the assumption that there is a fairly low correlation of 0.3 between the expected returns offered by the two shares. The combination of shares that offers the lowest risk, with a standard deviation of about 3%, is less risky than either of the two shares held in isolation, and offers a return of about 11.5%, which is some 2.5% higher than the return offered by the lower risk share, B, held in isolation (though less high than the 15% return offered by A held in isolation). We shall not provide the derivation of the formula for the standard deviation of a two-stock portfolio in this book (we refer the reader to any standard statistics textbook), but it is the simplest case of the 'variance/covariance' model and is as follows:

$$SD_{AB}=(W_A{}^2{}^*SD_A{}^2+W_B{}^2{}^*SD_B{}^2+2{}^*W_A{}^*W_B{}^*SD_A{}^*SD_B{}^*R_{AB})^{0.5}$$

Where W stands for weight within the portfolio, SD for standard deviation and R for correlation.

There are obviously more than two possible choices of asset to put into a portfolio, even if we restrict our analysis to equities only. For any group of shares, changing their weightings within the portfolio will result in the creation of an envelope of possible balances of risk and return. Evidently, an efficient portfolio is one that extends as far to the top and left (high return and low risk) of the chart as possible.

This was the point that Markowitz reached in his analysis. Its extension into the full CAPM model came later, developed independently by several economists.

CAPM's starting point was that as we increase the number of shares in the portfolio, its volatility declines until it reaches an irreducible minimum: the volatility of the equity market portfolio as a whole. Exhibit 2.5 illustrates what happens to the risk of a portfolio as more stocks are added to it. As specific risks are diversified away the investor is left only with un-diversifiable risk, which is otherwise known as market risk or systematic risk.

Exhibit 2.5: Diversification and risk

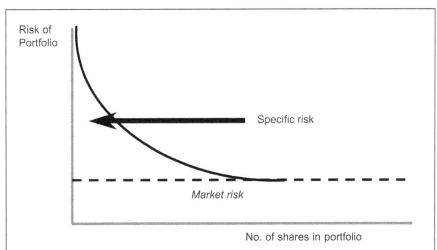

2.1 CAPM and the market line

We noted above that an efficient portfolio would be well diversified. We could, however, construct a portfolio badly (filling it, for example with lots of house-builders, all of whom would boom and bust together with the oscillations of the house-building cycle). The range of portfolios open to investors thus includes an envelope of efficient ones, those in which the trade-off between risk and return is relatively favourable, and a much larger choice of inefficient ones, where the return could be improved upon for any acceptable degree of risk.

In exhibit 2.6, the efficient frontier represents the risk-return characteristics of all of the available efficient portfolios. For any particular degree of risk there is no better available return than the one on the line. Above the line is unachievable.

Below the line is inefficient.

But in addition to assets that have risk attached to them there is also one asset that offers a risk-free return. This is a long-term government bond. The return is risk free because the risk of default is deemed to be negligible, and because the return is fixed, so long as the bond is held to redemption. Hence the position of the risk free asset on the chart. It offers a low return at no risk.

Exhibit 2.6: Capital market line

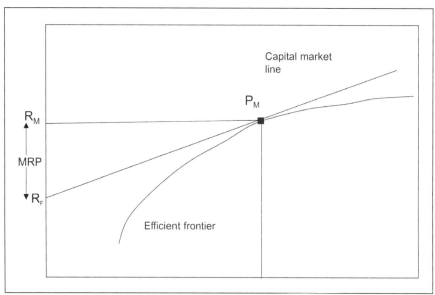

Since investors can hold a portfolio which comprises a combination of the risk-free asset and one portfolio, the one at the tangent of the efficient frontier and the capital line, it follows that they will always do this. Imagine an investor who held an equity portfolio on the efficient frontier to the left of the market portfolio. He could improve his returns at no additional risk by holding the appropriate mix of the risk free asset and the market portfolio, and would always benefit from doing this.

The extension of the capital market line to the right of the market portfolio is explained by the fact that investors can sell government bonds that they do not own (go short of the risk free asset) and buy more equities, thus increasing their risk and return through leverage.

The final stage in the argument is that the portfolio of choice must be the market portfolio. If it were not then presumably investors would shun the shares that made the portfolio sub-optimal and buy more of the shares that improved the portfolio's characteristics. As they did this they would force down the price of the former and drive up the price of the latter until they had eliminated the benefit that derived from selecting only certain stocks. In other words, in a perfect market the only optimal portfolio will be the market portfolio.

The CAPM theory results in a very simple formula for the required return on any individual asset. It is a function of three items: the risk-free rate, the market risk premium, and the impact that the asset has on the risk of the investor's portfolio, known as its Beta (see below). Mathematically, the formula is:

$$KE = RF + MRP * Beta$$

2.2 Pausing for breath

By this point the argument may seem to be distinctly unreal, and it may be worth briefly reviewing the steps in our argument, highlighting a few of the assumptions, and discussing the realism of the conclusion, which is that rational investors will only hold combinations of two assets: the risk-free asset and the market portfolio.

We began by defining return as mean expected return and risk as the standard deviation of expected returns. We went on to assume that risk was normally distributed, and then introduced the concept of correlation between expected returns and portfolio effects. This led us to the idea of an efficient frontier of investments. The fact that there is a risk-free asset implied that a line (a tangent, in fact), could be drawn from a portfolio holding the risk-free asset to a single portfolio on the efficient frontier implies that for all levels of risk, the relevant point on the line will offer the highest available return, so rational investors will all hold combinations of the risk-free asset and one portfolio, which, in an efficient market, must be the market portfolio.

How realistic is all this and how reasonable are the assumptions? Defining return as mean expected return is probably uncontroversial, but defining risk in terms of volatility is not, nor is the assumption of risks being normally distributed. A common sense approach would be to argue that it is the risk of company failure, of losing one's investment, that should weigh most heavily with investors, rather than the notional volatility of a portfolio over time. The cost of bankruptcy is ignored in CAPM, as it is effectively assumed that returns to assets are the product of a long succession of small incremental positive and negative movements during which investors can instantaneously adjust their portfolios with no transaction costs. One would therefore expect the model to be least successful at explaining the pricing of two types of assets: the capital of distressed companies, and assets which are highly illiquid, such as venture capital investments; or very large projects, where investors would find it impossible to diversify their portfolios effectively. This is exactly what we find in the real world. Pricing illiquidity is very difficult. Pricing default risk is easier, because option pricing techniques are applicable, and we revert to this approach later in this chapter.

Finally, there is the question of time horizons. The CAPM assumes that investors all measure risk and return over the same period. If they do not, or if the period is not what economists have assumed it to be, all historical measures aiming to prove or disprove the theory are unsound. Time horizons also complicate the notion of the risk-free rate and the market risk premium. The risk-free rate is actually a yield curve, not a single number. And there is no reason why the market risk premium should be a stable premium applied to each year's cash flows.

2.3 What is a Beta?

The CAPM analysis above implies that the factors that drive asset prices may be divided between two categories: specific risk, which is diversifiable, and for which investors therefore do not demand a return, and market risk, which is un-diversifiable, and for which they do demand a return. It follows from this that, under this approach, investors will demand returns from assets not because of the uncertainty of the returns from the asset, but because of the contribution of the asset to the uncertainty of the returns that they will obtain from their entire portfolios. An asset that increases the volatility of the portfolio is a high-risk asset, and one that reduces the volatility of the portfolio is a low-risk asset. To understand the point, imagine a share in a company which was very volatile, but which was not driven by fluctuations in the economic cycle; an oil exploration and production company might be a good example. Although it is itself volatile, it will not contribute to the volatility of the overall portfolio, and might even reduce it in times of crisis in the oil market. If CAPM is correct, investors will not demand a high return for undertaking the specific risk, and will be content with a fairly average return since they are undertaking only fairly average systemic (or un-diversifiable) risk.

Reverting to exhibit 2.6 for a moment, shares that have a high covariance with the equity market (that go up more than the market when it goes up and fall more than the market when it falls) will have the effect of increasing the volatility of the portfolio, as against the market portfolio. Increasing the weight of these shares would pull the investor's portfolio to the right of the market portfolio, and shifting the weight from these to shares with a lower covariance with the overall equity market would have the effect of pulling the overall portfolio to the left. Since we know that the two asset portfolio, represented by the risk-free asset and the market portfolio, is optimal, it follows that the premium over the risk-free rate that is required of any asset may be read straight off a line, the security market line, which related to its impact on the volatility of the overall portfolio. The security market line, which related required returns to covariance with the market portfolio, or Beta, is illustrated in exhibit 2.7.

Exhibit 2.7: Security market line

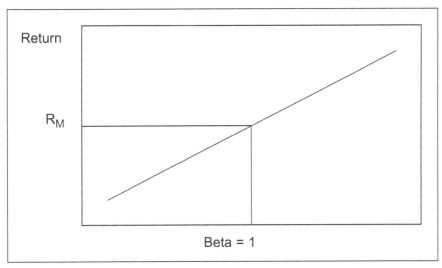

Beta is defined in terms of covariance with the market. Stocks with a higher than average covariance with the market are high Beta, and stocks with a lower than average covariance with the market are low Beta. It is important to understand that CAPM does not imply that all that drives share prices is equity market movements. What CAPM does is to assume that shares are driven by market movements and by stock specific factors, but that it is only their exposure to the former that determines their risk as part of an investor portfolio. Exhibit 2.8 illustrates the point.

Exhibit 2.8: Beta as measure of covariance

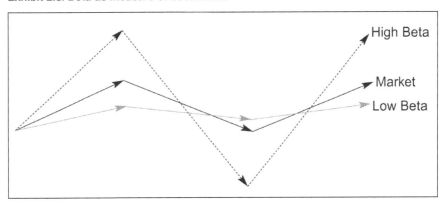

Examples of high Beta stocks are those where the company supplies one of the more volatile components of the overall economy, such as housebuilding, or those that are very sensitive to asset prices, such as life insurance companies. Examples of low Beta stocks are utilities, or food retailers. A point to which we shall return is the fact that the Beta of a share can be increased or decreased by the company financing itself with more or less debt.

Measuring Betas is normally done by a partial regression of the returns on the asset over a run of periods against returns on the overall equity market over the same periods. Exhibit 2.9 shows a plot of returns on a stock versus returns on a market over a series of periods, often, in practice, monthly returns over three or five years. The historical Beta of the stock is then estimated using the slope of the resulting line. There are clearly statistical problems with this. The correlation coefficients for individual companies are often very poor. And, in any case, the theory applies to expected Betas, not historical ones. In practice, Betas are generally calculated in this way, using databases such as those marketed by Bloomberg or DataStream.

There are two problems with standard calculations for Beta. The first is that they are backward looking, whereas it is prospective Betas that should drive discount rates. The second is that the statistical significance of many of the calculations is very poor. Finally, there is the usual problem with time-periods. Over what period should we be measuring Betas?

Exhibit 2.9: Estimating Betas

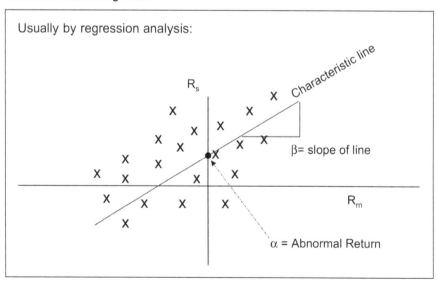

2.4 What is the market risk premium?

Let us return again to exhibit 2.6. An assumption that underlies it is that the market portfolio is expected to offer a higher return than a risk free asset. This is clearly sensible. While investors can diversify away all the specific risks to which equities are exposed, they cannot diversify away market risk, so they must be compensated for assuming it. Once we know what the price of market risk is, then we can draw the capital market line, and use it to read off the required return for any individual equity. But where do we get the market risk premium from?

As with Betas, one approach is to look at history. Data have been collected (in the UK in the form of the Barclays Equity-Gilt Study, in the USA by Ibbotson, and globally by Credit Suisse) that compare returns on different asset classes annually. There is a technical question that arises when doing this exercise. Should each year be treated as an individual entity, and the annual returns be arithmetically averaged, or should the whole period of decades be treated as a single entity, in which case the annual return derived will be a geometric average? We tend to the latter view, but would note that as with Betas the more crucial question is whether the expected future figures are the same as the actual historical ones.

Exhibit 2.10: Post 1900 market risk premia

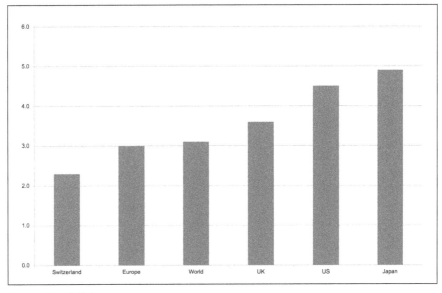

Source: Credit Suisse

Exhibit 2.10 shows estimates of measured historical annual returns from equities minus returns from holding long-term government bonds, over the period 1900–2018 for world markets, European markets and four main individual markets. In each case the returns are geometric annual averages (compound rates).

An alternative approach is to try to calculate expected returns from the equity market by estimating future dividend growth. The formula of the expected return from the equity market, derived by a very simple rearrangement of the Gordon Growth model discussed in chapter one, is as follows:

$$r = D*(1+g)/P + g$$

As at the end of 2018, the historical yield for the UK FTSE All-Share index was 4.54%. The prospective equivalent might be about 4.75%. Long-term nominal dividend growth could reasonably be estimated at about 2.5% annually, implying a return from holding the UK equity market of 7.25%. At the same date, the 10-year government bond had a redemption yield of 1.14%. Subtracting this from the prospective return implies a market risk premium of 6.11%. Given the inherent inaccuracy of the forecasts, about a 6.0% market risk premium seems a reasonable assumption. That this is significantly higher than the historical number for the UK in exhibit 2.10 probably reflects the extremely depressed level of bond yields after years of quantitative easing. In other words, it was probably the risk-free rate, rather than the cost of equity, that was distorted, though it should also be mentioned that the yield on the market was relatively high by historical standards, with doubts over the sustainability of some large company dividends.

2.5 Comments on CAPM

The CAPM tends to be used fairly unquestioningly by practitioners in the financial market. This is partly because it seems to work reasonably well and partly because it is simple to apply. Where it clearly breaks down, as in illiquid venture capital investments, it is simply ignored.

There have been two main attempts to provide an alternative. The first, Arbitrage Pricing Theory (APT), replaces the assumption that there is one factor driving required returns to a share (its exposure to market risk) with a multifactor approach, which requires a multiple regression analysis to identify coefficients for the different factors, generally including market risk. This may provide better explanations for historical share prices, and even more accurate measurements of Betas, but it is very time-consuming, and there is no strong evidence that the approach has a better predictive value in assessing the cost of equity than a simple CAPM approach.

The second is based on statistical work originally produced by Fama and French, which showed that equity returns may be better explained with reference to Beta and two different variables, size and price/book value. The significance of the latter factor has been the subject of much controversy, but a benefit of this approach may be its emphasis on liquidity. Other analysis has suggested that adjusting a market cost of capital for size and financial leverage offers better explanations for historical returns than does CAPM. But as Betas and financial leverage are closely connected, the main benefit from this approach may be the same as that of Fama and French, namely adjustment for liquidity. In practice, equity analysts do one of two things. They either (and this is the majority) use the standard CAPM approach, or they may use discount rates in which a market cost of capital is adjusted for leverage and liquidity.

3. The problem of growth

The literature on discount rates is more than usually bifurcated between the simplistic and the almost incomprehensible. Part of the problem is that practitioners, and practical training, all depend on theory that was developed by Miller and Modigliani more than half a century ago, while more recent economic studies have been largely ignored by practitioners. In addition, whereas all of the valuation methodologies discussed above represent demonstrably consistent variants on the same basic formula (so that the choices become those of convenience, and the issues those of implementation) this is not true of discount rates. Different formulae really do imply different assumptions about the world, and will result in different valuations if applied to the same accounting inputs. So it is even more important that we understand them.

Miller and Modigliani are chiefly remembered for the related propositions that, assuming no taxation and no default risk, the value of a company is unaffected by its financial leverage (because investors can manage their own balance sheets to create whatever leverage they want) and by its payout ratio (because today's over-distribution will have to be recovered tomorrow).

What was really important about their work was the conclusions that it implied for the cost of equity, as leverage increased. Since the value of the business was unchanged by altering the leverage (a stream of $100 a year that had been worth $1,000 a year if discounted at 10% was still worth $1,000) the effect on the cost of equity of any change in the given level of financial leverage could be computed readily. Exhibit 2.11 shows the annual cash flow, the discount rates, and the value, that attaches to the same assets, financed by different balances of financial leverage, with the debt, equity and capital valued separately.

Exhibit 2.11: Capital value decomposition

WACC and its components – No growth			
Source of capital	Annual receipt (CF)	Discount rate (k)	Capital value (V)	Note
Debt	25	5%	500	V=CF/k
Equity	75	15%	500	V=CF/k
Capital	100	10%	1,000	V=CF/k

If the value of the assets is unchanged by the shift in financing structure, then that is another way of saying that the Weighted Average Cost of Capital (WACC) does not change as the blend of debt and equity changes. Increasing the gearing has the effect of increasing the cost of a diminishing portion of equity and increasing the portion represented by low-cost debt. The weighted average remains unchanged. Exhibit 2.12 shows a chart of the movements in the cost of equity, the cost of debt, and the weighted average cost of capital as the gearing increases.

Exhibit 2.12: Leverage and WACC

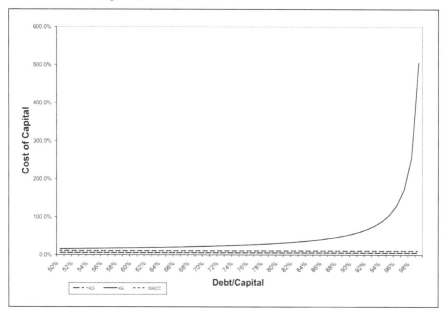

So far, so conventional. This is the point at which the textbooks move on to the talk about tax shelters and the cost of default risk. But let us stop here a moment and explore a point that often gets left out.

The valuations in exhibit 2.13 are derived by dividing annual cash flow by the discount rate. $100 a year discounted at 10% is worth $1,000. But what if the cash flows are growing? Well, we know how to value a growth perpetuity. So, just as an example, let us take the 50% debt financed example from exhibit 2.11, and assume that the company, instead of not growing, is going to grow at 3% annually. We use the Gordon Growth model to value the cash flow streams independently, and then to value the company using a weighted average cost of capital.

Exhibit 2.13: Impact of growth on values

WACC and its components – 3% growth				
Source of capital	Annual receipt (CF)	Discount rate (k)	Capital value (V)	Note
Debt	25	5%	1,250	V=CF/(k-g)
Equity	75	15%	625	V=CF/(k-g)
Capital	100	10%	1,429	V=CF/(k-g)

What is happening here? We do not get consistent value at all. The sum of the parts is bigger than the whole, which is not what we want to see. The reason is that in dividing by 'k-g' the impact on values is not linear as we increase 'g'. It will have a disproportionately large impact when applied to smaller values of k. This is very unsatisfactory, and illustrates an equally important truth about the original Miller and Modigliani analysis to the fact that it was based on a tax-free and default-free world. It was also premised on a no-growth world. Techniques for building tax and default risk into the original framework have been known and used for years. But the significance of the impact of growth on valuation has not been similarly emphasised, which is very odd since its potential impact on valuations is far greater, and most valuation models do assume constant growth after a forecast period.

Our approach to the practical calculation of discount rates is therefore going to differ from that conventionally followed in textbooks, since we shall take pains to think through the implications of all of our actions on growing, not merely on static, streams of cash.

> The customary practitioners' approach, unfortunately, is to use a theoretical structure that works perfectly in a static world, and then to misapply it to a growing one.

Unfortunately, the result is systematic overvaluation, of the sort illustrated in exhibit 2.13.

So as we build tax shelters and default risk into our discount rates we must try to establish an approach that is robust when applied to growth companies. It must be said at this point that the authors claim no originality with respect to the analysis, except, perhaps, to the manner of presentation.

4. Leverage and the cost of equity

Let us return to exhibit 2.12 for a moment. Because we are in a world with no default risk, the cost of debt does not change, and should be equivalent to a risk-free interest rate. The redemption yield on a long-term government bond is often used as a proxy. As the gearing changes, the cost of equity changes, so that the value of the company remains unchanged. The formula for the cost of equity under the standard Capital Asset Pricing Model (CAPM) is as follows:

$$K_E = R_F + (R_M - R_F) * B$$

where K_E is the cost of equity, R_M is the expected return on the overall equity market, R_F is the risk free rate, and B is the Beta of the share.

As we have seen, Beta is conventionally explained as a measure of covariance of returns on the share with returns on the equity market as a whole. The underlying assumption (with which we are not going to argue) is that investors hold equities as part of portfolios of assets. They are therefore unperturbed by the volatility of expected returns on individual assets. They only care about volatility of returns on the portfolio as a whole. Betas are typically measured by taking runs of historical data over specific periods (perhaps monthly data over five years) and measuring the slope of a line of best fit between returns on the share and returns on the market. An example is illustrated in exhibit 2.14.

Exhibit 2.14: Calculation of equity Beta

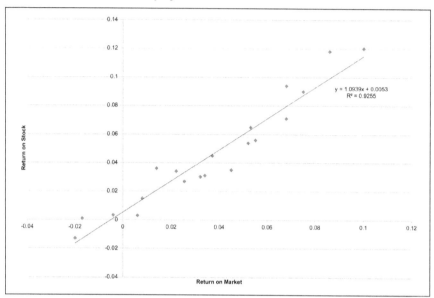

In this instance, the Beta is 1.09, which is barely above average, and market returns explain 92.6% of stock returns, which is high enough to be statistically persuasive. Real measurements are often not statistically significant.

In a perfectly efficient market, the intercept would be at zero. To the extent that there is a positive or negative intercept this is known as Alpha. Active portfolio managers seek positive Alpha shares. Unit tracking portfolios are built on the premise that Alphas are random and unpredictable. In this example, there is a negligible positive Alpha.

The main operational determinant to the Beta of a company's shares is the extent to which demand for its products is correlated with economic cycles. But there is also a direct link with financial structure. Even a very stable, non-cyclical business can be turned into a high Beta equity if it is largely funded by debt, as this will make the returns to the equity shareholder highly volatile. The basic formula that links Beta to leverage (if we ignore default risk) is the following:

$$B_L = B_A * (1 + V_D/V_E)$$

where B_L is the leveraged Beta, B_A is the unleveraged (or asset) Beta, V_D is the market value of debt, and V_E is the market value of equity.

Deleveraging measured, leveraged Betas into unleveraged Betas is done by using the equivalent formula:

$$B_A = B_L / (1 + V_D / V_E)$$

the easiest way to conceptualise this formula is to think about what happens if there is an equal weighting of debt and equity in the market value of a company. Then, the ratio V_D/V_E is equal to 100%. Any change in the value of the overall assets will be magnified by a multiple of 2 when applied to the equity, as illustrated in exhibit 2.15.

Exhibit 2.15: Leveraged assets

	Asset value	Debt	Equity
Opening	100	50	50
Closing	110	50	60
% change	10%	0%	20%

So we have a mechanism, in our risk free and untaxed world, for recalculating the impact of any level of gearing on the cost of equity. We just deleverage it to find the cost of equity to the underlying assets, and then releverage it back again.

5. Building in tax shelters

The simplest approach to a tax shelter is to see it as an addition to what the firm would be worth on an unleveraged basis. In other words, we value the company on the basis of its unleveraged cost of equity, and then add in a value for the cash that it conserves for its providers of capital, through paying less tax if it is leveraged than if it is unleveraged. This distortion arises because taxation is levied on profit after interest payments, so interest is deductible against corporation tax but dividend payments are not. In effect, what is happening is that three parties are sharing the operating profits generated: the bondholders, the government and the shareholders (in that order). If the providers of capital shift the balance from equity to debt, then their combined take increases at the expense of that of the government.

The conventional WACC/DCF approach is to handle tax shelters by alteration to the discount rate. This, it is argued, falls as leverage increases (because of the tax shelter), until the company becomes over-leveraged, and distress costs boom, at which point the discount rate starts to rise dramatically.

Our approach will be rather different. Instead of treating tax shelters as changing the discount rate, we shall begin by valuing them as an independent asset in their own right, and then add the result to the value of the unleveraged assets. This approach is known as Adjusted Present Value (APV). It will enable us to make explicit the connections between value and growth that get bundled up in the conventional WACC calculation. The formula that underpins APV is the following:

$$V_F = V_D + V_E = V_A + V_{TS} - DR$$

where V_F=value of firm, V_D=value of debt, V_E=value of equity, V_A=value of unleveraged assets, V_{TS}=value of Tax Shelter and DR is the value of the default risk.

The traditional WACC/DCF approach picks up the entire value in one calculation by adjusting the WACC for the impact of the tax shelter. We shall approach the valuation of the unleveraged assets and the tax shelter separately, and then make sure that we can reconcile our WACC with the APV valuations. As we shall see the differences between our recommended formulae and those in general use relate to the treatment of the tax shelter both in the formula for leveraging and deleveraging equity Betas and in the formula for adjusting WACC for changing leverage, for the same reason in both cases. We shall be discounting the tax shelter at the unleveraged cost of equity, and the standard approach discounts it at the gross cost of debt.

The discount rate that should be applied to unleveraged cash flows is obvious. It is the unleveraged cost of equity. The question is what is the discount rate that should be applied to the tax shelter. Miller and Modigliani assumed that the appropriate rate was the gross cost of debt. So, if a company pays 5% interest and has a 20% marginal rate of taxation then its net cost of debt for a WACC calculation is as follows:

$$5\% * (1-20\%) = 4\%$$

To see why this is so, look at exhibit 2.16.

For every $100 that I borrow, I pay $5 a year in interest, and reduce my tax bill by $1 a year. The net cost to me is $4 a year. Dividing all of these numbers by 5% (or multiplying by 20) gives us a total value of the debt of $100, comprising a value of the tax shelter of $20, and a net financial liability to the company worth $80. This analysis is so seductive that it is rarely questioned, yet there are severe problems with it.

Exhibit 2.16: Conventional tax shelter calculation

Tax shelter ($)	Capital amount	Interest rate	Cash flow
Gross debt	100	5.0%	5
Tax shelter	20	5.0%	1
Net debt	80	5.0%	4

The first problem is a practical one. We have seen in exhibit 2.13 above that if we move from a no-growth world to a growth world, the impact of growth unbalances calculations of value in favour of streams that are being discounted at a low discount rate. So if we discount growing tax shelters at the cost of debt, which is lower than the cost of equity, then relatively low growth rates can result in very large values for the tax shelter. In the extreme case, if the company is assumed to grow at its cost of borrowing then the value of the tax shelter becomes infinite. Exhibit 2.17 illustrates the value of unleveraged assets and tax shelters calculated for a constant growth company at three different growth rates, and the allocation of value between the two components.

Exhibit 2.17: APV for varying growth (1)

APV valuation	Annual CF	k	Value at different growth rates		
			0%	2%	4%
Assets	100	10%	1,000	1,250	1,667
Tax shelter	10	5%	200	333	1,000
Firm	110		1,200	1,583	2,667

The second problem is a theoretical one. Are tax shelters really equally risky (or, more properly, as riskless) as the company's outstanding debt? To generate a tax shelter a company has to generate a profit. The tax shelter is a function of a difference between two levels of pre-tax profit: that which the company would have generated on an unleveraged basis and that which it would generate after paying interest on a given level of debt. It is not the risk attaching to the interest payment itself that is relevant. It is the risk attaching to the marginal amounts of profit generated in the two examples.

Let us illustrate the point with a real example. Though rather old it is certainly dramatic. In 1996, the Kuwait Petroleum Corporation put up for sale its UK North Sea assets (held through a company called Santa Fe Petroleum). The assets were eventually bought by the Norwegian exploration and production company, Saga Petroleum, at a price that implied the use of a relatively low discount rate. This was partially justified by the fact that Saga borrowed the consideration, and that it had a marginal rate of taxation on its Norwegian operations of 78%. If you can pay interest at a net rate of 22 cents in the dollar then money seems cheap.

The two years that followed the acquisition, 1997 and 1998, were characterised by the Asian economic crisis. Oil prices collapsed. By the end of 1998 Saga was not making the profits that were required to shelter its interest payments. In its year-end accounts it was required to write down the acquired assets. This put a severe strain on its balance sheet, and the company responded with an attempted rights issue, which was not supported by its shareholders. During 1999, while oil prices were recovering, it lost its independence. At no point was Saga unable to pay the interest on its debts. So did it make sense to value the tax shelter by discounting it at the cost of debt? Clearly not. But that is exactly what happens when you say that the net cost of debt is the gross cost of debt times one minus the marginal rate of tax (the basis of almost all company valuation models)!

If what we are discounting is really a profit stream, not a stream that relates to interest, surely it should be the cost of equity, rather than the cost of debt, that is the relevant discount rate? In reality, the whole concept of a single cost of debt or equity (even in any one year) is oversimplified, but if we are going to use one number then it makes more sense to use the unleveraged cost of equity throughout. Exhibit 2.18 illustrates what happens to our previous example if we substitute the unleveraged cost of equity for the cost of debt in the valuation of the tax shelters. And the result looks a lot more plausible.

Exhibit 2.18: APV for varying growth (2)

APV valuation	Annual CF	k	Value at different growth rates		
			0%	2%	4%
Assets	100	10%	1,000	1,250	1,667
Tax shelter	10	10%	100	125	167
Firm	110		1,100	1,375	1,833

So we now have a perfectly workable methodology for valuing a company, if we continue to ignore distress costs resulting from over-leverage. We calculated the unleveraged cost of equity to the company by deleveraging its measured Beta. We then use that discount rate both to discount operating cash flows and tax shelters. We then add the two values together to derive a value for the company, deducting the value of the debt to derive a value for the equity.

5.1 Reconciliation with WACC/DCF

Not only is what has been outlined above not the standard approach, it is not even consistent with the standard approach. Traditionally, corporate valuations are done by discounting operating cash flows at a single discount rate, the weighted average cost of capital. This comprises in weighted components the leveraged cost of equity and the net of taxation cost of debt. We saw above in exhibit 2.11 that in a risk-free world with no growth it made no difference whether we valued the two components of capital as one or separately, but that it did start to matter once growth rates were built into the analysis. Ignoring growth for a moment (we shall return to it) even the no-growth value of a company will be different depending on whether we value tax shelters at the gross cost of debt or at the unleveraged cost of equity.

It is shown in the Appendix that the two approaches on the value of the company imply a difference between two equations for the calculation of equity Beta. The first is the one that we used above:

$$B_L = B_A * (1 + V_D / V_E)$$

where B_L=leveraged Beta, B_A=asset Beta, V_D=value of debt and V_E=value of equity.

And the more popular alternative is as follows:

$$B_L = B_A * [1 + V_D / V_E * (1-t)]$$

where the other variables are as above and t is the rate of corporation tax.

This formula still ascribes no risk to debt, but is consistent with the assumption that the tax shelter that accrues as a result of leverage should be discounted at the gross cost of debt, rather than (as we used above) the unleveraged cost of equity. Clearly, the second formula will make debt more attractive than the first, as it will result in a lower increase in the cost of equity. Its derivation also, quite explicitly, assumes no growth in the cash flows. For a growth company it is simply inaccurate.

The conventional WACC formula is as follows:

$$WACC = K_E * V_E / V_F + K_D * (1-t) * V_D / V_F$$

where the other variables are as above and V_F=value of firm (debt plus equity).

We are going to use our formulae for leveraging and in exhibit 2.19 show that the same cash flows produce the same value, whether the APV or WACC/DCF methodology is used, so long as we discount tax shelters our way, using the unleveraged cost of equity. Exhibit 2.19 shows the value of a company with a stream of free cash flow starting at 100% and rising at 3% annually, under a consistent set of assumptions about discount rates.

Exhibit 2.19: APV/WACC – risk-free debt

Row	Unleveraged value		Notes
1	Rf	4.00%	Risk free rate
2	MRP	3.50%	Market risk premium
3	B_A	0.8	Asset Beta
4	K_A	6.80%	Unleveraged cost of equity
5	FCF	100	Free cash flow
6	g	3.00%	Growth
7	**V_A**	**2,632**	**Value with no tax shelter**
	Leveraged APV		
8	BV_D	1,000	Book value of debt
9	V_D	1,000	Market value of debt
10	DRP	0.00%	Debt risk premium
11	I	4.00%	Interest rate
12	t	30.00%	Tax rate
13	$K_D*(1-t)$	2.80%	Net cost of debt
14	TS	12	Tax shelter
15	V_{TS}	316	Tax shelter valued at unleveraged cost of equity; not cost of debt
16	V_{A+TS}	2,947	Value including tax shelter
17	DR	0	Default risk
18	**V_F**	**2,947**	**Value including tax shelter and default risk**
	WACC/DCF value		
19	V_D/V_F	33.93%	Weighting of debt derived iteratively=weighting from APV
20	V_D/V_E	51.35%	Debt/Equity
21	B_D	0.0	$B_D=(I-R_F)/MRP$
22	B_L	1.2	$B_L = B_A*(1+V_D/V_E)-B_D*V_D/V_E$; not $B_A*[1+V_D/V_E*(1-t)]-B_D*V_D/V_E*(1-t)$
23	K_E	8.24%	Leveraged cost of equity
24	WACC	6.39%	Conventional weighed average
25	**V_F**	**2,947**	**WACC=APV**
26	WACC	6.39%	WACC = $K_A - I*t*V_D/V_F$

The unleveraged cost of equity in row 4 is calculated using the cost of equity formula discussed above. All the values are derived using the Gordon Growth model:

$$V = CF_{t+1} / (k-g)$$

where V=value, CF_{t+1}=next year's cash flow, k=discount rate and g=growth rate.

The tax shelter in row 14 is just the 1,000 debt times the interest rate of 4% (row 11) times the tax rate of 30% (row 12). The interest rate is the risk free rate (row 1), as there is as yet no default risk in our example. The tax shelter is valued using the unleveraged cost of equity, in accordance with our discussion above. The APV valuation (row 18) is the sum of the unleveraged value (row 7) and the value of the tax shelter (row 15), as there is no cost of default risk (row 17).

In the WACC/DCF value, the leveraged Beta in row 22 is calculated using the formula that is consistent with valuing tax shelters at the unleveraged cost of equity, not the gross cost of debt. (The version of the formula is that which also takes default risk into account, but as the Beta of debt in row 21 is zero, this does not affect the calculation.) The resulting leveraged cost of equity, in row 23, is then used as part of a standard WACC calculation, using the gearing in row 19 (derived iteratively) and the respective costs of debt and equity in rows 13 and 23. The iteration works because there is only one consistent pair of values for the value of the equity and the implied WACC.

To see this, it is helpful to think of leverage as working in two ways. For any given level of debt, if the gearing rises then this implies a lower value of the equity. On the other hand, in a risk-free world, a higher gearing implies a higher tax shelter, which implies a higher value for the equity. There is only one point at which the two factors are consistent, as illustrated in exhibit 2.20.

Exhibit 2.20: Iteration of WACC

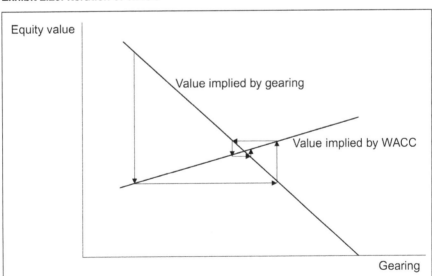

The result of all of this is that the value in row 18 (APV) is the same as the value in row 25 (WACC).

In row 26 of exhibit 2.19, WACC is calculated using the appropriate formula for discounting tax shelters at the unleveraged cost of equity:

$$WACC = K_A - I^*t^*V_D/V_F$$

where WACC=weighted average cost of capital, K_A=the unleveraged cost of equity, I=gross interest rate, t=tax rate, V_D=value of debt and V_F=value of firm.

This derives the same WACC as the conventional weighted average calculated in row 24. In both cases the figure is higher than would be derived if the tax shelter was discounted at the gross cost of debt. We have seen the difference between the two calculations for leveraged Betas above. We conclude with the differences for direct calculation of leveraged WACC (again, the proofs are in the Appendix).

The more common formula for WACC, using the assumption that the appropriate discount rate for tax shelters is the gross cost of debt, is as follows:

$$WACC = K_A - [(K_A - g)/(I - g)]^*I^*t^*V_D/V_F$$

where the variables are as in the last formula and g=growth.

The comparison is striking. The more usual formula will have two effects, the former of which is obvious, and the latter of which is not. It will produce lower answers for WACC and a higher value of the tax shelter because the cost of equity will be higher than the cost of debt. So far, so obvious. And it will produce progressively lower and lower discount rates the faster that the company is expected to grow.

> So, all other things being equal, a faster growing company, that distributes less of its cash flow and reinvests a higher proportion of it, will be subject to a lower discount rate than an otherwise identical company that distributes most of its cash flow and grows slowly!

Yes, this is probably ridiculous, but it is the inevitable effect of increasing g if K_A is higher than I, which it always should be.

Increasing the growth rate in the latter formula will have the effect of reducing the market leverage, which puts an upper limit on the gearing, but this does not alter the fact that the overall effect is for WACC to decrease as growth increases.

We therefore have two reasons for discounting tax shelters at the unleveraged cost of equity:

1. We are discounting a stream that relates to profit, not to interest payments.

2. If we discount tax shelters for growing companies at the gross cost of debt then the effect of increasing the growth rate is to reduce the discount rate, which seems implausible.

We have risked belabouring the question of tax shelters, but they loom large (implicitly and explicitly) in the discount rates that valuation models apply. During the era of low interest rates which began in the 1990s, companies were under unprecedented pressure from bankers and their shareholders to buy back equity in an attempt to increase shareholder value. The so-called TMT (telecoms, media and technology) crisis that followed the millennium was largely due to debt-funded acquisitions in markets that were perceived to offer fast growth. And the financial crisis of 2008 again illustrated the dangers of excessive leverage (though in the latter case mainly in the banking sector).

5.2 Default risk and the cost of debt

Liquidation rarely achieves an attractive value for a company's assets, which is why both debt and equity shareholders are often willing to accept financial reconstruction, despite the fact that the former may have to commute much of their debt into equity, and the latter to accept extreme dilution. Recovery rates depend on the type of business and are higher if assets are easily separable. But even with quite asset-rich companies, recovery rates even for senior creditors are generally well below 100%. Junior creditors often lose a significant proportion of their capital, and equity shareholders frequently lose all of it. Hence distress costs: as the risk of failure looms, it has a substantial impact on the cost of capital.

Let us defer discussion of companies that are teetering on the brink of failure for a moment, and begin with treatment of a relatively well capitalised company. Holders of debt in this company will only ascribe a very low probability to its failure during the life of its outstanding debt, whatever that may be. But there is some small risk of default, even in a safe company, and this probability, times the expected loss in the event of default, has to be loaded onto the cost of debt to the company. It takes the form of a risk premium, versus the cost of borrowing to the government over an equivalent period. The calculations that we have done up to now all ignored this risk, and assumed that the cost of debt to the company was equal to the cost of debt to the government.

Let us return to our APV and DCF valuations in exhibit 2.19 and repeat the exercise by assuming that the company has a cost of borrowing which is in excess of the risk-free rate, reflecting its market gearing, its interest cover, and the security of its assets (the latter of which is invisible in this example). The result in displayed in exhibit 2.21.

Exhibit 2.21: APV/WACC – implied Beta of debt

Row	Unleveraged value		Notes
1	Rf	4.00%	Risk free rate
2	MRP	3.50%	Market risk premium
3	B_A	0.8	Asset Beta
4	K_A	6.80%	Unleveraged cost of equity
5	FCF	100	Free cash flow
6	g	3.00%	Growth
7	V_A	**2,632**	**Value with no tax shelter**
	Leveraged APV		
8	BV_D	1,000	Book value of debt
9	V_D	800	Market value of debt
10	DRP	1.00%	Debt risk premium
11	I	5.00%	Interest rate
12	t	30.00%	Tax rate
13	$K_D{}^*(1\text{-}t)$	3.50%	Net cost of debt
14	TS	12	Tax shelter
15	V_{TS}	316	Tax shelter valued at unleveraged cost of equity; not cost of debt
16	V_{A+TS}	2,947	Value including tax shelter
17	DR	0	Default risk
18	V_F	**2,947**	**Value including tax shelter and default risk**
	WACC/DCF value		
19	V_D/V_F	27.14%	Weighting of debt derived iteratively=weighting from APV
20	V_D/V_E	37.25%	Debt/Equity
21	B_D	0.3	$B_D=(I\text{-}R_F)/MRP$
22	B_L	1.0	$B_L = B_A{}^*(1+V_D/V_E)\text{-}B_D{}^*V_D/V_E$; not $B_A{}^*[1+V_D/V_E{}^*(1\text{-}t)]\text{-}B_D{}^*V_D/V_E{}^*(1\text{-}t)$
23	K_E	7.47%	Leveraged cost of equity
24	WACC	6.39%	Conventional weighed average
25	V_F	**2,947**	**WACC=APV**
26	WACC	6.39%	$WACC = K_A \text{-} I{}^*t{}^*V_D/V_F$

To highlight the differences between this calculation and the previous one we shall concentrate on the consequences of the default risk on debt. This has been estimated in row 10 and results in a drop in the market value of the debt (row 9). (We have assumed that the interest stream is a perpetuity, whereas in reality corporate debt would have a finite duration so the impact on its value would be smaller. This in no way alters the rest of the analysis.)

The APV value in row 18 has been set to equal the DCF value derived in row 25, and the cost of default risk in row 17 is derived from the difference between the APV before the default risk and the WACC/DCF value. We showed in exhibit 2.21 above that if the gross cost of debt to the company is set at the risk-free rate, the APV and the WACC/DCF values are the same. If there is a default risk, then this is picked up in the discount rate calculated as a WACC, but not in the APV, as this uses unleveraged discount rates throughout.

In the WACC/DCF value, the gearing in row 19 is an iterated result as before. The Beta of debt is implied from its risk premium and calculated in row 21. The leveraged equity Beta in row 22 now makes use of the full leveraging formula, including the term relating to the Beta of debt, and the proof of this and the more common version are both provided in the Appendix. As with the risk-free valuation above, the formula for the WACC which is built up from the unleveraged cost of equity (in row 26) is consistent with the WACC calculated from its weighted components.

There is still a problem with this analysis. It is that the value of the company with default risk built into the cost of debt is the same as the figure that we derived earlier without default risk being built into the cost of debt. The reason is that we have used an implied Beta of debt and a leveraging formula for the cost of equity which has that Beta of debt embedded in it.

> In other words, the formulae are assuming that the higher cost of debt is entirely attributable to market risk and not to specific risk. The additional risk that has been loaded onto the debt is therefore being deducted in the Beta of the equity.

Let us try another approach, this time assuming that the Beta of debt in row 21 is zero, and that all of the debt-risk premium in row 10 can be ascribed to specific risk, with no market risk, and therefore no Beta of debt. Exhibit 2.22 below is in all respects identical with exhibit 2.21 above, except for the assumption that the debt has a Beta of zero.

Exhibit 2.22: APV/WACC – zero Beta of debt

Row	Unleveraged value		Notes
1	Rf	4.00%	Risk free rate
2	MRP	3.50%	Market risk premium
3	B_A	0.8	Asset Beta
4	K_A	6.80%	Unleveraged cost of equity
5	FCF	100	Free cash flow
6	g	3.00%	Growth
7	V_A	**2,632**	**Value with no tax shelter**
	Leveraged APV		
8	BV_D	1,000	Book value of debt
9	V_D	800	Market value of debt
10	DRP	1.00%	Debt risk premium
11	I	5.00%	Interest rate
12	t	30.00%	Tax rate
13	$K_D*(1-t)$	3.50%	Net cost of debt
14	TS	12	Tax shelter
15	V_{TS}	316	Tax shelter valued at unleveraged cost of equity; not cost of debt
16	V_A+_{TS}	2,947	Value including tax shelter
17	DR	(211)	Default risk
18	V_F	**2,737**	**Value including tax shelter and default risk**
	WACC/DCF value		
19	V_D/V_F	29.23%	Weighting of debt derived iteratively=weighting from APV
20	V_D/V_E	41.30%	Debt/Equity
21	B_D	0.0	Assume debt Beta is Zero
22	B_L	1.1	$B_L = B_A*(1+V_D/V_E)-B_D*V_D/V_E$; not $B_A*[1+V_D/V_E*(1-t)]-B_D*V_D/V_E*(1-t)$
23	K_E	7.96%	Leveraged cost of equity
24	WACC	6.65%	Conventional weighed average
25	V_F	**2,737**	**WACC=APV**
26	$WACC$	6.36%	$WACC = K_A - I*t*V_D/V_F$

In this instance, the value that we derive for the firm is lower than it was with a risk-free cost of borrowing, which looks more reasonable. None of the increased cost of debt is being absorbed by an assumed reduction in the leveraged equity Beta, because the Beta of debt is assumed to be zero. Here, we are explicitly assuming that the rules of CAPM do not apply to debt. It is all specific risk that is being priced into the premium, not market risk.

Notice also that in this case the calculated WACC in row 26 remains similar to that of the previous two examples, whereas the WACC based on a weighted average of the cost of debt and equity yields a higher discount rate, because the assumptions of CAPM are being infringed. Specific risk, as well as market risk, is being priced. (The small change in row 26 is attributable to the change in weight of debt and equity in the market value.)

Let us compare the three values. The first, in exhibit 2.19 assumed that the company borrowed at the risk-free rate. There is no default risk, just a tax shelter. This is clearly not possible in the real world. The second, in exhibit 2.21, assumed that the company pays a risk premium in its cost of debt, and attributes an implied Beta to the debt. Because the Beta on the debt then reduces the leveraged Beta of equity, the result is that the company is worth the same as it would have been worth in the absence of the premium on the cost of debt. Value has simply been shifted from debt to equity. The third, example, exhibit 2.22, example is the most realistic, though it flouts the assumptions of CAPM. In this case, all of the debt risk premium is deemed to be specific. The Beta of the debt is assumed to be zero. And the resulting value is higher than that of the unleveraged company but lower than that of the leveraged company with an implied Beta of debt.

The three calculations are charted in exhibit 2.23 below. The first bar is an impossibility, as no company can borrow at the risk-free rate. The first realistic alternative is not to borrow, and simply to be worth the value of the unleveraged assets. The middle bar shows what happens if we borrow and use an implied Beta of debt. The right bar shows what happens if we borrow and assume a zero Beta of debt. The truth lies somewhere between the two, but for many companies it may be reasonable to assume that most of the default risk on debt is unrelated to market risk, and in effect assume a zero Beta for the debt.

The obvious way to resolve the issue would be to measure the Betas of traded debt. Unfortunately, it is difficult enough to get statistically reliable measures for the Betas of equity. For debt, where the figures are clearly likely to be lower anyway, it is effectively impossible.

Exhibit 2.23: Value build-up

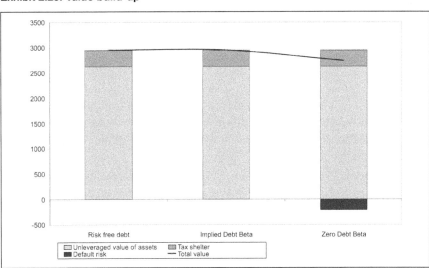

5.3 Implications of our analysis

We parted company with conventional approaches to discount rates by analysing the value of the assets and of tax shelters for a growing firm independently of one another, in a risk-free world. This enabled us to reconcile APV and WACC/DCF analysis, so long as we valued tax shelters at the unleveraged cost of equity, rather than at the cost of debt. We showed alternative formulae for leveraging of Betas and for calculations of WACC, which are often wrongly taken for granted and, in our view, abused. Finally, we introduced default risk into the analysis, and showed how the difference between the WACC/DCF and the APV approach could be used to derive an implied distress cost. This brought the analysis back to a conventional WACC/DCF framework, but left us with a choice between whether or not to assume that the risk premium on debt reflects market risk or specific risk. The latter seems more realistic but specifically breaches the assumptions underlying the CAPM.

It should be noted, moreover, that our formulae for calculation of WACC will derive significantly different conclusions with respect to the impact of increases in leverage from those commonly used. Our benefit from leverage will be lower. Our discount rates will be higher. And our resulting valuations will be lower.

6. Time-varying WACC

One of the more pernicious consequences of the traditional approach to discounting is that a WACC is conventionally calculated and then applied mechanically to all future cash flows, despite the fact that the appropriate discount rate for a particular year is a function of the company's market leverage in that year, and very few companies are expected to maintain a constant leverage over time. Since all of the formulae that we used for leveraging and deleveraging are consistent with one another, they can also be applied to models with specific forecasts followed by constant growth terminal values, of the kind that we shall be discussing in chapter five. This will require us to use the iterative process that we described above to calculate the value that produces consistent figures for the market value of the equity and the discount rate used for each year in our forecast, as a separate calculation. Each year's cash flow is then discounted at a different rate each year as it is brought back to the present. So, we start by iterating a value and a WACC for the terminus, and then bring it back year by year, discounting the year-end value of the company and that year's cash flow (or economic profit) at a different rate for each year of the specific forecast period.

We shall illustrate all this in chapter five, but would make two points now. Firstly, it is not correct to calculate time-varying WACCs using book leverage, any more than it is if a single rate is being used. Secondly, it is not correct to discount each item of cash flow or economic profit at the same rate compounded 'n' times if it is 'n' years away. If a company is equity financed now but will create tax shelters in future then it is not right to discount its year-10 cash flow ten times at the year-10 discount rate. It should be discounted ten times at different discount rates for each year.

An alternative to time-varying WACC (or APV, which values the tax shelter separately) is just to apply a single, target, gearing to the calculation of the WACC that will be used for all forecast years. This is slightly wrong, since in reality the rate should vary, but is an acceptable short-cut since it is the rate that applies to the long term cash flows that will have the main impact on the result. In this case, it should still be remembered that it is the market value of the debt and equity that sets the rate, not the book value.

Apart from leverage, there is an additional reason for changing the discount rate each year, which we have already discussed. This is that the risk-free rate is actually a yield curve, and it may be significant for firms that have high or low growth cash flows if we wrongly value them by assuming a discount rate based on a single risk-free rate.

7. The walking wounded – real options and capital arbitrage

Real options analysis has become extremely fashionable among academics, if not among practitioners. On this occasion, we tend to the view that the practitioners are generally right. There are considerable difficulties in translating a valuation methodology that was developed for financial derivatives and applying it to real assets. Derivatve valuation techniques depend on the possibility of creating equivalent portfolios comprising debt and the underlying asset, on instantaneous and cost-free arbitrage, and (often) on the range of expected returns on the underlying asset being normally distributed. Most real options breach all of these conditions. There is one clear exception. It is the put option conferred by limited liability on equity shareholders. This is generally not a particularly valuable asset. In severely distressed companies, it can be very valuable indeed.

Just how valuable is illustrated by the comment that is occasionally made that the best way to make money in the stock market is to buy shares that are being tipped as 'sell' by investment analysts. This is not a coincidence. It follows from the nature of the value offered by equity in barely solvent companies, and from the valuation methodology followed by most equity research analysts. Analysts mainly measure intrinsic value, and ignore option value.

Investment analysts generally value the equity in a company by using a discounting methodology to value the assets of the company, and then subtracting debt and other liabilities to derive an equity valuation. This result is often known as an intrinsic value.

Now imagine buying shares in a company which is almost insolvent. The intrinsic value of the shares is almost zero. If the value of the assets were to fall by even a small amount, the company would be insolvent and the shares would be worthless. But if the value of the assets rises by even a fairly small amount then the value of the shares will rise steeply. This is a classic payoff for a call option that is just in the money, as illustrated in exhibit 2.24. Equity investors start to make money when the value of the assets exceeds the sum of the par value of the debt and the price paid for the equity at time of purchase (equivalent to the price of the option).

Exhibit 2.24: Equity as call option

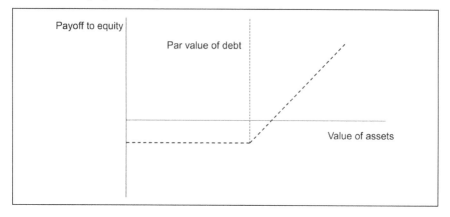

If the value of the assets is lower than the par value of the debt, shareholders in a limited liability company are free to walk away, leaving the company with the creditors. At above the par value of the debt, the intrinsic value of their equity rises in line with the value of the assets.

Another way to think about the nature of the option is to imagine that instead of buying a call on the assets, the shareholder had instead achieved the same effect as is achieved by limited liability through buying a put option from the creditors. In this instance, the value of the equity would rise as the value of the assets rose, but would fall only to the exercise price of the put. Below that, any further loss would be attributable to the writers of the put. If we think from the point of view of the writer of the put, not the buyer, he receives his payment so long as the value of the assets stay above the exercise price of the option. Below that price his receipts decline until if the asset falls in value to the exercise price minus the price that he received for the put option. Below that point, he loses money. This payoff is shown in exhibit 2.25.

Exhibit 2.25: Debt as written put

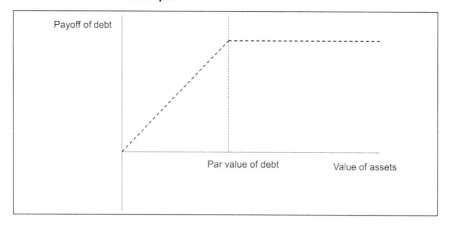

At any value of the assets which is above the par value of the debt, the creditor receives the par value of the debt. At values between the par value of the debt and zero, the value of his asset is eroded. At asset values of less than zero, he receives nothing. The payoffs to a creditor are therefore identical to those of a writer of put options.

Options are subject to a phenomenon known as put-call parity. That is to say that there is no difference between holding assets and a put option, which protects the downside risk (at a cost), or holding an equivalent value divided between cash and a call option. In both cases the portfolio will track that of the underlying asset upwards. And in both cases falls in value are limited, in the first case by the put option and in the second by the cash. Let us take an example. If I hold a portfolio of shares and a put option then I am exposed to the upside in the market, protected from the downside, and have paid an insurance premium (the cost of the put option). If I hold a call option and cash then I am also protected from the market falling (except for the cost of the call option, which I shall have lost). But if the market goes up then I participate, except for having paid a premium for the benefit of the call option. In both cases, I have given away a bit of value to protect myself against a market decline. If we exclude cash from the picture, put-call parity is as illustrated in exhibit 2.26.

Exhibit 2.26: Put-call parity

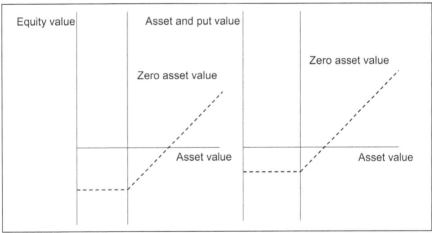

The two diagrams look almost identical, other than the lower base value on the left-hand side. The left half of exhibit 2.26 shows the payoff to equity as being identical to that of a call option, where the payoff only begins to be positive when the value of the assets exceeds the par value of the debt. The right-hand chart shows the payoff to holding the underlying asset, with a put option. The pattern is the same, but the portfolio starts to pay off at a lower asset value and is restricted on the downside at a higher value. This is because of the role of cash in the put-call parity equation discussed above. If:

Call + Cash = Asset + Put

Then:

Call = Asset + Put - Cash

Or, in the language of equity in limited liability companies:

Equity equals the assets of the business minus debt plus the value of the right to walk away if this is advantageous.

It is the right to walk away that is missed in standard, intrinsic value models.

The emergence of hedge funds as a significant asset class has been associated with an increase in so-called 'capital arbitrage', by which investors take net neutral positions in different capital instruments issues by the same company, in the hope of profiting from elimination of anomalies that may have emerged between their prices. The purest forms of capital arbitrage involve trading options against the underlying equity, or convertible bonds against a combination of debt and equity (or equity derivatives). But if a significant misevaluation of the option element of the relationship between debt and equity opens up, then this offers a further opportunity for arbitrage. It is one that should be negotiated with some care, as the example below illustrates.

7.1. Intrinsic value and time value: a refresher

This book is primarily concerned with intrinsic values, and for a full discussion of the valuation of options we refer the reader to one of the many textbooks on the subject. For those who already have some background in option theory, or who merely wish to be able to make some sense of the rest of this chapter, the basics are as follows.

Options comprise the right, but not the obligation, to buy or sell at a pre-arranged price either up to or on a particular date. The value of an option is set by five variables:

1. The option exercise price.

2. The price of the underlying asset.

3. The length of the exercise period.

4. The volatility of the underlying asset.

5. The risk-free rate.

An option price can be divided between its intrinsic value and its time value. Options will always trade at a premium to their intrinsic value, and the time value represents the largest part of their value when they are either out of the money (have a negative intrinsic value) or are just on the money. As their intrinsic value increases, the time value becomes a smaller part of their overall value, which is why option values are most important for distressed companies. Exhibit 2.27 shows the relationship between the intrinsic value and the time value for a call option as the value of the underlying asset changes.

Exhibit 2.27: The components of an option price

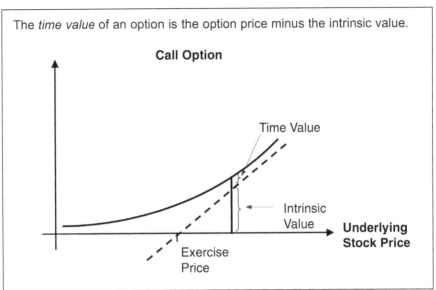

The *time value* of an option is the option price minus the intrinsic value.

Call Option

Time Value

Intrinsic
Value

**Underlying
Stock Price**

Exercise
Price

An example: Vivacious SA

The tables and charts in exhibit 2.28 illustrate a valuation of the equity and debt in Vivacious SA, at the high point of worries surrounding its debt level. It is fairly self-explanatory, though it should be noted that the valuation and forecast cash flows on part 2 of the model were those produced by an investment analyst at the time, based on information then available. Because the volatility of the underlying assets is not directly visible, this is derived in part 3 using the standard two-asset variance-covariance model, as illustrated in the BP/IAG portfolio discussed above. The Black-Scholes model in part 5 is adjusted to take loss of cash flow into account when valuing the option, and a period of two years was taken to be the life of the option, as that was the point at which a significant tranche of Vivacious's debt was payable. The chart illustrates the extent to which the company's equity was undervalued, and its debt overvalued, even if the fair asset values on which it was based were correct.

The commonsense way to think about this is to argue that if a company has an enterprise value that is very close to the par value of its debt, then there is a significant risk that it will default on its debt. So the debt must trade at a discount to its par value. In Vivacious's case it was trading at 95% of its value, but the model implied that it should at the time have been trading at 74% of its value. If value is being subtracted from the debt then it is being added to the equity. So the model shows that, if the valuations on which it is based were correct, the equity had an intrinsic value of €38,981 (fair enterprise value) minus €33,220m (net debt), a total of €5,761. The market was actually valuing the equity at €13,499m, versus a theoretical value of €14,538m. Not bad, but a disaster if you just said that it should be trading at €5,761m!

Readers may be reminded of our analysis of default risk above. At very high levels of risk, the debt starts to behave more like equity, and the assumption that debt has a significant Beta becomes more realistic. In addition to detracting from the value of the firm, the risk that attaches to debt does represent a diminution of the risk that attaches to equity.

What option pricing does is to provide a systematic way to allocate the shift in value between debt and equity. It can be thought of as either the value of the put option that the bond-holder confers on the equity-holder, or as the time-value of the call option inherent in the purchase of equity. Put-call parity says that they must be the same thing.

Exhibit 2.28: Vivacious SA

1. Accounting and market inputs to model (€m)

Equity market value:	
Price per share	12.40
Shares in issue	1,089
Market capitalisation	**13,499**

Book net debt calculation:	
Cash	(5,024)
Marketable securities	(1,713)
Cash and equivalent	(6,737)
Long-term debt	26,073
Short-term debt	13,884
Total debt	39,957
Net debt	**33,220**

Market value of debt:	
Market price of debt (% of book)	*95%*
Market value of debt	**31,559**

Enterprise value	**45,058**

2. Estimated fair value and cash flow of enterprise (€m)

Group interest:	
Media (consolidated)	22,716
Media (associates)	1,836
Telecoms	13,051
Environment	1,886
Other	630
Overhead adjustment	(1,138)
Group asset value	**38,981**

Cash flow to investors:	
Interest	635
Dividend	0
Cash flow to investors	**635**

Source: Deutsche Bank

3. Volatility calculations

Share price volatility:	
Period of measurement (days)	30
Measured S.D. over period	*46.6%*
Annual S.D.	*162.5%*
LN annual S.D. of share price	**96.5%**

Debt price volatility:	
Period of measurement (days)	30
Measured S.D. over period	*46.7%*
Annual S.D.	*162.9%*
LN annual S.D. of debt price	**96.6%**

Inputs for volatility calculation:	
Debt to capital ratio	*70.0%*
LN annual S.D. of stock price	*96.5%*
LN annual S.D. of debt value	*96.6%*
Correlation between values of debt and equity	**-0.559**

Volatility calculation:	
Weight of equity (We)	*30.0%*
Weight of debt (Wd)	*70.0%*
Variance of equity value (Ve)	*93.1%*
Variance of debt value (Vd)	*93.4%*
Correlation between values of debt and equity (CORRed)	*-0.559*
Annual variance of firm value (S.D.^2)	*32.3%*
LN annual S.D. of firm value	**56.8%**
[Var firm = We^2*Ve+Wd^2*Vd+2*We*Wd*S.D.e*S.D.d*CORRed]	

4. Option model inputs and results (€m)

Inputs to model:	
S = Estimated value of firm's assets	38,981
E = Book value of debt	33,220
S.D. = S.D. of enterprise value	*56.8%*
T = Weighted average duration of debt (years)	2
r = Risk-free rate	*4.0%*

Theoretical values of equity and debt:	
Value of equity	14,538
Value of debt	24,443
Enterprise value	38,981
Market value debt/book value debt (%)	*73.6%*
Target share price	13.35

5. Black Scholes option valuation model

Basic inputs:	
Asset value (S)	38,981
LN annual standard deviation of asset value (S.D.)	*56.8%*
Exercise price (E)	33,220
Annual periods (T)	2.00
Risk-free rate (R)	**4.0%**

Adjustment for project cash flow:	
Enter either: Annual cash flow from project	635
Or enter: Yield from project	
Yield for option calculation	*1.6%*

Model outputs:	
Value of call	14,538
Value of put	7,485

Model variables:	
Asset value	38,981
Exercise price	33,220
Years to expiry	2.00
Risk-free rate	*4.0%*
Standard deviation	*56.8%*
Variance (S.D.^2)	*32.3%*
Yield	*1.6%*
d1	0.65934
N(d1)	0.74516
d2	-0.14440
N(d2)	0.44259

Equity as a Call Option

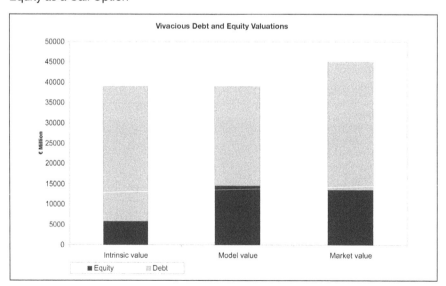

Clearly, rather than using an independent valuation of the assets, it is possible to use the market value implied by the sum of the market values of the equity and the debt, and then just to use the model to reallocate this value between the two components of the capital structure. Exhibit 2.29 shows what happens to the final slide if precisely the same model that was used above is amended to make the estimated fair value of the assets equal to the market value of the assets. The ascribed value to both equity and debt would have been greater in this case (rightly, as events turned out), and much of the upside would have been allocated to the equity.

Exhibit 2.29: Vivacious – market values

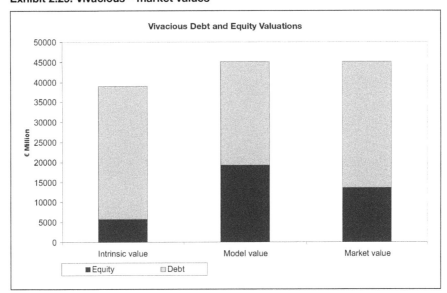

7.2 What happened to default risk?

Readers may remember that we had two extreme possibilities when interpreting the risk premium on debt when conducting an intrinsic valuation of a company. The first was to assume that all of the premium related to market risk, to ascribe a Beta to the debt, and to recycle that risk which was being assumed by the debt out of the cost of equity. The second was to assume that all of the risk relating to debt was specific.

> What we are doing in our option model is precisely equivalent to the first assumption above: that all of the loss of value resulting from risk that attaches to the debt gets transferred into additional value to the equity. But if we assume that all the risk that attaches to the debt is specific, then the full impact of the risk premium on the debt should be subtracted from the value of the company in the option model, as it is in the intrinsic value model.

The two choices are illustrated in exhibit 2.30.

Exhibit 2.30: Payoffs to equity and debt

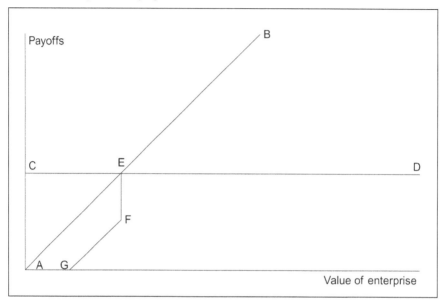

In this slide, the line from A to B is the set of possible enterprise values that we are considering prior to specific default costs, and the line from C to D denotes the par value of the company's debt. Then, as above, the intrinsic value of the equity is the standard call options payoff represented by the line from C to E to B. The payoff to the debt is the standard short put option payoff represented by the line from A to E to D.

Now suppose that the risk premium on debt does not represent market risk which is recycled back into the value of equity through a reduction in its Beta to reflect the Beta of debt, but that the debt has no Beta.

The line from B to E to F to G now represents the set of possible enterprise values for the company, with the vertical from E to F representing a default cost that is a specific risk. The payoff to the equity is still represented by the line from C to E to B, but the payoff to the debt is now represented by the line from G to F to E to D.

> There has been an overall loss of value to the firm versus the first case, just as there was when we considered the implications of zero Beta debt for intrinsic values.

The deduction from the value of the enterprise, which falls to the debt, is the area of the quadrilateral A to E to F to G. So the value of our enterprise can be represented as the sum of the value of the two options prior to the cost of the specific default risk, minus the cost of the specific default risk.

It is as if we took our second case from exhibit 2.21, in which all of the risk premium on the debt was ascribed to its Beta, and then decided that we were going to cut the value of the debt again, to reflect default risk, and that this time the loss of value would not be recycled via the Beta of the equity.

7.3 Implications for arbitragers

What this analysis implies is that just as ignoring the option relationship between debt and equity holders may result in a massive undervaluation of the equity in a company if that option is valuable, so might naïve application of the standard option model result in considerable overvaluation of the entire enterprise. If we start with an estimated enterprise value and then allocated it using option models between debt and equity we may ignore default risk. Starting with the market value of the enterprise value, rather than an estimated enterprise value, should avoid this, but is clearly very limiting. We may not always believe that the market is right about the enterprise value.

Readers may be interested to refer back to the Vivacious example. There, the analyst's estimates of fair value were significantly below, not above, the market enterprise value. It is reasonable to suppose that the analyst's sum-of-the-parts valuation represented a fairly cautious approach to the market values of the business in the event of forced liquidation.

The market value of the enterprise may or may not include a deduction for specific risk. As we have seen, whether the capital market demands compensation only for market risk or for specific risk as well remains an open question. One sample is not enough to support the contention that the analyst's value includes default costs while the market value does not.

The question of whether or not specific risk is priced will not merely affect the resulting estimate of enterprise value. It will also change the allocation of that enterprise value between debt and equity, because the loss of value resulting from the specific risk of default represents a deduction from the payoffs that attach to the debt, but does not alter the payoffs to the equity.

8. International markets and foreign exchange rates

Before concluding our analysis of discount rates, some comment should be made about the practical problem that shares are traded on different stock exchanges, and that companies are priced, report and operate in different currencies.

The CAPM works from only two assets: the risk-free asset and the market portfolio. Both are deemed to be global, and the latter includes all asset classes, including property, works of art, etc. In practice is it not easy to establish the Beta of a Titian painting, so the assumption is ignored. It is customary to use local risk-free rates and

Betas against the local market. But this creates more problems. Imagine a European chemicals company that for some reason delisted from the German market and relisted in Paris. The German market has more cyclical stocks on it than the French, so it would have a higher Beta against the French market than against the German. One could compensate for this by saying that the equity risk premium is higher in Germany. CAPM would say that it is not, and that the German market is higher Beta than the French market against the global portfolio, but this is hard to measure in practice.

Foreign exchange issues matter mainly because of the risk of applying a euro or dollar-based discount rate to a stream of cash flow that is generated in a high inflation country. In this situation, it is important (and should be possible) to make sure either that the fast growth stream of local forecasts is translated into a slower growth stream of hard currency forecasts, or that an appropriate (higher) discount rate is applied to the higher inflation stream of forecasts.

9. Conclusions on discount rates

The theory surrounding discount rates is probably the most interesting aspect of valuation, but it is also complicated. The result is that practitioners tend to apply a series of formulae for WACC and for leveraging and deleveraging Betas whose implications are not generally understood, and that are in any case inappropriate for growing companies, even though most models finish up with a terminal value that explicitly assumes a growth rate to infinity.

We built up our analysis of discount rates by starting with the unleveraged cost of equity, then adding tax shelters, and then subtracting the cost of distress, but checked for consistency in the case of constant growth companies all the way through. This, as well as common sense, dictated that tax shelters should be discounted at the unleveraged cost of equity, not the gross cost of debt.

From the point of view of the holder of debt, the risk premium is a measure of the value of the put option that has been transferred to the equity shareholder. This insight implies an alternative approach to valuing debt and equity which is particularly appropriate in the case of companies that are on the brink of insolvency, because the option will have a relatively high value relative to its intrinsic value. Standard approaches to valuation, including those that we shall be working with for the rest of this book, ignore this option value, as it is relatively small for well capitalised companies.

This still begs the question of where the unleveraged cost of equity comes from, and, as we have indicated, there are problems with the CAPM. It remains the most widely-used approach, but there are good empirical reasons for replacing Betas with alternative factors reflecting size, leverage and liquidity. And there is a very real risk, even if we discount tax shelters at the unleveraged cost of equity, that we shall add back the value of the tax shelter to the company and not properly subtract the cost associated with default risk, unless we make the assumption that the risk premium that attaches to debt is all related to specific risk, and that the Beta of debt is zero.

The two extreme assumptions are either to assume that all of the default risk that attaches to debt is attributable to market risk, which is probably very unrealistic, or to assume that none of it is attributable to market risk, which is probably closer to the truth for most companies. In the case of very risky companies, it will clearly not be true, and a deduction for the specific cost of default needs to be made.

9.1 Practical recommendations

The practical and theoretical difficulties with the theory surrounding discount rates (both CAPM and the impact of leverage) have not been fully resolved. Because they are difficult they are often ignored by practitioners, which may be very dangerous. As with the choice of valuation model to use out of the four discussed in chapter one, we would recommend a pragmatic approach to deciding how to handle discount rates, depending on what the key issue is that is to be addressed. Points to bear in mind are the following:

1. Are the cash flows and the discount rate in the same currency?

2. Does it matter if we use one risk-free rate or do we need to model using the yield curve (which would require a time-varying model, whether WACC or APV)?

3. Do we have a group of homogenous enough companies to try to get to an industry asset Beta in which we can have some confidence?

4. Is a significant proportion of what we are valuing attributable to tax shelters, in which case we want to use APV?

5. What are we going to assume about the Beta of debt?

6. Is the company's balance sheet structure going to change enough for this to be significant to its value, in which case we need to use either APV or time-varying WACC (in both cases being sure to discount the tax shelter at the unleveraged cost of equity, and to adjust the cost of debt for default risk)?

7. Is the company so risky that there is a significant option component to the value of the equity?

Rather than providing a single menu for the selection of discount rates, we should prefer to leave readers equipped to determine which approach to use after answering for themselves the questions above. Our examples in chapters five and six will include selection of and calculation of appropriate methodologies and discount rates for valuation.

Chapter Three

What Do We Mean By 'Return'?

Introduction

Economists and accountants do not mean the same thing when they use the term 'return'. To an economist, an Internal Rate of Return (IRR) is a term of art with a specific mathematical meaning. It means the discount rate that if applied to a stream of cash flows will provide a present value that equates to the cost of the investment. Put another way, the IRR is the discount rate that gives a result such that the Net Present Value (NPV) of the investment is exactly zero.

To an accountant, a Return on Capital Employed (ROCE) is a fraction, of which the numerator is operating profit generated in a particular year and the denominator is the amount of capital that was employed to generate the profit.

There are two important differences between the two definitions. The first is that the IRR is a figure that is calculated using cash flows over the life of the project, not just for one year. The second is that the IRR is based on cash flow numbers and the ROCE is based on accounting profits and balance sheets. We went to some lengths in chapter one to demonstrate that it was not practically possible to forecast corporate cash flows without having recourse to profits and balance sheets. Surely, we are not now going to reverse that conclusion? No, we are not, but we are going to temper it with a recognition that if we use accounting returns on capital as a proxy for economic returns, which is what we really want, then in most real-life examples the former is only an approximation for the latter. This obviously begs the question of whether or not it would be possible to restate accounts in such a way as to permit accurate measures of returns. There is at least one methodology that is commercially available and marketed to address this problem, and there are also some sectors of the equity market in which companies often provide information that makes more accurate assessment of returns possible. Our approach will be as follows. First, we shall explore the problem. Then we shall look at the solution proposed by Cash Flow Return On Investment (CFROI). Finally, we shall comment on ways in which accounts are, and could be made more representative of, value creation, a direction in which accounting practices are already moving. Thus, the last of our theoretical chapters connects with one of the more important issues to be addressed in chapter four: the capitalisation and depreciation or revaluation of fixed assets.

1. IRR versus NPV

Exhibit 3.1 illustrates the cash flows for a project as they are often portrayed in financial literature. The 'down' bars in year zero represents the initial investment, and reflects cash outflow for the investor. The up bars in subsequent years represent annual cash flows, and reflects prospective cash inflow for the investor. Discounting has the effect of diminishing the cash flows as they are brought back to year zero values.

Exhibit 3.1: Project cash flow

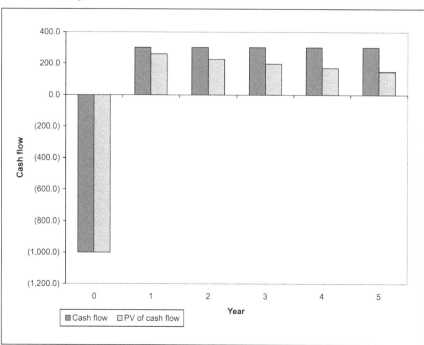

If we calculate the cumulative cash flows over the six years, without discounting, then the cumulative cash flow from the project is a positive 500. If we use a discount rate of 15.2%, which is the IRR for the project, then the NPV (which comprises the initial cash outflow and the present value of the subsequent cash inflows) is zero. This is illustrated in exhibit 3.2 below.

Exhibit 3.2: Project cash flows and NPV

Project cash flows						
Year	0	1	2	3	4	5
Cash flow	(1,000.0)	300.0	300.0	300.0	300.0	300.0
Cumulative cash flow	500.0					
Factor	1.000.0	0.8678	0.7530	0.6534	0.5670	0.4921
PV of cash flow	(1,000.0)	260.3	225.9	196.0	170.1	147.6
NPV	0.0					
Discount rate	*15.2%*					

We can illustrate the fact that the IRR is 15.2% in a different way. Suppose that we recalculated the present value of the project at the beginning of each year. Then if we calculated the profit for the year as the cash flow that the project generated minus the impairment to its value each year, then the result should reflect a 15.2% return on the opening capital. Let us have a look. The calculations are represented in exhibit 3.3.

Exhibit 3.3: ROCE=IRR

Economic accounting						
Year	0	1	2	3	4	5
Cash flow	(1,000.0)	300.0	300.0	300.0	300.0	300.0
Opening PV of cash flows	0.0	1,000.0	852.4	682.3	486.2	260.3
Closing PV of cash flows	1,000.0	852.4	682.3	486.2	260.3	0.0
Impairment of value	1,000.0	(147.6)	(170.1)	(196.0)	(225.9)	(260.3)
Profit	0.0	152.4	129.9	104.0	74.1	39.7
ROCE (opening capital)	*0.0%*	*15.2%*	*15.2%*	*15.2%*	*15.2%*	*15.2%*

The first row repeats the undiscounted cash flows from exhibit 3.2. The second calculates the present value of the project at the beginning of each year. As the discount rate used is 15.2%, the project's IRR, this is tautologically zero at the start of year 0. The third row calculates the present value of the project at the end of the year, at the same discount rate. Again, the figure of 1,000 is tautological. Profit is then calculated as the cash flow from operations for the year minus the impairment of value for the year (the fall in present value for the project). In year 0, 1,000 is spent to create 1,000 of value. In subsequent years, cash flow exceeds the impairment of value, and if the resulting profit is divided by the opening present value then the resulting return is always 15.2%. This calculation is analogous to calculation of a lease payment, in which interest would substitute for profit and amortisation of principal for impairment of value.

But, of course, this is not what happens in conventional accounting. Exhibit 3.4 shows the same calculation performed for the same asset, but substitutes straight line depreciation for impairment of value and opening and closing capital for opening and closing present values.

Exhibit 3.4: Conventional ROCE calculation

Conventional accounting						
Year	0	1	2	3	4	5
Cash flow	(1,000.0)	300.0	300.0	300.0	300.0	300.0
Opening capital	0.0	1,000.0	800.0	600.0	400.0	200.0
Closing capital	1,000.0	800.0	600.0	400.0	200.0	0.0
Depreciation	0.0	(200.0)	(200.0)	(200.0)	(200.0)	(200.0)
Profit	0.0	100.0	100.0	100.0	100.0	100.0
ROCE (opening capital)	0.0%	10.0%	12.5%	16.7%	25.0%	50.0%

The difference between this and exhibit 3.3 above lies in the depreciation being calculated as a straight line figure derived by taking the investment amount and dividing by the useful life. In reality, the impairment of value that results from retirement date for the asset approaching accelerates. The cost of losing something in 24 years rather than 25 years is much less than the cost of losing something in two years rather than three years. Yet conventional accounting does not accommodate this, with only two approaches to depreciation being acceptable: straight line, or declining balance. The latter is even worse from the point of view of misrepresenting economic reality.

In fairness, the problem for accountants is that our exercise involved the assumption that we can predict future cash flows. Traditionally, this would have been regarded as an imprudent basis for accounting. But the dividing line between traditional historical cost accounts and fair value accounting has become much more blurred in recent years. This is partly because of the pressure to reflect the value of derivatives and other assets on balance sheets at market value. In addition, both in the areas of capitalisation of intangible assets acquired on consolidation, and in the application of ceiling tests to all fixed assets, there is a gradual shift towards a greater reflection of market values in published balance sheets. If ever taken to its logical conclusion, this would eliminate our problem, or rather, replace it with a new one: assessing the reasonableness of the assumptions that underlie the claimed market values. This is already an issue for insurance companies (see discussion of accounting for insurance contracts in chapter six), oil companies ('SEC 10' NPVs) and all companies with complex derivatives in their balance sheets, which are subject to what Warren Buffett has memorably described as 'mark to myth' accounting. We shall return to all of these issues later, but first would note two things about our calculations.

The first is that the difference between internal rate of return and accounting returns on capital will tend to be worst in the case of companies with assets that have long asset lives and whose cash flows are expected to rise over the life of the asset. It will tend to be most acute for utilities, natural resource companies and insurance companies, and it is no surprise that managements, bankers and investors in all of these sectors set little store by unmodified historical cost accounts.

The second is that the problem will be mitigated considerably if the company maintains a portfolio of similar assets in it, all of different ages. Let's return to our example one last time but instead of assuming a one-asset company instead assume that our company has within it five assets, of differing ages. Exhibit 3.5 shows its simplified accounts for the year.

Exhibit 3.5: Mature company ROCE

Mature company	
Cash flow	1,500.0
Opening capital	3,000.0
Closing capital	3,000.0
Depreciation	(1,000.0)
Profit	500.0
ROCE (opening capital)	16.7%

This is better than the results for a new or an old asset, but there is still a significant difference between 16.7% and the right answer, which is 15.2%. And the closeness of the results will depend on the shape of the cash flows that are generated by the assets over their lives, and by the phasing of capital expenditure within the company. In reality, company capital expenditure often goes in waves. This will tend to result in companies that have recently undergone a period of low investment achieving high accounting returns on capital employed, and companies that have just undergone a period of high capital expenditure looking rather unprofitable.

Before we rush to the conclusion that accounts are treacherous things after all, and that we should return to discounting cash flows and ignoring profit and balance sheets, reflect on a question that we discussed in chapter one: where do we get our forecasts of cash flows from? Generally, the answer is: from accounting projections of the corporation that we are trying to value. So we are stuck with accounting numbers. The question is how we can try to make them as meaningful as possible.

The best known attempt to construct a valuation model that is explicitly aimed at solving this problem is Cash Flow Return On Investment (CFROI), popularised by HOLT (now owned by Credit Suisse).

2. Calculating CFROI

One approach to the problem, as we have seen, is for accounts to reflect fair values. In this instance the simple ratio of profit divided by capital equates to the IRR that the company is achieving. But accounts are not created that way and (from the outside, at least) it is generally impossible to recreate them by revaluing all the assets every year.

If we cannot revalue the assets we want then to go back to modelling cash flows directly, as we did in exhibit 3.2, but then we run into another problem. We do not get corporate cash flows by asset. Often, we just get the information for the business as a whole. CFROI starts with this constraint and makes a simplifying assumption: that we can use the company's cash flow from operations, its historical stream of capital expenditure, and the life of its assets to construct a model that looks like exhibit 3.6, but which applies to the corporate entity as a whole. Exhibit 3.6 illustrates what CFROI sets out to do.

Exhibit 3.6: Basics of CFROI calculation

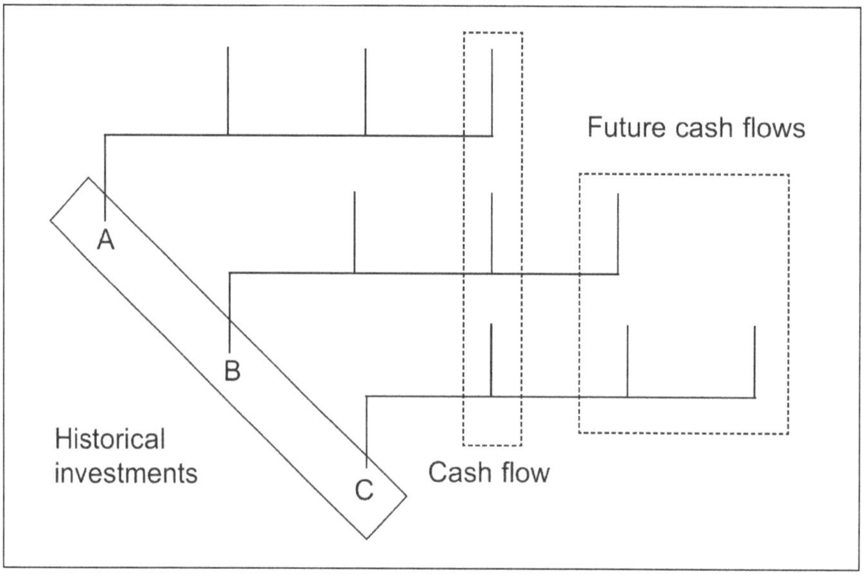

In this example, the company has assets with a life of three years. Investments A are in their third year of life, B in their second and C in their first. All that we can ascertain from the accounts about their cash generation is the total cash flow in the current year. The insight is that if we add together the three historical annual investments, and then relate this total to a series of three annual corporate cash flows, then we can use this to calculate an internal rate of return for the company as a whole. This calculation is illustrated in exhibit 3.7.

Exhibit 3.7: CFROI=corporate IRR

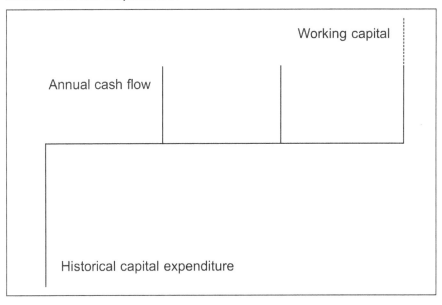

The company's CFROI is simply the IRR calculated for this model. Notice that the cash flow for the final year includes release of working capital, as if the company were to be liquidated.

Let us return to the previous exhibit, 3.6. Two of the years of investment, B and C, comprise assets that have a remaining life. We do not know what they are generating, but we can calculate their average remaining lives as their net book values divided by the annual depreciation charge. In our example this figure will approximate to one year, so we calculate the value of the existing assets as being one year's cash flow, discounted for one year with working capital released at the end. Clearly, if the company had assets with an average remaining life of five years, the value of the existing assets would be calculated as a discounted stream comprising five years' cash flow, again with working capital released at the end.

And what about future investments? That is why we needed to calculate the CFROI. Suppose that the company is currently achieving a return on investments that is in excess of its cost of capital, then the standard assumption would be that over time this would be driven by competition back into line with its WACC. We can then model the value that will be added by a future stream of investments by assuming that although each year's capital expenditure will be higher than the last, the spread that it earns over the WACC is less than the last, with the result that after a reasonable period (whatever that might be), no further value is added, so no further calculations need to be undertaken to value the company. This concept is known as a 'fade', and we shall return to it when we look at practical issues in valuation in chapters five and six.

There are some additional complications if the approach that we have now discussed is to be applied in the way that HOLT applies it. The first relates to inflation. Our company had assets with a life of only three years. Many capital intensive companies have assets with a life of 15 years or more. In this case just adding up the stream of historical investments and relating them to current cash flow is misleading, as inflation will result in understatement of the capital required to generate current cash flow. The solution is to restate everything in real terms, escalating the historical investments into current day money. The resulting CFROI is then real, rather than nominal, and should be related to a real cost of capital.

The second complication relates to the tapering of returns. Rather than assuming that existing assets continue to generate their current cash flows, and that new investments generate even cash flows over their lives, HOLT applies the fade not just to cash flows generated by new assets in their first year, but also to individual annual cash flows from existing and new assets on a year-by-year basis. So each component of the cash flows that is being discounted is fading year by year to a level that implies that the return on the individual investments fades towards the cost of capital. Exhibit 3.8 illustrates the effect of the fade on cash flows from existing assets.

Exhibit 3.8: Cash flow from existing assets

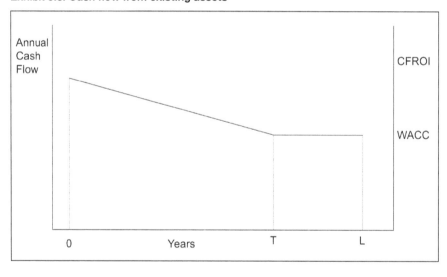

In this chart, L is the remaining life of the assets. T is the point in the future at which it is assumed that competition has beaten down returns so that CFROI=WACC. The period from o to T is the fade period. The left-hand Y axis shows projected cash flow from the existing assets, ignoring release of working capital. The right-hand Y axis shows the CFROI that was used to calculate them.

New assets are modelled in exactly the same way. Each year's investment is bigger than the last, inflated at the real growth rate of the firm. It generates a stream of cash flow that declines each year until it reaches a level, at year T, that equates to a level at which, if it had been maintained over the life of the investment, its IRR would be equal to the WACC. There is no need to model investments made after year T, since they have no impact on the value of the firm. The life of the model needs only to be to the point at which all investments made before year T have generated all of their annual cash flows, so the model life will be T plus L. Clearly, for a company whose CFROI is expected to fade into line with its WACC over a period of, say, eight years, and whose assets have a total life of 15 years, this implies that the full model will extend over 23 years.

We have discussed CFROI with the use of diagrams because, unlike the valuation models discussed in chapter one, it makes minimal use of formulae but is instead a large, detailed, calculation which has to be done on a year-by-year basis for a specific company. There is no terminal value based on a constant growth formula, and the annual cash flows are derived separately for the existing assets and for the projected new investments. We shall talk through a set of detailed exhibits for a real company in the next section. Our methodology may not be exactly identical to that used by HOLT, but it is very similar, and in any case one of the attractions of the CFROI approach is that it is extremely flexible. We shall defer discussion of its disadvantages until it has been adequately explained.

2.1 CFROI example

Exhibit 3.9 below illustrates the outputs from a real, detailed, CFROI model. Again, we shall spare the reader all the numbers, but have represented the outputs graphically, in the hope that this will make the methodology as clear as possible. The model is of the food retailer, Singleton PLC. At the time, Singleton's assets had a gross asset life of 21 years, and a remaining net asset life of 13 years, implying an average asset age of eight years. It was assumed that an appropriate fade period during which the company's CFROI would fade from its then current level to equal its WACC was eight years, implying that only investments made prior to year eight needed to be modelled. Thus, the model needs to extend out by a total of 29 years, comprising eight years of fade period and the 21-year life for the investments made in year eight. The template used was designed to handle up to 40 years of combined fade period and asset life, and the charts illustrate the full 40-year period in each case, to give a sense of chronological proportion.

Exhibit 3.9: CFROI model of Singleton PLC

1. CFROI and forecast CFROI

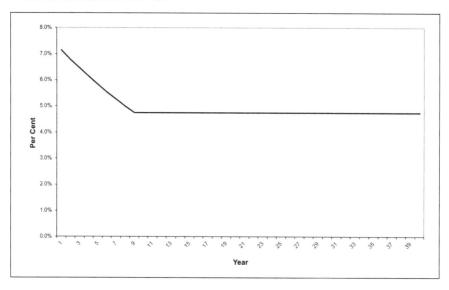

2. Cash from existing assets

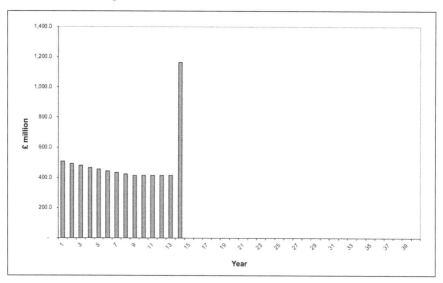

3. Forecast investments (incl. W.C.)

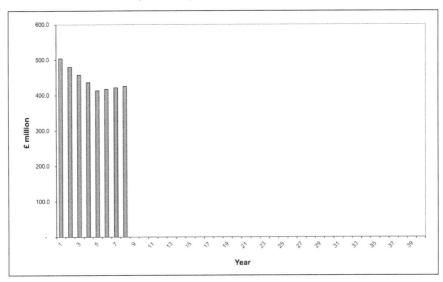

4. Cash from new assets

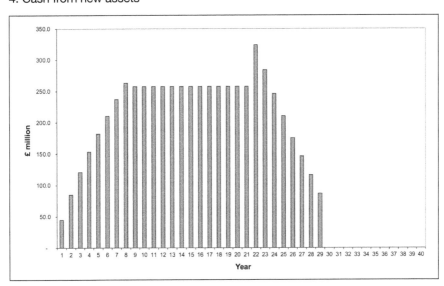

5. Net cash flow (new assets)

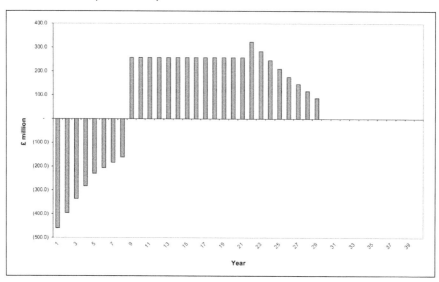

6. Net cash flow (all assets)

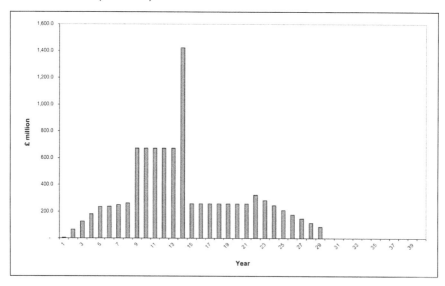

Chart 1 simply shows what happens to CFROI over time. It is assumed to fade over eight years into line with the company's WACC, after which it remains at that level.

Chart 2 shows the cash flows that are projected from the existing assets. They have a remaining life of 13 years, and the large amount for year 13 reflects release of the company's existing working capital. Annual cash flows fall over the 13 years because the firm's CFROI is fading towards its WACC.

Chart 3 shows forecasted investments, and extends only eight years because all new investments undertaken after year eight have an NPV of zero (IRR=WACC). Capital expenditure for the first five years is explicitly forecast to start high and then fall. The company had been through a period of underinvestment. After year five the model takes over, with an assumed real underlying growth of 1% annually.

Chart 4 shows the cash flows that are projected from new investments. They rise to year eight as new investments are made, and they are flat from year eight to year 21, as cash flows stop fading after year eight (IRR=WACC). In year 21 they bounce with the release of the non-depreciated working capital from the year-one investment. And after that they fall as assets are retired.

Chart 5 shows the net cash flows that are projected from new investments. The difference between this and the previous chart is the assumed cash outflows related to the investments in new assets shown in chart 3.

Chart 6 pulls together all of the above. Discounting these cash flows gives the value of the company, as does adding together the discounted value of the cash flows in charts 2 and 4.

2.2 Conclusions regarding CFROI

The first point to make about the CFROI methodology is that it is a subset of the standard discounted cash flow to capital approach discussed in chapter one. What is different about it is the way in which it goes about projecting what the cash flows are actually going to be. Instead of using corporate projections for a period, followed by a terminal value based on an assumed growth rate and return on capital employed, it separates the task of modelling existing assets and future assets, and generates separate streams of cash flow for the two. Existing assets are assumed to produce streams of cash that fade towards that which is implied by a CFROI that equals the company's WACC. Each new year of new investments generates its own stream of cash, and is modelled as if it were an individual asset, with a stream of cash receipts that fades in line with the returns assumed for the old assets. After year T, when CFROI=WACC, new investments can be ignored, and the model need only run off the cash flows from investments that have already been made before year T.

But look again at chart 6 in exhibit 3.9. Do these cash flows really look like those that you would expect any stable, low growth company to generate? Probably not. They are an artificial construction, not a realistic projection. Moreover, they are highly dependent on the assumed asset life. Growth rates and fades are issues with which analysts have to grapple, whatever the methodology used. But asset lives are not. One could say that what CFROI does is to replace one problem with another. Using conventional accounts leaves us dependent on return on capital calculations that are economically inaccurate. Breaking with them and switching to CFROI leaves us dependent on calculations of internal rate of return that are in turn highly dependent on the assumed life of the company's assets. And what about companies whose assets do not generate flat streams of real cash flow?

Finally, there is the question of what to do about accruals. It was bad enough thinking through what to do with them in a standard WACC/DCF model. Easier in an economic profit model: we just left them in. But they are hard, though not impossible, to build into a CFROI model. The latter is explicitly based on cash flows and net present values, and provisions of all kinds would really also have to be built into the cash flow streams. In the case of decommissioning costs, this should not be impossible. Just as non-depreciating assets could be released, decommissioning costs could be deducted. But when it comes to pension provisions, life could get harder.

Overall, our suggestion would be that the problems created by converting forecasts into a CFROI structure exceed the benefits for most companies. Exceptions might be companies that have very long asset lives, and very regular cash flows from operations. Some utilities would be candidates for this treatment.

3. Another approach: CROCI

We should in fairness make reference to another approach, namely Cash Flow Return on Capital Invested (CROCI). This was originally developed as a proprietary methodology by Deutsche Bank equity research department, and in principle is an adjusted version of an economic profit model. The main adjustment is to restate all of the accounts on a current cost basis, to avoid overstatement of profitability resulting from inflation. But the methodology also allows for the use of different approaches to depreciation, including that used by the company, a standard asset life set by the investment bank (based on industry norms), and amortisation (effectively what we called impairment of value in exhibit 3.3 above). As used by Deutsche Bank, the main point of their methodology is to emphasise returns to capital, rather than equity, and to eliminate the impact of inflation, but it can also be used to substitute impairment of value for depreciation in the calculation of achieved returns on capital employed.

4. Uses and abuses of ROCE

Companies and analysts need to be aware of the distortions introduced by straight line depreciation. In particular, there is likely to be a systematic bias whereby companies that have invested heavily look less profitable than they really are and companies that have underinvested look more profitable than they really are. As investment often goes in medium-term cycles, this is an important effect.

The impact of the effect is likely to be greatest with companies that have long-lived assets, especially if cash flows are expected to grow over the life of the asset. A gas pipeline would be a fine example.

Something clearly needs to be done to correct for this when valuing companies. One approach is to model existing assets and then to assume additional value added from new investments. This need not take the form of a CFROI analysis, which aggregates cash flow from existing assets. In many cases they can be modelled separately. Indeed, CFROI could be seen as a special case (complete aggregation) of an asset-based company valuation.

It is unlikely to be helpful to model most companies in this way. Separating out the existing and future assets of Procter and Gamble, for example, would be very hard. Most of the assets are intangible. How do we separate investments in building new brands from the marketing costs associated with this year's sales? And, as intangible assets are mainly not capitalised, we shall get no help whatever from looking at notes regarding fixed assets in the accounts, either with respect to the scale of historical investments, nor with gross and remaining asset lives.

So in general we shall be thrown back on corporate, accounting-based models. Of course, it would be nice if companies were to provide us with information that would permit us to adjust fixed assets to fair value, and to accrue fair value additions and impairments through the profit and loss account. In some sectors of the equity market we already can.

Chapter Four

Key Issues in Accounting and Their Treatment Under IFRS

Introduction

The premise of much of the material in this book is the importance and value relevance of accounting information. This importance extends both from the detail and disclosure provided to users by financial statements and the inadequacies of other alternative sources of information.

Furthermore, the move toward consistent accounting across the globe increasingly makes rigorous comparison and analysis of accounting information more feasible than was previously the case. For example, joint projects between the IASB and the FASB on areas such as leasing and revenue recognition, both addressed in this text, move us towards a more common suite of accounting standards. Even if some differences remain on these new standards, there is still more commonality than previously existed. The 'fair value' orientation of many recent accounting standards means balance sheets in the main reflect more up-to-date values. In many cases, even though fair values are not without difficulty themselves, balance sheet values will be more relevant for users.

Accounting and valuation

At the risk of repeating oneself, it is still worth restating some of the key themes in the text so far. First, accounting information is highly relevant for valuation. The level of disclosure, recognition of non-cash economic flows (as well as lots of cash ones), matching and substance over form principles all lead to an investor-friendly information source. Second, the linkages between the balance sheet, income statement and cash flow, once properly understood, can bring users closer to an understanding of the profitability and efficiency of the business through the calculation of economically meaningful returns. Third, alternative sources of information, such as using cash measures of performance, suffer from a number of potential flaws:

- Ignore key economic flows merely because they have not been paid/received in cash.

- Tend to be highly volatile if capital expenditure is included.

- Lack detailed disclosure (e.g., no segmental analysis of cash flow numbers).

- Vulnerable to manipulation (e.g., delay paying suppliers or offering generous discounts both would enhance cash flow but are potentially very damaging for the business).

- Do not fully integrate with balance sheets making it more difficult to use return measures as we do not have an integrated balance sheet that reflects cumulative retained 'cash' earnings.

Notwithstanding the above, we are well aware of the potential difficulties of using accounting information. In particular, history has shown that management will often seek to manipulate subjective accounting rules to maximize the short-run performance of the firm. Therefore, it is often useful to carefully examine cash earnings in addition to accruals-based profit. However, we do not accept that cash flow represents a superior basis for establishing the enterprise value and ultimately equity value of a company.

Finally, it should also be emphasised that accounting information will often need to be adjusted for specific valuation methodologies. This does not mean that the information itself is necessarily flawed. Instead the IASB, and others, have developed a very general model of accounting with the broadest appeal. It has ensured that the major disclosures and information content exists, but it is up to users to decide on how to employ it in their valuation processes. This text, and in particular this chapter, is themed around how we think accounting information can most effectively be integrated into valuation models.

This chapter addresses key areas of accounting that tend to present problems for valuation. Each financial statement issue is addressed in a structured way around six themes:

- Why is the issue of relevance to investors?

- What is existing GAAP under IFRS?

- What is the US GAAP treatment if different from IFRS?

- What are the financial analysis implications?

- Case study examples

- What are the modelling and valuation implications, together with any adjustments, leading from GAAP?

Issues relating to accounting for business combinations are covered in chapter seven. Specific accounting issues relating to banks, insurance, utilities, oils and real estate are addressed in their respective specialist chapters although many of the issues in this chapter would be relevant for these sectors. The key topics addressed are illustrated in exhibit 4.1.

Exhibit 4.1: Technical accounting areas covered

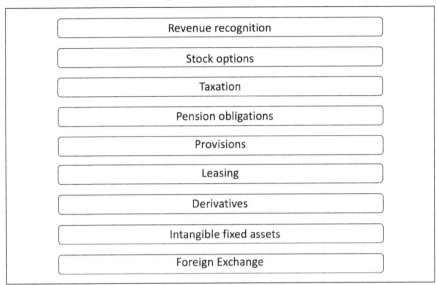

1. Revenue recognition and measurement

1.1 Why is it important?

When interpreting historical accounts, importance is generally ascribed to revenue because it is seen as a key driver of both profitability and cash flow. But it is important to recognise that revenue does not actually equate to a stream of cash inflows. This is why, for example, the widely-used EBITDA figure should not be treated as a measure of cash flow. It includes sales made on non-cash terms, provisions and accrued expenses, to name but a few, none of which are cash flow items. This is not a problem that can be addressed by reverting to cash-based measures, since if a company is actually accruing revenue, that will be paid subsequently, this is clearly material to its value. Moreover, some businesses, such as publishing and airlines, receive cash upfront as consideration for a stream of product or service that will be delivered over the rest of a year, or longer. In that situation, it would clearly be inappropriate to allocate all of the revenue to the quarter in which it was received.

So, we need a realistic measure of accrued revenue, not of cash received. Obviously, this creates a risk – that the measure of revenue that is accrued in a company's accounts, and possibly extrapolated in forecasting models, is not realistic. During severe downturns there have been several cases of companies that booked large amounts of revenue, and therefore of profit, that were subsequently reversed in later quarters. The message for the user of accounts, therefore, is that we need a measure of accrual, but one that is realistic.

1.2 What is current GAAP under IFRS for revenue recognition?

In a broad sense, the term revenue refers to sources of income for a business enterprise. Most forms of business activity generate revenues from a range of different sources. For our purposes it is useful to distinguish between operating and non-operating revenues. Exhibit 4.2 below illustrates such an approach with examples.

Exhibit 4.2: Sources of income

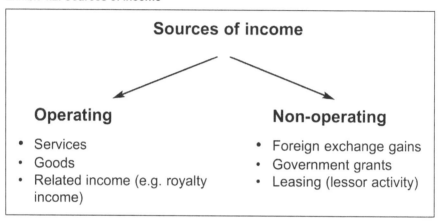

For most analysts the key topic for analysis is those streams of income derived from core business activity, i.e., sales of core products and services. Therefore, this section will focus on these operating streams. This is not to say that non-operating revenues may not be important and significant. A summary of the accounting treatments that apply to such ancillary revenue sources is provided in exhibit 4.3 below.

Exhibit 4.3: Non-operating revenues

Source of revenue	Accounting treatment
Government grants	Revenue grants (to cover operating costs) are treated as income as related expense is incurred; *Capital grants (to cover the cost of non-current assets) treated as deferred credits.*
Foreign Exchange	Gains on trading transactions are reported as reductions in operating expenses; Gains on *financing transactions are reported as part of finance charges.*
Leasing (lessors)	If capital leases then immediate recognition of total sale value of assets under lease treated as revenue *If operating lease then spread profit over lease term giving revenue, in the form of rental receipts, in each year of the lease term*

We ascribe the term revenue recognition to the issue of when a particular source of revenue should be recognised. This timing issue is of crucial importance for calculating profit margins and for gaining an appreciation of historical performance. This is especially so where the product of historical analysis will be a view about future sales and growth. Almost all valuations for industrial concerns entail a forecast of revenues. Indeed, many other facets of valuations and associated models are driven off sales forecasts. For example, operating costs are typically linked to sales forecasts. Furthermore, most models also use revenue figures as drivers for less obvious items such as property, plant and equipment. Therefore, revenue numbers and related information, such as segmental disaggregations, are of significant importance to valuers. An analyst must have a strong knowledge of the revenue recognition issues in his/her sector in order to forecast this core number competently.

In addition to the issue of timing we also have the issue of measurement of the revenue i.e., what number appears in the financials. This tends to be less problematic than the recognition point. In common with many other accounting topics, fair values should be used in the measurement of revenues. This would mean that revenue would have to be discounted if the terms of the transaction where such that the time value of money was material. Given the relatively straightforward nature of the measurement issue, the remaining parts of this chapter will concentrate on the timing issue.

1.2.1 The approach to timing of revenue

There are two broad approaches to revenue recognition: revenue recognition at a point in time and revenue recognition over time. The critical event approach essentially recognises revenues when a significant event occurs. For example, in the real estate sector the critical event might be when contracts are exchanged or when transactions are legally complete. The passage of time approach might also be used in the property sector to recognise rental income as time passes. Companies can employ both approaches for different sources of revenue.

Historically revenue recognition derived from industry practice rather than being addressed explicitly by accounting standards. Two basic conditions had emerged as the drivers for revenue recognition timing which supplement the more general approaches outlined above. The first condition is that prior to recognising revenue the 'sale' must be realised i.e., either the company has received the cash or expects to (for example, the customer is of good credit worthiness). This condition could be satisfied by a company having an appropriate credit control system in operation. The second condition is that the revenues must be earned. In other words, the work relating to the revenue under consideration for recognition must be complete.

In many ways GAAP based on these principles existed without many difficulties for a considerable period of time. However, increasingly complex business activity eventually exposed the inadequacies of relying on these simple conditions. Therefore, the IASB and the FASB embarked on a significant project which eventually resulted in the issuance of IFRS 15 *Revenue from Contracts with Customers* by the IASB and an equivalent, ASC 606 under US GAAP.

Below we outline the major features of IFRS 15 and, in particular, when revenue should be recognised in the income statement. The subsequent sections address some of the contemporary issues surrounding revenue recognition. This is a significant accounting issue as incorrect recognition could lead to a misstatement of income and misjudgements about historical performance.

Let us examine the sales cycle for a basic transaction involving the sale of goods.

Exhibit 4.4 Sales cycle for goods

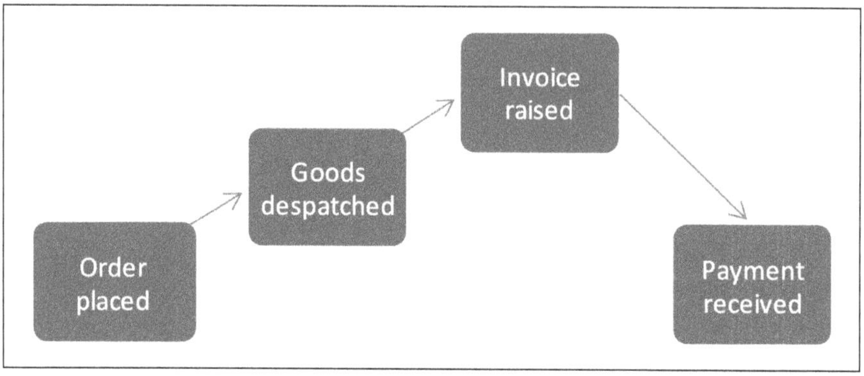

At which stage of the above cycle should the sale be recognised as revenue?

IFRS 15 *Revenue from Contracts with Customers* provides guidance on this accounting issue. It states that revenue should be recognised when control of a promised good or service is transferred to a customer. For the sale of goods, transferring control to the customer would ordinarily occur when most (but not necessarily all) of the following conditions are met:

- The vendor has a right to payment for the goods sold.
- The customer has legal title of the goods.
- The customer has physical possession of the goods.
- There has been a significant transfer of risks and rewards of ownership from the vendor to the customer.
- The customer has accepted the goods.

In many cases, most of the above criteria are satisfied at the point of despatch (typically, goods are transferred using 'free on board' shipping point terms, where the buyer is deemed to have taken delivery at the point of despatch). It can therefore be assumed that normal practice is to record the sale once the goods have been despatched.

The accounting issue of cut off should also be considered at this point. Financial statements are prepared using the accruals or matching concept. This means that all revenues earned, and all costs incurred during the accounting period should be reflected in the financial statements regardless of date of cash receipt or payment.

At the end of the financial year, particular attention should be given to the matching of goods despatched pre-year end and the corresponding sales invoices. The sales invoices for these goods should be accounted for in the current financial year in order to match revenue and costs. Even in this apparently straightforward situation, there is significant room for error and manipulation.

The timing of revenue recognition is therefore a significant accounting issue and IFRS 15 provides detailed instruction and guidance to help address this.

1.2.2 The approach to measurement of revenue

Measurement of revenue for the sale of goods is a less contentious issue than for long-term contracts. In general, revenue is based on the transaction price, which is defined as:

"The amount of consideration to which an entity expects to be entitled, in exchange for transferring promised goods and services to a customer."

There are a few key areas of complexity that should be considered and where IFRS 15 provides some guidance:

- Variable consideration – offering discounts, rebates or even a right of return to customers will cause some uncertainty as to the amount of consideration that the vendor eventually receives. The vendor is required to recognise revenue based on an estimate of the net amount they expect to receive (i.e., after adjusting for discounts, rebates and returns).

- Non-cash consideration – payment by the customer may be in the form of other goods or services. If this occurs, the vendor needs to estimate the fair value of the goods and services received and include them in the amount of revenue recognised.

- The existence of a significant financing component – if a significant period of time elapses between payment by the customer and transfer of the goods, the vendor needs to consider whether the consideration includes a financing component (e.g., the amount payable by the customer has been adjusted to reflect payment being made significantly before or after the goods are transferred). If this is identified then the amount of revenue recognised needs to exclude any estimated interest income or expense (and the interest income or expense separately presented in earnings).

1.2.3 Revenue recognition and long-term contracts

So far, we have considered transactions which are completed within an accounting period. In practice, that is not always the case. The area of long-term contracts is a particular revenue recognition 'grey area'. Long-term contracts are contracts that straddle a year end.

Exhibit 4.5: Long-term contract timing schedule

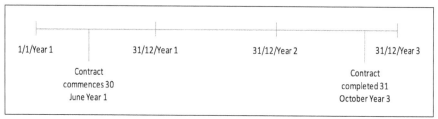

The accounting issues which arise from this scenario are:

- When should the revenue on the contract be recognised?

- When should the costs on the contract be recognised?

In practice, there are two possible approaches for recognising the revenues (and costs) as demonstrated in the diagram below:

Exhibit 4.6: Point in time versus over time forms of revenue recognition

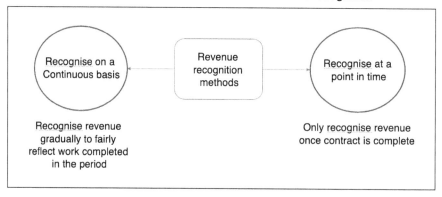

We have already seen that IFRS 15 requires revenue to be recognised when control of a promised good or service is transferred to a customer. For a long-term contract, this transfer of control can occur either on a continuous basis (and therefore revenues would be recognised over time) or at a point in time (and therefore revenues would be recognised at that point in time).

Although the concept of 'transferring control' on a continuous basis might seem unusual, it essentially means that the vendor is providing a service to the customer, even where this service results in the construction of a physical asset. The accounting rules provide some guidance on how to determine when control is transferred over time:

- The customer simultaneously receives and consumes the benefits of the vendor's efforts (e.g., can the customer enjoy the benefit of any work performed to date?).

- The vendors efforts create (or enhance) a physical or intangible asset that the customer controls (e.g., the customer bears the risks and rewards of ownership of the asset).

- The vendor has a right to payment for work completed to date and any asset created has no alternative use (e.g., the work is sufficiently bespoke that the vendor could not sell the item to another customer).

In reality, determining whether these criteria can be satisfied will depend on the detail contained within the customer contracts.

Assume the following:

	€m
Contract value	20
Total estimated costs	(16)
Profit	4

If it is determined that the control transfers only on completion of the contract:

- Revenue will be accounted for on completion.

- Costs recorded as 'contract assets' (i.e., part of current assets).

This would result in the following:

	Year 1 €m	Year 2 €m	Year 3 €m
Revenue	–	–	20
Costs	–	–	(16)
Profit	–	–	4

Although this example demonstrates a prudent approach to the accounting, it is questionable whether it is particularly relevant for users. It does not assist the users in their understanding of how the profit of €2m was earned, nor what was happening in years one and two.

Fortunately, for the majority of long-term contracts, revenue recognition over time will be the most appropriate method. This method does however raise the question of how to measure progress on the contract, since this will determine how much revenue is recognised each year:

Revenue recognised = % progress on contract X total contract revenue

IFRS 15 addresses this issue and stipulates that one of the following two methods should be used to determine contract progress:

1. Output method: expert survey of work to date is used to determine value of work completed relative to total value of contract.

2. Input method: compare the input costs incurred to date (e.g., labour and materials) relative to the total expected input costs for the contract. This is also known as the 'cost-to-cost' method.

Returning to the example from above, we now determine that control transfers on a continuous basis and the company decides to use the input method to determine contract progress. 25% of input costs are incurred in year one, 50% in year two and the remainder in year three.

This would result in the following:

	Year 1 €m	Year 2 €m	Year 3 €m
Revenue	5	10	5
Costs	(4)	(8)	(4)
Profit	1	2	1

This approach can only be adopted if there is reasonable certainty as to the outcome of the contract and at a point where progress under the contract can be measured with reasonable certainty. Where this is not the case, then revenues are only recognised to offset any costs recognised (i.e., no profit is recognised). Once there is sufficient certainty on the outcome and progress, the approach described above would then be applied.

This again illustrates the play off between the fundamental concepts of prudence and accruals.

1.2.4 Further thoughts on revenue recognition

The sections above on revenue capture some of the broad concepts about the timing of recogition.

The introduction of IFRS 15/ASC 606 represented a significant development in accounting by introducing a single, core principle which determines how revenues are recognised, regardless of industry and contract type:

> "Revenue [shall be recognised] to depict the transfer of promised goods and services to customers, in an amount that reflects the consideration to which the company expects to be entitled in exchange for those goods and services."

This principle means that similar transactions in different industries would result in the same pattern of revenue recognition. We shall now turn to some more detailed aspects of IFRS 15 and look at how this principle is applied in a variety of situations beyond the examples we have considered up until now.

Multiple element contracts

In recent years, companies have increasingly sold goods and services together, under a single contract. These contracts often have payment schedules requiring both upfront and on-going payments from customers, with the timing of the payments often unrelated to the timing of when the goods and services are delivered. This is particularly the case in the software and telecoms industry where hardware, licences and data may all be included in the customer contract. These 'multiple element contracts' present a significant accounting challenge, in determining how and when the revenue for each element should be recognised.

IFRS 15 has introduced a five-step framework which explains how revenues should be recognised for all the goods and services promised in a single contract:

Exhibit 4.7: Steps in revenue recognition under IFRS 15

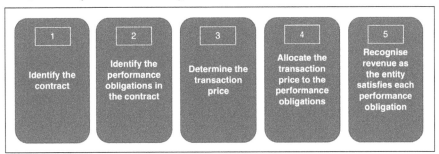

1. The contract determines the rights and obligations of a company and customer.

2. Performance obligations are distinct goods and services promised to a customer.

3. The total payments the company expects to receive from the customer, including an estimate of any uncertain amounts or discounts.

4. Allocation is made based on the estimated relative standalone values of the goods and services.

5. Revenue is recognised as each good or service is delivered to the customer.

One of the most important steps in this framework is that companies must allocate revenue to each of the goods and services, based on their relative standalone values; this means allocating revenue based on how much they are worth if they were to be sold separately. It should be noted that this allocation occurs even if the goods are never sold separately, and in that situation the company would need to make an estimate of the values (e.g., based on the value of similar goods and services or based on cost plus a mark-up).

Principal verses agent

Companies can either be acting as a principal (on their own behalf) or as an agent (on behalf of a third party). This is an important distinction for revenue recognition as it determines whether the company is required to present the gross revenues and costs in relation to a customer contract (if they are acting as principal) or just the net fees or commissions that they derive from the contract (if they are acting as agent).

Indicators that a company is acting as an agent would include where the company:

• Does not have the primary responsibility for fulfilling the contract.

- Does not take on significant inventory risk or credit risk (i.e., would not incur losses from inventory damage or non-payment by customer).

- Does not have discretion in setting prices for the goods and services.

If these indicators apply, then the company would recognise only their fees or commissions as revenue, rather than including the total value of goods and services delivered to the customer.

Warranties

Companies frequently provide warranties to customers in connection with the goods and services they provide. The question therefore arises as to whether the warranty is a 'distinct service' and therefore whether revenue should be separately allocated to the warranty (thus reducing the amount of revenue allocated to the underlying goods or services).

The accounting rules distinguish between warranties which provide assurance to the customer that the goods or services will function as expected (which are not considered a distinct service) from warranties which provide the customer with additional assurance or services (which are considered a distinct service).

Where warranties are not considered a distinct service, then they do not impact on revenue recognition; instead the company would need to recognise a provision (i.e., liability) for any expected warranty claims.

Where warranties are considered a distinct service, then the company would need to allocate revenue to the warranty and recognise the allocated revenue over the warranty period.

Consignment sales

Companies may transfer inventory to a third party (dealer) but retain ultimate control for the inventory. This is known as a consignment sale and an example of this would be where any unsold inventory is returned to the company at the end of a specified period.

No revenue is recognised by the company until the inventory is sold by the dealer to the ultimate customer, as this is the point where control is transferred.

Non-refundable upfront fees

Companies may require customers to pay a non-refundable upfront payment at the start of a contract; examples would include joining fees for a health club or set-up fees in service contracts.

Upfront fees cannot be recognised at the start of the contract except where the payment relates to a good or service which is being provided at that point. In practice, this is rarely the case so these fees are usually deferred and recognised when the underlying goods and services in the contract are delivered.

Summary of probable treatment for a range of sources of revenues

Understanding accounting rules for revenue recognition is a real challenge for analysts. Businesses (and their contracts with customers) are complex and often difficult to understand as an outsider. The following table should provide a starting point for analysing the revenue recognition rules for a range of activities.

Issues	Commentary/Treatment
Subscriptions	Revenue is recognised as service is delivered. Treat as deferred (unearned) income until then.
Media revenues	Advertising revenue is recognised on publication or transmission of the advertising. Production revenues (e.g., television production) are recognised on delivery of content and acceptance by the customer. Licence and distribution revenues are recognised in full as soon as the customer is able to benefit from the license or content.
Software revenues (how to account for those in the vendor's financials)	If the company is not required to provide any material updates or hosting, revenue is recognised in full at the start of the licence period (even if the licence is for a fixed term). If the software and hosting are provided together (software-as-a-service or cloud services), revenue is recognised as service is delivered. If significant customisation is required, then follow a 'long term contract' approach. If multiple elements exist (e.g., sale of standard software with support) then generally, the fee should be allocated to software and support services, and recognised as earned.
Real estate transactions	Revenue could be recognised at either: Exchange of contracts Completion of the transactions
Barter transactions (exchange)	IFRS 15 provides that: If the exchange is like for like (i.e., similar goods/services) then no revenue is generated If dissimilar goods/services are exchanged, then revenue will be recognised at the fair value of the goods/services received

1.3 US GAAP

US GAAP and IFRS are now aligned on the material aspects of revenue recognition following the publication of IFRS 15 and ASC 606 in the US.

1.4 Financial analysis implications

Analysts need to be aware that there are a number of different areas where revenue recognition issues are complex and deserve attention. What can users actually do to help gain a reasonable understanding of such a broad and important area?

The following identifies some basic analytical steps:

1. Gain a thorough understanding of the revenue recognition issues in their sector. This is particularly important in the early years of implementation of IFRS 15.

2. Understand the accepted practice and related GAAP in the sector recognising that this may change given the new standard.

3. Document the accounting policy chosen by each entity in the sector. Highlight any companies with policies outside the norm and the likely impact on the financial statements. How might this impact on comparable company analysis?

4. Watch out for signs of difficulty relating to revenues:

    i.   Unexpected changes in revenues

    ii. Increasing disparity between profit and cash

    iii. Unexpected ballooning of accounts receivable in working capital

    iv. Change in the segment mix, especially if unexpected and or inconsistent with strategy

    v.   Significant revenues or increasing proportion coming from a related party

    vi. Substantial revenues from non-operating sources

    vii. Change in the proportion between contract assets and accounts receivable. For example, increases in contracts assets may indicate that a company is struggling to get to a position where they can actually invoice the client. It is only at the invoicing stage that a contract asset becomes an account receivable balance.

1.5 Case example

It's actually quite difficult to use case studies to illustrate revenue recognition points as the disclosures under various GAAPs have tended to be somewhat limited and IFRS 15 has only recently been issued.

The main issue to look at, as outlined in the paragraph above, is the revenue recognition policy for the company. To illustrate the point, we have reproduced extracts from the accounting policies of two companies:

Exhibit 4.8: Property company revenue recognition

Revenue and profit recognition

Revenue comprises the fair value of the consideration received or receivable, net of value added tax, rebates and discounts. Revenue does not include the disposal value of properties taken in part exchange against a new property. Surpluses or deficits on the disposal of part exchange properties are recognised directly within gross margin.

Revenue is recognised on house and apartment sales at legal completion. For affordable housing sales and other sales in bulk, revenue is recognised upon practical completion and when substantially all risks and rewards of ownership are transferred to the buyer.

Revenue is recognised on land sales and commercial property sales from the point of unconditional exchange of contracts. Where unconditional exchange of contracts has occurred but the Group still has significant obligations to perform under the terms of the contract, such as infrastructure works, revenue is recognised when the obligations are performed.

Profit is recognised on a plot-by-plot basis, by reference to the margin forecast across the related development site. Due to the development cycle often exceeding one financial year, plot margins are forecast, taking into account the allocation of site-wide development costs such as infrastructure, and estimates required for the cost to complete such developments.

Provision is made for any losses foreseen in completing a site as soon as they become apparent.

Source: Crest Nicholson Annual Report 2017

As we can see, Crest recognises revenues based on 'legal completion', whereas another choice would be on the basis of unconditional exchange of contracts, which is the revenue recognition approach for commercial property sales. Note the caveat about a situation where there are infrastructure, or similar, obligations remaining at the point of exchange. In such circumstances revenue recognition is delayed further until these are completed.

We can see the direct impact of IFRS 15 *Revenue Recognition* in the Deutsche Telekom extract below. This addresses a multi-part contract involving the sales of a phone plus related services which are now looked upon as separate performance obligations. Under this new accounting policy, the obligation to provide the handset is complete once it has been handed over at the inception of the contract. Previously, there would have been a lower initial amount recognised. As the customer shall pay over the period of the contract a receivable is recognised for this.

Exhibit 4.9: Deutsche Telekom revenue recognition

- In the case of multiple-element arrangements (e.g., mobile contract plus handset) with subsidized products delivered in advance, a larger portion of the total remuneration is attributable to the component delivered in advance (mobile handset), requiring earlier recognition of revenue in future. This leads to the recognition of what is known as a contract asset – a receivable arising from the customer contract that has not yet legally come into existence – in the statement of financial position.

- At the same time, it results in higher revenue from the sale of goods and merchandise and to lower revenue from the provision of services.

Source: Deutsche Telekom AG Financial statements as of December 31, 2017

1.6 Building valuation models: What to do

Whether the model is constructed in the form of a DCF or an economic profit model, the relevant figure is clearly the accrued revenue, not cash receipts. For companies in which there is a significant difference in any one period between these two items, extrapolating cash receipts is likely to be highly misleading. This implies two conclusions for valuation models. The first is that it is necessary to assess what is an appropriate accrual, which will be dependent on the accounting rules discussed above. The second is that when running DCF valuations we shall actually be valuing a stream of notional 'cash flow' which will include accruals. Otherwise only one side of a coin is being taken into account. If a contractor has fulfilled a significant part of a contract, but has only incurred expenses then it is clear that his cash flows may be significantly understating his value creation. If a publisher sells a large number of subscriptions over a period considerably longer than that of the accounting period just reported, he has received cash that creates liabilities against which supply of the product will be made in subsequent period. Ignoring this fact overstates value creation.

These points do not seem as odd if the form of valuation model chosen is an economic profit model, since we are accustomed to non-cash items appearing in profit and loss accounts. But it is crucial to understand that the same issues apply even within the format of a DCF model.

2. Stock options

2.1 Why is it important?

In many sectors, such as technology and telecommunications, the remuneration of executives contains a significant component of stock options. These options provide management and other employees the opportunity to participate in the capital growth of the business. At the same time, they achieve a level of goal congruence, i.e., harmonising the objectives of management and shareholders. In order to understand corporate performance fully, analysts must appreciate the cost of this significant component of remuneration. If it bypasses the income statement then this may have significant implications for comparable company analysis as well as accurate profitability assessment. Furthermore, if a P/E approach to valuation is to be employed then the analyst needs to be aware of how the potential dilution resulting from stock option compensation is reflected in EPS numbers. And the same point applies to intrinsic value models; there is a cost associated with the dilution.

2.2 What is current GAAP under IFRS for stock options?

Essentially, there are two key accounting issues relating to stock options that must be resolved. First, what is the compensation charge to be recognised in the income statement? Second, what is the impact, if any, on diluted EPS?

2.2.1 The compensation charge

The relevant IFRS and US GAAP accounting standards are IFRS 2 *Share-based payment* and SFAS 123 and APB 25 *Accounting for Stock Issued to Employees,* respectively.

Both standards take a similar approach to accounting for stock based compensation, by requiring that the fair value of, say, stock options must be calculated at grant date and charged to the income statement over the vesting period. It is important to note that this approach is taken regardless of whether the company intends to settle the options by issuing new shares or by buying back its own shares in the market (even if only the latter would impact on cash).

In the rare cases that fair value cannot be reliably determined, both IFRS and US GAAP allow the use of intrinsic value.

2.2.2 Intrinsic value approach

The intrinsic value of a stock option is calculated as the difference between the market price of the underlying and the strike price of the option.

So, if a share is trading in the market at €5 and an option offers the holder the right to buy it for €4 then this option has an intrinsic value of €1. Options with intrinsic value are termed 'in-the-money'. If the right to buy (strike or exercise price) is the same as the current market price then the option is said to be 'at-the-money'. If the market price is lower than the strike it is called an 'out-of-the-money' option. Intrinsic value can never be negative; it is simply zero. A crucial point to note is that generally the intrinsic value is measured at grant date only.

2.2.3 Fair value approach

The intrinsic value approach fails to recognise that options have more than intrinsic value. Even if an option is currently out-of-the-money, the price of its underlying could rise and bring it into-the-money. This other element of value is termed 'time value'. One broadly accepted method of calculating the fair value of an option is to use some form of Black-Scholes model, although approaches such as those involving a binomial model (often called a 'binomial lattice') may also be appropriate, especially for income-bearing assets, such as equities.

For our purposes, we merely need to appreciate that Black Scholes provides a means of ascertaining the fair value of an option and has six key inputs:

Exhibit 4.10: Inputs to Black-Scholes option pricing model

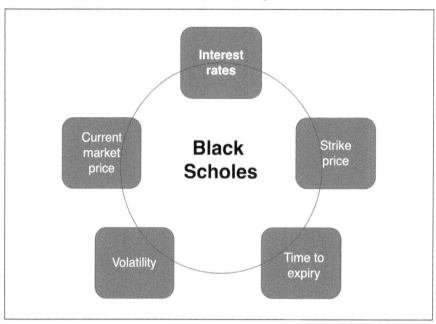

IFRS 2 does not require the use of any specific valuation approach for stock options. However, it does outline the advantages of the binomial lattice approach.

A few simple examples will illustrate the fair value approach set out in IFRS 2.

Example 1

- Johnson Plc gives 2000 options to a member of staff.

- The options have a strike price of €5. The current market price is €5.

- The options are given to the staff member in return for his services.

- The vesting period is three years.

- A Black Scholes model of the option would produce a fair value per option of €3.

Total Options	2,000
Value (at fair value)	€6,000
Vesting period	3 years
Annual charge to EBIT	€2,000

Note that in the example above, the vesting period is the period between option grant date and vesting date.

Exhibit 4.11 The vesting period

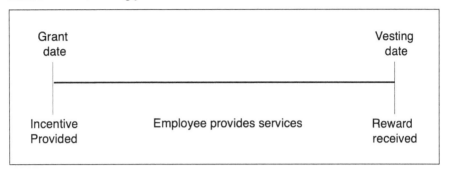

Example 2

- A corporate grants 100 share options to each of its 500 employees (50,000 options). The vesting period is three years and a binomial lattice model of the option gives a fair value of €15. The expectation is that 20% of employees will leave over the period and therefore the forfeiture rate is 20%.

Year	Calculation	Expense	Cumulative Expense
1	[50,000 × 80% × €15] × 1/3	€200,000	€200,000
2	[[50,000 × 80% × €15] × 2/3] – 200,000	€200,000	€400,000
3	[50,000 × 80% × €15] – 400,000	€200,000	€600,000

2.2.4 How are options reflected in diluted EPS?

IAS 33 *Earnings per Share* states that the treasury stock method should be used to reflect the dilutive element for stock options. The key point to note is that under this approach options are only reflected if they are in-the-money. Out-of-the-money or at-the-money options are not included at all. Therefore, there is potential for 'latent dilution' and thus diluted EPS may fail to fully reflect the dilutive potential of stock options. Given this, it is unlikely that it is an acceptable alternative to stock option expensing.

2.3 US GAAP focus

The FASB standard is, for all intents and purposes, similar to IFRS 2 discussed above.

2.4 What are the implications for financial analysis?

Some years ago, US companies were given a choice of approaches to stock option expensing; intrinsic value or fair value. Most US corporates chose the intrinsic value approach with fair value disclosures. Presumably this is based on the fact that it would enhance EBIT when compared to the fair value approach (fair value is always greater than intrinsic value). European companies had typically followed an intrinsic value approach as well. By adopting this form of treatment, companies were able to ensure that they could achieve a zero compensation charge for the stock option component of remuneration by simply issuing stock options at-the-money.

Irrespective of what accounting standards say, there has been no unanimity about whether options should be expensed. However, now that companies have used the standard in practice, the objections appear more muted. To the authors the arguments for expensing are cogent. The most important argument is that options have value. If a company grants generous options to its employees then for an investor this may make the company a less attractive investment due to the potential future dilution. There must be a reflection of this cost in the income statement.

A fundamental issue will be whether the user of the financials truly believes that the expense is a real economic cost. Many companies continue to reverse out option expenses in measures of underlying earnings. We firmly believe it is a real cost and such non-GAAP adjustments are unhelpful and economically misguided. Once an acceptance is made of the validity of option expensing, attention should turn to the credibility of the number itself. Naturally if one is fair valuing anything which does not have a liquid market then there will be a significant degree of subjectivity. In particular, certain inputs to any option valuation model, such as volatility, tend to influence the result greatly, and yet there is no accepted methodology for estimation. This has lead one commentator to suggest that IFRS 2 was a standard in 'random number generation'.

However, we must bear in mind that these numbers will be audited. Audit firms are unlikely to accept volatility and other estimates that are inconsistent with their observations of the markets and of other clients.Furthermore, disclosures will allow users to assess the quality of the calculation, at least to some degree.

The other area of concern is that companies are free to make estimates of the number of employees who will actually forfeit their options. The most common form of forfeiture is where the employee leaves the company. Exhibit 4.12 illustrates how the numbers work under IFRS 2.

Exhibit 4.12: Stock option forfeit example

Problem	Year	Expense	Cumulative expense
A corporate grants 100 share options to each of its 500 employees (50,000 options). The vesting period is three years and a binomial lattice model of the option gives a fair value of 15. The expectation is that 20% of employees will leave over the period and therefore the forfeiture rate is 20%. Assume these forfeiture rates turn out to be accurate.	1.	[50,000 X 80% X €15]X 1/3 = 200,000	€200,000
	2.	[[50,000 X 80% X €15] X 2/3] - 200,000 = 200,000	€400,000
	3.	[50,000 X 80% X €15] - 400,000 = 200,000	€600,000
If the forfeiture estimate changes as time progresses then the company will make adjustments in each year to ensure the overall result is up to date on a cumulative basis. So, the example is as above except: In year 1 20 people leave and the company reassesses its estimated forfeiture rate at 15%. In year 2 a further 22 employees leave and the company reassesses the forfeiture rate at 12%. In year 3 a further 15 employees leave meaning that over the 3 years 57 employees left.	1.	[50,000 X 85% X €15] X1/3 = 212,500	€212,500
	2.	[[50,000 X 88% X €15] X 2/3] - 212,500 = 227,500	€440,000
	3.	[50,000 X 88.6% X €15] - 440,000 = 224,500	€664,500

Source: Adapted from IFRS 2 (IASB, 2004)

[1] The final cumulative total of €664,500 is based on the 44,300 options at €15 each

The key point to note is that the forfeiture rate could be used to smooth the income statement number. For example, a company could accelerate cost recognition if it set a low forfeiture rate in the early periods. Alternatively, costs could be deferred if a high forfeiture rate was initially set.

2.5 Case example

The detailed note for RBS below has a number of important aspects to it. First, the note specifies various conditions that must be satisfied in order for share based compensation to vest. Second, the core treatment, fair valuing the options, recognises a 'cost of employee services'. Third, the valuation is based on a set of inputs which very much align with the inputs for a Black-Scholes type valuation model. Lastly, the valuation is expensed on a straight-line basis over the vesting period with the other entry being to equity (share settled awards) or a liability (cash settled awards).

Exhibit 4.13: Stock option expensing policy

The Group operates a number of share-based compensation schemes under which it awards RBSG shares and share options to its employees. Such awards are generally subject to vesting conditions: conditions that vary the amount of cash or shares to which an employee is entitled. Vesting conditions include service conditions (requiring the employee to complete a specified period of service) and performance conditions (requiring the employee to complete a specified period of service and specified performance targets to be met). Other conditions to which an award is subject are non-vesting conditions (such as a requirement to save throughout the vesting period).

The cost of employee services received in exchange for an award of shares or share options granted is measured by reference to the fair value of the shares or share options on the date the award is granted and takes into account non-vesting conditions and market performance conditions (conditions related to the market price of RBSG shares). An award is treated as vesting irrespective of whether any market performance condition or non-vesting condition is met. The fair value of options granted is estimated using valuation techniques which incorporate exercise price, term, risk-free interest rates, the current share price and its expected volatility. The cost is expensed on a straight-line basis over the vesting period (the period during which all the specified vesting conditions must be satisfied) with a corresponding increase in equity in an equity-settled award, or a corresponding liability in a cash-settled award. The cost is adjusted for vesting conditions (other than market performance conditions) so as to reflect the number of shares or share options that actually vest. If an award is modified, the original cost continues to be recognised as if there had been no modification. Where modification increases the fair value of the award, this increase is recognised as an expense over the modified vesting period.

Source: RBS 2017 Annual report

2.6 Building valuation models: what to do

The argument that stock options are not an expense to the business and should therefore not be reflected in the profit and loss account is analogous to the argument that a provision for decommissioning a manufacturing plant is a non-cash item and should not be included in a discounted cash flow valuation. The latent dilution that is likely to result from the exercise of stock options will be a cost to existing shareholders if and when it occurs, and the challenge is to build this cost into our valuation methodology.

It is necessary to make an important distinction here. This is between options that have already been granted, and options that are based on expectations the company may grant in the future. Treatment of options that have already been granted is fairly straightforward.

The more sophisticated, and more accurate, approach is to subtract the fair value of the outstanding options from the value of the company, and then to calculate the value of the shares by dividing the result by the number of shares currently in issue and outstanding. In this version, the options are treated as a financial liability, and this fully reflects their latent value.

The less sophisticated, though more common, approach is to calculate a diluted value per share by increasing the number of shares used in the calculation to include the dilutive options. This calculation takes into account only the in-the-money options, and then calculates the proportion of them that are dilutive by dividing the average exercise price by the current share price and subtracting the result from one, to derive a percentage. The logic is that if options are exercised at a price of 100p and the share price is 150p, then the cash raised by the exercise would permit the company to cancel two thirds of the options, and the remaining one third would be dilutive.

There is no doubt that the former approach is more accurate if all that we are worried about is history, but suppose that we were confronted by a company that was clearly likely to continue to remunerate its employees through the issue of share options. A naïve cash flow approach to valuation would fail to pick up this projected cost. It will appear in the profit and loss account as a non-cash cost, and it has not yet been reflected in the grant of share options. So, what do we do with it?

The answer must be that it is an accrual that we should deduct from our forecasts of cash flow or NOPAT in our valuation models, just like any other accrual. If we are running a DCF model, the projected costs associated with stock options should be deducted from the cash flows that we value. We are not arguing that they are actual cash cost but merely if we do not make an adjustment our value will be distorted. If we are running an economic profit model, NOPAT should be calculated after deducting these costs. As with the treatment of other accruals, the correct treatment of stock options is more intuitive in the framework of an economic profit analysis, but it can be handled correctly whichever valuation approach is used.

As mentioned above, failure to deduct for the accrual will result in overvaluation of the company. To see why, imagine two otherwise identical companies. One states that from now on it will only pay its employees in cash, and raises their salaries to reflect this. The other evidently intends to continue to pay them in a combination of cash and stock options issued at the money, with no intrinsic value. (We assume that fair value of the stock options brings the value of their remuneration into line with that of the employees in the first company.) Failure to take into account the cost associated with projected issues of new options – not just with the historical already existing ones – will result in the second company appearing to be worth more than the first one.

3. Taxation

3.1 Why is it important?

Taxation is one of the more confusing areas of accounting. The terminology is opaque and the numbers are often driven by rules embedded in complex legislation that have little to do with sensible economics. However, for analysts a clear understanding of taxation is important. Firstly, it is a core cost for all companies irrespective of the specific sector. Secondly, there can be significant value attached to certain tax numbers such as tax losses. It is not untypical to find a complete mistreatment of these potentially important items in valuation models. Thirdly, tax has important implications for the cost of capital as discussed in chapter two.

3.2 What is current GAAP under IFRS for taxation?

3.2.1 Taxation refresher

It is very important to distinguish between the two types of tax that we see in a typical set of financials; current taxation and deferred taxation. We shall deal with current taxation initially prior to returning to the thorny issue of deferred taxation.

Current taxation

During each accounting period the company must estimate how much taxation is due on the profits that are generated in the accounting period. This is calculated as:

Profits chargeable to tax x local tax rate

Profits chargeable to taxation are pre-tax accounting profits adjusted for tax purposes. A typical calculation of taxable profit is shown in exhibit 4.14:

Exhibit 4.14 Corporate tax calculation

Profit before taxation (per the accounting income statement)	**X**
Add back disallowables:	
Accounting depreciation and amortisation	X
Certain non-cash expenses such as general provisions	X
Less allowables	
Tax depreciation	X
Cash expenses (i.e. the cash equivalent to the disallowed costs)	X
Profits chargeable to tax	X

Once calculated the entry to record the current taxation will be:

Increase taxation liability in the balance sheet   *X*

Increase taxation expense in the income statement   *X*

3.2.2 Deferred taxation

As we have seen above, there are differences between accounting profit as determined by accounting standards on the one hand, and taxable profit as determined by the tax authorities on the other. These differences give rise to an accounting concept known as deferred tax. We will use a simple example to explain this (exhibit 4.15).

Exhibit 4.15: Deferred tax example

(Figures in £)

Income statement

	Year 1	Year 2
Profit before tax and royalty income	200,000	200,000
Royalty income	50,000	-
Profit before taxation	250,000	200,000
Taxation		
Current	(80,000)	(100,000) ◄ - ┐
Deferred	(20,000)	20,000
Profit after taxation	150,000	120,000
Tax computation		
Accounting profit before taxation	200,000	200,000
Royalty income (cash basis)		50,000
Taxable profits	200,000	250,000
Taxed @ 40%	**80,000**	**100,000** ----┘

From this example we can see that royalty income is taxed on a cash receipts basis but accounted for on an accruals basis. If the royalty is received in a different period from when it is earned then there will be a timing difference, i.e., an item has gone through both the income statement and the tax computation, but in different periods. The income statement as presented pre-deferred taxation does not reflect the economics of the business. In the year with the higher profit we have a lower tax charge and vice versa. This means that the income statement does not show the underlying profitability of the business. It distorts trends; year one is indeed better than year two but the difference is exacerbated by taxation. In addition, insufficient liabilities have been recognised in the first year. At that stage the company has essentially crystallised a tax liability by earning profits but while the profit has been recognised, the associated taxation liability has not.

We can use deferred taxation to make appropriate adjustments to overcome these problems. We have adjusted the taxation charge to reflect the tax cost of earning the royalty income in the first year. This transfers the taxation cost to the year when the income is recognised in the income statement. In addition, this also achieves proper recognition of liabilities as we have a tax liability (deferred tax provision) on the balance sheet. This provision is then paid in the second year as the tax moves from being deferred to being current.

A simple way to calculate the required adjustment is to calculate the timing difference and apply the relevant tax rate to it. So, for example in the first year the originating timing difference is £50,000. At a tax rate of 40% this gives rise to a deferred taxation adjustment of £20,000. A similar but reversing entry takes place in year two.

The entries are:

- **Year 1**: Increase tax cost and increase deferred tax provision by £20,000

- **Year 2**: Decrease tax cost and decrease provision for deferred taxation by £20,000

3.2.3 Balance sheet focus

It is important to note that IFRS, in this case IAS 12, actually uses a balance sheet approach to deferred taxation. This means that IFRS use a concept known as temporary differences, rather than the conceptually more straightforward timing differences. Temporary differences arise where the tax value of an asset/liability is different from the accounting value. In many cases this will provide the same answer as timing differences; it is just a difference in emphasis. However, it does mean that more differences relating to deferred taxation will arise than under a timing difference system. For example, revaluations of fixed assets must be reflected in deferred taxation under IAS 12 as the tax base of the asset will not reflect the revaluation, whereas the accounting value for depreciation purposes will do so.

3.2.4 Advanced example

Exhibit 4.16 below is more difficult. Here we can see that the temporary differences (note, we shall use this term from now on rather than timing differences) arise from the difference between the tax and accounting bases for this asset. In reality this will reflect the difference between accounting depreciation and tax depreciation.

The various columns in the table work as follows:

Column 1: This is the Net Book Value (NBV) of the asset calculated as cost less accumulated depreciation.

Column 2: This is the tax base calculated as cost less tax allowances at an accelerated 75% per annum on a reducing balance basis.

Column 3: This represents the difference between the accounting and tax asset values i.e., temporary differences.

Column 4: Deferred taxation is calculated as the temporary differences multiplied by the tax rate, in this case 30%. This is a liability (see below).

Column 5: This is the change in the deferred tax liability and would be included in the income statement charge.

Columns 6 & 7: Both sum to the initial investment of £200,000.

Note the inputs underneath the spreadsheet that are driving the computations.

Exhibit 4.16: Temporary differences

Temporary differences (£)

	1	2	3	4	5	6	7
Period	NBV	Tax base	Temp. Diff	Deferred taxation @ 30%	Movement to P&L	Tax Allowances	Accounting Depreciation
1	180,000	50,000	130,000	39,000	39,000	150,000	20,000
2	160,000	12,500	147,500	44,250	5,250	37,500	20,000
3	140,000	3,125	136,875	41,063	-3,188	9,375	20,000
4	120,000	781	119,219	35,766	-5,297	2,344	20,000
5	100,000	195	99,805	29,941	-5,824	586	20,000
6	80,000	49	79,951	23,985	-5,956	146	20,000
7	60,000	12	59,988	17,996	-5,989	37	20,000
8	40,000	3	39,997	11,999	-5,997	9	20,000
9	20,000	1	19,999	6,000	-5,999	2	20,000
10	0	0	0	0	-6,000	1	20,000
					0	200,000	200,000

Inputs:

Cost	200,000
Useful life (years)	10
Tax rate	30%
Allowance (declining balance)	75%

Why in this example do we have a deferred taxation liability? It is because profits in year one have only been reduced by a £20,000 depreciation charge whereas taxable profits have suffered a £150,000 deduction. This means that taxable income would be £130,000 lower than accounting income (£150,000–£20,000). We know from the earlier part of this section that current tax is based on taxable profits (rather than accounting profits). Therefore, if we were just to 'plug in' the current tax charge we would show a high profit in the accounts with a small tax charge. In addition, from a balance sheet perspective we would not be showing a full liability for the tax cost of the profits being recognised. We can see from the example that ultimately accounting depreciation does catch up with tax allowances and so the deferred taxation cancels. However, in the meantime deferred taxation ensures that the income statement and balance sheet produce superior, and more complete, information.

It is also important to note that the temporary differences (and therefore deferred tax liabilities) calculated above are calculated based on undiscounted amounts – reflecting the accounting requirement under IAS 12 that deferred tax assets and liabilities are undiscounted in order to 'simplify' the calculations.

3.2.5 Deferred tax assets

The most important source of deferred tax assets is operating losses – these have been recognised in the income statement but not in the tax computation which merely reported a 'nil' result. Another way of thinking about this is to imagine that if a company makes a loss of, say £10m, it should be able to recover this against future tax liabilities. Therefore, the actual economic cost of the loss is £10m X (1-t) – i.e., less than the actual loss recognised. This 'shield' is an asset as it will be available to decrease future tax liabilities.

This analysis assumes that sufficient future profits will be earned to recover the value of these losses. However, it should be noted that under IFRS deferred tax assets can only be recognised where recovery of those tax losses is *probable*. This is a significant hurdle given that – by definition – the company is, or has recently been, loss-making. It may not be expected to be profit-making for some time. Recent tax rule changes in many countries have raised this hurdle further since tax losses are now generally restricted in terms of the amount that can be offset against profits in any given year, thus increasing the period over which the tax losses will need to be recovered. However, even where a company has not been able to fully recognise deferred tax assets in relation to tax losses, the disclosures in the notes to the accounts will provide detail on the value of any tax losses not yet recognised.

Therefore, the asset associated with these losses only has value if future profits are earned. Hence the risk relating to deferred tax assets is the same as the risk of earning future profits. This point is essentially the justification, outlined in chapter two, for discounting tax shields at the unlevered cost of equity rather than the much lower cost of debt. The ability to earn future profits is riskier in terms of recovery than the returns on debt instruments.

3.3 US GAAP Focus

In broad terms the standards are similar. The differences here relate to the detailed application. Key differences:

- Under US GAAP deferred tax assets are always recognised in full, with a valuation allowance used to adjust this amount for amounts where it is 'more likely than not' that the benefit will not be realized. Under IFRS deferred tax assets are recognised only to the extent it is probable that they will be realized.

- US GAAP provides exemptions from the idea that all temporary differences should be recognised. These relate to leveraged leases, undistributed earnings of subsidiaries and certain (development) costs in the oil and gas industry.

- US GAAP requires the use of an enacted rate of tax for deferred tax purposes whereas IAS 12 will allow the use of a 'substantially enacted' one. For example, if a government was expected to change the future tax rate then this new rate would be more readily useable under IFRS rather than US GAAP.

- Classification of deferred tax assets and liabilities under IFRS is generally non-current. Under US GAAP the classification follows the asset/liability to which it relates.

- Different rates are used for deferred taxes on inter-company transactions. IAS 12 requires the use of the buyers' tax rate whereas US GAAP requires the seller's rate

---

3.4 Implications for financial statement analysis

Deferred taxation makes financial statements more useful. There are a number of useful deferred taxation disclosures that valuers should master in order to glean as much information as possible about the nature of the company's tax charge:

- The current taxation charge note explains what elements of the tax charge come from current, as against deferred, taxation.

- The current tax charge also highlights any overseas tax issues (e.g., non-reclaimable tax credits on the remittance of overseas earnings) as well as over/under provisions relating to the accuracy of estimating historic tax charges.

- The deferred tax reconciliation explains why the accounting profit before tax multiplied by the statutory tax rate in the home country does not equal the tax expense in the income statement. Examples of typical differences would include:

  - non-deductible expenses (e.g., entertainment expenditure in most tax jurisdictions);

  - non-taxable income;

  - different tax rates from overseas.

Calculating an effective tax rate is an important step in analysing tax information. Because of deferred taxation we know that some of the distortions to the tax charge have been eliminated. Therefore, the normal way to calculate this is to take accounting PBT and divide this into the tax expense (both current and deferred). This is in essence a blended rate as, for multinational companies, it will reflect the tax rates in all the jurisdictions in which the enterprise operates. The alternative, calculating tax numbers in different countries on a divisional basis, is fraught with difficulties but may offer some interesting insights.

If a user has reversed out any non-recurring items from a post-tax earnings number, such as net income , then the associated taxation will need to be eliminated as well. Unfortunately, this information is often not disclosed in which case the user can do worse than simply apply the effective rate to the exceptional item or the home rate if it appears reasonable to assume that the item most relates to that geographical region. Clearly, if one could specifically identify a country where the exceptional had occurred then a more specific adjustment might be possible.

3.5 Case example

We have reproduced the three key tax notes that need to be examined:

- Breakdown of the tax expense from the income statement (exhibit 4.17).

- Reconciliation of the tax expense to the accounting profit times the 'home' statutory rate (exhibit 4.18).

- Deferred taxation note (exhibit 4.19).

Exhibit 4.17: Income statement analysis of tax charge

Recognised in the income statement	2018 £m	2017 £m
Current tax – current year	(52.1)	(72.7)
Current tax – adjustment in respect of prior years	(0.4)	5.8
Total current tax charge	(52.5)	(66.9)
Deferred tax – current year	22.4	(38.3)
Deferred tax – rate change	(7.3)	9.3
Deferred tax – adjustment in respect of prior years	7.6	(2.8)
	(29.8)	(98.7)

Tax (charged)/credited to other comprehensive income	2018 £m	2017 £m
Current tax on pension scheme[1]	17.2	24.7
Deferred tax on pension scheme	(57.4)	46.1
Deferred tax on cash flow hedges	5.9	0.3
	(34.3)	71.1

1. An additional deficit funding contribution of £89.8m has been paid by the Partnership during the year (2017: £124.8m) in relation to the defined benefit pension scheme, resulting in a tax credit of £17.2m (2017: £24.7m) to the statement of other comprehensive income/(expense) and a corresponding reduction in our current tax liability.

Source: John Lewis Annual Report 2018

- Adjustment in respect of prior years – as taxation calculations are not finalised by the reporting date for the company, estimates are used. Once the final figures come through the estimates are adjusted but only against next year's taxation expense.

- Deferred taxation will result from the application of the tax rate to timing differences as described in the body of the chapter.

- The last section relates to tax items that have not gone through the income statement but instead are shown in other comprehensive income. These relate to specific items where the related gain and loss has gone to comprehensive income along with the associated tax.

Exhibit 4.18: Reconciliation of tax expenses

The tax charge for the year is higher (2017: higher) than the standard corporation tax rate of 19.2%[1] (2017: 20.0%). The differences are explained below:	2018 £m	2017 £m
Profit before tax	103.9	452.2
Profit before tax multiplied by standard rate of corporation tax in the UK of 19.2% (2017: 20.0%)	(19.9)	(90.4)
Effects of:		
Changes in tax rate	(7.3)	9.3
Adjustment in respect of prior years	7.2	3.0
Depreciation on assets not qualifying for tax relief	(14.0)	(12.3)
Difference between accounting and tax base for land and buildings	4.9	(5.1)
Differences in overseas tax rates	(0.1)	2.0
Sundry disallowables	0.2	(5.1)
Other permanent differences on sale of property	(0.8)	(0.1)
Total tax charge	(29.8)	(98.7)
Effective tax rate (%)	28.7	21.8

1. Based on a blended corporation tax rate comprised of two months at 20.0% relating to the 2016/17 fiscal year and ten months at 19.0% relating to the 2017/18 fiscal year.

Source: John Lewis Annual Report and Financial Statements 2018

This note is often referred to in the accountancy profession as a 'tax reconciliation'. It links the reported profit before tax multiplied by the tax rate in the country of the holding company (UK in this case) with the actual tax charge in the income statement. Note that in our example the difference, in 2018, is substantial with the first calculation resulting in a charge of £19.9m but the actual tax charge much higher at £29.8m.

The major points of comment are as follows:

- Difference between accounting and tax base for land and buildings – this means that the actual 'value' of land being depreciated in the accounts is different from the equivalent tax based valuation.

- Differences in overseas tax rates simply refers to other countries in which the group has operations having different statutory rates.

- Depreciation on assets not qualifying for tax relief – essentially this means that capital allowances (also known as tax depreciation) are not available on certain assets which are being depreciated for accounting purposes. This reconciling item is particularly common for UK companies where, in recent years, capital allowances have not been available on commercial property, yet these assets must be depreciated for accounting purposes.

- Adjustments in respect of prior years – appear to show that the company has overestimated its tax liability in the last two years. It has therefore reduced subsequent estimates and hence the effective rate in the current year.

Exhibit 4.19: Deferred taxation note

Deferred tax is calculated in full on temporary differences under the liability method using a tax rate of 19% for deferred tax assets and liabilities expected to reverse before 1 April 2020, and 17% for those assets or liabilities expected to reverse after 1 April 2020. In the year to 28 January 2017, a tax rate of 20% was used for deferred tax assets or liabilities expected to reverse before 1 April 2017, 19% for those assets or liabilities expected to reverse before 1 April 2020, and 17% for those assets or liabilities expected to reverse after 1 April 2020.

The movement on the deferred tax account is shown below:

Deferred tax	2018 £m	2017 £m
Opening net asset	48.2	33.6
Credited/(charged) to income statement	22.7	(31.8)
(Charged)/credited to other comprehensive income/(expense)	(51.5)	46.4
Closing net asset	19.4	48.2

Source: John Lewis Annual Report and Financial Statements 2018

This note explains the movement in the deferred taxation numbers. Note that some deferred tax is charged to the income statement and the other portion is charged to comprehensive income consistent with the earlier note.

3.6 Building valuation models: what to do

Deferred tax represents a significant problem both when modelling company accounts and when converting those forecasts into a valuation. We shall take the two separately.

From inside the company, or outside if it provides adequate information, it is possible to calculate future deferred tax assets/liabilities and the utilisation of these throughout the explicit forecast period. The utilisation of the deferred tax balance is used to adjust the forecast P&L tax charge to derive the expected tax paid (or 'cash taxes') each year in our cash flow forecasts.

But what happens if we do not have this information? In most cases it is not plausible to try to model on an asset by asset basis. Instead, it may be reasonable to look at the history of the company's tax charges over the past few years. In a simple case, if the company is mature, but still growing slowly, there may be a reasonable proportion of its annual tax charge that may be assumed to accrue as deferred tax each year and never to be paid, because as the company continues to grow, it continues each year to create tax depreciation in excess of its depreciation charges.

Even in the case of growing companies it cannot necessarily be assumed that deferred taxation provisions will not reverse. If capital expenditure is switched from one subsidiary to another then capital allowances created in the new market cannot be utilised to lower taxable profits in the mature market. The risk is that the opposite happens. Tax that has been charged but not paid in previous years becomes payable.

There is also one very common example of the accrual of simple timing differences that is worth remembering. When companies make provisions for restructuring, they generally do apply tax to them, because when the severance payments and other costs are incurred, they will probably be allowable costs. So, in the year of the provision, there is likely to be a negative deferred tax charge, as tax is paid on profit before the charge. But this will probably reverse in the years afterwards, in which there is no impact on the profit and loss account but cash costs of restructuring are incurred, and reduce the tax liability. During this period, there will probably be positive deferred tax, as tax payments are lower than the tax charge in the profit and loss account.

Turning to valuation, there are two key questions to ask about any provision. The first is, 'Will the liability in the balance sheet ever crystallise?' and the second is, 'Do the future provisions in the cash flow statement represent a stream of cash that will ultimately have to be paid out to somebody or not?'. In the case of deferred tax liabilities, unusually, it may be reasonable to assume that the answer to both questions is 'No', in which case we are assuming that the balance sheet provision is effectively equity and that the cash flow stream is effectively profit. But it is very dangerous to assume this without considering the implications of your forecasts for taxation. What would happen to a company that had large amounts of provision for deferred taxation in its balance sheet if, perhaps as a result of being subject to a Leveraged Buy-Out (LBO), it were to dramatically reduce its rate of capital expenditure? All that tax would suddenly become payable...

4. Accounting for pension obligations

4.1 Why is it important?

Anyone reading the financial press over the last decade cannot fail to have seen the various headlines about pension liabilities, their magnitude and how companies are planning to finance what they owe employees. It is no surprise that accounting is central to this debate. For many traditional industrial firms in sectors such as engineering, automotive and chemicals the provision of retirement benefits has been an important component of employee remuneration – and these companies have been highly labour intensive resulting in substantial liabilities. Accounting for these pension benefits is complicated by the different types of pension, the uncertainty associated with asset returns as well as the complex interplay between domestic legislation and accounting concepts. Here we shall attempt to demystify some of the major areas of uncertainty as well as focusing on the financial analysis and modelling implications.

4.2 What is current GAAP under IFRS for pensions?

In relation to financial reporting there are two key issues: the income statement charge and the balance sheet asset/liability. Neither of these is straightforward. Before proceeding to explore each of these components of pension accounting let us deal with a few of the fundamental aspects of pensions.

4.2.1 Forms of pension scheme:

There are two main categories of pension.

Category 1: Defined contribution schemes

These schemes define the contributions that the employer will make to the fund on behalf of the employee. The contributions are typically expressed as a percentage of gross salary. Once the transfer is made by the employing company then no further obligations rest with the company. The residual risk remains with the employee.

Accounting for these schemes is very straightforward and simply involves charging the contributions as an operating expense. They are in effect extra salary. There would not normally be any balance sheet obligation save for some delay in making the contributions.

Category 2: Defined benefit

These schemes define the target benefits to be paid to employees on retirement in the future. Normally the target is expressed as a fraction of final salary (i.e., salary on leaving the company or retiring). The fraction normally changes as extra years of service are completed. So, a scheme might provide that an employee would generate an annual pension of 2% of her final salary for each year of employment. So, if she worked for ten years then she would generate an annual pension of 20% of her final salary.

As the company has made a promise to pay the risk resides with it. This risk is not easy to control as there are so many uncertainties associated with the ultimate outcome. For example, how long will the employee be in service? What will the final salary level be? How much should be invested now to meet the estimate of the obligation? How long will the employee live? It is these uncertainties that make the accounting complex.

4.2.2 Funded and unfunded schemes

A certain level of confusion also emanates from the fact that pension schemes may be funded or unfunded. In the US and the UK for example, it is mandatory for defined benefit plans to be funded. This means that any contributions that the actuary determines are necessary must be made to a separate funding vehicle. Therefore a scheme will have both a fund (i.e., the equities, bonds and cash invested to satisfy future obligations) and an obligation (i.e., amounts to be paid to employees on retirement). The difference between the actuary's current estimation of the fund on the one hand and the obligation on the other can either be a deficit or surplus. In other jurisdictions there is no funding requirement (e.g., Germany and Japan). Therefore, while there is an obligation with such schemes, the investment is effectively in the corporate's assets.

Economic status of the fund

The level of funding required for a defined benefits pension plan is determined by the actuary. The actuary will base estimates of funding requirements based on forecasts of various factors such as:

- salary levels;
- retirement age;
- life expectancy;
- employee turnover;
- investment performance of the fund's assets;
- level of benefits guaranteed.

Due to the difficulty of forecasting such variables, deficits (under funding) and surpluses (over funding), commonly arise on defined benefit plans.

For example, for a funded scheme the relevant deficit or surplus could be ascertained by comparing the current market value of the plan assets ('fair value') with the present value of the obligations. We shall explore this further below.

4.2.3 Types of obligation

The level of salary at retirement has a significant impact on the ultimate defined benefit plan obligation. There are two alternative approaches to estimating this: Accumulated Benefit Obligation (ABO) and Projected Benefit Obligation (PBO). The only difference between these two calculations is that whilst the former ignores expected future increases in salary, the latter includes an estimate of such increases. It is the latter calculation that is required under IFRS and US GAAP. Given the lengthy period that most pension liabilities span, embedding future salary increases can have a dramatic impact on the calculated liabilities.

The calculation of the PBO is as follows:

	€
Opening PBO	X
+ Service cost	X
+ Interest on PBO	X
+/- Actuarial gains/losses	X
+ Prior service costs	X
Gross pension costs	X
- Benefits paid	(X)
Closing PBO balance	X

Notes:

- IFRS uses the term DBO (Defined Benefit Obligation) but this is the same as the more widely used PBO.

- ABO and PBO are identical in schemes not related to pay (flat benefit plans).

- Both ABO and PBO are based on present values and hence each measure is very sensitive to the discount rate used. The required discount rate is that for a high-quality corporate bond of equivalent maturity and currency. IAS 19 suggests a corporate bond with a AA rating (so-called double 'A' rating).

4.2.4 Pension plan assets

This can be calculated as the assets at the start of the year plus returns and contributions less the payments to pensions. The assets (equities, bonds, real estate and cash instruments) are marked to market for the purposes of calculating the funded status of the scheme. Remember that if the scheme is unfunded then there will be no assets, just a PBO.

4.2.5 IAS 19 Key aspects of pension accounting

IAS 19 sets out the treatment of pensions under IFRS. Exhibit 4.20 summarises the overall treatment in the income statement and balance sheet.

A defined benefit pension scheme will be reflected in the financials as follows:

Exhibit 4.20: Overview

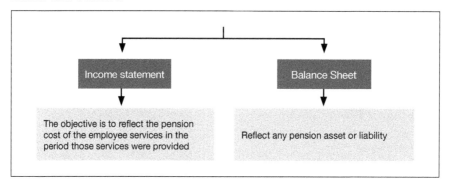

Income statement charge

The actual cost of providing a defined benefit scheme in any year will be the increase in the obligation minus the increase/plus a decrease in the fund assets. This concept is reflected in the income statement calculation below although it is presented differently.

	£	
Service cost*	X	Real events
Interest cost	X	
Less: Interest on assets	(X)	Smoothed event
Pension cost	X	

* The service cost represents the core operating cost. It is the extra pension benefits that an employee has accrued by working for the year in question.

Notes:

- The interest cost on the PBO less the interest income on plan assets is referred to as the net interest cost. The net interest cost is generally included within finance costs whilst the service cost is included in operating costs (i.e., in EBIT).

- The interest income on plan assets is a 'smoothed' number rather than representing the actual return on fund assets as this will be volatile from one year to another. It is calculated by applying the discount rate used in the obligation (PBO) liability determination to the value of the pension assets.

- Under US GAAP (and until relatively recently under IFRS), the income statement charge includes the expected return on plan assets, rather than the interest income on plan assets. This is calculated using management's expectation of the rate of return that the plan assets will generate each year. IFRS switched to the interest income number because of a concern that management could 'game' the assumptions to boost earnings.

Computation of balance sheet asset/liability

The balance sheet asset or liability is calculated thus:

	€
PV of future obligation (i.e., the PBO)	X
– Fair value of plan assets	(X)
+ Effect of asset ceiling	X
Pension liability/ (asset)	X

Essentially, this is the funding status of the plan adjusted for the effects of the asset ceiling (discussed below).

The asset ceiling

If the fair value of the plan assets exceeds the PBO, IFRS may restrict the potential asset that can be recognised in the balance sheet. This restriction applies where the company cannot access the benefits of surplus funding either through:

- A refund of contributions from the pension fund.

- A reduction in future pension contributions.

Therefore, where a company has a surplus in its pension fund, this might not be reflected in full in balance sheet assets.

Comprehensive example

Lamy plc has the following disclosures in its notes regarding its pension fund on 1 January, year 5:

	€
Pension fund assets (@ fair value)	10,000,000
Pension fund liabilities (@ present value)	(10,400.000)
	(400,000)

There were no unrecognised gains and losses at the start of the year.

The following information relates to the year ended 31 December, year 5:

Current service cost	€800,000
Expected long-term return on assets	5.1%
Contributions to the fund	€1,020,000
Pensions paid	€900,000
Actual return on assets	€400,000

The present value of liabilities at 31 December, year 5 is estimated to be €11,000,000. The relevant discount rate is 5%.

What would be the treatment under IAS 19?

Please note:

• Assume actuarial gains/losses are spread over a useful service life of 10 years.

• Experience losses arising from changing actuarial assumptions amount to €180,000. There were no carried forward experience gains/losses. In addition, for simplicity assume that, in the past, actual and expected gains had always been identical.

Solution

Income Statement

All included in Operating Costs €

Service cost	800,000
+ Interest cost	520,000
- Interest on plan assets	(510,000)
	810,000

Balance Sheet Liability

PV of future obligation	11,000,000
- FV of plan assets (W1)	(10,520,000)
	480,000

W1 Fund Assets

Opening balance	10,000,000
+Actual return	400,000
+Contributions paid	1,020,000
-Pensions paid	(900,000)
	10,520,000

4.3 US GAAP focus

Although US GAAP and IFRS are well aligned in respect of the valuation of defined benefit pension liabilities and plan assets, there are differences in the income statement pension cost. These differences include:

- US GAAP allows actuarial gains/losses either to be recognised immediately in earnings or to be amortised to earnings using a corridor approach. Under IFRS actuarial gains/losses are recognised immediately in Other Comprehensive Income.

- US GAAP requires a calculation of the 'expected return on plan assets', based on the companies' estimation of the rate of return the plan assets will generate in the year ahead. This expected return is included in earnings. IFRS applies the PBO discount rate to the plan assets to derive 'interest income on plan assets' as explained in section 4.2.5 above.

- US GAAP recently amended guidance so that the service cost must be separately presented alongside other employee costs within operating profit. Other pension cost components outside of EBIT. IFRS allows a choice over pension cost presentation, although most companies follow the same presentation as the new US GAAP guidance.

4.4 Case example

Pension liabilities are included in the provisions section of a balance sheet. The notes to the financials must be reviewed in order to make any sense of the numbers. Remember we are trying to deal with two aspects: the income statement charge and the balance sheet 'debt'. Typically, information about both would be disclosed in the 'provisions' note, as in the case for BMW below (exhibit 4.21).

The balance sheet disclosure for BMW shows a recognised liability of €3,236m. This arises from a gross obligation of €22,710m and plan assets of €19,477. In our view the full economic status of the fund is the best picture of a scheme, i.e., the full deficit. Where relevant, when we are undertaking a valuation, the figure included should be net of deferred tax as, unlike debt principal repayments, pension payments are typically tax deductible.

Exhibit 4.21: BMW pension provisions

in € million	Germany 31.12.2017	Germany 31.12.2016	United Kingdom 31.12.2017	United Kingdom 31.12.2016	Other 31.12.2017	Other 31.12.2016	Total 31.12.2017	Total 31.12.2016
Present value of defined benefit obligations	11,641	11,112	9,594	10,311	1,475	1,476	22,710	22,899
Fair value of plan assets	9,604	8,643	8,908	8,714	965	958	19,477	18,315
Effect of limiting net defined benefit asset to asset ceiling	–	–	–	–	3	3	3	3
Carrying amounts at 31 December	2,037	2,469	686	1,597	513	521	3,236	4,587
thereof pension provision	2,037	2,469	702	1,597	513	521	3,252	4,587
thereof assets	–	–	–16	–	–	–	–16	–

Source: BMW Group Annual Report 2017

Exhibit 4.22 above shows the income statement charge. The crucial aspect is *where* each element has been included in the income statement. In our view it is only the service cost that should be included in the EBIT number. All other charges are financial in nature.

Exhibit 4.22: BMW pension costs

in € million	Defined benefit obligation	Plan assets	Total
1 January 2016	19,926	−16,930	2,996
EXPENSE/INCOME			
Current service cost	557	–	557
Interest expense (+)/ income (−)	557	−479	78
Past service cost	−171	–	−171
Gains (−) or losses (+) arising from settlements	−8	–	−8

Source: BMW Group Annual Report 2017

4.5 Implications for financial analysis

In an environment where there is a shortage of highly skilled and experienced staff, pension benefits can be used as a means of attracting employees. However, offering generous pension terms can be very expensive. Therefore, analysts will want to explore the underlying assumptions and status of the plan closely. Such analysis may well involve going beyond the financial statements data and adjusting the financials.

One of the key problems for analysts is the significant amount of 'netting off' that occurs under IAS 19. Given the smoothing nature of some of these numbers there is an argument that, if the numbers are significant, some level of disaggregation should be undertaken by the analyst.

Typical adjustments that might be made would include:

- The only charge that should go into EBIT is the service cost. This is the true ongoing regular cost.

- IAS 19 does not specify where the various elements of the pension expense should go. Therefore, it is important that the analyst understands where each item is prior to attempting to carry out reversals and other adjustments. IAS 19 requires the location of the various components to be disclosed but we have seen instances when this important disclosure has been omitted. In any event other items that are included in EBIT should really be reversed out. Interest and return on assets are both financial items and the amortisation of actuarial gains and losses should not really be spread but instead should go to equity, in total, immediately.

- Adjustment of pension numbers to align assumptions across peers within an industry. This is not a straightforward matter but is important if divergence in assumptions exists.

Impact on key variables

The following table illustrates the impact of changes to key assumptions on the balance sheet liability:

Exhibit 4.23: Impact of pension assumptions on key metrics

Assumptions Underlying Pension Accounting						
Variable	Disclosed in Financial Statements	Pension Accounting Elements				
		Pension Cost	ABO	PBO*	FV of Plan Assets	Plan Status
Discount rate increase	Yes	Decrease	Decrease	Decrease	–	Improved
Rate of compensation increase	Yes	Increase	–	Increase	–	Dis-improved

* Called DBO in IAS 19

4.6 Building valuation models: What to do

There are two distinct issues that need to be addressed. First is the treatment of the liability relating to years of service already worked. The second issue is the burden on the company in the future of offering 'new' pension benefits to employees as further years of service are undertaken.

In relation to the former, it is important that both under-funded and unfunded pension liabilities are included in the valuation as a form of debt as they represent a loan from employees to the company. If the pension is unfunded, then future profits will also incorporate a provision for future liabilities. This cannot be ignored in valuations.

There are a variety of ways in which pension liabilities can be calculated: using accounting values, using actuarial funding values or even the present value of committed funding contributions. However, it is our view that accounting values – that is, the PBO less the fair value of any plan assets – provides the most appropriate basis for use in a valuation model. This is because the accounting values reflect the debt-like nature of pension commitments (in reference to the discount rate used for the PBO calculation), are comparable across jurisdictions regardless of regulatory funding rules, and are also updated for market moves at each balance sheet date.

In summary, the valuation implications are therefore:

- **Unfunded schemes**: treat the Projected Benefit Obligation (PBO), net of any related deferred tax asset, as debt.

- **Funded schemes: net off the fair value of plan assets from the obligation to derive over or under-funding.** Adjust this amount for any deferred tax balances and treat as debt.

We now turn to dealing with the second issue, future pension benefit promises. We suggest free cash flow should be net of the pension charge, even though this will be shown in the accounts as a non-cash item. This is because it is a real cost. The alternative is to attempt to identify what cash flows would actually be paid out, a task that would often be impractical. If we use the service cost in our free cashflow calculation then we are assuming that, in the long run, the service cost will approximate to the normalised contributions. Therefore, we would suggest forecasting the service cost based on a percentage of staff costs and reflecting this in free cash flow. If this is done then the only value that is lost is the difference between the time value of when the service cost forecast goes through free cash flows and when it is actually contributed to the fund. This is something most valuers can live with.

When constructing valuation models, it is not always easy to establish what the free cash flow net of service costs would be. For most practical purposes it is reasonable to assume that, to the extent that forecast free cash flows include an element that contains provisions for pension obligations, we simply want to detach that amount from the cash flows that we are discounting. This is because it represents an accrual of a liability that is attributable to someone other than the shareholders (in this case, the employees). For the same reason, we should not add back the change in the provision for pension obligations into NOPAT when we calculate economic profit (see chapter five on valuation), because although it is a non-cash item, it represents a real cost to the business. And when thinking about returns on capital employed, it is important to remember that pension obligations are part of the financial capital of the company, equivalent to debt.

5. Provisions

5.1 Why is it important?

Although the thesis of this book is that valuers, including those using discounted cash flow methodologies, need to carefully examine accounting earnings, we are not immune to some of the vagaries of accounting information. Provisioning is one area which historically has been troublesome for interpretation. The nature of provisions is such that they are subjective and non-cash. This means they are vulnerable to manipulation. If a user is to understand the operating performance of an entity, and to use this as a basis for valuation, then a sound understanding of provisions is important. Note that this section addresses provisions other than those which are covered by speciifc accounting standards such as deferred taxation and pensions which have been dealt with above.

5.2 What is current GAAP under IFRS for provisions?

IAS 37 defines a provision as simply a liability of uncertain timing or amount. So, for example if a company is subject to a lawsuit, and it anticipates this loss in its financials, then this would be called a provision. Given the centrality of estimation and uncertainty surrounding provisions, it is little surprise that they can be used to manipulate earnings. The example below illustrates this point.

Example:

Build Bob PLC is a manufacturing company. A chemical leakage occurred at a production facility that unfortunately has led to a lawsuit for $10m environmental damage to a local canal. The legal counsel acting on the company's behalf believes that there is a probable chance of the lawsuit succeeding against the company. The various transactions and entries proceeded as follows.

- Year 1: Given that there is a probable chance of the litigation succeeding the company must record the lawsuit:

  - Increase provisions $10m, increase expenses $10m.

- Year 2: Let us assume that the case has not yet been settled. Lawyers are now of the opinion that it will be a claim of $15m. In this case the following entry would be recorded:

  - Increase provisions $5m and increase expenses $5m.

- Year 3: New evidence has undermined the case against the company and the legal team now think a claim of only $12m will succeed. The following entry would be made:

  - Decrease provisions $3m and decrease expenses $3m.

Note that it is the decrease in the provision that goes through the income statement as income.

- Year 4: The case is settled for $9m. The closing entry would be:

  - Decrease provisions $12m, decrease cash $9m, decrease expenses $3m.

- Note that the cash movement only happens in year 4. All the other movements are purely bookkeeping adjustments leaving them highly susceptible to manipulation.

In an attempt to stop excessive provisioning being used as an income smoothing technique, IAS 37 sets out strict criteria that must be satisfied prior to the recognition of a provision. A decision tree is provided in the appendix to the standard which we have reproduced here as exhibit 4.24 together with some explanatory notes.

Exhibit 4.24: Provisions recognition decision tree

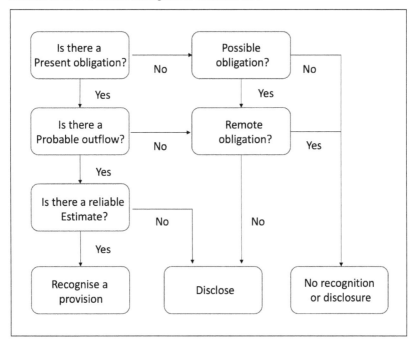

Explanatory notes

Note that in order to recognise a provision various criteria must be met:

- Present obligation, i.e., there must be an existing quasi-legal liability.

- Obligating event, i.e., the event leading to the liability must already have occurred.

- It must be probable that the outflow will occur.

- Measurability – the liability must be capable of expression in monetary units.

If any of these conditions are not met then no numbers will be recognised on the financial statements. Instead there is either disclosure, or no recognition at all. Disclosure will also happen if there is a possible outflow. This is then termed a contingent liability. If the probability is remote, then no action is required at all.

5.3 US GAAP focus

Very substantial overlap exists between the two standards. However, there are a few differences:

- IAS 37 requires discounting if material whereas under US GAAP certain provisions are not discounted.

- Restructuring provisions can only be recognised under IAS 37 if a detailed formal plan is announced publicly or implementation has begun. Under US GAAP a provision is only recognised if a transaction occurs that leaves little or no discretion to avoid the future liability. A mere plan does not create a sufficient obligation.

5.4 Case example

The provisions note for Lufthansa is reproduced below in exhibit 4.25. Note that it delineates provisions into those expected to be settled within a year (current) and non-short term items (non-current).

Exhibit 4.25: Lufthansa provisions note

T127 NON-CURRENT AND CURRENT OTHER PROVISIONS						
	31.12.2017			31.12.2016		
in €m	Total	Non-current	Current	Total	Non-current	Current
Obligations under partial retirement contracts	30	14	16	21	14	7
Other staff costs	186	145	41	167	125	42
Obligation to return emissions certificates	31	–	31	28	–	28
Onerous contracts	103	54	49	115	56	59
Environmental restoration	28	25	3	28	25	3
Legal proceedings	119	21	98	104	20	84
Restructuring/severance payments	208	94	114	219	82	137
Fixed-price customer maintenance contracts	148	42	106	167	5	162
Maintenance of operating lease aircraft	292	149	143	291	124	167
Warranties	41	–	41	50	–	50
Other provisions	405	57	348	379	52	327
Total	1,591	601	990	1,569	503	1,066

Source: Lufthansa Annual Report 2017

Exhibit 4.26: Operating profit disclosure note with provision reversal

T077 OTHER OPERATING INCOME		
in €m	**2017**	2016
Foreign exchange gains	885	886
Commission income	272	250
Income from the reversal of provisions and accruals	151	255
Income from the reversal of impairment losses on fixed assets	83	10
Compensation received for damages	64	45
Reversal of write-downs on receivables	46	27
Income from operating-leasing aircraft	44	13
Income from the disposal of non-current assets	38	13
Rental income	33	31
Services provided by the Group	27	34
Income from staff secondment	26	28
Income from the disposal of non-current available-for-sale financial assets	5	51
Income from sub-leasing aircraft	1	3
Miscellaneous other operating income	601	538
	2,276	**2,184**

Source: Lufthansa Annual Report 2017

Some points to note:

1. The overall level of other provisions has increased during the year. This would therefore be an expense in the income statement. We would also expect to see this as an adjustment in the cash flow statement (see further extract above).

2. The provision note is disaggregated into its various constituent parts. The largest part of the provision is for aircraft maintenance undertaken on those aircraft held under operating leases.

3. The second note shows that £151m of previously recognised provisions have been reversed which will act as a boost to earnings. Note that this is included in other operating income.

5.5 Implications for financial analysis

There are two aspects to the analysis of pensions: identifying the existence or otherwise of income smoothing and the classification of provisions as debt or equity. We shall deal with the former here whilst the latter is dealt with in the valuation section below.

In order to be able to determine whether provisions have been used for the purpose of income smoothing a user must be able to identify what provisions have passed through the income statement. There are a number of ways to identify this:

- Examine the cash flow statement – what does the reconciliation of profit to cash flow show for provisions?

- Examine the increase/decrease in the provision numbers in the balance sheet. Remember it is the *movement* that goes through the income statement.

- Examine the expenses notes and look for the existence of provisions either increasing or decreasing.

The user must try to ascertain if the provision is genuine, or is instead an attempt to control the reporting of results. The use of excessive provisioning in good years and reversals in poor years is a classic form of income smoothing. The user may choose to reverse out those provisions which are 'unnecessary' and reverse out the reversals when they occur! One way of doing this is to accept an ongoing 'average' level of provisions and reverse out accruals above or below this benchmarked norm.

5.6 Building valuation models: What to do

In a similar way to pension provisions discussed above, we have to consider both provisions that exist at the point of our valuation and also provisions that may arise in the future. In general terms, for valuation purposes, provisions in the balance sheet are either treated as quasi debt (similar to debt) or quasi equity (not a real liability), and provisions in future cash flows are treated as if they were a cash cost, or as if they were profit. A balance sheet provision that is unlikely to be paid out in cash will be treated as equity whereas a provision, such as those for pensions, which will certainly be paid out in cash, will be classified as debt.

Looking at this in slightly more detail:

- Provision is equity (ie it will not result in a cash payment)

As equity it is no longer being looked upon as a cost. Therefore, it should be added back to both free cash flow and NOPAT. Examples of this might be deferred taxation provisions in a growing company.

- Provision is debt – one-off

If we are dealing with a liability that will only crystallise once, for example a restructuring cost, then we should treat this as debt in our enterprise value calculation, unless the provision reverses during our forecast period.

- Provision is debt – continuing

Pensions are a good example of this type of provision. Here we have two distinct problems. We have the existing obligation which, in a similar manner to the one above, should be treated as debt. Then we have the ongoing cost in our forecasts. As we saw in the discussion of pensions in section four above, this is a real cost, and we must deduct it from both NOPAT and free cash flow even though we cannot with any real precision forecast the actual cash cost. This is very tricky to do and the pensions section explored some compromise solutions to this some of which might apply to other forms of provsion.

6. Leasing

6.1 Why is it important?

Leasing is a popular source of finance for a wide range of corporates. They are of special interest to users of financial statements as the accounting for these agreements is far from straightforward. In addition, there is ample evidence that companies take advantage of accounting definitions in order to understate the true leverage of the company. It is important that any user who wants to perform reasonably sophisticated analysis becomes familiar with the accounting rules underpinning these legal agreements.

6.2 What is current GAAP under IFRS for leases

Following years of deliberating and debating, the IASB and FASB have now finalised their new lease accounting standards. These apply to accounting periods beginning on/after 1 January 2019. Although the two standards are similar there is an important divergence in the income statement approach which we shall address below.

Before moving on to describe the changes that are being introduced we shall first explain briefly the treatment under IAS 17 which was changed by IFRS 16 *Leases*. Many of the historic numbers valuers will use will be from periods where this standard applied.

6.2.1 Previous accounting of leases: operating versus finance leases

Central to the treatment under the previous accounting rules is the difference between an operating lease and a finance lease. A finance lease was a leasing contract that transferred the substantial risks and rewards of an asset to the lessee. The standard used a range of criteria to assess whether a lease was a finance lease and these are set out in exhibit 4.27

Exhibit 4.27: IAS 17 Finance lease criteria

Criteria	Comment
Ownership is transferred at the end of the lease	This would effectively be payment by instalments
There is a bargain purchase option	If the asset can be bought below its fair value then according to IAS 17 it is a bargain
Lease term is for the major part of the asset's economic life	Typically 75% of the asset's life is the benchmark
Present value of minimum lease payments is substantially all of the fair value of the leased asset	Here, fair value can be read as cash price. Substantially all normally equates to c90%
Assets are of a specialised nature	If only the lessee can use them it's the lessee's asset
Residual value fluctuations belong to the lessee	This would be an indicator of where the economic risks and rewards lie
Lessee can extend the lease at a below market rental	The secondary period brings the lessee closer to economic ownership

Under the old standard finance leases are capitalised in a similar manner to how all leases will now be capitalised under IFRS 16. Operating leases are leases that are not captured by the criteria in exhibit 4.27. Under the old standard they were simply treated like rental agreements. Therefore, a stream of rental expenses are recorded in the years to which they relate and a corresponding entry is made to reflect the reduction in cash. There is no balance sheet recognition of any committed future payments under this approach to operating lease accounting.

6.2.2 What are the key changes in IFRS 16 *Leasing*?

The most significant change is that all leases are 'on balance sheet'. This is achieved by requiring companies to recognise a 'lease asset' and a 'lease liability' on the balance sheet. The amounts to be capitalised are based on the present value of the future lease rental payments. Under IFRS 16, the accounting also results in a different cost recognition profile for leases and is likely to have a negative effect on net income for companies which are expanding, as they have more 'newer' leases (explained further below). Importantly, the US GAAP income statement treatment of leases has not changed from the previous standard.

Operating vs financial lease classification

Central to the conceptual shift in the accounting is the elimination of the previous classification of leases as either 'operating leases' or 'finance leases'. Instead all leases (with a lease term greater than 12 months) are now treated in a similar way to how finance leases have previously been accounted for. They are 'capitalised' by recording the present value of the lease as part of their property, plant and equipment. The capitalised value reflects the company's estimate of value of the right to use the asset over the term of the lease. This calculation, based on present values, is described below. In addition, companies recognise an equal and opposite financial liability to reflect the obligation to pay future lease rental.

The present value of the lease is calculated by:

• Including all contractual rental payments but excluding any payments which vary in line with the performance or usage of the asset (such variable rentals are common in the retail sector for example).

• Adjusting the lease term for any renewal options or early break clauses where the company is 'reasonably certain' to exercise these options. These provisions effectively extends the lease term to include optional periods if the conditions are satisfied.

• Using a discount rate which reflects the rate implicit in the lease. In many cases this can be broadly expected to reflect the company's cost of borrowing.

Income statement treatment

Under IFRS, the income statement cost of the capitalised lease differs from the current 'straight-line' recognition of operating lease rentals. Instead, the rental cost is replaced with a depreciation charge from the lease asset (included within EBIT) and an interest cost on the lease liability (included within finance costs). Although the depreciation charge would be a straight-line cost, the interest cost reduces over the life of the lease, resulting in a reducing overall lease cost as the lease contract matures. The reduction in interest cost is intuitive. The lease rentals pay down the principal of the 'obligation' over the life of the lease. Therefore, in the early years interest is higher as the loan is higher. The situation reverses in later years.

This difference in cost profile is illustrated in the chart below:

Exhibit 4.28: Income statement treatment under IFRS 16 *Leases*

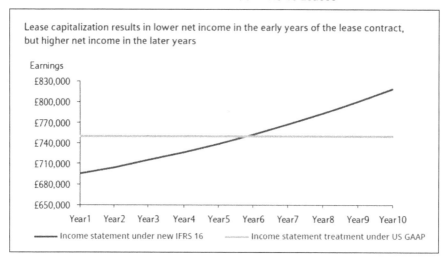

This negative impact on earnings is particularly acute for companies which have been expanding in recent years utilising leases as a financing source. This is because a greater proportion of their leases are less than halfway through their lease term. However, where a company holds a portfolio of leases where the start/end dates are evenly distributed, the earnings impact should be more neutral, as the expense profiles of all the leases would result in a broadly stable expense each year.

None of this applies to the FASB model, which will determine US GAAP. It is designed to ensure that the lease cost in the income statement is on a straight-line basis and is all included within EBIT.

The following example illustrates the treatment of lease capitalisation.

Comprehensive example

Shortcut Inc. needs to acquire an asset with a value of €560,200.

The firm decided to finance the asset with a lease. The document was signed at the company's solicitors on the 1 January year 1. The details of the lease are as follows:

Lease term: 5 years

Rentals: €144,000 payable in arrears

Depreciation Policy: Straight line

The relevant calculations are shown below.

Annual Finance Charge

Year	Opening Loan Balance	Interest at 9%	Lease Rental	Capital Repayment	Closing Loan Balance
	€	€	€	€	€
1	560,110	50,410	(144,000)	93,590	466,520
2	466,520	41,987	(144,000)	102,013	364,507
3	364,507	32,806	(144,000)	111,194	253,313
4	253,313	22,798	(144,000)	121,202	132,111
5	132,111	11,889*	(144,000)	132,111	-

*Adjusted for rounding errors of approximately €78

Lease obligations

	1	2	3	4	5
	€	€	€	€	€
Current liability	102,013	111,194	121,202	132,111	-
Non-current liability	364,507	253,313	132,111	-	-
Total obligation	466,520	364,507	253,313	132,111	-

Non-current assets: Right of use asset

	1	2	3	4	5
	€	€	€	€	€
Cost	560,110	560,110	560,110	560,110	560,110
Accumulated depreciation	(112,022)	(224,044)	(336,066)	(448,088)	(560,110)
Net book value	448,088	336,066	224,044	112,022	

Points to Note

- As an alternative to using the incremental rate of borrowing, the lessee could use the lessor's implicit rate in the lease if practicable (unfortunately, this rate is not disclosed in the lessee's financials).

- At inception of the lease

  ↑ Equipment ('Right of use' asset) €560,110

  ↑ Lease obligations €560,110

- The equipment is depreciated over five years, assuming that this is the shorter period between lease term and useful life of the asset.

- The amount of borrowing increases each year by the finance charge which accrues at 9% and decreases each year by the rental payments of €144,000. The table splits the €144,000 between interest and capital payments.

- The income statement will reflect the interest charge each year.

6.2.3 What will the impact of the changes be?

The standards eliminate one of the key benefits of using operating leasing, namely that liabilities are 'off balance sheet'. However, companies lease assets for a wide range of reasons. These include the taxation advantages provided by leases in certain regions, costs relating to operation and maintenance which can often be project managed in a efficient way by lessors, and limited availability of alternative sources of leverage such that leasing has to be used. The accounting standard setters recognised that there is a risk that companies might seek to circumvent IFRS 16 by negotiating shorter leases with frequent renewal options. Therefore, the standards contain anti-avoidance provisions which require lease terms to include:

- Periods covered by an extension/renewal option where there is a 'significant economic inducement' to exercise that option.

- Periods covered by an early termination option (e.g., a 'break clause') where there is a significant economic inducement *not* to exercise that option.

6.2.4 How will the market interpret the adjustments?

Given the implementation of IFRS 16 is a recent accounting change we address the impact on key metrics here.

Net income (and EPS)

Companies are required to replace operating lease rentals (previously reported as a cost in EBIT) with amortisation on the leased asset and interest on lease liability. For companies with large individual leases, this translates into lower net income in early periods which is then offset by higher reported profits towards the end of the lease term. However, for companies with a portfolio of leases, with differing lease start/end dates, this impact is reduced as the expense profiles of all the leases would result in a broadly stable expense each year. Note under US GAAP no changes take place as the income statement charge is not being changed.

EBITDA

Given that the new approach substitutes rental payments for interest and amortisation and EBITDA is clearly before amortisation and interest, the new rules will lead to higher EBITDA.

Multiples

Share prices should remain relatively unchanged, unless the accounting rules change perceptions of risk or reveal new information. However, if there are changes to EPS or EBITDA (as discussed above) which are not accompanied by a change in price, multiples are likely to change. Where the impact of the changes is significant, companies could experience a material distortion to multiples such as P/E or EV/EBITDA. It will not be straightforward to 'unwind' the new accounting treatments, so it is likely that the market will take the new earnings as the starting point going forward.

6.3 US GAAP

The balance sheet treatment of leases is now essentially the same under IFRS and US GAAP. However, as shown in exhibit 4.28 above, the income statement treatment is significantly different. The US retain an operating lease model that results in a consistent 'rent' charge over the lease term whereas all leases are capitalised under IFRS. This means that, under IFRS, there will always be an upfront cost on leases as the interest plus depreciation outweighs a flat rental charge.

6.4 Case example

IFRS 16 *Leases* was introduced for accounting periods beginning on or after 1 January, 2019. Therefore at the time of publication of this text only 'early adopters' have disclosed detailed information about leases under the new regime. Air France-KLM Group show the impact of adoption of the new standard and this can provide a useful window into the line items impacted in the financial statements. Exhibit 4.29 shows the income statement impact of the adoption of a number of different accounting standards. Here our focus is on IFRS 16. The first thing to note is that there are two columns. The second column is for maintenance services. IFRS 16 allows companies to treat these contracts as if they are leases even though they do not technically meet the definition in the standard given there is no 'asset'. We shall focus on the first IFRS 16 column entitled 'Impact – contracts capitalisation'. The overall impact of applying the standard is to increase net income by €62m. This comes from reversing out lease rentals (€285m) and replacing these with extra depreciation of €220m and interest of €84m. There are other items, unique to the Air France-KLM Group, which net out to £62m, but it is these first items that are most relevant from a general learning perspective.

The second exhibit addresses the impact on the balance sheet. The right of use asset of €4,900m is new to the asset side of the balance sheet and on the liability side 'lease debt' of €5,141m reflects the capitalisation required by IFRS 16. Note that they are not the same number as the Air France-KLM Group has adopted the full retrospective approach. Therefore, although on the first day of any lease the asset and liability would normally equal each other subsequently the two numbers diverge. The asset will be depreciated on a straight line basis whereas the liability will be increased by finance charges and decreased by lease rental payments.

Exhibit 4.29: Impact of IFRS 16 Leases on income statement and balance sheet

Impact on the consolidated income statement

In € millions **Period from January 1 to March 31, 2017**	Published accounts	IFRS 9 impact	IFRS 15 impact	IFRS 16 impact – contracts capitalization	IFRS 16 impact – maintenance of leased aircraft	Restated accounts
Sales	**5,709**	-	**(4)**	-	-	**5,705**
External expenses	(3,508)	-	(15)	49	9	(3,465)
Salaries and related costs	(1,812)	-	-	-	-	(1,812)
Taxes other than income taxes	(45)	-	-	-	-	(45)
Other income and expenses	210	-	-	-	55	265
EBITDAR	**554**	-	**(19)**	**49**	**64**	**648**
Aircraft operating lease costs	(285)	-	-	285	-	-
EBITDA	**269**	-	**(19)**	**334**	**64**	**648**
Amortization, depreciation and provisions	(412)	-	1	(220)	(50)	(681)
Income from current operations	**(143)**	-	**(18)**	**114**	**14**	**(33)**
Income from operating activities	**(142)**	-	**(18)**	**114**	**15**	**(31)**
Net cost of financial debt	(56)	-	-	(84)	-	(140)
Other financial income and expenses	(31)	29	-	59	(11)	46
Income before tax	**(229)**	**29**	**(18)**	**89**	**4**	**(125)**
Income taxes	9	(7)	6	(27)	(2)	(21)
Net income of consolidated companies	**(220)**	**22**	**(12)**	**62**	**2**	**(146)**
Net income	**(216)**	**22**	**(12)**	**62**	**1**	**(143)**
Earning per share (basic and diluted)	(0.74)	0.07	(0.04)	0.21	-	(0.50)

Impact on the consolidated balance sheet

Only accounts impacted by IFRS 9, IFRS 15 and IFRS 16 are presented hereafter.

In € millions **Balance sheet as of December 31, 2017**	Published accounts	IFRS 9 impact	IFRS 15 impact	IFRS 16 impact – contracts capitalization	IFRS 16 impact – maintenance of leased aircraft	Restated accounts
Asset						
Flight equipment	9,921	32	-	(294)	(25)	9,634
Other property, plant and equipment	1,492	-	-	(74)	-	1,418
Right-of-use assets	-	-	-	4,900	963	5,863
Deferred tax assets	234	(10)	32	164	59	479
Trade receivables	2,136	-	29	-	-	2,165
Other current assets	1,264	(1)	23	(52)	8	1,242
Equity and liabilities						
Return obligation liability and other provisions (current and non-current term)	2,198	-	(109)	-	1,122	3,211
Financial debt (current and non-current)	7,442	(4)	-	(141)	-	7,297
Lease debt (current and non-current)	-	-	-	5,141	-	5,141
Deferred tax liabilities	11	-	(5)	-	-	6
Deferred revenue on ticket sales	2,889	-	128	-	-	3,017
Other current liabilities	3,100	-	146	-	(3)	3,243
Equity	3,015	25	(76)	(356)	(115)	2,493
• Holders of Air France-KLM	3,002	25	(76)	(355)	(115)	2,481
• Non-controlling interests	13	-	-	(1)	-	12

Source: Air France KLM June 2018 interim report

6.5 Implications for financial analysis

Any user will need to understand the nature of an entity's financing to understand its performance. A core part of this understanding will be the use and treatment of leases. For example, comparing two airlines, one that uses finance leases against one that predominantly uses operating leases, requires judicious adjustments for leasing contracts irrespective of the accounting treatment preferred under IFRS. These are discussed in the modelling section below. IFRS 16 will greatly improve the comparability given that if companies utilise leases of whatever form the committed payments will appear on the balance sheet.

In the next section we analyse the impact on a variety of measures of capitalising. For simplicity's sake, let us assume that we have a company that has used operating lease extensively. The company is now required to apply IFRS 16. As we have seen, this standard requires the capitalisation of outstanding lease commitments. Exhibit 4.30 describes the impact on some key metrics measures of this capitalisation process.

Exhibit 4.30: Impact of capitalising lease

Issue	Impact	Comment
Net income	Lower (early years)	In contrast to the consistant nature of the net income charge under operating leases, capitalised leases make higher charges in the earlier years of a lease and as the 'principal' is repaid the charges comes down because the interest element of the charge falls.
EBIT	Higher	As a major part of the capitalised lease charge is interest then we would expect EBIT to be higher over all years. An exception to this might be if the lessee charged very high levels of accelerated depreciation but this would be very rare.
Debt:equity	Higher	We get extra debt on the balance sheet with capitalised leases.
Return on equity	Lower (early years)	Net income is lower early in the lease period and higher later in the lease period so this ratio will first fall and then increase.
Return on capital employed	?	Capital employed is higher but so is operating profit. Therefore the outcome here is a function of the relative change in the numerator and denominator.
EBIT/Interest	?	EBIT is higher but so is interest and they both change by different amounts so again we need to look at the numbers.

6.6 Building valuation models: What to do

From a valuation perspective, all leases are a form of debt irrespective of the accounting treatment. The implementation of IFRS 16 is therefore helpful in fully aligning the accounting with the way in which leases should be incorporated into a valuation model. Post-IFRS 16 it is therefore simply a matter of identifying the total lease assets and lease liabilities reported by the company and ensuring that they are included:

- In the operating capital employed when thinking about capital turns and the return on operating capital.

- In the debt figure when calculating weighted average cost of capital and when deriving a value for the equity from an enterprise value perspective.

- As part of capital expenditure forecasts in discounted cash flow models. This means that expected increases in leased assets should be treated as a cash outflow when forecasting free cash flows. This is to ensure a that company growing its leased asset portfolio is appropriately captured in cash flow forecasts. Such increases represent capital expenditure and so are critical to valuing the business. In practice, this can be done for each forecast year by deriving free cash flow as forecast net operating profit after tax, minus the forecast growth in operating capital employed between the beginning and the end of the year. Historically, this point has frequently been forgotten when dealing with finance leases – possibly because the increases in lease liabilities were not recorded as investments in the cash flow statement. However, omitting this step risks understating the capital intensity of the business.

7. Derivatives

7.1 Why is it important?

Derivatives have become an integral tool used by almost all companies of reasonable size. Their use varies but typically the vast majority of corporates use derivatives to hedge exposures. The exposures might be:

- **Future price of raw materials** (e.g., aviation kerosene for an airline, cocoa beans for a manufacturer)

- **Foreign currency** (e.g., customer balances in a foreign currency)

- **Interest rates** (e.g., protect against rising interest rates where the company has predominantly variable rate debt)

Analysts need to understand how these instruments are reflected in the financials. This is especially the case as the accounting issues are not straightforward. The investor needs to be in a position to appreciate the entries that are made for these items prior to considering a logical approach for analysis.

7.2 What is current GAAP under IFRS for derivatives?

7.2.1 Derivative refresher

Technically, a derivative is simply an instrument whose value is dependent on the value of something else. A forward contract to buy euros to fund a summer holiday will, by the time the holiday arrives, have been either a winning or a losing 'bet'. The value of the derivative, in that instance, is the gain or loss versus just buying the money when you needed it.

All derivatives are ultimately made up of four types of entity, or a combination of more than one of them.

Forward contracts

These are the simplest, and take the form described above in the foreign currency example. They are not tradeable instruments, but an Over The Counter (OTC) contract between two parties.

Futures contracts

Futures contracts are just forward contracts that are tradeable on regulated markets. The advantage is liquidity. The disadvantage is that the terms of the contracts have to be standardised to facilitate trading.

Swaps

Swaps are portfolios of forward contracts. If a company swaps its fixed coupon debt into floating rate, with a bank as counterparty, what the bank has actually done is to sell a series of forward contracts on interest rates over the duration of the debt.

Options

These represent the right, but not the obligation, to buy (call) or sell (put) an asset at a pre-arranged price. The option element makes these instruments complex to value.

In general derivatives are interchangeable, and arbitrageable, with one another. The choice of instrument, and whether to deal on regulated exchanges or use OTC contracts, is one of convenience. So-called 'exotic derivatives' are merely bundles of contracts of the type described above, though valuing them can be horribly complex.

7.2.2. Derivative accounting tutorial

IFRS 9 *Financial instruments* is the core standard under IFRS for derivatives. It is a complex standard and was the subject of extensive debate during its development, as it was swiftly (and recently) introduced as a replacement for the previous standard (IAS 39) which was deemed to have exacerbated accounting concerns during the 2008 financial crisis.

Although IFRS 9 covers the accounting for all financial instruments, here we will focus primarily on accounting for derivatives. In this respect, IFRS 9 has a single basic premise: derivatives must be recognised on the balance sheet at fair value. Historically, under many national GAAPs, driven by a historical cost perspective, derivatives remained unrecognised. This is because there is no real concept of cost at the initiation of, for example, a swap. The only recognition of their effect may be the matching of the relevant underlying with the derivative on settlement. Therefore, a company could have an entire portfolio of derivatives at the year end with little or no recognition in the financials as there is no upfront cost as such. This position would continue to prevail until the relevant hedged transaction took place. The IASB viewed this 'deferral and matching' system as a privilege (rather than a right) and therefore tore up the book on how derivatives were accounted for. The simple step of insisting that derivatives be marked to market at fair value means that recognition is now mandatory.

In many ways it is the other entry that is of most interest – if an asset/liability is recognised by marking a derivative to market on the balance sheet, does the other side of the entry capturing the change in value go to the income statement or, alternatively equity? IFRS 9 has devised a system to discern where such gains and losses are recognised. The example below shows the three different classifications for derivatives and the consequent treatments. The following comments will help in understanding the nature of these categories:

No hedge

This applies to derivatives not entered into for hedging purposes and, perhaps more importantly, those that fail to qualify for hedge accounting. Hedge accounting is an accounting treatment that allows the symmetircal offset of gains and losses on derivatives and underlying hedged items. So, for example, a gain on an asset would be offset with a loss on the derivative. Hedge accounting presents a smoother picture in the accounts. In this case, where hedge accounting treatment is not achieved the change in value of the derivativee goes through the income statement.

Fair value hedge

If the derivative does meet the definition of a hedge, and there is an existing asset/ liability, then both are valued at fair value and gains/losses offset in the income statement thereby reflecting the economics of the situation.

Cash flow hedge

Again this applies if the hedge criteria are satisfied but it is future cash flows that are being protected rather than the fair value of an existing asset/liability. In this case the derivative is still marked to market. However, as no underlying yet exists (it will only happen when the future cash flows materialise) the movements in value go directly to equity. Once recognised in equity the gains/losses await the underlying and, when it happens, they are 'recycled' to income (i.e., matched).

In practice there are quite complex entries so IFRS 9 produces a range of examples with numbers. The following examples are based on the rules in IFRS 9.

Example 1 – Fair value hedges

Six months before year end, a company issues a 3-year €10m fixed interest note at 7.5% with semi-annual interest payments. It also enters into an interest rate swap to pay LIBOR (London Interbank Offer Rate) and to receive 7.5% semi-annually; swap terms include a €10m notional principal, 3-year term and semi-annual variable rate reset.

LIBOR for the first six month period is 6%. By year end, interest rates have fallen and the fair value of the swap (after settlement) is €125,000 (asset).

What entries are required?

1. If traditional historic accounting is used.

2. IFRS 9 with no hedge accounting.

3. IFRS 9 with hedge accounting.

Solution

1. If traditional historic accounting is used

Borrowings

1. Loan is recognised at net proceeds

↑	Cash	€10,000,000
↑	Creditors	€10,000,000

2. Interest on loan for period

↓	P&L account – net interest payable	€375,000
↓	Cash	€375,000

Derivatives

1. Swap is recognised, measured at cost

↑	Financial asset – held for trading	€0
↓	Cash	€0

2. Settlement under swap in period

↑	Cash (€375,000-€300,000)	€75,000
↑	P&L account – gain on hedge	€75,000

2. IFRS 9 with no hedge accounting

Borrowings

1. Loan is recognised at net proceeds

↑	Cash	€10,000,000
↑	Creditors	€10,000,000

2. Interest on loan for period

↓	P&L account – net interest payable	€375,000
↓	Cash	€375,000

Derivatives

1. Swap is recognised, measured initially at cost

↑	Financial asset – held for trading	€0
↓	Cash	€0

2. Settlement under swap in period

↑	Cash (€375,000-€300,000)	€75,000
↑	P&L account – gain on hedge	€75,000

3. Swap is subsequently remeasured to fair value

↑	Financial asset – held for trading	€125,000
↑	P&L account – gain on hedge	€125,000

3. IFRS 9 with hedge accounting

1. Loan is recognised at net proceeds

↑	Cash	€10,000,000
↑	Creditors	€10,000,000

2. Interest on loan for period

↓	P&L account – net interest payable	€375,000
↓	Cash	€375,000

Derivatives

1. Swap is recognised, measured initially at cost

↑	Financial asset – held for trading	€0
↓	Cash	€0

2. Settlement under swap in period

↑	Cash	€75,000
↑	P&L account – gain on hedge	€75,000

3. Swap and loan are subsequently remeasured to fair value

↑	Financial asset – held for trading	€125,000
↑	Financial liability (loan)	€125,000

Example 2 – Cash flow hedges

Delta Limited has tendered for a contract. The price quoted is $10m. However, Delta's functional currency is the Euro. Therefore, as prices would be fixed, Delta wishes to hedge this exposure. It enters into an FX future with a nominal value of $10m.

The treatments under various scenarios are summarised below:

Traditional transaction approach

The hedge will be ignored until the contract flows occur at which point the gain/loss on the derivative would be recognised. If the contract tender is not successful, the derivative would be settled and reported in income.

Hedge accounting conditions not met

The FX derivative is marked to market at period end through the income statement as it is classified as speculation per IFRS 9.

Hedge accounting conditions are met

Phase I: Derivative is marked to market on the balance sheet with gains/loss going to equity.

Phase II: Once cash flows occur, the gain/loss on derivative is matched with the relevant portion of the hedged inflows.

7.3 US GAAP focus

IFRS and US GAAP are broadly similar in terms of their application to derivatives. However, there are significant differences between the two frameworks in other aspects of accounting for financial instruments. These differences have increased since the introduction of IFRS 9. The key differences include:

1. Offsetting financial assets and liabilities entered into with the same counterparty is generally easier under US GAAP than IFRS, since US GAAP requires only a legal right to net settle, whereas IFRS requires both the legal right *and* the intention to net settle.

2. US GAAP contains more onerous criteria for qualifying for hedge accounting than IFRS; US GAAP requires a rigorous assessment of hedge effectiveness before hedge accounting can be applied, whilst IFRS requires only an economic relationship between the derivative and the hedged item.

3. US GAAP has retained the classification system used by the previous IFRS accounting standard (IAS 39), which means that financial assets are classified based on the legal form of the instrument and the intent of the holder (loans and receivables, held to maturity instruments, available for sale instruments and held for trading instruments). IFRS now classifies instruments by their cash flow characteristics and the business model (resulting in classification as either amortised cost, fair value through OCI or fair value through P&L). In general, more financial asset will be recorded at FVTPL under IFRS than US GAAP.

4. The impairment model for financial assets differs, with US GAAP using a 'full expected loss' model, whereas IFRS uses a 'partial expected loss model'. This means that impairment losses are recognised in full at an earlier point in time under US GAAP than under IFRS.

7.4 Financial analysis implications

There is no accepted systematic approach to dealing with derivative gains and losses. In addition to the general complexity surrounding some of the instruments, the reported numbers may be material and volatile making it a challenge for analysts to discern what elements should be reflected in underlying earnings.

Perhaps the most straightforward approach to this issue is to consider a number of interpretation points that must be considered.

1. Simply reversing out gains/losses on derivatives is not an option. For example, a gain/loss on a derivative that relates to a cash market transaction recognised in the financials is a real economic cost/income. Reversing out may, for example in the case of an interest rate hedge, mean the interest expense is under/overstated.

2. It is also difficult to see how analysts can deal with comparable analysis of companies where one qualifies for hedge accounting and another does not, yet both are

economically similar. Our favoured approach is only to reverse any derivative gains/losses recognised in the income statement that relate to underlying transactions that are not recognised in the same income statement. Ineffective hedges should be treated as financial income/charges.

3. It should be borne in mind that for accurate forecasting a good appreciation of the hedges a company has in place is important. Therefore, analysts and investors can utilise the information in the financials to develop this understanding. It should always be borne in mind that current hedging conditions are unlikely to persist beyond a certain time horizon. But, a company can always hedge if it is prepared to pay the price.

7.5 Case example

We have included two extracts from the financials of Commerzbank to illustrate certain points of interest on financial instruments. The first example in exhibit 4.31.

Exhibit 4.31: Commerzbank fair value hedges

€m	31.12.2017	31.12.2016	Change in %
Positive fair values micro fair value hedges	1,184	1,721	−31.2
Positive fair values portfolio fair value hedges	274	348	−21.4
Positive fair values cash flow hedges	7	7	2.6
Total	1,464	2,075	−29.4

€m	31.12.2017	31.12.2016	Change in %
Negative fair values micro fair value hedges	2,198	3,041	−27.7
Negative fair values portfolio fair value hedges	38	10	
Negative fair values cash flow hedges	19	29	−34.9
Total	2,255	3,080	−26.8

Sources: Commerzbank annual report, 2017.

Exhibit 4.31 discloses the instruments that have been fair valued and included on the balance sheet. Derivatives with negative and positive values are disclosed separately. This is to provide more information to users and minimizes netting off that might obscure the underlying economics. Note that the classification into micro, portfolio and cash flow hedges.

If a user wishes to identify what amount of derivative fair value differences has passed through the income statement then this will be disclosed in the cash flow statement. The cash to profit reconciliation is reproduced below in exhibit 4.32 below. The gains on derivatives are a highly significant reconciling item. These are reversed out as they are non-cash losses and hence do not have an effect on cash.

Exhibit 4.32: Commerzbank cash to profit reconciliation

€m	Notes	2017	2016[1]
Consolidated profit or loss		250	382
Non-cash positions in consolidated profit or loss and reconciliation with cash flow from operating activities:			
Write-downs, depreciation, write-ups on fixed and other assets, changes in provisions and net changes due to hedge accounting		1,925	1,457
Change in other non-cash positions		−7,082	1,647
Net gain or loss on the sale of fixed assets	(17)	14	76
Other adjustments		−3,973	−3,937
Sub-total		**−8,866**	**−376**
Change in assets and liabilities from operating activities after adjustment for non-cash positions:			
Financial assets – Loans and Receivables	(24)	11,470	17,178
Financial assets – Available for Sale		8,456	3,370
Financial assets – Fair Value Option	(28)	1,098	11,676
Financial assets – Held for Trading	(30)	9,954	12,893
Other assets from operating activities		825	−244
Financial liabilities – Amortised Cost	(26)	−1,615	−28,883
Financial liabilities – Fair Value Option	(29)	−3,236	−5,672
Financial liabilities – Held for Trading	(31)	95	−695
Net cash from contributions into plan assets	(54)	12	9
Other liabilities from operating activities		−1,292	−5,604
Interest received	(8)	7,111	7,403
Dividends received	(9)	106	164
Interest paid	(8)	−3,244	−3,630
Income tax paid	(21)	−443	−337
Net cash from operating activities		**20,432**	**7,251**

Source: Commerzbank Annual Report 2017

7.6 Building valuation models: What to do

Taking the three categories of hedge separately, gains or losses on fair value hedges offset changes in value of the hedged entity, so there should be no impact on the profit or cash flow that is being discounted. However, when thinking about returns on capital employed, it is marked to market capital that we should ideally be using, so the net value of fair value derivatives should be included in the calculation.

With cash flow hedges, we only want to reflect the profit or cash effect of the hedge when the underlying transaction crystallises, which is as it will be reflected in the accounts. But, for the same reason, it would make sense to reverse gains and losses on cash flow hedges out of equity in calculations of return on equity or return on capital.

Unless it is known that a company is speculating (in which case the trading gain or loss is clearly a trading gain or loss!) it might seem sensible to reverse out the profit or loss from derivatives that are not classified as hedge transactions. The problem with this is that if the derivative is effectively hedging a future transaction then the gain or loss on the derivative will substantially offset a loss or gain on the transaction, and leaving it in would provide a clearer impression of the real economic position than leaving it out. If in doubt, it is probably better to leave it in.

Most analysts do not model future gains and losses on derivatives. For most practical purposes, what is key is to remember that transaction hedges to protect the company against foreign exchange risk, for example, will run out typically after a year to eighteen months. So if there has been an adverse currency movement which has not yet been reflected in trading profits, it will be! Unless the exchange rate is expected to reverse, the risk is that a substantial impairment to the value of the business is ignored. The marking to market of cash flow hedges should at least alert analysts to this problem.

8. Non-current assets

8.1 Why is it important?

Much of the balance sheet of today's typical listed company is made up of intangible fixed assets i.e., those with no physical presence. Therefore, in order to analyse a company's asset base and return on invested capital appropriately, we must have a good understanding of how financial statements reflect this important asset group. In many ways the accounting appears to obfuscate and confuse rather than show the underlying economics of a company's dealings in intangibles. Tangible fixed assets are also of importance, although the accounting under IFRS is generally more straightforward.

8.2 What is current GAAP under IFRS for intangibles?

Before proceeding to focus on intangible assets it is worth addressing briefly tangible non-current assets. The accounting for these assets is a much more straightforward task at one level – recognition does not tend to be a problem. The acquisition of an asset, such as a building or piece of equipment is recognised initially at purchase cost plus other costs required to get the asset into a useable condition and location (legal costs and transport costs for example). There are a few aspects of IFRS tangible asset accounting that should be drawn to investors' attention:

- Under IFRS fixed assets can be revalued to market value, although this is not required. A key asset we might see revalued would be property, plant and equipment. As this is optional under IFRS it is likely that companies will carefully consider whether to take advantage of it. On the plus side, if a company revalues its assets then debt-equity measures would be lower. However against this, earnings will be lower due to higher depreciation. Return on equity will suffer due to this earnings effect as well as the higher equity. When companies in the UK had this choice they tended to adopt a non-revaluation stance, especially given the rigorous rules regarding keeping the valuations up to date. For these reasons few companies make extensive use of this option.

- Investment properties are defined as those properties not used in the operations of a company but, instead, are held for investment purposes. IAS 40, *Investment properties*, allows the adoption of either a cost or a fair value (through the income statement) model. If the choice is made to adopt a cost model then the fair value of these assets should still be disclosed (see the section on real estate companies in chapter six).

Both of these treatments could cause problems for our clean surplus assumption. Remember to achieve clean surplus accounting all gains/losses recognised during a period should go through the earnings number that is being used in the valuation. If a company revalues an asset and this change goes through equity then our 'clean' assumption is violated. This might encourage valuers to treat such gains and losses as income for valuation purposes (as against for performance analysis or comparables where these items should clearly be excluded). The same problem does not apply to property companies that adopt the fair value model as in this case clean surplus accounting is not violated as the fair value movements go through the income statement.

- Residual values used for depreciation calculations (intangibles rarely have residual values) must be based on updated information. In some countries residual values have historically been ignored for depreciation purposes so this may reduce depreciation charges. From an economic perspective it makes obvious sense to charge the real cost of an asset rather than ignoring the future residual value or using an out of date one.

The difficulty of accounting for intangible fixed assets lies in the difficulty of attaining an appropriate valuation. This is especially the case for assets that are not generic such as customer loyalty, brand recognition, trademarks, licenses and franchises. Therefore the accounting rules reflect a high degree of conservatism when dealing with intangibles.

IAS 38 *Intangible assets* only allows recognition of an intangible asset if it meets a challenging asset definition. An asset is defined as a resource which is controlled by an entity as a result of past events and from which future economic benefits are expected to flow to the entity. These two conditions (control and future benefits) often mean that potential intangibles do not meet the definition of an asset. For example, advertising costs would not meet the definition as the benefits that may flow are in no way controlled by the enterprise. Therefore such costs are expensed.

Many of the accounting issues surrounding the recognition of intangible fixed assets can be distilled into one question: has the intangible been purchased or internally generated?

8.2.1 Purchased intangibles

By their nature a purchased intangible has a much better chance of recognition than internally developed. This is simply due to the fact that a company will normally only buy something over which it has control and from which they would expect to enjoy future economic benefits. If the purchase of the intangibles is in the context of a business combination then again recognition is highly likely. This recognition may well be in the form of a specific intangible (such as brands) or as part of the residual goodwill. The treatment of goodwill is considered in chapter seven.

8.2.2 Internally developed intangibles

As stated above, most intangibles will not meet the recognition criteria as they are not purchased. R&D, or more precisely 'D', is one notable exception. IAS 38 specifies two phases that an internal intangible passes through, the research phase and the development phase.

Research phase

This is the original and planned investigation undertaken with the prospect of gaining new scientific or technical knowledge. All of the costs associated with this phase should be written off as incurred.

Development phase

The application of research findings or other knowledge to improve or substantially develop company products, services or processes. Development costs that meet the following conditions *must* be capitalised otherwise they are written off as an expense.

- The project is technically feasible.

- There is an intention to complete the intangible asset and use or sell it.

- The enterprise has the ability to use or sell the asset.

- It must be clear how the intangible can be used or how it could be sold.

- The company has adequate resources to complete the project.

- The expenditure associated with the intangible asset can be reliably measured.

Once an intangible asset has been capitalised then it should be initially recognised at cost. Subsequent to initial measurement at cost the preferred IFRS treatment is to show the asset at cost net of accumulated amortisation and impairment charges. Theoretically IAS 38 does allow revaluations of intangibles but this is only where there is an active market in the intangible. Given the unique nature of many intangibles this is unlikely to be the case and so we very rarely see revaluations of intangibles.

The amortisation period is assumed to be less than 20 years. However, in certain industries a longer period may be acceptable. This might apply for example in the aerospace industry where expenditure might be expected to generate benefits over periods as long as 30 years although we doubt very much whether such amortisation periods would be used in practice. The normal approach to amortising an intangible is to use a straight-line depreciation method with a zero residual value.

8.3 US GAAP focus

There are two key areas of divergence between US GAAP and IFRS on accounting for intangibles:

Research and development expenditure is generally expensed in the US, although certain software and technology costs may qualify for capitalisation. Under IFRS development expenditure must be capitalised.

Intangibles can be revalued under IFRS if they are traded in an active market (highly unlikely for most intangibles). This is prohibited under US GAAP.

8.4 Case examples

A typical accounting policy for a company that capitalises development costs is reproduced below in exhibit 4.33. The last paragraph essentially reproduces the criteria required in IAS 38.

Exhibit 4.33: Capitalising development costs

A. **Accounting policies**
Research and development expenses include the cost of scientific and technical activities, industrial property, and the education and training necessary for the development, production or implementation and marketing of new or substantially improved materials, methods, products, processes, systems or services.
Under *IAS 38 – Intangible Assets*, development expenditure is recognised as an intangible asset if the entity can demonstrate in particular:
• its intention to complete the intangible asset and use or sell it, as well as the availability of adequate technical, financial and other resources for this purpose;
• that it is probable that the future economic benefits attributable to the development expenditure will flow to the entity;
• that the cost of the asset can be measured reliably.
Capitalised development costs include related borrowing costs (see Note 12.2.A).
Expenses for the year include research costs, non-capitalised study and development costs under the above criteria, and the amortisation of capitalised development costs.

Source: Peugeot Annual Report 2017

The second extract below (exhibit 4.34) show the intangible assets note. In addition to development capitalisation, software costs and other intangibles are also capitalised and amortised. Amortisation policies are very much at the discretion of the company and if we are to view these as real costs then some level of normalisation must be applied to the reported numbers. Note that amortisation of intangibles is almost universally straight line. The numerical disclosures are in the normal format of cost plus additions less amortisation equals book value.

Exhibit 4.34: Peugeot intangible assets

B. Change in carrying amount

31 December 2017 (in million euros)	Goodwill	Development expenditure	Brands, software and other intangible assets	Intangible assets
At beginning of period	**1,514**	**4,860**	**594**	**5,454**
Purchases/additions [1]	-	1,619	150	1,769
Amortisation for the year	-	(845)	(98)	(943)
Impairment losses	-	(80)	-	(80)
Disposals	-	(1)	(46)	(47)
Change in scope of consolidation and other [2]	1,829	8	1,824	1,832
Translation adjustment	(22)	(70)	1	(69)
At period-end	**3,321**	**5,491**	**2,425**	**7,916**

[1] Including borrowing costs of €88 million capitalised in accordance with **IAS 23 (Revised) - "Borrowing Costs"** (see Note 12.2.A).

[2] including 1,810 million in goodwill for the Opel acquisition.

Of which Opel Vauxhall Automotive segment		40	1,795	1,835

31 December 2016 (in million euros)	Goodwill	Development expenditure	Brands, software and other intangible assets	Intangible assets
At beginning of period	**1,382**	**4,352**	**417**	**4,769**
Purchases/additions [1]	-	1,365	102	1,467
Amortisation for the year	-	(825)	(100)	(925)
Impairment losses	-	(47)	2	(45)
Disposals	-	(19)	(2)	(21)
Change in scope of consolidation and other	127	13	176	189
Translation adjustment	5	21	(1)	20
At period-end	**1,514**	**4,860**	**594**	**5,454**

[1] Including borrowing costs of €92 million capitalised in accordance with **IAS 23 (Revised) - "Borrowing Costs"** (see Note 12.2.A).

Source: Peugeot, Annual Report 2017

8.5 Implications for financial analysis

This is a relatively simple area in terms of accounting complexities. However, there are still important issues from an analytical perspective.

Firstly, accounting for intangibles does not typically reflect the underlying economics of these key assets. This is especially the case for internally developed intangibles which have almost universally been written off. These are real assets resulting from discretionary investments. Management must be held accountable for decisions relating to these. If we want to establish the real size of a balance sheet then we will need to consider the capitalisation and and amortisation of intangible assets. This will directly affect our interpretation of profitability and returns on capital.

Secondly, intangibles offer room for manipulation. This is normally through the choice of a useful life. As this decision is highly subjective users need to be aware that profitability can vary substantially depending upon the life chosen. There are therefore two choices available to users: ignore the amortisation by using a profit number such as EBITA or normalise the amortisation charge across the sector under analysis. The decision taken will be a function of the objective of the analysis.

8.6 Building valuation models: What to do

We have seen in the earlier chapters of this book how valuation is ultimately dependent on expected returns on incremental capital. Chapter three dealt with the fact that straight line depreciation did not reflect impairment of value, and looked at alternative approaches. These would apply equally to the point relating to the manipulation of amortisation periods referred to above. But intangible assets represent a far more difficult problem for company valuation when they do not appear on the balance sheet at all, and that is the case for many companies, for the accounting reasons already explained.

Really, this leaves the modeller with two choices. Pursue a strategy of recapitalisation or instead employ a shortcut methodology. Unsurprisingly, the short cut approach, is much more common.

Let's consider a recapitalisation approach. This is achievable when the company gives the necessary information to identify what its intangible investments actually are. For example, all of the research and development programme of a pharmaceuticals company is associated with what in economic terms is investment; none of it is likely to be expenditure required to generate this year's sales. And it is separately identified in the financial statements. If we make the assumption that we know what an appropriate amortisation period is there is no difficulty in going back through historical accounts, adding back the research cost, capitalising it and amortising it. Assuming that the appropriate amortisation period is ten years then we need to do this for nine years of history. The result will be an uncertain impact on profit, but a huge increase in capital employed, which should permit the calculation of what the actual, rather than accounting, returns on investment have been. If the historical data is not available, it is possible to approximate these adjustments with an assumed historical growth formula, which we shall discuss in chapter five in the section on modelling fixed assets.

Unfortunately, it is often impossible to separate out the capital from the operating element of costs that create intangible assets. There is also a challenge in separating out the effective expenditure from the ineffective and furthermore inherent difficulties exist with discriminating between spending that is building sales for the future and spending that is generating sales this year. The least bad solution is to capitalise all of it. But sometimes, the relevant information on the expenditure is simply not there at all. The analyst is therefore left to estimate for example, the proportion of the wage bill of a software company that is related to development of new products. This is an almost impossible task.

So we fall back on option two which is acceptance of the inherent flaws in the accounting model that are not easily repaired. Due to this tension in the capitalisation and write off of costs we effectively have to accept that for large parts of the equity market there will be no reversion of returns on capital, based on accounting numbers, into line with the economic cost of capital, however far forward we extrapolate. This is a recognition that the accounting returns will be overstated, and that they should therefore not be assumed to drop into line with economic reality over time.

9. Foreign exchange

9.1 Why is it important?

For most multinational companies the accounting treatment of foreign exchange items is a significant item. Depending on the exact nature of the underlying foreign currency activity, it can have implications for earnings, equity and debt numbers reported in the financial statements. Analysts must be in a position to deal with these important and complex numbers. Some of the major questions that arise are in this area:

- What is the difference between transaction and translation exchange gains and losses?

- When do gains/losses go through income and when through equity directly?

- What are the implications from an analysis and modelling perspective of these reported gains and losses?

9.2 What is current GAAP under IFRS for transactions in a foreign currency?

IAS 21 *The effect of changes in foreign exchange rates* addresses two crucial issues relating to foreign exchange transactions. First, it provides rules for translating individual transactions that are denominated in a foreign currency. Second, it addresses the issues relating to the translation of foreign entities into consolidated financial statements.

9.2.1 Individual transactions

Here we will focus on the aspects of IAS 21 that relate to foreign currency transactions which would include:

1. buying or selling goods and services which are invoiced in a foreign currency,

2. borrowing or lending in a foreign currency, or

3. acquiring/disposing of assets/settlement of liabilities in a foreign currency.

Initial measurement

The fundamental rule is that a foreign currency transaction, such as the sale of goods mentioned above, is initially translated at the spot rate on the date of the transaction. In practice a rate that approximates to that may well be acceptable, such as a weekly or monthly average, assuming rates do not fluctuate significantly.

Example I

Rendle SA purchases a major piece of mechanical equipment from a UK supplier. The functional currency of Rendle SA is the euro and the price of £10,000,000, is quoted, and must be paid in, sterling.

The exchange rate is 0.668.

Applying the fundamental rule would require the following entry:

Increase fixed assets [10,000,000/0.668]	€14,970,060
Increase creditors	€14,970,060

Subsequent valuation

The subsequent measurement of these items is based on the distinction between monetary and non-monetary items. Monetary items are those that involve the right to receive, or an obligation to deliver, units of a foreign currency. The obvious examples of these are payables, receivables and loans. Non-monetary assets lack this right to receive or pay monetary amounts and would include inter alia inventory and property and equipment. IAS 21 quite logically provides that monetary items will be translated using the closing rate (i.e., the rate on the balance sheet date) whereas non-monetary items will not be retranslated.

Suppose at the year end the £/€ exchange rate was 0.778, the entries would be:

Decrease creditors by	€2,116,590
Increase fx gain	€2,116,590
£10,000,000/0.778 = 12,853,470-14,970,060	= €2,116,590

Settlement

To finish the example assume that settlement took place when the £/€ = 0.745.

Decrease cash [10,000,000/0.745]	€13,422,819
Decrease creditors	€12,853,470
Increase fx loss	€569,349

Note that IAS 21 is silent on exactly where these gains and losses are recognised. However, it is reasonable to assume that fx gains and losses that relate to operations would be reported in operating profit whereas those relating to financing, would be reported as finance charges or income. The latter example might arise on the retranslation of a foreign currency loan.

9.2.2 Consolidated financials

If a parent company has a number of independent subsidiaries then their financials are likely to be prepared in the functional currencies of these entities. The functional currency is the key operating currency of that entity. For example, an independent subsidiary of a UK corporation operating in Germany will typically have its costs and revenues in euro, and will prepare its financial statements in euro as well. Therefore a set of rules is required to translate these amounts into the presentation currency, i.e., that used in the consolidated financial statements.

This is not as complex a topic as it might sound. All that is needed is a rate. IAS 21 requires most of the balance sheet to be translated at the closing rate and the income statement at the actual rate. In the latter case an average rate is often used for pragmatic reasons. For the purposes of this chapter it is important to note that the gains and losses on this translation exercise are recognised as a separate component of equity. This means that the gains and losses arising from the consolidation process do not pass through the income statement. The rationale for this is that the exchange gains are not under managerial control, have little or nothing to do with performance and, in any event, have little discernible impact on present and future cash flows.

In many cases the foreign exchange movement on the translation of foreign subsidiaries is the major gain/loss that bypasses the income statement and is recognised directly in equity. Therefore it throws up valuation issues. To ignore it would result in dirty-surplus accounting and so this issue is discussed below.

9.3 US GAAP focus

There are no major differences between the GAAPs in this area.

9.4 Case example

The statement of comprehensive income for Dow Du Pont group plc is reproduced below in exhibit 4.35. The statement begins with net income and then lists the other gains and losses that have been recognised in the financial statements outside of net income. These would typically be recognised directly in equity. The exchange movements are highlighted on the third line and described as 'Cumulative translation adjustments'. Such adjustments must relate to either the retranslation exercise for subsidiaries mentioned above or the hedge of a foreign currency asset, as they have been reported in equity rather than earnings. There would also be foreign exchange movements reported through earnings and these are effectively included in the net income number at the top of this comprehensive income calculation.

Exhibit 4.35: Dow Du Pont statement of comprehensive income

(In millions) For the years ended Dec 31.		2017	2016	2015
Net Income	$	1,592	$ 4,404	$ 7,783
Other comprehensive income (loss), net of tax				
Unrealized losses on investments		(46)	(4)	(94)
Cumulative translation adjustments		446	(644)	(986)
Pension and other postretirement benefit plans		466	(620)	552
Derivative instruments		(16)	113	(122)
Total other comprehensive income (loss)		850	(1,155)	(650)
Comprehensive Income		2,442	3,249	7,133
Comprehensive income attributable to noncontrolling interests, net of tax		174	83	65
Comprehensive Income Attributable to DowDuPont Inc.	$	2,268	$ 3,166	$ 7,068

See Notes to the Consolidated Financial Statements.

Source: Dow Du Pont group, Report & Accounts 2017

9.5 Building valuation models: What to do

9.5.1 Transaction effects

Foreign exchange transaction effects would normally exemplify themselves in terms of a widening or narrowing of margins. If a company manufactures products in its home market, with a domestic cost base (not all imported raw materials) then a weakening of the domestic currency will result in higher revenues if it retains its price to customers abroad in their local currency. The opposite, of course, occurs if the domestic currency strengthens.

Over time, this effect should probably unwind. For most economies, a fall in the exchange rate is likely to be associated with inflation, which will ultimately drive up domestic costs. But the time lags can be quite substantial.

So there should be an impact on forecasts resulting from recent foreign exchange movements if the company is a large exporter or importer.

The picture is complicated if the company operates a policy of transaction hedging, and this may extend for prolonged periods into the future. Such long term hedges may well not achieve hedge designation for the relevant derivatives positions, which complicates things further. The impact on valuation is usually less acute than it is on specific annual forecasts of profit. Companies cannot hedge their sales forward forever, and when the protection afforded by the hedges runs out, the full impact of the currency will be felt. Since even two or three years' worth of profits and cash flows have only a small impact on value, the main worry for the modeller is likely to be the accuracy of individual annual forecasts. Where hedges are not designated as cash flow hedges, this will also mean that large gains or losses will occur on the derivatives long before the transactions that are being hedged occur.

9.5.2 Translation effects

Where currencies are forecast to move against the reporting currency of the group, translation effects will ensue. Projecting the detailed impact on the balance sheet, as explained in the accounting discussion above, is very difficult from outside the company, because it is generally not possible to get enough information on the assets and liabilities concerned to re-translate the balance sheet at different rates. More common might be an approximate apportionment taken through the entire balance sheet with the adjustment to equity taken to other consolidated income. Companies generally borrow in the currency of the relevant subsidiary, so it is often, though not always appropriate to assume that all of the balance sheet items can be apportioned more or less proportionately. It is clearly important to check this.

Also important is that, even though it may be non-recurring, a one-off fall in the exchange rate for an overseas subsidiary does represent a real fall in the value of the business to its shareholders. The future stream of cash flows and profits in the parent company has been impaired. In discounted cash flow terms, the stream of cash that we are discounting is reduced. In economic profit terms, we are now making the same return on a smaller balance sheet, with exactly the same negative impact on value.

A different problem arises where a group has operations in high inflation countries with endemically weak currencies. In that situation, we are not looking at a one-off event, but at a likely sequence of annual currency losses. In addition to the forecasting issues raised, this also involves a point with respect to discount rates. It is crucial that the profits or cash flows that are being discounted, and the rates that are used to discount them, are consistent with another. In general, the preferred approach is to use the discount rate that equates to the group's reporting currency, and then to make sure that the accounts are translated so that profits, balance sheets and cash flows are as they are projected to be represented in that currency. So a large Brazilian subsidiary may be growing fast, but when translated into euros, the rate of growth will be reduced, and there will be negative translation effects on the balance sheet size, creating translation losses. Cash flow growth will be reduced in line with the impact on profits.

The point has already been made that it is a feature of economic profit models that they rely on clean value accounting: that all of the increase or decrease in shareholders' equity must be attributable to profits, dividends, share distributions and share buy-backs. If this is not the case then there will be a mismatch between what is happening to balance sheets and what is happening to profits, which will throw out the identity between cash flow valuation and economic profit valuation. So when we construct our economic profit models it is important that, if translation gains or losses are being forecast, then they must be included in the NOPAT that is used to derive the calculation of forecast economic profit.

Currency of debt

The point was made above that companies generally borrow in local currency as a natural fair value hedge. If the assets are in dollars and I borrow in dollars then I have to some degree hedged my dollar exposure. But what if I am a Norwegian oil producer, with most of my assets in Norway, but with cash flows that are largely (not entirely, if I am selling gas into continental Europe in euros) denominated in dollars? A company might respond to this by denominating its borrowing almost exclusively in dollars. What happens to it when the dollar falls against the krone?

First, it books a substantial unrealised profit on the retranslation of its dollar debt into fewer krone. Second, its revenues in that year and in all subsequent years fall in krone terms because the dollar stream converts into fewer krone (unless oil and gas prices go up).

If one were modelling the company's assets, it would make sense to model them in dollars and to value them using a dollar discount rate. If one were modelling the company, then it would still probably be easier to model it in dollars, value it in dollars, and then convert the projected accounts into krone.

A currency crisis and the consequent losses can eliminate large portions of a company's equity through the recognition of currency translation losses.

Many years ago a UK company went spectacularly bankrupt during the 1980s. Polly Peck, as the company was called, had large financial assets and debts, with the assets mainly denominated in Turkish lira, and its loans mainly denominated in Swiss francs. The result was large positive financial items in the profit and loss account, and large currency losses recorded as other gains and losses and taken straight to shareholders' funds. It was still looking quite profitable as it became insolvent with the huge diminutions in equity.

There are two messages from this sad tale. Firstly, other consolidated gains and losses may or may not be ongoing, but they do count. Secondly, it should not be assumed that all debt is automatically borrowed in the functional currency of the company.

Chapter Five

Valuing a Company

Pulling things together

It is time to pull together the theory from the early chapters of this book with the accounting issues raised in chapter four. We are going to look at valuation models for a series of companies, selected to illustrate specific issues in forecasting and valuation. In all cases, whether or not there are difficult accounting issues involved, valuing a company comprises two elements: projecting its accounts for a specific period (often five years) and putting a value on what happens after the five years, often treated as a single, so-called 'terminal value'.

So we shall start with a fairly simple company and how to produce a five-year forecast for its financials. We shall then calculate its cost of capital, for the purposes of producing a valuation. Once we know the appropriate discount rate, we need something to discount, so we shall calculate the free cash flow and the economic profit that we think the company will generate over the five years of our forecast. Initially, we shall use a single terminal value calculation to complete both the DCF and the economic profit valuation, and shall incidentally demonstrate that, as the theory in chapter one implied, they do indeed produce the same answer.

Then it will be time to move on to some examples that illustrate some more of the problems that often arise in the real world that tend to be ignored by the textbooks. These break into several groups.

1. There are the companies that are hard to model and value because they exemplify the kinds of accounting issues raised in chapter four. These points will be picked up throughout the examples below.

2. There are companies that are expected to have a dramatic change to their balance sheet structure, perhaps through a share buy-back. This is a pure valuation point.

3. There are highly cyclical companies, in which the key question often boils down to what is a normal year, for the purpose of long-term extrapolation.

4. There are companies with a large component of intangible assets, frequently not capitalised, which raises the question of what their returns on capital actually are.

5. There are fast growing, and also often highly profitable, companies, where the issues are the rate at which both of these elements will fade to maturity.

Obviously, we are not going to be able to illustrate everything. But we hope to be able to show you enough to ensure that, whatever the problem, you have a systematic approach to dealing with it to produce realistic values. Most of the issues are generic to groups of industrial companies, often known as the 'cyclicals', the 'growth stocks' or whatever. There are some sectors that require very different treatment, and we shall defer consideration of these until the next chapter.

1. Building a forecast

One of the simplest sorts of company to forecast and value is a food retailer. Its accounts are usually fairly transparent. It often conducts one business in only one country, which means that different business streams do not have to be modelled individually and then consolidated, though we are going to do so here merely to illustrate the methodology. It operates in one currency. It is not cyclical and if it is a market leader it is unlikely to grow very fast, since its market is already mature. For this reason, we shall start with a food retailer, which we shall analyse under the name, Magna Group.

The entire forecast is printed in exhibit 5.1, and in the commentary that follows we shall refer to the different pages of the model: EBIT, fixed costs, profit and loss, balance sheet, cash flow, fixed assets, working capital, equity, debt and ratios. When referring back to the model it would be useful to bear in mind some conventions that we have followed. Firstly, entered numbers (either from historical accounts or forecast drivers) are boxed. Secondly, all percentages, rather than numbers, are italicised. Thirdly, year 0 refers to the last financial year and years 1–5 are forecasts.

Exhibit 5.1: Magna accounts forecasts

1. Magna operating profit (Euro million)

Year	-1	0	1	2	3	4	5
Net sales							
Wholesale	23,972	25,093	25,846	26,679	27,603	28,631	29,776
Real	8,198	8,205	8,287	8,396	8,542	8,736	8,998
Extra	2,835	2,773	2,801	2,838	2,887	2,953	3,041
Media	9,583	10,563	10,880	11,231	11,620	12,052	12,534
Trader	2,584	2,811	2,895	2,989	3,092	3,207	3,336
Online	3,900	3,819	3,857	3,908	3,976	4,066	4,188
Total sales	**51,072**	**53,264**	**54,566**	**56,040**	**57,719**	**59,645**	**61,873**
Other companies	454	331	334	338	341	344	348
Magna group	**51,526**	**53,595**	**54,900**	**56,378**	**58,060**	**59,990**	**62,221**
Growth in sales							
Wholesale		*4.7%*	*3.0%*	*3.2%*	*3.5%*	*3.7%*	*4.0%*
Real		*0.1%*	*1.0%*	*1.3%*	*1.7%*	*2.3%*	*3.0%*
Extra		*(2.2%)*	*1.0%*	*1.3%*	*1.7%*	*2.3%*	*3.0%*
Media		*10.2%*	*3.0%*	*3.2%*	*3.5%*	*3.7%*	*4.0%*
Trader		*8.8%*	*3.0%*	*3.2%*	*3.5%*	*3.7%*	*4.0%*
Online		*(2.1%)*	*1.0%*	*1.3%*	*1.7%*	*2.3%*	*3.0%*
Total sales		***4.3%***	***2.4%***	***2.7%***	***3.0%***	***3.3%***	***3.7%***
Other companies		*(27.1%)*	*1.0%*	*1.0%*	*1.0%*	*1.0%*	*1.0%*
Magna group		***4.0%***	***2.4%***	***2.7%***	***3.0%***	***3.3%***	***3.7%***
EBIT							
Wholesale	709.1	799.6	904.6	933.8	966.1	1,002.1	1,042.2
Real	147.0	160.5	165.7	185.8	209.2	236.8	269.9
Extra	(47.2)	(75.7)	28.0	33.7	40.8	49.7	60.8
Media	280.2	345.2	380.8	393.1	406.7	421.8	438.7
Trader	(41.6)	(13.8)	29.0	35.5	43.7	53.9	66.7
Online	131.4	94.1	96.4	102.3	108.9	116.6	125.6
Total EBIT	**1,178.9**	**1,309.9**	**1,604.5**	**1,684.2**	**1,775.5**	**1,880.9**	**2,004.0**
Other companies	(13.4)	8.2	8.4	8.4	8.5	8.6	8.7
Magna group	**1,165.5**	**1,318.1**	**1,612.9**	**1,692.7**	**1,784.0**	**1,889.5**	**2,012.7**
EBIT margin							
Wholesale	*3.0%*	*3.2%*	*3.5%*	*3.5%*	*3.5%*	*3.5%*	*3.5%*
Real	*1.8%*	*2.0%*	*2.0%*	*2.2%*	*2.4%*	*2.7%*	*3.0%*
Extra	*(1.7%)*	*(2.7%)*	*1.0%*	*1.2%*	*1.4%*	*1.7%*	*2.0%*
Media	*2.9%*	*3.3%*	*3.5%*	*3.5%*	*3.5%*	*3.5%*	*3.5%*
Trader	*(1.6%)*	*(0.5%)*	*1.0%*	*1.2%*	*1.4%*	*1.7%*	*2.0%*
Online	*3.4%*	*2.5%*	*2.5%*	*2.6%*	*2.7%*	*2.9%*	*3.0%*
Total EBIT	***2.3%***	***2.5%***	***2.9%***	***3.0%***	***3.1%***	***3.2%***	***3.2%***
Other companies	*(3.0%)*	*2.5%*	*2.5%*	*2.5%*	*2.5%*	*2.5%*	*2.5%*
Magna group	***2.3%***	***2.5%***	***2.9%***	***3.0%***	***3.1%***	***3.1%***	***3.2%***
Other operating income	1,532	1,461	1,476	1,490	1,505	1,520	1,536
Annual growth		*(4.6%)*	*1.0%*	*1.0%*	*1.0%*	*1.0%*	*1.0%*

2. Magna fixed costs (Euro million)

Year	-1	0	1	2	3	4	5
Selling expenses	(10,377)	(10,636)	(10,901)	(11,174)	(11,452)	(11,738)	(12,031)
Annual growth		*2.5%*	*2.5%*	*2.5%*	*2.5%*	*2.5%*	*2.5%*
General administrative expenses	(1,013)	(1,031)	(1,049)	(1,068)	(1,087)	(1,106)	(1,126)
Annual growth		*1.8%*	*1.8%*	*1.8%*	*1.8%*	*1.8%*	*1.8%*
Other operating expenses	(115)	(112)	(109)	(106)	(103)	(101)	(98)
Annual growth		*(2.6%)*	*(2.6%)*	*(2.6%)*	*(2.6%)*	*(2.6%)*	*(2.6%)*

3. Magna profit and loss account (Euro million)

Year	-1	0	1	2	3	4	5
Net sales	51,526	53,595	54,900	56,378	58,060	59,990	62,221
Cost of sales	(40,126)	(41,687)	(42,431)	(43,556)	(44,866)	(46,403)	(48,217)
Gross profit	11,400	11,908	12,469	12,822	13,194	13,586	14,004
Gross profit margin	22.1%	22.2%	22.7%	22.7%	22.7%	22.6%	22.5%
Other operating income	1,532	1,461	1,476	1,490	1,505	1,520	1,536
Selling expenses	(10,377)	(10,636)	(10,901)	(11,174)	(11,452)	(11,738)	(12,031)
General administration expenses	(1,013)	(1,031)	(1,049)	(1,068)	(1,087)	(1,106)	(1,126)
Other operating expenses	(115)	(112)	(109)	(106)	(103)	(101)	(98)
EBITA	1,427	1,590	1,885	1,965	2,056	2,161	2,285
Amortisation of intangible assets	(261)	(272)	(272)	(272)	(272)	(272)	(272)
EBIT	1,166	1,318	1,613	1,693	1,784	1,889	2,013
Investment income	38	(60)	(11)	(11)	(11)	(11)	(11)
Net interest	(378)	(425)	(477)	(434)	(395)	(356)	(315)
Other financial items	4	(16)	(6)	(6)	(6)	(6)	(6)
Net financial items	(336)	(501)	(494)	(451)	(412)	(373)	(332)
Earnings before tax	830	817	1,119	1,241	1,372	1,517	1,681
Income tax	(328)	(246)	(392)	(435)	(480)	(531)	(588)
Tax/Earnings before tax	39.5%	30.1%	35.0%	35.0%	35.0%	35.0%	35.0%
Group net income	502	571	728	807	892	986	1,092
Non-controlling interests	(59)	(75)	(96)	(106)	(117)	(129)	(143)
NCI/group net income	11.8%	13.1%	13.1%	13.1%	13.1%	13.1%	13.1%
Attributable net income	443	496	632	701	775	856	949
Dividend distribution	(334)	(334)	(425)	(471)	(521)	(576)	(638)
Retained earnings	109	162	207	230	254	280	311
Common stock							
Weighted average shares (m)	324.1	324.1	324.1	324.1	324.1	324.1	324.1
Year end shares (m)	324.1	324.1	324.1	324.1	324.1	324.1	324.1
Preferred stock							
Weighted average shares (m)	2.7	2.7	2.7	2.7	2.7	2.7	2.7
Year end shares (m)	2.7	2.7	2.7	2.7	2.7	2.7	2.7
Shares outstanding							
Weighted average shares (m)	326.8	326.8	326.8	326.8	326.8	326.8	326.8
Year end shares (m)	326.8	326.8	326.8	326.8	326.8	326.8	326.8
Earnings per share (Euro)	1.36	1.52	1.93	2.15	2.37	2.62	2.90
Common stock dividend (Euro)	1.02	1.02	1.30	1.44	1.59	1.76	1.95
Preferred stock dividend (Euro)	1.12	1.12	1.43	1.59	1.75	1.94	2.15
Payout ratio (common stock)	75.2%	67.2%	67.2%	67.2%	67.2%	67.2%	67.2%
Preferred dividend/common dividend	110.0%	110.0%	110.0%	110.0%	110.0%	110.0%	110.0%

4. Magna balance sheet (Euro million)

Year	-1	0	1	2	3	4	5
Fixed assets							
Intangible assets	4,070	3,987	3,715	3,443	3,171	2,899	2,627
Goodwill	188	326	326	326	326	326	326
Tangible assets	7,201	10,490	10,741	11,062	11,447	11,891	12,389
Financial assets	229	238	238	238	238	238	238
Total fixed assets	**11,688**	**15,041**	**15,020**	**15,069**	**15,182**	**15,354**	**15,580**
Current assets							
Inventories	5,506	5,941	6,047	6,207	6,394	6,613	6,872
Trade receivables	369	339	347	357	367	379	394
Other receivables and other assets	2,857	2,061	2,111	2,168	2,233	2,307	2,393
Cash and cash equivalents	1,323	1,593	2,071	2,503	2,932	3,372	3,840
Total current assets	**10,055**	**9,934**	**10,576**	**11,235**	**11,926**	**12,672**	**13,498**
Deferred tax assets	1,084	1,456	1,456	1,456	1,456	1,456	1,456
Prepaid expenses and deferred charges	96	149	149	149	149	149	149
Total assets	**22,923**	**26,580**	**27,201**	**27,909**	**28,713**	**29,630**	**30,683**
Equity							
Capital stock	835	835	835	835	835	835	835
Additional paid-in capital	2,558	2,551	2,551	2,551	2,551	2,551	2,551
Reserves retained from earnings	305	279	441	648	878	1,132	1,412
Group net profit	443	496	632	701	775	856	949
Treasury stock	0	0	0	0	0	0	0
Total equity	**4,141**	**4,161**	**4,459**	**4,735**	**5,039**	**5,374**	**5,747**
Non-controlling interests	105	188	259	333	415	505	605
Provisions							
Pensions and similar commitments	960	1,012	1,132	1,259	1,396	1,542	1,699
Other provisions	725	758	758	758	758	758	758
Total provisions	**1,685**	**1,770**	**1,890**	**2,017**	**2,154**	**2,300**	**2,457**
Other liabilities							
Financial debts	5,587	7,802	7,802	7,802	7,802	7,802	7,802
Trade payables	9,119	9,907	10,084	10,351	10,663	11,028	11,459
Other liabilities	1,965	2,097	2,148	2,206	2,272	2,347	2,435
Total other liabilities	**16,671**	**19,806**	**20,034**	**20,359**	**20,736**	**21,177**	**21,695**
Deferred tax liabilities	196	526	431	336	240	145	50
Deferred income	125	129	129	129	129	129	129
Total equity and liabilities	**22,923**	**26,580**	**27,201**	**27,909**	**28,713**	**29,630**	**30,683**
Check	0.000	0.000	0.000	0.000	0.000	0.000	0.000
Net debt	4,264	6,209	5,731	5,299	4,870	4,430	3,962
Operating capital (including goodwill)	9,107	11,140	11,055	11,006	11,003	11,040	11,107
Operating capital (excluding goodwill)	8,919	10,814	10,729	10,680	10,677	10,714	10,781

5. Magna cash flow (Euro million)

Year	0	1	2	3	4	5
EBIT		1,613	1,693	1,784	1,889	2,013
Depreciation and amortisation		1,521	1,551	1,587	1,628	1,674
Changes in pension provisions		60	61	63	64	66
Changes in other provisions		0	0	0	0	0
Changes in net working capital		63	99	115	135	160
Income taxes charged		(392)	(435)	(480)	(531)	(588)
Changes in deferred tax assets and liabilities		(95)	(95)	(95)	(95)	(95)
Changes in prepayments and deferred income		0	0	0	0	0
Cash flow from operating activities		**2,770**	**2,874**	**2,973**	**3,091**	**3,229**
Capital expenditure		(1,500)	(1,600)	(1,700)	(1,800)	(1,900)
Cash flow from investing activities		**(1,500)**	**(1,600)**	**(1,700)**	**(1,800)**	**(1,900)**
Dividends to Magna shareholders		(334)	(425)	(471)	(521)	(576)
Dividends to NCI shareholders		(25)	(32)	(35)	(39)	(43)
Equity issued		0	0	0	0	0
Equity bought back		0	0	0	0	0
Change in debt		0	0	0	0	0
Net interest paid		(417)	(368)	(321)	(274)	(225)
Investment income		(11)	(11)	(11)	(11)	(11)
Other financial items		(6)	(6)	(6)	(6)	(6)
Cash flow from financing activities		**(792)**	**(841)**	**(845)**	**(851)**	**(861)**
Opening cash	1323	1,593	2,071	2,503	2,932	3,372
Change in cash	270	478	433	429	440	468
Closing cash	**1593**	**2,071**	**2,503**	**2,932**	**3,372**	**3,840**
Average cash	1,458	1,832	2,287	2,718	3,152	3,606
Interest received	158	199	248	295	342	391
Interest rate on cash	*10.8%*	*10.8%*	*10.8%*	*10.8%*	*10.8%*	*10.8%*

6. Magna fixed assets (Euro million)

Year	0	1	2	3	4	5
Tangible fixed assets						
Opening gross value	**12,597**	**16,408**	**16,803**	**17,272**	**17,809**	**18,410**
Additions	1,421	1,500	1,600	1,700	1,800	1,900
Disposals and transfers	(499)	(1,105)	(1,131)	(1,163)	(1,199)	(1,239)
Other items	2,889	0	0	0	0	0
Closing gross value	**16,408**	**16,803**	**17,272**	**17,809**	**18,410**	**19,071**
Historical long term growth	2.0%					
Opening net value	**7,201**	**10,490**	**10,741**	**11,062**	**11,447**	**11,891**
Additions	1,421	1,500	1,600	1,700	1,800	1,900
Depreciation	(959)	(1,249)	(1,279)	(1,315)	(1,356)	(1,402)
Other items	2,827	0	0	0	0	0
Closing net value	**10,490**	**10,741**	**11,062**	**11,447**	**11,891**	**12,389**
Opening gross assets/depreciation	13.1					
Closing cumulative depreciation	5,918	6,063	6,211	6,363	6,520	6,682
Opening fixed asset turn	7.4	5.2	5.2	5.2	5.2	5.2

7. Magna working capital (Euro million)

Year	0	1	2	3	4	5
Inventory days	52	52	52	52	52	52
Trade receivables days	2	2	2	2	2	2
Other receivables (% sales)	*3.8%*	*3.8%*	*3.8%*	*3.8%*	*3.8%*	*3.8%*
Trade payables days	87	87	87	87	87	87
Other liabilities (% sales)	*3.9%*	*3.9%*	*3.9%*	*3.9%*	*3.9%*	*3.9%*
Total non-cash working capital	(3,663)	(3,726)	(3,825)	(3,940)	(4,076)	(4,235)
Opening working capital turn	(23)	(15)	(15)	(15)	(15)	(15)

8. Magna equity (Euro million)

Year	0	1	2	3	4	5
Share price (Euro)	36.76					
Par value (Euro)	2.56					
Equity issued		0	0	0	0	0
Equity bought back		0	0	0	0	0
Shares issued		0	0	0	0	0
Shares bought back		0	0	0	0	0

9. Magna debt (Euro million)

Year	0	1	2	3	4	5
Opening financial debt	5587	7,802	7,802	7,802	7,802	7,802
Change in finance debt	2215	0	0	0	0	0
Closing finance debt	**7802**	**7,802**	**7,802**	**7,802**	**7,802**	**7,802**
Average finance debt	6,695	7,802	7,802	7,802	7,802	7,802
Interest paid	**(528)**	**(615)**	**(615)**	**(615)**	**(615)**	**(615)**
Interest rate on debt	7.9%	7.9%	7.9%	7.9%	7.9%	7.9%
Opening pension provision	960	1,012	1,132	1,259	1,396	1,542
Interest on pension provision	55	60	67	74	82	90
Changes in pension provisions	(3)	60	61	63	64	66
Closing pension provision	**1012**	**1,132**	**1,259**	**1,396**	**1,542**	**1,699**
Provision/fixed costs	*0.0%*	*0.5%*	*0.5%*	*0.5%*	*0.5%*	*0.5%*
Average pension provision	986	1,072	1,195	1,328	1,469	1,620
Interest on pension provision	(55)	(60)	(67)	(74)	(82)	(90)
Interest rate on pension	5.6%	5.6%	5.6%	5.6%	5.6%	5.6%

10. Magna ratios (Euro million)						
Year	0	1	2	3	4	5
Revenue growth	4.0%	2.4%	2.7%	3.0%	3.3%	3.7%
Dupont including goodwill						
Opening operating capital asset turn	5.9	4.9	5.1	5.3	5.5	5.6
Net operating margin	1.6%	1.7%	1.8%	1.8%	1.9%	1.9%
Return on opening operating capital	9.2%	8.6%	9.1%	9.7%	10.3%	11.0%
Opening net debt/operating capital	46.8%	55.7%	51.8%	48.1%	44.3%	40.1%
Dupont excluding goodwill						
Opening operating capital asset turn	6.0	5.1	5.3	5.4	5.6	5.8
Net operating margin	2.1%	2.2%	2.3%	2.3%	2.3%	2.4%
Return on opening operating capital	12.5%	11.3%	11.9%	12.5%	13.2%	13.9%
Opening net debt/operating capital	47.8%	57.4%	53.4%	49.6%	45.6%	41.3%

When forecasting, it may be desirable to rearrange the profit and loss account with the aim of achieving two objectives: separating out cash costs from non-cash costs, and where possible splitting cash costs between variable costs and fixed costs. Variable costs are those that move in line with units sold. Fixed costs do not. Often, the largest fixed cost is represented by employment, and it is often desirable to forecast this as a separate item. Non-cash costs comprise depreciation and amortisation. To make the Magna model as intelligible to readers as possible, we have almost completely followed the layout of the company's financial accounts, but if modelling a group of companies, there is much to be said for imposing your own standardised formats.

A problem arises immediately for companies which do not undertake a single business in a single country. In this case information is often provided broken down either by business or by location (but never the full matrix), for sales and for EBIT. This leaves the modeller with a choice. Either the benefit of the operating split is retained, and the detail of the cost structure is lost, or the other way round. Unfortunately, this dilemma arises more often than not, and it arises in the case of Magna. We have opted here to break out the operating forecasts by business line, and to project revenue growth and margin for each business.

We have also projected fixed costs on page two of the model, escalating individual line items independently of volumes sole. But this means that when we get to the profit and loss account, the calculation runs upwards from EBIT, with the fixed costs added back to derive gross profit, and the cost of goods sold derived as the difference between revenues and gross profits. This is clearly the opposite of what one would like to do. It is also inevitable, given the way that the information is presented in their accounts, for many companies. The only solution is to watch movements in the gross margin very carefully, since it is a result that reflects assumptions made about revenue growth rates, EBIT margins and growth in fixed costs.

A second question is treatment of unusual items. Obviously, it is the underlying trends in revenues and costs that should inform our forecasts. While it is not always desirable to follow the company's guidance on what constitutes an unusual item (for some companies, if it is positive it is in the normal line of business and if it is negative then it is obviously an aberration to be ignored!), some decisions regarding what to leave in and what to remove are required. And sometimes it is not left clear by the accounts what the impact of unusual items has been on the taxation charge. As a broad rule of thumb, restructuring costs reduce tax charges because when actually incurred they will be allowable against taxable profit (but not in the year in which the provision is made, note). Impairments of goodwill are generally irrelevant to the tax charge since goodwill is not usually an allowable expense, but write-ups and write-downs of other fixed assets generally increase or decrease deferred tax liabilities. And gains and losses on disposals are hard to model as the cost allowable against tax and the book value are not necessarily the same nor is the rate of capital gains tax necessarily the same as the rate of corporation tax. But one must do one's best to guess. Where you do strip out items to get at an estimate of underlying net income, then it is important to show both the stated and the adjusted figures, especially in the forecasts, as will become clear when we move on to discussing the valuation.

Just as the profit and loss account needed to be rearranged, so, often, does the balance sheet. In general one wants to keep the number of line items to the list of elements that it makes sense to forecast independently. Thus, on the asset side of the balance sheet we shall want to separate the different elements of fixed assets, and to separate cash and cash equivalent, from trade receivables and from other current assets. But it makes little sense in most cases to penetrate further than that, and published balance sheets will separate out cash from short-term investments (a distinction that we can generally safely ignore) but may not separate out trade receivables and trade payables from other current assets and other current liabilities, which we shall definitely want to do. Trade receivables and trade payables are an important part of the capital employed in the business whereas, for example, other current liabilities are often dominated by tax liabilities that have accrued to be paid within the next twelve months.

Notice that under IFRS accounting, which Magna adopts, shareholders' equity includes the earnings generated during the year but does not exclude the dividend announced with respect to the year. This is deducted from equity when it is paid, and the following year's earnings are added. So cash dividends and accrued dividends are aligned and there is no current liability relating to dividends announced but not yet paid.

We would also often suggest lumping provisions (other long-term liabilities) together in the printed balance sheet, though their component parts may well need to be modelled separately if they comprise, for example, deferred taxation, provisions for pension obligations and provisions to cover restructuring costs. But, as with the profit and loss account, we have kept the format of the Magna model as close to that of the company's accounts as possible.

1.1 Forecasting the business drivers

Whereas most of the components of a model of an industrial company are similar to one another, as we shall see shortly, the main differences relate to the drivers to revenue and cash operating costs. These are clearly industry specific. We are not going to be able to cover all eventualities, though, as already indicated, we shall try to give as many generic examples as possible. So, how are we going to forecast our food retailer?

One approach would be to start from the macro: estimate annual expenditure in food retailers in general, and then allocate an assumed market share to our company. The other is to start from the bottom up. How many square feet of space do we have, and what value of goods do we sell per square metre? The latter also relates to the specific retailing concept of 'like for like' sales: the value sold off the same space as the previous year, as opposed to increases (or decreases) due to changes in the size or number of stores. Clearly, the two should relate to one another.

As we are not trying to turn you into a food retail specialist, in our model we shall take the second approach and ignore the first, but if you are a food retail specialist it would be a good idea to add up all your revenue projections and see if they come to a sensible figure. In addition, we have stopped at the level of revenue growth forecasts by division, without relating them back to per square metre numbers, though this would not be difficult. What we shall be careful to do is to ensure that our forecasts of capital expenditure are consistent with our forecasts of revenue, a point to be returned to when modelling fixed assets.

1.2 Fixed assets, capital expenditure and depreciation

There are three sorts of company, when it comes to capital expenditure. The first is non-cyclical and has a large number of assets. Magna clearly falls within this category, and we shall defer detailed discussion of the others for now, but will mention them here for completeness.

Some companies have very small numbers of large assets that need to be modelled specifically. Imagine a gas pipeline. It costs a large amount to build. It is generally built with a capacity that considerably exceeds its initial likely throughput. For some years, volumes might rise without any required capital investment. Then it reaches its capacity, so some incremental expenditure is required to add compression facilities to the pipe. Eventually, no further additions are possible. We need another pipe. Toll roads, bridges, airports, many utilities and others of the same kind come in this category.

Then there are the cyclicals. At the low point in the cycle a cement manufacturer is probably not operating plant at full capacity. As the upturn occurs, not only do prices recover but volumes may increase considerably without any attendant need for additional capacity. Clearly, as the economy continues to grow and demand increases, capacity will be stretched to the point at which additions are required.

A food retailer is not like either of these examples, nor would be a food manufacturer, or a pharmaceuticals company, or many others. In all of these cases it makes little sense to ask what the additional capital expenditure is that would be required to add 4% to sales next year, except in the most general of senses. All other things being equal, it is probably reasonable to assume that the relationship between sales and fixed assets is a fairly constant one. In other words, if we can project depreciation then we can project the necessary capital expenditure to ensure that assets grow in line with expected sales. The ratio of sales to fixed assets is generally known as the 'fixed asset turn', and is a crucial, and often under-analysed, component of company forecasts. One of the more frequently encountered errors in company valuations results from models having perfectly reasonable projections of profit, but far too low a level of net investment (capital expenditure and increase in working capital minus depreciation) to fund the projected expansion in profit. Since free cash flow is the difference between two items, profit and net investment, the result is systematic overvaluation.

It is of course possible to make the capital expenditure dependent on an assumed fixed asset life, but that is probably a little too rigid. Companies often provide guidance regarding planned capital expenditures, and in any case investment flows are not even, but tend to move in waves with cycles in demand. We would therefore recommend inserting forecasts as independent variables, but checking the resulting capital turns for plausibility.

Turning to depreciation, this is difficult to forecast because in reality assets are depreciated individually, and we do not have enough information to do this. In addition, although models often relate depreciation to net fixed assets, this is in fact incorrect. As exhibit 3.4 showed, if an asset is depreciated using the straight line method over a period of five years, then depreciation will be a fifth of its opening book value in the first year, but equivalent to 100% of it in the last year. It is true that a company with a portfolio of assets may approximate to the mid-point, at which depreciation will equal 33% of opening net book value. But most companies are subject to waves of capital expenditure followed by periods in which it is lower. In this instance, the average remaining life of the company's assets will fluctuate.

Let us try an alternative approach. Depreciation may not be a fixed proportion of net assets, but it should be a fixed proportion of the gross cost of fixed assets, if it is calculated on a straight line basis. So dividing a company's opening gross fixed assets by its depreciation charge will give us the appropriate asset life by which to divide all future opening gross fixed assets to calculate annual depreciation, if we assume that it carries on investing in the same sort of assets.

How do we forecast gross assets? The additions are easy. They are annual capital expenditure figures. And the deductions? Assets get retired at the end of their life, so we need to project asset retirements. Obviously, one way to do this would be to go back through the relevant number of annual reports and accounts so if the asset life is 10 years, then we retire the capital expenditure that grew the gross fixed assets 10 years ago. This could get laborious, and assets may have been bought and sold in the meantime.

A simpler approach is formulaic. If we assume that we know roughly how fast the company has, on average, been growing, then we can work out what the capital expenditure should have been 10 years ago that, if grown each year at a constant rate, would have left us with the gross fixed assets that we have in the balance sheet now. The opening balance sheet value of our gross fixed assets must be the following, if capital expenditure has grown at a constant rate each year:

$$F = R*[1+(1+g)+(1+g)^2+...(1+g)^{n-1}]$$

where F=opening gross fixed assets, R=this year's retirements, and n=asset life.

To see why, return to exhibit 3.4 The asset that was bought at the end of year 0 is fully depreciated (and therefore retired) at the end of year 5. So what is in the balance sheet at the beginning of year 5 is the partially depreciated assets bought during years 0-4. At the end of year 5, the assets bought during year 0 are retired. Retirement in year 5 will thus be capital expenditure in year 0. Making retirements the subject of the equation gives:

$$R = F/[1+(1+g)+(1+g)^2+...(1+g)^{n-1}]$$

This is another geometric expansion, rather like the perpetuity that gave us the Gordon Growth model in chapter one. We shall as usual relegate the proof to the mathematical appendix, but the general solution is as follows:

$$R = F^*g/[1-(1+g)^n]$$

We can forecast next year's retirements by taking closing gross fixed assets from the last report and accounts, calculating the asset life in years, and then applying a constant growth factor to retrospectively approximate the stream of capital expenditure that will be retired over forecast years. This version of the formula will give us a negative figure for R, the amount to deduct from fixed assets.

Clearly, if the asset life is low then it may be practicable to look the numbers up. And if our forecast period is longer than the asset life then we can start to use the capital expenditure numbers that we have in our model. So if the asset life is 5 years and we have a 10-year forecast, then retirements in year 6 should equal capital expenditure in year 1. In our example, the asset life is a lot more than 5 years, so we shall be entirely dependent on the formula for our forecasts of retirements.

To explain the detail of page six (titled Magna fixed assets) of the Magna model, additions to gross assets are projected capital expenditure, taken to the cash flow. In the absence of disposals, disposals and transfers represent the retirements forecast by formula as discussed above. Depreciation is derived by dividing opening gross assets by the gross asset life, and is also taken to the cash flow. Closing net assets are taken to the forecast balance sheets. Moving from one forecast year to the next, it is the net between capital expenditure and depreciation that represents a cash outflow and an increase in net fixed assets.

We have not discussed acquisition or disposal of fixed assets, but it is not uncommon to know that a company has a policy of trading assets (perhaps the tail of its portfolio), and to need to model this. In the case of disposals, it will be necessary to estimate the gross asset value as well as knowing the net book value. Companies will often announce both the consideration and the profit associated with a sale, but will not generally state the gross value of the assets sold. Unless advised otherwise, there is little choice but to assume that the asset is of the same age as the average of the group's assets, so the ratio of gross to net is just assumed to be the average for the group.

1.3 Amortisation of intangible assets

The accounting treatment of goodwill is discussed in chapter four. Acquisition of new goodwill will have to await chapter seven, and discussion of mergers and acquisitions. For the time being, we are merely concerned with building intangible assets into our accounting forecasts of a going concern. It follows that there can be no acquisition of new goodwill in the model. Goodwill is not amortised under IFRS but may be written down if its value is impaired.

Other intangible assets may be capitalised for one of two reasons. They may be created as part of the writing up and down to fair value of assets assumed as part of an acquisition. In this case, they may be amortised over their useful lives, or may be deemed to not to have a determinable life and be carried unamortised. Alternatively, the company may capitalise some of its expenditure on the creation of patents or brands, in which case they will both be amortised and added to by future investments, and will be systematically retired.

Intangible assets of the second kind should be modelled in exactly the same fashion as tangible assets, with amortisation run off gross fixed assets and an asset life. And it is reasonable to assume retirements in the same way as we did for tangible fixed assets. For simplicity, we have assumed that Magna is amortising intangibles at a constant rate each year (until they are fully written down, which does not happen in our forecast).

1.4 Changes in working capital

It is most convenient to separate operational from financial items when modelling companies. We shall therefore treat working capital as comprising inventory, trade debtors (trade receivables) and other non-cash current assets, minus trade creditors (trade payables) and other non-cash current liabilities. Cash and short-term debt will be modelled separately as part of financing (though in Magna's case the balance sheet shows total debt and we have left this unallocated). This should not be taken to imply, however, that all cash should automatically be netted off against debt when valuing the equity in a company. That would be fine if it were really practical to run a company with no cash whatsoever in its balance sheet, clearly an impossibility. So, when we model the company's finances, we shall take minimum operating cash requirements into account. But we shall treat them as part of the cash and debt calculation, and keep them separate from non-cash items.

Working capital used to be referred to by classical economists as 'circulating capital', and this is a useful way to conceptualise it. At any one time our company will have a given stock of goods on its shelves. It will owe its suppliers for that which has been delivered to it during the credit period under which it buys, and it will be owed small amounts, mainly relating to the fact that some customers use credit cards, with the result that there is a small interval between the purchase and receipt of payment.

All of this is best handled in terms of days of purchases or sales. Inventory clearly relates to purchases (cost of goods sold). If inventory in the balance sheet represents one twelfth of annual COGS, then it is reasonable to assume that a normal stock turn is one month. Similarly, if the company makes its purchases under credit terms averaging between 30 days and 60 days, then trade creditors might represent some 45 days' worth of annual COGS. In the case of this company, it would be surprising if trade receivables represented more than a very small number of days of sales (because people usually pay cash in supermarkets), but it is to sales that they relate, not to COGS.

For a non-cyclical business, it is reasonable to assume that the resulting figures are likely to remain stable in forecast years. This is clearly not the case for cyclical companies (imagine what happens to the stock turn of an auto manufacturer in a recession) but we can probably hold the numbers of days flat in the case of a food retailer, unless there was a clear industry trend towards tighter stock management, or different credit periods for purchases.

When we turn to the other components of non-cash working capital, life becomes more difficult. Other current assets may largely comprise prepayments. Other current liabilities, whatever else it contains, is likely to have as one of its larger items the tax that has accrued for the year but which had not, as at the year end, been paid.

It makes little sense to regard either other current assets or other current liabilities in terms of days of anything. Accrued tax may in some cases be modellable but the current liability is generally less important to model than possible long-term assets or liabilities created as a result of deferred tax. We discussed the accounting treatment of deferred taxation, and ways in which it could possibly be modelled, in chapter four.

To keep the model comprehensible, we have simply escalated other current assets and liabilities in line with sales, but it is important to be aware that if this is unacceptably simplistic additional line items can be split out and forecast separately. We are forecasting the three main components (inventory, trade receivables and trade payables) and lumping other items together. Although we forecast the line items with respect to sales or costs depending on whether they relate to one or the other, it is useful to take the resulting net non-cash working capital figure and relate it to sales. In the same way that we did for fixed assets, we are answering the question of how much capital we need to tie up to produce one unit of sales. It is a 'working capital turn' which can be related to the 'fixed asset turn' to derive an overall 'capital turn'. In Magna's case the negative figure implies that its trade creditor item so exceeds inventory and debtor items that the overall balance is a negative non-cash working capital.

To elaborate the mechanics of page seven of the model (titled Magna working capital), the historical numbers for days of sales of receivables, payables, etc are calculated from the balance sheet items, as is the working capital and the opening working capital turn. The forecast drivers are shown, and the results of those drivers are taken to the forecast balance sheet items. These are then aggregated to show total non-cash working capital in the tab, and the movements in the total non-cash working capital are then taken to the cash flow statement. So the balance sheet forecasts are driving the forecast cash flows.

1.5 Unleveraged profits

With revenues, margins, fixed assets and working capital all modelled, we have essentially finished with the operating assets of the company. What still needs to be dealt with, apart from minorities and associates, is how the assets are financed: the balance between equity, debt and provisions. There is nothing to prevent us from completing our profit and loss account, other than the fact that we shall not know, until we have completed the model, what the movements in cash and debt are going to be, and therefore what to assume for interest received and charged. At this point, we complete the profit and loss account, leaving the interest items blank. (Obviously, exhibit 5.1 is complete, and has the interest line items in, but for reasons that will become apparent later in the text, it is necessary to leave hooking up the interest lines in the profit and loss account until the model is in all other respects built.)

As will become clear when we turn to valuation, we should always strike EBIT to exclude profits from joint ventures and associates, whether or not the company includes them in operating profit. What we want is the operating profit that is generated by the operating assets of the business that we are trying to model and value. Profits from associates are returns on financial assets, and where they are material the associates need to be forecast and valued separately.

Although we are not populating the rows represented by interest charges, it is important to separate out what the company will usually show as one net line into three components: interest received, interest paid and other financial items. The point is that we shall forecast the first two as a function of average cash and average debt balances for the year. The third may or may not be predictable. Dividends received are. Gains and losses incurred on swaps contracts are not. Magna shows a single item for net interest in its profit and loss account, and we have again followed its format, though it would be usual in models to show the two items separately, and they are forecast separately in our model as we shall see.

As we have no interest calculations in the model yet our pre-tax profits will be simply EBIT plus profits from associates, and are therefore higher than they will be when the model is complete. In fact, what we are projecting is unleveraged profits, a concept to which we shall return when we move on to valuation issues.

Taxation is a complex subject which we have already met in chapter four. It is best to keep separate two questions: What is the tax charge in the profit and loss account going to be? And what is the tax paid going to be? At this point we are merely concerned with the tax charged to the profit and loss account.

In principle, one would expect a tax charge to be the pre-tax profit times a statutory tax rate. In practice, there are a variety of reasons why it might not be: goodwill impairment, profits from associates, international operations, tax losses brought forward, consolidation effects, gains or losses on disposals, and so on. Goodwill impairment is not generally recoverable against tax. So when calculating taxable profit, it should simply be added back to pre-tax profit. The impact of amortisation of assets capitalized on acquisition is more complicated. As discussed in chapter four, when assets are written up on consolidation a deferred tax liability is created. This is unwound through their lives, which may result in tax charges that are lower than cash tax payments. As discussed in detail below, we make this assumption for Magna. Profits from associates are generally consolidated net of taxation, and if they are then clearly they will have no impact on the group tax charge. So they should be subtracted from pre-tax profit to arrive at taxable profit.

When it comes to the other items, a more subjective approach is often required. For example, if the model works on business, rather than geographical, lines, then a geographical shift in profits will have to be dealt with by an intuitive adjustment to the effective rate of taxation. We have discussed tax losses in chapter four, but would merely make the point here that if a company has accounted for the loss by creating a deferred tax credit then the tax loss will not have any impact on the tax charge in future years, because in terms of the profit and loss account, the credit was recorded in the year in which the loss was incurred. But if the loss was merely noted in the accounts but no deferred tax asset was created then the taxable profit will be reduced to the extent of the tax loss carried forward.

Consolidation effects occur if a group has subsidiaries, some of which are loss-making and do not create deferred tax assets. In this case the marginal rate of tax in the consolidated profit and loss account will look very high, as losses reduce pre-tax profits but not the tax charge. Clearly this would reverse if the loss-making subsidiary returns to profit and incurs a reduced tax charge.

Finally, it is very hard to model the impact of disposals on tax. Capital gains are not necessarily taxed at the statutory rate of corporation tax, and the book value of the asset may be very different from the cost that is allowed when selling it for the purpose of calculating taxable gains. The default assumption is that book profit equals taxable profit, and that the corporation tax rate equals the tax rate on the disposal profit, but this is all highly unlikely to be correct. In the absence of better information, however, it is what has to be assumed.

Below the tax line on page three of the model there are two lines for potential deductions before we get to profit attributable to ordinary shareholders. The first is the deduction for Non-Controlling Shareholders' Interests (NCI) in group profits. The second is for the deduction of dividends payable to preference shareholders.

Whereas profits from associates accrue from businesses outside the group, and should be forecast independently, profits attributable to NCIs are clearly a part of profits generated by group companies. There is an important distinction here, between groups in which the NCIs represent third party interests in large numbers of subsidiaries, and groups in which there are a few large third party interests in a few large subsidiaries. In the former case it is clearly sensible to escalate the profit attributable to NCIs in line with group profit before NCIs, assuming a constant proportion of group profit is attributable to third parties. In the second case the issue is one of materiality. If the NCIs matter and the number of subsidiaries is small, then it may be worth trying to model them separately. We shall adopt the constant percentage interest approach here.

The dividends on preference shares are usually fixed as a percentage of par value, though this may not be in the currency of the company, so there may be some translation effects in the reporting currency of the group. German companies represent an exception, in that preference shares often receive a variable dividend in excess of the dividend to ordinary shares, and this is the situation with Magna.

Finally, we come to the calculation of the per share statistics. Earnings per share are calculated using the weighted average number of shares issued and outstanding (net of treasury stock) during the year, whereas the dividend will be paid to the shares outstanding on a specific date. We have handled this by forecasting the number of shares in issue at the year end (to be discussed below) and then using the average of the opening and closing shares in issue to derive a weighted average. For most companies, the relevant earnings figure would be after preference dividends, which are treated as being akin to interest. Because Magna's preference shares receive variable dividends, they are treated as akin to equity, and the earnings per share calculation is based on income after the NCI and the weighted average total number of shares (preferred and ordinary) that are outstanding for the year.

Finally, we have to forecast the dividend per share. For a non-cyclical company, a constant payout ratio may be appropriate. For a cyclical it would not be, as the company would be forever halving and doubling its dividends, which few companies set out to do. In our case we shall set what looks like a sensible payout ratio and then use share issues and buy-backs to manage the balance sheet structure, which is exactly what most companies are now doing. We have maintained a constant premium of preference over ordinary dividends in our forecasts.

1.6 Provisions

Provisions represent charges to the profit and loss account which reflect costs that have accrued, but have not yet been paid. Examples are provisions for restructuring (we are going to make lots of severance payments associated with a redundancy programme that we have now announced, but we have not made them yet), provisions for deferred taxation, and provisions for underfunded or unfunded pension liabilities.

Although it is often easiest to aggregate provisions in the cash flow statement and balance sheet, to make the model more compact and easy to read, we usually need to forecast provisions separately, generally in the three categories: pension provisions, deferred tax provisions and restructuring provisions. Accounting issues relating to all of these items have been discussed in chapter four. What we are concerned with here is the application of the accounting rules to models of future corporate accounts. Often the most important provision to model carefully is the pension provision, and in the Magna model this is the line-item on which we have concentrated (see page nine of the model). Other provisions, which are relatively small, have been held constant in the forecast balance sheet on page four of the model.

The key to modelling pension provisions is to separate out the two elements of pension costs that appear in the income statement. The service cost is the only part of pension costs that applies to operating costs, and should be modelled as part of employment costs. The net interest charge applied to the PBO and the net interest credit applied to plan assets (see chapter four on pensions) should be allocated to financial items. Since unexpected returns and actuarial adjustments are probably unpredictable, these are the only items that it is probably prudent to forecast. We shall deal with historical accrued surpluses or deficits as a deduction or addition to net debt when we value the company. In other words, we shall treat a company with an underfunded pension scheme as if it immediately borrowed the money to fund it, with the payments into the scheme precisely matching its accrued obligations in all future years.

For companies with unfunded pension schemes, we shall also treat the outstanding provision as akin to debt, but we cannot assume a future matching between contributions to the scheme and accrued liabilities, as there is no scheme. Pensioners are paid directly by the company. The service cost of the pension should be part of employment costs. The interest charge should be part of financial items. The accrued provision in the balance sheet should be treated as debt. But there will also be an annual provision contribution to forecast cash flow, which reflects the difference between the accrued liability for the year and the payments that the company has made to retired employees during the year. This is clearly an item for which we are not going to want to pay, when we value the shares in the company. It is analogous to the provisions for decommissioning costs that we discussed in chapter one. The cash stream ultimately reflects a liability that will ultimately be reflected in pensions paid to our employees. So why should we pay for it when we buy the shares?

In the debt page of the Magna model (page nine), there is a set of calculations that relate to the modelling of the pension liabilities. The interest charge is not a cash payment, but an unwinding of a discount rate. For this reason, it is included in the financial items in the profit and loss account, but then backed out of the cash interest paid in the cash flow statement, because it does not represent actual cash paid. Instead, it accrues as part of the addition to the pension provision each year. So the pension provision in the balance sheet expands both with the increase in the provision for the year (notionally, the service charge, in our forecasts) and with the interest charge.

From outside a company it is highly unlikely to be possible to establish the differences between the book value of assets for tax purposes and for reporting purposes. One is generally left with the rather cruder option of looking at the history of its tax paid as a percentage of tax charges, and should generally assume that if the company continues to grow then its cash flows will continue to benefit from continued deferred tax provisions, and that the provision in the balance sheet will never crystallise. This happy assumption has several dangers attached to it. The first is that since tax is collected at the level of the operating company, it is quite possible that a group could continue to grow, but would be unable to offset tax depreciation created in one business against tax liabilities that have accrued in another. The second is that the rate of growth of the business may slow, in which case it will not continue to create new capital allowances at the pace necessary to continue to defer a constant proportion of its tax charge.

When assessing acquisition targets this last point may be particularly important if the strategic intention is to redirect the cash flows of the target to fund more attractive investment opportunities in the portfolio of the acquirer.

In Magna's case, the balance sheet on page four of the model shows that the company has net deferred tax assets. These may be created by losses brought forward and while it is reasonable to assume that they will eventually be utilised, the timing of this is often uncertain. Deferred tax assets also arise because net pension liabilities are reported gross, but the cost of funding them is allowable against tax.

Finally, we have the one-off provisions, most commonly exemplified by restructuring costs. These may generally be expected to reverse within the forecasting period of the model, so the main point to remember is that if provisions have been taken through the profit and loss account but the money has not yet been spent, then future cash flows should suffer from the cash outflow and the reversal of the provision.

1.7 Shareholders' funds

If we ignore items that are taken straight to shareholders funds but which have not been reflected in the profit and loss account (such as unrealised gains or losses on currency translation, gains or losses on cash flow hedges that have not yet been recycled, and so on) then the annual movement in shareholders' equity is simply explained by retained net income and any increase or decrease in equity through the issuance, or buy-back, of shares.

For now, we are not going to project other consolidated gains or losses which go straight to shareholders' equity but do not go through the profit and loss account. As we have seen in chapter one, it is vital to economic profit valuations that clean surplus accounting is used, so that the profit used to derive economic profit is consistent with the increases or decreases in equity from year to year. We discussed this point with respect to both derivatives and foreign exchange in chapter four. In this model, we are not assuming any other consolidated income, so clean value accounting applies.

Rather than having a single line item for shareholders' equity, it is not difficult to project the components separately, divided between paid up capital, share premium account, retained earnings and the profits generated during the past year. Other items, such as revaluation reserves, may arise from time to time but are unlikely to be forecast.

In its basic state, the model has no share issues or buy-backs built into it, so we shall discuss the modelling of simple accrual of earnings first, and then revert to how to model changes in capital.

In this case there is no change either to capital stock or additional paid in capital during the forecast years. The two relevant line items on page four of the model are thus reserves retained from earnings and group net profit. To understand how they work, let us take the estimates for year 1. Starting with the profit and loss account, the company is forecast to make attributable net income of €632m (see page three of the model, Magna profit and loss account). This figure is added to its equity on page four, because the year 1 dividend, of €1.30 and €1.43 per share for ordinary and preference shares, respectively, will not be paid in cash until year 2. What is paid during year 1 is the dividends that were announced for year 0, which represent a total of €334m (see the cash flow statement on page five). In the end year 0 shareholders' funds on page four of the model, the figure of €496m of attributable earnings was included. This drops out of the equity in year 1, replaced by an addition to retained earnings of €162m from page three of the model. In year 2, the figure of €632 will disappear from shareholders' funds on page four of the model, to be replaced by additional retained earnings of €207m (because the year 1 dividend of €425m will have been paid), and year 2 attributable earnings of €701m will be added to the total. And so on.

This is the logical place to address the mechanics of share issues or buy-backs. They represent the first of our special cases to be discussed in the later sections of this chapter, after the basic model is completed, so we shall return to them, and illustrate the text with an example, when we get there.

If you are in a company planning a schedule of share buy-backs, of course you would want to be accurate about the implications. From the outside, the main use to which we shall put this facility is to realise (when the model is complete) that we are projecting wildly improbable balance sheets and to conclude that over the next few years the company is likely either to issue or to buy back a large amount of equity. The detail of the timing is unknowable, so the best that we can generally do is to forecast the year end number of shares outstanding and assume that the weighted average is equal to the arithmetic average of the opening and closing number. If you know that the company is going to have a large issue on 30 September, then it would clearly be more sensible to weight the weighted average number of shares accordingly.

Another important question regarding share issues or buy-backs is the price at which the share transactions are assumed to happen. All other things being equal, share prices are expected to rise over time. So using the current share price is presumably pessimistic if we are issuing new shares to raise new equity in five years' time, and optimistic if the idea is that we shall buy back equity. Here, a more sophisticated approach than just using the current share price is to use the cost of equity (see chapter two for a definition) and the Gordon Growth model (from chapter one) to derive an expected annual share price appreciation. If the company has a cost of equity of 7% and a dividend yield of 3% then presumably its shares are expected to rise in value at 4% a year.

In our model we have shareholders' funds rising with retained earnings unless we assume a share issue or buy-back. In this case, we calculate the number of shares bought or sold by using the forecast share price. This number must then be carried back to the year end shares in issue on the profit and loss account tab, so that each year's shares outstanding is equal to the number outstanding in the previous year, plus or minus the new shares issued or bought back. The resulting changes in shares issued must be carried back to the profit and loss account for the purpose of calculating earnings per share and dividends.

One consequence of an earlier decision should be noted. Because we set the payout ratio as the basis for determining the dividend per share, earnings accretion or dilution resulting from share buy-backs or issues will automatically be compensated for in higher or lower dividend payments per share. When modelling cyclical companies, for which a fixed payout ratio is not suitable, it is likely to be necessary to reconsider the dividend stream in the light of expected issues or buy-backs of equity.

A final point is the allocation of the funds raised or spent between the various categories of shareholders' equity. If the change is a new issue, then the par value of the new shares is added to paid up capital, and the surplus over par value is added to the share premium account, or, as Magna describes it, additional paid in capital. In the event of a buy-back, the full value of the distribution represents a negative item in shareholders' funds, namely, treasury stock.

1.8 Non-controlling interests

Both associates and NCIs are consolidated into group accounts with line items for earnings, dividends and shareholders' equity, but no further information. The accounting treatment for NCIs is that their interest in group profit is shown as a charge to the profit and loss account. It is a part of cash flow from operations, but the dividend paid by the relevant subsidiaries to the third party shareholders (who lie outside the group) is shown in the cash flow statement as an item of cash flow to and from finance. And the difference between the two, which represents the accrual of retained income that is attributable to third party shareholders, accumulates as third party interest in group equity in the balance sheet.

In our discussions of the relationship between growth, return on equity and payout ratios in chapter one we made the observation that if two of these are set independently, then the third is a dependent variable. This is as true on an annual basis as it is in a constant growth model. Setting the earnings growth rate and the payout leaves return on equity and shareholders' funds as results. Setting the earnings growth rate and the return on equity (which implies a figure for equity) determines the dividend and therefore the payout ratio.

In this model we have let the earnings grow with those of the group as a whole and we have set the dividend stream to grow with those of the group as a whole, with the future level of return on equity to associates as an implicit result. Naturally, whichever way round the forecast is constructed, it will be important to ensure that all three figures and ratios seem reasonable.

As we shall see when we turn to valuation, the value of the NCIs will be included in the value that is put on the operations of the group by both DCF and economic profit models. This implies that it has to be independently calculated and deducted from the value of the group, alongside debt and other liabilities, before ascribing a value to the equity of group shareholders.

1.9 Associates

The accounting treatment for associates is for the profit attributable to the group to be shown as a separate line item in the profit and loss account. Since the cash flow statement begins with an income figure that includes all profit consolidated from associates, an adjustment item subtracts the difference between the profit consolidated from associates and the dividends received from associates, so that the figure for cash flow from operations merely reflects the dividend stream. The difference between the profit consolidated from associates and the dividend received from associates comprises the group's retained profits in its associated companies. Investments in associates are shown in the balance sheet under financial assets (a part of fixed assets), and it is the group's net interest in the shareholders' funds of the associates that is displayed. So the item in the balance sheet grows each year to the extent of its interest in the retained earnings of the associated companies.

As Magna does not have significant equity associates, let us take a simple example. Suppose that group A has a 40% interest in associated company B. If B makes $100 of net income, A will book $40 of profit from associates. Suppose that B pays out 25% of its profits and retains 75%. Then A will receive $10 in dividend from B. A's cash flow statement will include the $10, and there will be a line item which attributes the negative figure of –$30 to the difference between profit booked from associates and dividend received from associates. The $30 will accrue to the financial assets in A's balance sheet as retained net income in associates. Overall, we are adding $40 to A's equity, $10 to A's cash, and $30 to A's fixed assets, so everything balances.

There is one point that should be noted here, to which we shall return in chapter seven. In the case of there being goodwill associated with the acquisition of an interest in an associate, the goodwill is booked along with the net interest in the associate, as part of the financial assets of the group. And profits from associates are shown net of impairment of goodwill (if it is impaired). The goodwill is not separately shown as part of group goodwill either in the balance sheet or as part of the amortisation charge, because the associate is not part of the group. It really is a case of 'two line accounting'.

By contrast to the situation regarding minority interests, associates lie outside the group, and it makes little sense to forecast their contribution as a fixed proportion of group profits. It probably makes more sense to make independent estimates of growth in earnings and either return on equity or payout ratios, and then to check the results for realism.

1.10 The cash flow statement

While it may be useful for presentational reasons, or to draw conclusions from historical trends, it is not essential to enter historical cash flows into our model.

We do need a historical profit and loss account and balance sheet from which to build our forecasts. We do not need a cash flow statement. Moreover, for many companies it is highly unlikely that it will be possible fully to reconcile historical cash flows with movements in balance sheet items. An important reason for this is that foreign assets and liabilities are generally translated at closing exchange rates, while revenue accounts are translated at average exchange rates, with the difference going straight to equity as a gain or loss on translation of foreign activities.

Whether or not history is being shown in the model, we recommend using a structure of the cash flow that facilitates modelling. This implies breaking it into three components: cash flow from operations, cash flow to and from investment, and cash flow to and from finance. The intuition is that the former shows what our business is expected to generate. The second shows what our business is expected to absorb by way of new investment. And the balance between the two is a measure of cash flow available to or required from finance, which will be distributed to or required from the providers of capital. Companies have discretion to arrange their cash flows either starting with net income or with EBIT. In the latter case there will be a line item for taxes paid, in the former a possible adjustment for deferred taxation.

If deferred taxation is being assumed then the cash tax would be lower, offset by the creation of a deferred tax provision. Or if a deferred tax liability is being unwound, then the reverse occurs: cash tax higher than the tax charged to income. That is what happens in the Magna model. We are assuming that the deferred tax liability in the balance sheet reflects capitalisation of intangible assets on acquisition, and that their amortisation reduces the tax charge on page three of the model, but not the tax paid, hence the cash outflow relating to deferred tax on page five, and the fall in the balance sheet deferred tax liability on page four of the model.

Although we shall obviously retain the right to revisit the question of equity issues or buy-backs when we have seen the resulting forecast balance sheets, if we simply take the figures as we have them, most of the forecast cash flows can be completed. We have profit, depreciation and amortisation, provisions and changes in working capital, which together comprise cash flow from operations. We have capital expenditure, which is our cash flow to and from investments unless we start to model asset acquisitions and disposals. And we have line-items for equity issued or bought back, dividends paid to our shareholders, and dividends paid to minority shareholders. All that is left is the allocation of the remaining elements of cash to and from finance: changes in short-term debt, changes in long-term debt, and changes in cash and cash equivalents.

Before we move on the treatment of the components of net debt, we should return briefly to the treatment of disposals of fixed assets, because this is not treated in the Magna model, though we shall return to it in chapter seven. If an asset is sold for a sum of £150m, with a book value of £100m, a profit of £50m will result. This will be subject to a tax charge which may or may not be that of the group, and may be levied on something other than £50m, depending on the tax carrying value of the asset. But from outside if the marginal rate of corporating tax is 30% then we probably have little option other than to assume that the resulting tax charge will be £15m.

How does all this appear in the accounts? The profit and loss account would show a pre-tax exceptional gain of £50m, with the tax charge rising by £15m, implying that the net of tax impact on earnings is £35m. The line-item in the cash flow for net profit on disposals will contain a negative figure of −£35m, so that the figure for cash flow from operations is not affected by the disposal. When we get to the movements to and from investments, the net proceeds from the disposal have to be included in the cash flow. What are they? Not £150m, clearly, since we have paid some tax. The net receipt is £150m minus tax of £15m, which equals £135m. This could also be thought of as £100m of book value plus £35m of net of tax profit on the disposal.

Thinking in terms of the impact of all of this on the balance sheet, equity has risen by £35m (the net profit on the disposal). Fixed assets have fallen by £100m (the book value of the assets). And cash has risen by £135m (net cash receipts). Both sides of the balance sheet have expanded by £35m.

As a general point about modelling, it is worth thinking through all of the implications of an event for the profit and loss, the cash flow statement and the balance sheet before you start to insert numbers into your spreadsheet. If you can see how the changes to assets and liabilities will balance, the probability of success is high!

1.11 Net debt

Many models simply stop at forecasting net debt as a single line item. This is rather unsophisticated and has a number of disadvantages. It obviously cannot reflect different interest rates applying to cash, short-term debt and long-term debt. It looks ugly if the company turns net cash positive because one is left with a negative net debt item on the liability side of the balance sheet. And it eliminates from analysis the whole question of a company's future funding requirements which, depending on the use to which the model may be being put, may or may not be half of the point of building the model.

Equally, if you are in the Treasury department of a company, or in a bank advising the Treasury department of a company, then you are going to want to model the debt tranche by tranche, and to be much more specific about the composition of short-term debt, and of cash and cash equivalents. What we are going to produce is of intermediate detail, but it should provide an adequate indication of how one could go further.

As Magna's balance sheet shows total debt as a single item, this is how we have modelled it, but we describe below an approach that can be used to separate out forecasts of long term debt and short term debt.

The general approach is to model long-term debt as the independent variable. Reports and accounts will let us know the maturities of the group's debt, so we can enter that into our model. We can also enter discretionary changes in long-term debt as a separate entry for each year. Clearly, it will only make sense to do this when we have seen the projected balance sheets, and know what the financial structure of the company would be in the absence of voluntary issuance or retirement of debt.

Cash and short-term debt will be the dependent variable, with a simple rule to allocate between them. We shall decide what the minimum operating cash requirement for the company is, and any surplus cash over and above that will be used to pay down short term debt. Clearly, it is not possible to pay off short-term debt below zero, so in the event of our forecasting the elimination of short-term debt then any additional cash piles up over and above the minimum operating requirements.

In the event of a shortfall, then the logic for the model is as follows. You did not have an equity issue. You did not have a bond issue. We need a certain minimum level of cash, so there is nowhere to go to find it other than from additional short-term debt. So short-term debt rises to ensure that cash levels are not lower than the minimum operating level.

There is one small point implicit in all this that should be highlighted in passing. The short-term debt is being treated as a 'revolver' in that rather than forecasting the movement in short-term debt we are effectively assuming that it is all paid off and that new short-term debt is assumed each year, as required. Or none is borrowed if none is required.

Reverting to the treatment of long-term debt, the reality is that when this becomes due for payment in less than one year it moves out of long-term debt into short-term debt, and is then paid 12 months later. We therefore want to pick up as short-term debt in the balance sheet the sum of the balance under the revolver and the repayment of long-term debt that falls due in the following year, and to pick up as long-term debt in the balance sheet the total long-term debt liability minus the portion that falls due in the following year.

Our Magna model is less sophisticated than that, following the company's balance sheet format. On the debt tab we have as a default assumption that there is no increase or decrease in debt. This will be reviewed once we are able to assess the full forecast. The pension provision, which is the only provision to be modelled, is on the debt tab, as it contributes to interest charges and will be treated as debt in our valuation. The change in debt, or absence of it, is reflected in the relevant line of the cash flow forecast, and is one of the drivers to movements in cash balances.

1.12 The balance sheet

In much the same way that double-entry bookkeeping had as one of its objectives the ability to check records for consistency, so our projected balance sheets should permit us to ensure that all of the calculations that we have done so far are consistent with one another.

> For this to work it is essential that each item in the balance sheet is separately estimated, and that assets and liabilities are separately summed and checked against one another. As soon as one item in the balance sheet is introduced as a 'fudge factor' (all the assets minus the other liabilities, or whatever), it will stop fulfilling its function as a check on our model.

The corollary to this is that if the balance sheet does balance unaided, then it is almost impossible that the rest of the model is not hooked up correctly. Individual estimates for certain line items may be crazy, but they are at least consistent. We shall worry about how to avoid silly, rather than inconsistent, forecasts later.

It will be remembered that we are still forecasting with no interest in the profit and loss account at this stage. To spare the reader two lots of balance sheet to look at, we shall make the point here that connecting up the balance sheet should be done first, and that the interest charges from the debt calculation should then, and only then, be inserted into the profit and loss account. The reason is that (whatever the software package that is being used) insertion of the interest charge creates a circularity in the model.

Interest is a function of average debt. Average debt is a function of year end debt. And year end debt is a function of interest. Packages such as Microsoft Excel can cope with circularities, but they make the models harder to audit. So it is worth getting the balance sheet to balance first, and inserting the interest into the profit and loss account afterwards. Exhibit 5.1 above illustrates restated profit and loss account, balance sheet, and cash flow statement, all with interest charges already connected into the profit and loss account.

2. Ratios and scenarios

An understandable mistake that is often made by those who have limited experience of modelling and valuing companies is to imagine that if they make sensible estimates for the key inputs to a model then this implies that the outputs will also be sensible. Sadly, this is not the case. The reason is that for any input there is a range of plausible numbers that could be used. But certain combinations of plausible inputs will themselves produce implausible outputs.

A simple example relates to growth and capital expenditure. The two are clearly related. A sensible range could be applied to both. But if we take the most optimistic plausible growth rate for revenue, and the lowest plausible value for capital expenditure over the next 5 years, we shall end up with some highly implausible forecasts.

This was a simple case, but there are others that are more complicated. Suppose that you are analysing an industry that is highly cyclical, with the driver to the economic cycle being the impact of fluctuations in Gross Domestic Product (GDP) on demand. Analysis of the company's history might suggest that there are two main drivers to profitability: sales and margin. But it will almost certainly turn out that there is a close relationship between periods of high sales growth and periods of high margins (because capacity is being fully utilised), and between periods of weak or negative sales growth and of low margins (because of low capacity utilisation). Where there seemed to be two variables determining profit there is in reality only one (sales), with the other (margin) a dependent variable. Spotting these connections is not always easy, but is the key to producing intelligent forecasts.

Although not all of this can be automated, and there is a skill to understanding the relationships that apply to particular industries, you can help yourself by always concentrating on a single output tab, combining all the key ratios that are implied by your model. These should be broken into the following categories: growth rates, margins, capital turns, returns on capital and financial leverage.

Taking the ratios by group, the annual growth figures are fairly self-explanatory. Both they and the margin figures should be separated between what they are telling you about the operations (everything down to EBIT) and what they are telling you about financing, because from pre-tax profit downwards the figures are affected by the amount of interest that is forecast to be paid or received.

We have addressed the question of capital turn as we proceeded through the construction of the model. At the time we made the point that the fixed asset turn and the working capital turn should be monitored for realism. They have an additional importance in that margins and capital turns in combination determine return on capital employed, as shown in the following formula:

$$R=P/CE=P/S*S/CE$$

where R is return on capital, P is net operating profit after tax (NOPAT), CE is capital employed, and S is sales.

We do not need a mathematical appendix for this, since it is obvious that the figures for sales just cancel out to give us profit over capital.

The point of the expansion is that the ratio of profit over sales is a margin, and the figure for sales over capital is a capital turn. The latter may be split out again to separate capital between fixed and working capital. So we can break out our assumptions for future returns on capital employed into their business drivers: margin and capital turn. If we wish, we can also break these factors down further.

Before we proceed, it will be remembered that in our discussion of valuation in chapter one, we made the point that a constant growth company could be valued from just three inputs: growth rate, return on capital and weighted average cost of capital. And the equity in a company can be valued from growth rate, return on equity and cost of equity. What our present analysis does is to allow us to break down the crucial return element of the equation into its determinants. This is why it is often referred to as the 'value driver' approach to valuation. Instead of just discounting a stream of cash, we can break the determinants of the stream down into margins and capital turns, and then subdivide those further if required.

The principles underlying this analysis are known as 'DuPont Analysis', and in their full form are aimed at extending down to the return on equity. This can be represented in a number of ways, but given where we have started with gross margins and capital turn giving us a return on capital, the natural extension is to leverage up the return on capital to a return on equity. This is done using the following formula:

$$r=Y/E=R+(R-I)*D/E$$

where r is return on equity, R is return on capital, Y is net income, I is net cost of interest, D is debt and E is equity.

Again, the proof is in the mathematical appendix, but the intuitive explanation is that our return on equity is the same as the return on capital, plus an additional spread that we earn on the portion of our assets that are funded by debt. The spread is the return on capital minus the cost of debt. Returns and interest rates are all net of tax in this formula, though they could clearly be grossed up by dividing by one minus the tax rate.

So the margins and capital turns define our return on capital (feel free to check this!) and when we forecast the long-term future offer us a way to project long-term returns on capital employed as a result, rather than as an input. If we progress to thinking about returns to equity we have three drivers: margin, capital turn and leverage.

In practice, extending the analysis down to a return on equity is often complicated by the facts that there are non-operating assets in the balance sheet, and that liabilities comprise not just debt on which a spread is being earned but also various different sorts of provisions and minority interests. Our pragmatic recommendation, when it comes to the valuation of industrial companies (but not banks and insurance companies) is to concentrate on valuing the operating capital, and then derive a value of the equity by adding the market value of non-operating assets and subtracting the market value of financial liabilities. For this reason our DuPont analysis on the ratios page of the Magna model stops at capital and merely illustrated the capital gearing (including only finance debt as debt, not, for example, the pension provision, as we shall do in our valuation).

Given the importance of return on capital employed to the interpretation of history, the construction of forecasts and the derivation of a terminal value (see below), we should linger briefly on what we mean by it. We are looking at the operating profit generated by the operating assets of the business, so the profit excludes both financial items and profits from associates, and the denominator represents only the fixed and working capital that is deployed in the business. It excludes financial investments, associates, and so on.

There are two specific points to be made to avoid confusion. The first is that the returns in this table have been calculated by dividing taxed operating profit for the year (NOPAT) by opening capital employed, not average capital employed. The reason for this will become apparent when we get to economic profit valuation below.

The second point is that while companies often refer to capital employed as meaning debt and equity (ours and third party), our definition includes all provisions as part of the capital base. Some modellers use the phrase 'invested capital' to mean the total and 'capital employed' to mean merely finance capital. Our reasons for rejecting the distinction are simple. Firstly, if we are looking at the operations of a company we want to know how well it is doing with its assets, irrespective of how they are financed. Finance is a separate question. Secondly, when we come to value a company we cannot ignore provisions. In the last analysis they are either a liability or they are not, in which case they are effectively equity, in economic terms. Magna's opening year 1 capital employed, for example, included €1,012m of pension provisions on which it is accruing interest and which is clearly debt. It also includes €758m of other provisions that will either crystallise or they will not. If so they are a financial liability to be netted off the value of the equity (unless they will reverse within our forecast) or they are effectively part of equity.

Returning to exhibit 5.1, the last block of ratios relate to balance sheet leverage, and will drive our choice of decisions regarding share issues and buybacks and bond issues on the equity and debt tabs, since it is leaving us with a balance sheet structure that dramatically reduces financial leverage during our forecast period.

We shall defer a detailed discussion of goodwill until chapter seven, but would make a few quick points here.

- Firstly, when a company makes an acquisition it must ultimately justify the goodwill that it paid.

- Secondly, this does not imply that it must earn more than its cost of capital on the capital base including goodwill in the early years after the acquisition. This depends on whether long-term investment opportunities comprised a large part of the value.

- Thirdly, it does not really matter whether economic profit models are set up to include or exclude goodwill in the calculation (because what I gain in book value by including it is knocked off again in capital charges), but *what is absolutely crucial is that, when companies are forecast, the return that they are expected to make on incremental capital investments should relate to the returns that they are making excluding goodwill. When a company builds a new asset it does not put a pile of goodwill on top of it.*

When using a model, rather than building it, there is a correct order in which it makes sense to approach the assumptions which drive it. We should start with the determinants of sales growth, and then work through the drivers to variable and fixed margins. Capital investment and changes in working capital follow. This fixes the operating cash flows of the business. We should then move on to the balance between debt and equity, and finish (if we progress this far) with the balance between long- and short-term debt. It is evident that if the forecasts are approached in the other direction, you are likely to chase yourself around them several times, as later changes make earlier ones look unrealistic.

We have now built and discussed at some length a detailed model of a fairly simple company. Our strategy now will be to add a valuation procedure to it, and then to devote the remainder of the chapter to considering some of the more common cases in which the standard approach is inadequate. Be warned that we shall not display the full construction of the models in each case, only the deviations from what we are doing with Magna. So now is the time to ensure that you are happy with what we have done so far.

3. Building a valuation

When we value a company we need to do two things. The first is to decide what we are going to discount, and the second is to decide the rate at which we are going to discount it. We had an extensive discussion of the cost of equity and cost of capital in chapter two, and in chapter one we proved that if models are applied consistently then there are four approaches at arriving at the same answer: to value capital or equity, and to value it by discounting cash or by discounting economic profit. We are not going to use all four models for each company we analyse, and in any case as the projected market gearing for most companies alters throughout the forecast period it is a complicated matter to reconcile the results in practice, rather than in the theoretical world of constant growth models. It can be done, but we would need to recalculate all of the components of the cost of capital by annual iteration (time varying WACC) to do it. We shall look at this technique later in the chapter when we turn to difficult situations that need special treatment, but many companies do have fairly stable balance sheets, which means that this refinement is often unnecessary. Put brutally, errors in the forecasts will considerably exceed errors in the discount rate so there is no point worrying too much about the impact of small changes in balance sheet structure.

This also militates in favour of discounting economic profits and cash flows to capital, rather than to equity, as within a wide range (a cash pile at one end and imminent financial collapse at the other), changes in financial gearing are largely mutually offsetting as far as WACC is concerned. As leverage rises, so do both tax shelters and default risks. They largely cancel one another out. This is not true of the cost of equity, where quite small changes in gearing can have a quite large impact on the appropriate discount rate.

So we shall calculate one WACC for our company, and carry it through the forecast years. Our problem now switches back to the first question. What are we supposed to be discounting? Since there is no difficulty in reconciling DCF with economic profit we shall calculate both valuations, and would strongly recommend that you do so in your models. They slice the value in different ways, and this can be highly illuminating. If forced to come off the fence, we would prefer economic profit to DCF, because it conveys more information about how the valuation is derived, and because it is easier to avoid losing accruals in a valuation methodology that goes with the grain of accrual accounting, rather than butchering the accounts to get at the operating cash flows.

3.1 Defining free cash flow

In the section of the note that follows we shall be commenting at length on the valuation routine attached to the basic Magna model, which derives a WACC and intrinsic values for the company both using the DCF and the economic profit methodology. As with the previous section, we reproduce the full printout of the two pages below, in exhibit 5.2, and shall then refer back to them in what follows.

Exhibit 5.2: Magna valuation

11. Magna cost of capital

Risk free rate	4.02%
Equity risk premium	4.00%
Beta	0.83
Cost of equity	7.34%
Risk free rate	4.02%
Debt premium	1.50%
Gross cost of debt	5.52%
Tax rate	35.00%
Net cost of debt	3.59%
Share price	36.76	
Shares issued (m)	324	
Market capitalisation	11,914	65.7%
Net debt (book)	6,209	34.3%
Enterprise value	18,123	100.0%
WACC	**6.05%**	

12. Magna DCF/EP valuation (Euro million)

Year	1	2	3	4	5	Terminus
WACC	6.05%					
Incremental ROCE	9.0%					
Long term growth	2.0%					
EBITA	1,613	1,693	1,784	1,889	2,013	
Notional taxation on EBITA	(660)	(688)	(720)	(757)	(800)	
NOPAT	**953**	**1,005**	**1,064**	**1,133**	**1,213**	**1,237**
Depreciation & amortisation	1,521	1,551	1,587	1,628	1,674	
Capital expenditure	(1,500)	(1,600)	(1,700)	(1,800)	(1,900)	
Change in working capital	63	99	115	135	160	
Free cash flow	**1,038**	**1,055**	**1,067**	**1,096**	**1,147**	**962**
Opening capital employed	**11,140**	**11,055**	**11,006**	**11,003**	**11,040**	**11,107**
Earnings growth	13.6%	5.4%	5.9%	6.4%	7.1%	2.0%
Return on opening capital employed	8.6%	9.1%	9.7%	10.3%	11.0%	9.0%
Cost of capital	6.05%	6.05%	6.05%	6.05%	6.05%	6.05%
Investment spread	2.5%	3.0%	3.6%	4.2%	4.9%	2.9%
Economic profit	**279**	**336**	**398**	**467**	**545**	**565**

DCF valuation

+ PV 5 year cash flow	4,531	20.4%
+ PV terminal value	17,691	79.6%
= Enterprise value	**22,222**	**100.0%**
+ Financial assets	238	
- Non-controlling interests	(188)	
- Pension provisions	(1,012)	
- Net debt	(6,209)	
= Equity value	**15,051**	
Value per share	46.06	

Economic profit valuation

+ Opening balance sheet (excl. financial assets)	11,140	50.1%
+ PV 5 year economic profit	1,670	7.5%
+ PV terminal value (ex incremental investment)	6,953	31.3%
+ PV terminal value (incremental investments)	2,459	11.1%
= Enterprise value	**22,222**	**100.0%**
+ Financial assets	238	
- Non-controlling interests	(188)	
- Pension provisions	(1,012)	
- Net debt	(6,209)	
= Equity value	**15,051**	
Value per share	46.06	

In our discussion of discount rates in chapter two we devoted considerable space to the question of whether tax shelters should be discounted at the unleveraged cost of equity or at the gross cost of debt, and concluded that (whatever the lack of guidance from the theoreticians) it made more sense to discount them at the unleveraged cost of equity. This choice also had implications for the formula that we use for leveraging and deleveraging Betas.

Whichever choice we make about how to treat tax shelters, however, there is no doubt that since we are treating the tax shelter as an item to be adjusted for in the discount rate (via a net of tax cost of debt), we should not also be taking it into account in the cash flows that we discount. To do so would clearly be double-counting. So when we calculate free cash flow we do so by restating the cash flows as if the company had no debt in its balance sheet. We discount deleveraged free cash flow. This is true whether we apply a single WACC, or whether we value the unleveraged assets and the tax shelter separately, as in an APV analysis.

Turning to the forecasts of economic profit and cash flow, notice a number of points relating to the calculation.

- The first is that, because we want unleveraged free cash flows, we start not with pre-tax profits but with EBIT.

- Secondly, the calculation of tax is a notional one. It is what the tax would have been in the event that we were not in fact going to be creating tax shelters through the payment of interest. Tax in our forecast profit and loss account is in fact lower than the tax shown here, and the difference is the tax shelter that the company will create if it carries the levels of debt that we are projecting. As with our actual forecast, we add back amortisation of acquisition intangibles into taxable profit, so the notional tax charge is arrived at by multiplying EBITA by the marginal rate of taxation.

- Thirdly, we would include as part of our NOPAT those provisions for which we want to pay (deferred taxation, for example), because we do not believe that they represent a real accrual of liability. The reason for including them in the NOPAT, rather than putting them alongside depreciation will become apparent when we move on to discussing the economic profit calculation of value. Clearly, where we put them in a DCF calculation will make no difference to the calculation of free cash flow.

- Fourthly, the remaining items (comprising depreciation and amortisation, capital expenditure and change in non-cash working capital) can conveniently be netted off against one another to derive a figure for net investment. This is the extent to which the company grows its balance sheet size from one period to the next.

So free cash flow can either be thought of as unleveraged cash flow from operations less investment, or, much more usefully, as NOPAT minus net investments: profit less the proportion of profit that we have to plough back into the business to fund future growth. The reason why this is a much better way to look at the problem is that we have a formula for retentions, which we discussed in chapter one. It is that retentions must equal projected growth divided by projected returns on incremental capital.

3.2 Terminal value calculations

It is clearly very easy to discount back 5 figures for free cash flow to derive a present value. But it will also not get us very far towards the valuation of the company, since the larger part of the value will be attributable to the stream of cash that Magna is expected to generate after the end of the forecast period. Since it is not practical to forecast to infinity, the most common approach to what happens after the forecast period is to apply a terminal value formula, using the Gordon Growth model that we discussed in chapter one. This implies our knowing two things: what free cash flow will be in the first year after the forecast period (the Terminus), and knowing what growth rate to apply to it.

In chapter one we discussed the connection between growth, retentions and return, so here we shall merely refer back to that discussion and make the point that, for most companies, the best approach to calculating free cash flow in the Terminus is to apply the formula:

$$FCF_{t+1}=NOPAT_t*(1+g)*[1-g/ROCE_i]$$

where t+1 is the Terminus and i refers to incremental capital.

This is often referred to as the 'value driver' formula for terminal value, since it uses the retentions approach to work out what proportion of profit needs to be reinvested to derive the projected growth, and then derives free cash flow as profit minus required retentions. As we discussed earlier in this chapter, the DuPont approach can then be used to disaggregate the expected return on incremental investment into a margin and a capital turn. The capital turn can be split between fixed assets and working capital. And if required the margins could be split between gross (before fixed costs), operating (after fixed costs) and net (after tax), so it is possible to make the terminal value the result of a detailed breakdown of value drivers.

We shall keep the model simple and just run the Terminus off two assumptions: earnings growth and return on incremental capital. But it is important to note how flexible this approach can be made to be.

If we add together the net present value of the free cash flows in exhibit 5.2, and the value that derives from applying the Gordon Growth model to the free cash flow in the Terminus, then we can add them together to derive a value for the operating assets of the company.

Before we move on there is one frequent error that must be avoided at all costs.

Remember that the Gordon Growth model applied to the free cash flow in the Terminus will derive a value as at the end of the forecast period (a future value of the terminal value). For our purposes we want a present value of the terminal value, so the formula for the terminal value that we want in our valuation is as follows:

$$TV_0=FCF_{t+1}/(WACC-g)/(1+WACC)^t$$

This gives us the terminal value at the end of year zero (the last financial year) based on free cash flow in the first year after our explicit forecast period (the Terminus year), capitalised as a growth perpetuity (by the Gordon Growth model) and discounted back for the length of the forecast period. In the case of our model the discounting of the terminal value will be over five years, even though the terminal value relates to cash flow in year six. Do not forget that the Gordon Growth model capitalises a growing perpetuity which starts with a payment in a year's time, so a stream starting at end year six is valued at end year five, and then brought back for five years to end year zero.

Exhibit 5.2 shows the breakdown of the value that we are putting on the operating assets of the company, comprising two present values, one for the forecast free cash flows, and one for the terminal value.

3.3 From enterprise value to equity

If we want to put a value on the equity of the company, we need to adjust the value of the operating assets. In the simplest case, this simply involves making a deduction for debt. But in almost all real examples, there are a number of adjustments to be made for three other categories of item: accrued provisions that we regard as representing real liabilities, non-operational assets, and the element of our derived value for operational assets that is attributable to third party shareholders (NCIs).

The key point relating to all of these items is that what we want is their market value, but what we see in the balance sheet is a book value. A judgement about materiality is required. If it matters, because the debt is trading at 30p in the pound, or because the minorities are worth five times book value, then make an adjustment. In particular, the P/B and P/E formulae that we derived in chapter one can be used to derive fair value multiples for associates and NCIs, to be respectively added to and subtracted from the basic valuation of the operating assets. To make the connection with Magna's report and accounts as transparent as possible we shall work with book values, but it would be a fairly simple matter to make them better approximations to market value.

3.4 Economic profit valuation

As we say in chapter one there is no difference between an economic profit valuation and a discounted cash flow valuation, and the Mathematical Appendix has a proof that for an all-equity company residual income and dividend discounting always result in the same value. But they do allocate the value in very different ways. The insight offered by DCF has to do with duration. If I buy the company, how much of the value is returned over the first five years and how much after that? The insight offered by economic profit valuation is that the company may be seen as being worth the book value of it assets plus a premium, to reflect its success in earning a return on capital employed which is above the cost of the capital employed.

Deriving economic profit for one year is not hard, and can be achieved in either of two ways. We can calculate the spread between the return on capital and the cost of capital as a percentage spread, and then multiply it by the opening capital to arrive at a figure.

Or we can calculate a capital charge by multiplying the opening capital by the cost of capital and deducting the result from NOPAT.

Imagine a company that starts the year with capital of $1,000. It earns NOPAT of $120 during the year, a return on capital employed of 12%. Its cost of capital is 10%. Our first approach would be to say that 12% less 10% is 2%, so the company is earning an investment spread of 2%. On capital of $1,000, this implies economic profit of $20. Our second approach would be to say that the cost of $1,000 capital at 10% is $100, and we made NOPAT of $120, so the economic profit was $20. In both cases, we are deducting from the company's profits not just an interest charge but a full cost of capital, so any resulting surplus or deficit comprises value added or subtracted.

Before we reproduce these calculations for Magna, let us pause over one point. We are using the opening amount of capital in this calculation, not the average, which would be the more usual number to quote. The reason is this. Just as in a DCF model we treat cash flow as if it all arrives on the last day of each year, discounting the first year for one year and the second for two, and so on, we do the same with an economic profit model. We assume that the year one profits arrive all at the end of the year, and represent a return on the capital that was invested at the beginning of the year. The resulting economic profit is discounted for one year at the WACC. For year two, the same applies, but the resulting economic profit is then discounted for two years. Handling the numbers this way guarantees that the results of the two analyses will be identical, and it is not generally worth the effort involved in adjusting either valuation to a mid-year discounting convention.

As with the DCF valuation, we shall simply discount the five years' economic profit at the WACC to derive a present value of the forecast economic profit.

3.5 Terminal values in economic profit

When we were discussing valuation methodologies in chapter one we made the point that the two key drivers were assumed growth rate and assumed return on incremental capital. This is not necessarily the same as the return on historical, already installed capital. To see why not, consider a company that is currently earning £100 a year of NOPAT. If the company is to grow its profits at 4% annually and will make a 10% return on incremental capital then it needs to reinvest 4/10 of its profit, a total of £40, and it can distribute 6/10 of its profit, a total of £60. We met these calculations both in chapter one and in the discussion of the value driver terminal value for DCFs earlier in this chapter. But stop a moment and consider what is happening here. We need to reinvest £40 in new capital because at a 10% return this will give us the required additional £4 of profit. If we did not want to grow our profit, then we could happily distribute all of our profit and leave the balance sheet size unchanged.

There is no reason at all to assume that the existing capital is earning the same rate of return as that which we want to assume for the Terminus. In both the DCF and the economic profit model, we assume that the capital that is already installed at the end of the forecast period is capable of generating the same returns, and the same stream of profit, forever. The growth and retentions formula relates merely to the amount of new capital that we shall need to generate new streams of profit in future years.

We shall consider later the question of what to do in the event that we do not believe that existing capital will continue to generate stable returns into the long-term future. For the time being let us just remain with, and understand, the convention that once a pound of capital is invested it earns the same return in perpetuity. Now, if we have a company that is projected to earn a high return on capital by the end of the forecast period, several per cent above the WACC, for example, we are free to make whatever assumption that we want to about the return that will be made on new capital invested after the forecast period. Since new capital may generate a different return from existing capital, the blended return may be different every year, as the balance between old and new capital changes.

Although we did not worry about it at the time, this is happening in our DCF model as well. There it was implicit, since we were valuing the stream of cash that the company pays out, and were only using the assumed return on incremental capital to derive the stream. Here, the distinction between treatment of old capital and new capital (at the Terminus) will have to be explicit, as otherwise we shall be trying to model a company that is earning a differing return on capital, and therefore a different investment spread, each year.

The solution is simple. We start with the economic profit that is generated in the Terminus. This is easy for us to calculate, because we know the opening capital (it is the closing capital at the end of our forecast period), and we know the NOPAT (as in the DCF it is NOPAT in year t bumped up for one year's growth). If the company were never to make another investment, and the lump of capital earned the same return for ever, then the value that results is just a no-growth perpetuity:

$$PV_t = EP_{t+1}/WACC$$

where PVt is the present value at the end of the forecast period of the perpetuity represented by the economic profit from the Terminus held flat to infinity. Of course, as with the terminal value in the DCF, this has to be discounted back to a present value in year zero, so its contribution to the firm's value is:

$$PV_0 = PV_t/(1+WACC)^t$$

but we are assuming that the company will grow by reinvesting some of its profit in year t+1 and beyond. So we need another calculation to derive the incremental value that will be created by the incremental investments that the company makes after the forecast period. We do this by calculating how much it will invest in the first year, then by calculating how much value this investment will create, and finally by applying the Gordon Growth model to the result, because each following year's investment will be bigger by the growth rate than the one before. Because all new investments are assumed to earn the same return on capital, the application of a constant growth formula here will work.

To calculate the investment made in year t+1 we use:

$$I_{t+1} = NOPAT_{t+1} * g / ROCE_i$$

which is essentially the same formula that we used to calculate free cash flow in the DCF model but spun round to calculate retentions.

We then calculate the value added by this one year's investment by calculating the investment spread that it achieves, and valuing it as a flat perpetuity:

$$PV_{i,\,t+1} = I_{t+1} * (ROCE_i - WACC) / WACC$$

where $PV_{i,t+1}$ is the present value of an infinite flat stream of economic profit derived by multiplying the net investment made in year t+1 by the investment spread that it generates.

But we shall invest more in year t+2, and more again in year t+3, with a constant growth rate of g, so we can now derive the value of the whole investment programme to infinity as:

$$PV_t = NOPAT_{t+1} * g / ROCE_i * (ROCE_i - WACC) / [WACC * (WACC - g)]$$

even those readers that have understandably shunned the Mathematical Appendix will need to grasp this unpleasant looking formula if they are to use economic profit models. A formal derivation is, as ever, in the Mathematical Appendix. Intuitively, the first part of it calculates the investment that will be made in year t+1, as a function of growth and incremental return. The second part converts this into a stream of economic profit by multiplying by an investment spread. And the third part contains two capitalisations. The first capitalised the stream represented by the t+1 year investment. The second applies the Gordon Growth model to it to calculate the present value of an infinite stream, with each year's investment being bigger by (1+g). Do not forget that, as ever, this is a value at the end of our forecast period, and will need to be brought back to a current value:

$$PV_0 = PV_t / (1 + WACC)^t$$

before we go ahead and enter these two components of the terminal value into our model, let us just linger a moment on what the PV_t formula above is telling us. It is giving us the present value of a stream of investments that will be made to infinity, starting in one year's time, by capitalising the value that each annual investment will create. This has an application that goes well beyond the construction of economic profit models.

> The economic profit terminal value formula is applicable to all sectors of industry in which it is practical to value the existing assets of the company and separately to put a value on the future investment stream. This allows operating assets to be valued without reference to consolidated accounts, if the assets (franchises, properties, oil fields, drug patents) can be valued directly, and then an additional component of value be put on the firm's incremental investment opportunities.

So we now have two components to our economic profit terminal value.

The first represents the present value of a flat stream of economic profit generated by the assets as at the end of the forecasting period, valued as a flat perpetuity, and then brought back to year zero.

The second represents the value that will be added by incremental net investments made after the forecasting period, derived from the same retention formula that we used in the DCF model. The value added by the first year's investment is then calculated and extrapolated as a constant growth series of additions to value. We are not valuing an annual cash flow here. We are valuing an annual accrual of additional value to the company.

So, does it give us the same answer as the DCF? Exhibit 5.2 illustrates the complete economic profit valuation of Magna, with the same balance sheet adjustments that we used for the DCF valuation. And, yes, it gives us the same answer.

What is very different about this analysis is its attribution of that value, which is sliced four ways: the current balance sheet, the economic profit that is expected to be generated over the next five years, the economic profit that would be generated after five years if no additional investments were undertaken, and the value that we are putting on the investment programme after the forecast period.

In our discussion of the DCF valuation, we did not concentrate on the assumptions made to derive the terminal value, so let us do so here, as we are now in possession of far more insight into what they mean. The growth figure is generally uncontentious. If a company grows faster than nominal GDP for ever then it will end up taking over the world, which has yet to happen. In reality, mature companies grow less fast than nominal GDP, so the growth rate used in terminal values should be around 3-4% as a maximum.

What about the return on incremental investment? In theory, this should drop into line with the cost of capital with the result that economic profit erodes away and there is no need to put a value on incremental investments. In practice, as we shall discuss later, balance sheets for many companies do not fully reflect the investments made to establish the brand, develop the drug, and so on. We then have two choices: we can rebuild the balance sheet as if large amounts of operating cost had been capitalised, or we can just accept that it is unrealistic to assume that incremental returns, as shown in the published accounts, will not be higher than the WACC. In the latter case we are explicitly assuming a positive investment spread to correct for the inadequacy of published accounts to meet our requirements.

This is why it is common for valuations to assume that incremental returns will be lower than that achieved at the end of the forecast period, but higher than the WACC. One of the advantages of the economic profit approach is that it makes explicit in the print-out of the valuation how much value is dependent on this assumption.

3.6 Sensitivities

What we have discounted is cash flows and economic profits derived from a base case assumption. True, we have used a discount rate that has some risk premium built into it, but so long as we remain within the CAPM framework this merely reflects market risk, and ignores specific risk. What this means is that the onus is on the modeller, when a base case has been generated, to put high and low cases round it, typically by flexing the assumptions for growth rates, margins and capital requirements during the forecast period, and for growth and return on incremental capital after the forecast period. Experimenting with this will quickly establish where the really important assumptions lie, and also how sensitive the resulting valuation is to each of the individual variables. It will also establish the extent to which valuations are skewed, as upward or downward changes in assumed margins, for example, will probably not have symmetrical effects on the derived valuation.

If it is possible to ascribe probabilities to the different input assumptions, then the resulting values can be probability weighted, to produce a possibly more meaningful number than the base case value. Pushing this analysis to its logical conclusion results in so-called Monte-Carlo analysis, which requires as input probability distributions for the drivers to value, and which produces a probability distribution of resulting values for the asset or company.

4. Frequent problems

This completes our discussion of basic DCF and economic profit valuation, and we repeat our warning from the end of the section related to forecasting. Although we shall devote some time to discussion of issues in which the basic approach does not work well, we shall not again reproduce an entire model and both valuations with full explanations of how they were derived. So be sure that you are comfortable with what we have done before moving on through this book.

We began this chapter by saying that in addition to explaining a basic model, we would also move on to discussion of some commonly encountered problems. The first of these, the accounting issues discussed in chapter four, pepper the book. The explicitly modelling issues that remain are four:

1. Varying balance sheets

2. Cyclical companies

3. 'Asset light' companies

4. Growth companies

They all require very different treatment, and we address them one by one below.

4.1 Changing balance sheet structures

It is not unusual to find yourself analysing a company in which the balance sheet structure is projected to change quite dramatically. This may arise because the company has been forecasted without any specific projections for share issues or buy-backs, or because it is clear that the company can and should change its balance sheet structure. In the first case, it is probably sensible to address the problem by building share issues or buy-backs into the model, so that the balance sheet structure remains stable. On this basis, it is not unreasonable to use a single discount rate throughout the forecasts, as we did for Magna above.

But there are other cases where this will not do. Suppose that you are modelling a biotechnology company, which is currently financed entirely with equity, not least because it has unpredictable cash flows and few separable assets. The company may fail, but if it succeeds, then it will probably become, as it matures, a large, stable, cash generative entity, which can support a reasonable amount of debt, and should do so to benefit from the resulting tax shelter. In this case it is absolutely unacceptable to use a single discount rate through time. In addition, as we discussed in chapter two, there is also a real question as to whether its cost of capital should not be reduced on the grounds of liquidity and general stability, whether or not this is in accordance with the principles of the CAPM. Before we turn to growth companies, which we shall address below, there is a simpler case in which varying discount rates are required. This is where the company is already mature and stable. Nothing is going to happen to the riskiness of the existing business. But the company may have indicated that it was its intention to substitute debt for equity simply in an attempt to reduce its cost of capital.

As we saw in chapter two, increasing the proportion of debt in a balance sheet does two things. It increases the size of the tax shelter, and it increases the risk to both the debt and the equity. There is dispute about both the appropriate treatment of the tax shelter and the treatment of the risk premium on the debt. We shall take the simplest (and, we believe, probably the best, approach) here. We shall discount the tax shelter at the unleveraged cost of equity, and we shall assume that 100% of the risk premium on debt is default risk, and that debt has a zero beta. We explored the implications of these conclusions in chapter two and will merely assume them here.

Whatever the stand that we take on theoretical questions, there is also a practical issue as to which of the two methodologies to adopt: Adjusted Present Value (APV), which we discussed in chapter two, or Time-Varying WACC (TVW). The former works by valuing the assets and the tax shelter as separate components. The latter works by iterating a different annual solution for WACC each year. We shall use TVW as our methodology for this exercise, for two reasons. The first is that whereas APV is intuitively easy to understand, TVW requires some explanation if it is to be replicated. The second is that TVW is in many ways more flexible, because it is possible to build default risk into the cost of debt. As we saw in chapter two, APV cannot handle default risk, which has to be derived by running a WACC calculation to derive a value that can be compared with an APV, with the difference attributable to default risk.

We shall continue to use Magna as our example. It is a perfectly reasonable candidate for a share buy-back, and using it will have the additional benefit that we can illustrate to readers the mechanism modelled on the equity tab, and the impact of the buy-back on a valuation that has already been established using a constant discount rate.

Before we do this exercise, look again at Magna's ratios of debt to capital in the model reproduced above. Debt is falling steadily. In the event that this really happened, the company's cost of capital would rise steadily, making our valuation above over-optimistic. So there are two possibilities: either that the forecast above is right, and that the valuation above is too high, or that the company will maintain a more leveraged balance sheet, perhaps through buy-backs, in which case the valuation above could be more or less correct. Let us test these hypotheses.

In exhibit 5.3, we reproduce the three main financial statements, the equity tab, and two new valuation tabs for Magna (pages 13 and 14). It is the same model, with a €1bn share buy-back built into it in year 4, and a somewhat different valuation routine to cope with TVW. The other parts of the model are not reproduced since all the operating figures are assumed to be the same as in exhibit 5.1 above.

Exhibit 5.3: Magna valuation with buy-back

3. Magna profit and loss account (Euro million)

Year	-1	0	1	2	3	4	5
Net sales	51,526	53,595	54,900	56,378	58,060	59,990	62,221
Cost of sales	(40,126)	(41,687)	(42,431)	(43,556)	(44,866)	(46,403)	(48,217)
Gross profit	11,400	11,908	12,469	12,822	13,194	13,586	14,004
Gross profit margin	22.1%	22.2%	22.7%	22.7%	22.7%	22.6%	22.5%
Other operating income	1,532	1,461	1,476	1,490	1,505	1,520	1,536
Selling expenses	(10,377)	(10,636)	(10,901)	(11,174)	(11,452)	(11,738)	(12,031)
General administration expenses	(1,013)	(1,031)	(1,049)	(1,068)	(1,087)	(1,106)	(1,126)
Other operating expenses	(115)	(112)	(109)	(106)	(103)	(101)	(98)
EBITA	1,427	1,590	1,885	1,965	2,056	2,161	2,285
Amortisation of intangible assets	(261)	(272)	(272)	(272)	(272)	(272)	(272)
EBIT	1,166	1,318	1,613	1,693	1,784	1,889	2,013
Investment income	38	(60)	(11)	(11)	(11)	(11)	(11)
Net interest	(378)	(425)	(477)	(434)	(395)	(412)	(429)
Other financial items	4	(16)	(6)	(6)	(6)	(6)	(6)
Net financial items	(336)	(501)	(494)	(451)	(412)	(429)	(446)
Earnings before tax	830	817	1,119	1,241	1,372	1,461	1,567
Income tax	(328)	(246)	(392)	(435)	(480)	(511)	(548)
Tax/Earnings before tax	39.5%	30.1%	35.0%	35.0%	35.0%	35.0%	35.0%
Group net income	502	571	728	807	892	949	1,019
Non-controlling interests	(59)	(75)	(96)	(106)	(117)	(125)	(134)
NCI/group net income	11.8%	13.1%	13.1%	13.1%	13.1%	13.1%	13.1%
Attributable net income	443	496	632	701	775	825	885
Dividend distribution	(334)	(334)	(425)	(471)	(521)	(531)	(595)
Retained earnings	109	162	207	230	254	294	290
Common stock							
Weighted average shares (m)	324.1	324.1	324.1	324.1	324.1	310.5	296.9
Year end shares (m)	324.1	324.1	324.1	324.1	324.1	296.9	296.9
Preferred stock							
Weighted average shares (m)	2.7	2.7	2.7	2.7	2.7	2.7	2.7
Year end shares (m)	2.7	2.7	2.7	2.7	2.7	2.7	2.7
Shares outstanding							
Weighted average shares (m)	326.8	326.8	326.8	326.8	326.8	313.2	299.6
Year end shares (m)	326.8	326.8	326.8	326.8	326.8	299.6	299.6
Earnings per share (Euro)	1.36	1.52	1.93	2.15	2.37	2.63	2.95
Common stock dividend (Euro)	1.02	1.02	1.30	1.44	1.59	1.77	1.98
Preferred stock dividend (Euro)	1.12	1.12	1.43	1.59	1.75	1.95	2.18
Payout ratio (common stock)	75.2%	67.2%	67.2%	67.2%	67.2%	67.2%	67.2%
Preferred dividend/common dividend	110.0%	110.0%	110.0%	110.0%	110.0%	110.0%	110.0%

4. Magna balance sheet (Euro million)

Year	-1	0	1	2	3	4	5
Fixed assets							
Intagible assets	4,070	3,987	3,715	3,443	3,171	2,899	2,627
Goodwill	188	326	326	326	326	326	326
Tangible assets	7,201	10,490	10,741	11,062	11,447	11,891	12,389
Financial assets	229	238	238	238	238	238	238
Total fixed assets	**11,688**	**15,041**	**15,020**	**15,069**	**15,182**	**15,354**	**15,580**
Current assets							
Inventories	5,506	5,941	6,047	6,207	6,394	6,613	6,872
Trade receivables	369	339	347	357	367	379	394
Other receivables and other assets	2,857	2,061	2,111	2,168	2,233	2,307	2,393
Cash and cash equivalents	1,323	1,593	2,071	2,503	2,932	2,336	2,778
Total current assets	**10,055**	**9,934**	**10,576**	**11,235**	**11,926**	**11,635**	**12,436**
Deferred tax assets	1,084	1,456	1,456	1,456	1,456	1,456	1,456
Prepaid expenses and deferred charges	96	149	149	149	149	149	149
Total assets	**22,923**	**26,580**	**27,201**	**27,909**	**28,713**	**28,594**	**29,621**
Equity							
Capital stock	835	835	835	835	835	835	835
Additional paid-in capital	2,558	2,551	2,551	2,551	2,551	2,551	2,551
Reserves retained from earnings	305	279	441	648	878	1,132	1,426
Group net profit	443	496	632	701	775	825	885
Treasury stock	0	0	0	0	0	(1,000)	(1,000)
Total equity	**4,141**	**4,161**	**4,459**	**4,735**	**5,039**	**4,342**	**4,696**
Non-controlling interests	105	188	259	333	415	500	594
Provisions							
Pensions and similar commitments	960	1,012	1,132	1,259	1,396	1,542	1,699
Other provisions	725	758	758	758	758	758	758
Total provisions	**1,685**	**1,770**	**1,890**	**2,017**	**2,154**	**2,300**	**2,457**
Other liabilities							
Financial debts	5,587	7,802	7,802	7,802	7,802	7,802	7,802
Trade payables	9,119	9,907	10,084	10,351	10,663	11,028	11,459
Other liabilities	1,965	2,097	2,148	2,206	2,272	2,347	2,435
Total other liabilities	**16,671**	**19,806**	**20,034**	**20,359**	**20,736**	**21,177**	**21,695**
Deferred tax liabilities	196	526	431	336	240	145	50
Deferred income	125	129	129	129	129	129	129
Total equity and liabilities	**22,923**	**26,580**	**27,201**	**27,909**	**28,713**	**28,594**	**29,621**
Check	0.000	0.000	0.000	0.000	0.000	0.000	0.000
Net debt	4,264	6,209	5,731	5,299	4,870	5,466	5,024
Operating capital (including goodwill)	9,107	11,140	11,055	11,006	11,003	11,040	11,107
Operating capital (excluding goodwill)	8,919	10,814	10,729	10,680	10,677	10,714	10,781

5. Magna cash flow (Euro million)

Year	0	1	2	3	4	5
EBIT		1,613	1,693	1,784	1,889	2,013
Depreciation and amortisation		1,521	1,551	1,587	1,628	1,674
Changes in pension provisions		60	61	63	64	66
Changes in other provisions		0	0	0	0	0
Changes in net working capital		63	99	115	135	160
Income taxes charged		(392)	(435)	(480)	(511)	(548)
Changes in deferred tax assets and liabilities		(95)	(95)	(95)	(95)	(95)
Changes in prepayments and deferred income		0	0	0	0	0
Cash flow from operating activities		**2,770**	**2,874**	**2,973**	**3,110**	**3,268**
Capital expenditure		(1,500)	(1,600)	(1,700)	(1,800)	(1,900)
Cash flow from investing activities		**(1,500)**	**(1,600)**	**(1,700)**	**(1,800)**	**(1,900)**
Dividends to Magna shareholders		(334)	(425)	(471)	(521)	(531)
Dividends to NCI shareholders		(25)	(32)	(35)	(39)	(40)
Equity issued		0	0	0	0	0
Equity bought back		0	0	0	(1,000)	0
Change in debt		0	0	0	0	0
Net interest paid		(417)	(368)	(321)	(330)	(338)
Investment income		(11)	(11)	(11)	(11)	(11)
Other financial items		(6)	(6)	(6)	(6)	(6)
Cash flow from financing activities		**(792)**	**(841)**	**(845)**	**(1,907)**	**(926)**
Opening cash	1323	1,593	2,071	2,503	2,932	2,336
Change in cash	270	478	433	429	(597)	443
Closing cash	**1593**	**2,071**	**2,503**	**2,932**	**2,336**	**2,778**
Average cash	1,458	1,832	2,287	2,718	2,634	2,557
Interest received	158	199	248	295	285	277
Interest rate on cash	*10.8%*	*10.8%*	*10.8%*	*10.8%*	*10.8%*	*10.8%*

8. Magna equity (Euro million)

Year	0	1	2	3	4	5
Share price (Euro)	36.76					
Par value (Euro)	2.56					
Equity issued		0	0	0	0	0
Equity bought back		0	0	0	(1,000)	0
Shares issued		0	0	0	0	0
Shares bought back		0	0	0	(27)	0

13. Magna unleveraged cost of equity

Risk free rate	*4.02%*
Equity risk premium	*4.00%*
Beta	0.83
Cost of equity	*7.34%*
Share price	36.76
Shares issued (m)	324
Market capitalisation	11,914	65.7%
Net debt (book)	6,209	34.3%
Enterprise value	18,123	100.0%
Market debt/equity	*52.1%*
Deleveraged Beta	0.55
Deleveraged cost of equity	*6.20%*

14. Magna time varying WACC valuation (Euro million)

Year	1	2	3	4	5	Terminus
WACC	*6.05%*					
Incremental ROCE	*9.0%*					
Long term growth	*2.0%*					
NOPAT	953	1,005	1,064	1,133	1,213	1,237
Free cash flow	1,038	1,055	1,067	1,096	1,147	962
Opening capital employed	11,140	11,055	11,006	11,003	11,040	11,107
Opening net debt	6,209	5,731	5,299	4,870	5,466	5,024
PV of future cash flows	**21,944**	**22,241**	**22,541**	**22,850**	**23,150**	**23,415**
Return on opening capital employed	*8.6%*	*9.1%*	*9.7%*	*10.3%*	*11.0%*	*9.0%*
Time varying cost of capital	*6.08%*	*6.09%*	*6.10%*	*6.11%*	*6.10%*	*6.11%*
Investment spread	*2.5%*	*3.0%*	*3.6%*	*4.2%*	*4.9%*	*2.9%*
Economic profit	**276**	**332**	**393**	**461**	**540**	**559**
PV of future economic profit	10,804	11,186	11,535	11,846	12,109	12,309

DCF valuation

= Enterprise value	**21,944**
+ Financial assets	238
- Non-controlling interests	(188)
- Pension provisions	(1,012)
- Net debt	(6,209)
= Equity value	**14,773**
Value per share	45.21

Economic profit valuation

+ Opening balance sheet (excl. financial assets)	11,140	50.8%
+ PV economic profit	10,804	49.2%
= Enterprise value	**21,944**	**100.0%**
+ Financial assets	238	
- Non-controlling interests	(188)	
- Pension provisions	(1,012)	
- Net debt	(6,209)	
= Equity value	**14,773**	
Value per share	45.21	

Starting with the equity page, we have assumed that the company buys back 27m shares at €36.76 a share, with a total cost of €1bn. This is a relatively large buy-back, but still leaves the company with adequate shareholders funds to maintain its dividend policy. If you turn to the balance sheet you will see the impact of the buy-back on the equity of the company. In the profit and loss account, the impact of lower interest receipts, fewer shares and higher earnings per share are all visible.

To construct a TVW model, we need two additions to the methodology used in the last section. Firstly, we need to deleverage the company's Beta, so that it can be releveraged each year to reflect different market gearing. Secondly, we need to rearrange the valuation model so that it applies each annual discount rate successively to the stream of cash flow or profits. Let us start with the discount rate. The deleverage page of the model contains some of the information previously provided on the discount rate page (we have excluded the debt calculations as they remain unchanged), but shows the figures used to deleverage Magna's Beta and to derive a deleveraged cost of equity. This cost of equity will be releveraged each year as part of an annual WACC calculation.

On the valuation page, there are two important differences between the calculations as done here, and as done above. As with the discount rate, some of the information on the previous calculation has been left out, so that we can concentrate on the new elements.

First, rather than each item of cash flow or economic profit being discounted once if it occurs in year 1, twice if it occurs in year 2, and so on, here we have to work backwards from the end. So the terminal value is discounted at its own discount rate. Then, it and the cash flow or economic profit for year 5 are both discounted back for one year at the discount rate for year 5. In year 4, the start year 5 value and year 4 cash flow or economic profit is discounted at the unique rate for year 4, and so on back to year 1. The effect of this is that an item that relates to the terminal value is discounted at six different rates as it migrates back to start year 1.

This would be a pointless restatement of what happens in a normal model (you can restate any model to work this way) unless it were coupled with an individual reworking of the discount rate each year. The insight here, explained in chapter two, is that there is only one combination of value for equity, ratio of market values of debt to equity, and discount rate, that leaves them all compatible with one another. So each year gets its own discount rate, and changing the level of projected debt by repurchasing shares alters the rate for that year and for subsequent years. In terms of the model reproduced above, the net debt number is that forecast in the company's projected accounts, but the enterprise value is a function of the TVW, and the TVW is a function of the enterprise value.

We should note that the leveraging and deleveraging uses the formula that assumes that the tax shelter is discounted at the unleveraged cost of equity, so that:

$$B_L = B_A * (1+D/E)$$

(See chapter two for discussion and definitions.)

We have not altered the assumed cost of debt to the company, partly for the sake of transparency and partly because the impact of the buy-back on Magna's coverage and gearing ratios is not huge. In fact, as we shall discuss in a moment, the buy-back merely stabilises a balance sheet that was otherwise becoming less efficient.

Looking at the results, it may at first be surprising that the value derived is lower than that in the simple single discount rate model. But look at the annual WACCs. They are actually rising, as the company's market leverage is falling, despite the buy-back. For comparison, we reproduce below this valuation page for the company based on the assumption (used in exhibit 5.1) that it does not buy back shares. The discount rate rises faster and the derived value is lower again.

Exhibit 5.3 continued

14. Magna time varying WACC valuation (Euro million)

Year	1	2	3	4	5	Terminus
WACC	6.05%					
Incremental ROCE	9.0%					
Long term growth	2.0%					
NOPAT	953	1,005	1,064	1,133	1,213	1,237
Free cash flow	1,038	1,055	1,067	1,096	1,147	962
Opening capital employed	11,140	11,055	11,006	11,003	11,040	11,107
Opening net debt	6,209	5,731	5,299	4,870	4,430	3,962
PV of future cash flows	21,860	22,152	22,446	22,749	23,043	23,306
Return on opening capital employed	8.6%	9.1%	9.7%	10.3%	11.0%	9.0%
Time varying cost of capital	6.08%	6.09%	6.10%	6.11%	6.12%	6.13%
Investment spread	2.5%	3.0%	3.6%	4.2%	4.9%	2.9%
Economic profit	276	332	393	461	537	557
PV of future economic profit	10,720	11,096	11,440	11,745	12,002	12,199

DCF valuation

= Enterprise value	21,860
+ Financial assets	238
- Non-controlling interests	(188)
- Pension provisions	(1,012)
- Net debt	(6,209)
= Equity value	14,689
Value per share	44.95

Economic profit valuation

+ Opening balance sheet (excl. financial assets)	11,140	51.0%
+ PV economic profit	10,720	49.0%
= Enterprise value	21,860	100.0%
+ Financial assets	238	
- Non-controlling interests	(188)	
- Pension provisions	(1,012)	
- Net debt	(6,209)	
= Equity value	14,689	
Value per share	44.95	

This tells us several things about balance sheet structures and capital efficiency, as well as about valuation modelling.

1. The first is that the impact of share buy-backs of a practicable size (we cannot buy back all our equity!) on value is generally fairly small. Getting the operations right matters much more than getting the balance sheet right.

2. The second is that balance sheets that 'drop out' of forecasts without active financial management being assumed often drift in the direction of piling up surplus cash. In this case, assuming a flat discount rate is wrong: it would rise unless something is done about it.

3. There are generally limits to the extent of a company's practical ability to leverage up. Most buy-backs are exercises in returning surplus cash to avoid balance sheet deterioration, not fundamental transformations of the financial structure of the company.

It is notable, incidentally, that the last valuation, with TVW and no buyback brings us much closer to the actual share price of the company at the time of writing (€36.76) than the assumption of a flat discount rate.

4.2 Cyclical companies

The problems associated with cyclical companies are not that they require a different type of model from the one we applied to Magna, but that it is much harder to work out what to put into it. What is generally required is not more sophisticated modelling but a more sophisticated understanding of history. The reason is that across the cycle, their profitability tends to vary dramatically, and we need to be sure that our forecasts get us back to a 'mid-cycle' set of figures, at least before we arrive at the terminus.

Remember that cyclical companies will tend to be high-Beta. This means that they will have a high calculated cost of capital. We do not, therefore, need to build the risks from cyclicality into our forecasts. They are already built into our discount rate. This is why, in practice, five-year forecast periods are common for mature companies. If they are mature, but cyclical, it is long enough to make it plausible that we have moved from the current state of boom or bust back to a normal year. The issues then becomes what a normal year actually looks like, and clearly this requires an interpretation of history.

There is clearly a trade-off involved in the length of time period that one uses for analysing the history. A decade is necessary to pick up a sense of full cycles, and it could be argued that longer would be better. As against that, over ten years a company will probably change its business mix. There may be secular changes in the margin structure and capital requirements. And inflation, interest and returns may all rise or fall. So it is important not merely to look at averages but also at the slope of trend lines, and we shall do both in the analysis below.

Rather than build a model of a cyclical company, which would look exactly like Magna but with more volatile inputs, we are instead going to analyse historical accounts for a cyclical Swedish engineering company, which we shall name the Swordfish Group, over a 15-year period. We begin, in exhibit 5.4, with its history of return on capital employed.

Exhibit 5.4: Swordfish ROCE

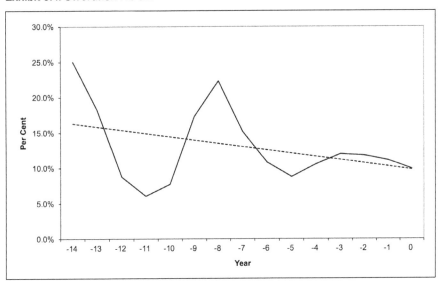

The recession of years -5 and -11 are clearly visible, as is the boom at the start of the historical period and of year -8. There is a further trend, it would appear, towards lower volatility and to lower overall returns on capital employed. These are in part attributable to business mix, and in part to changes in the local economy related to convergence to rates of inflation and growth of other European Union economies.

Return on capital is a result, not a driver. The drivers are sales growth, operating margins and capital turns, which can be split between working capital requirements and fixed asset requirements. It therefore makes sense, when forecasting these items, to look at their histories in turn.

Exhibit 5.5 shows the history for annual sales growth for the Swordfish Group as a whole. Clearly, a more detailed approach would be to model the separate businesses independently, but even the consolidated figures tell a story.

Exhibit 5.5: Swordfish sales growth

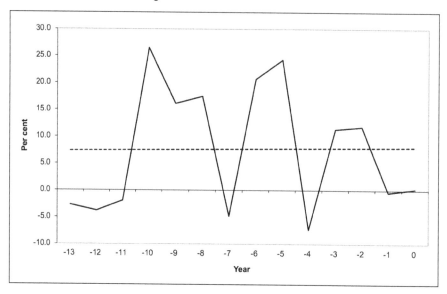

Movements in sales growth have to be interpreted carefully. In addition to economic cycles, consolidated sales for an international business will also reflect movements in currencies, and may also be affected by acquisitions and disposals. A more detailed analysis would clearly permit these items to be separated out from one another. Here, we merely note that the recessions of the first two years and the last two years are clearly visible, but with a rather more volatile pattern in between than would be explained merely by the economic cycle. The underlying trend in growth in sales is very stable, which should permit a reasonable sense of long-term growth rates.

Turning to margins, these can of course be split between gross trading margins and the impact of fixed costs. Exhibit 5.6 below merely concentrates on the consolidated operating margin over the period.

Exhibit 5.6: Swordfish EBIT margin

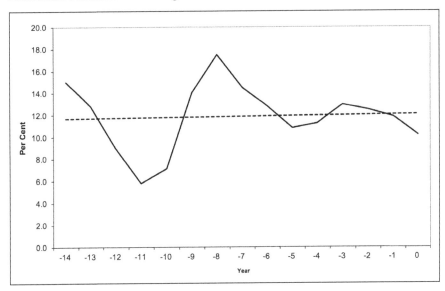

Less distorted by acquisitions, disposals and currency, this very much follows a cyclical pattern that we might expect, with a boom at the start, followed by a severe recession, some falling away from year –3, and a very bad year to end the series. It also shows that the underlying trend in operating margin is almost completely stable, which should again make it reasonable to use this as a basis for extrapolation.

Remember that it is not only sales and margins that are cyclical. There tends to be a build-up of inventory as companies enter recession, and a working off of the surplus as they move out of it again. This basic cycle can be broken by price discounting, changes in credit terms to customers, and other business responses, or even changes in revenue recognition (see chapter four) so a perfect correlation with economic activity is unlikely. And, again, there is a question of trend. Exhibit 5.7 shows inventory days for Swordfish, expressing inventory in terms of cost of goods sold.

Exhibit 5.7: Swordfish inventory days

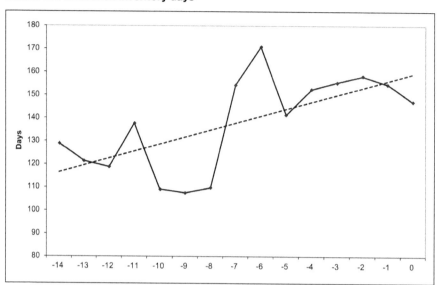

The most notable factors in this chart are the lack of a simple correlation with economic cycles, though inventory days were low during years −10 to −8, and inflected dramatically in year −7, and, even more strikingly, the surprisingly upward-sloping line, implying that the underlying inventory requirements of the business increased quite considerably over the 15-year period. This is an area in which anyone trying to model the company would clearly have to do some work to identify whether the trend is likely to be maintained, or even what the best reasonable assumption about the underlying mid-cycle level of inventory days actually is.

Fixed assets can be thought of, as we have seen, in terms of fixed asset turn: the amount of sales generated for a unit of fixed assets. Trends through time may also be usefully presented in terms of the ratio of capital expenditure to depreciation. Clearly, for any growing company this ratio should average at more than one. Exhibit 5.8 shows the history for Swordfish.

Exhibit 5.8: Sandvik capex/depreciation

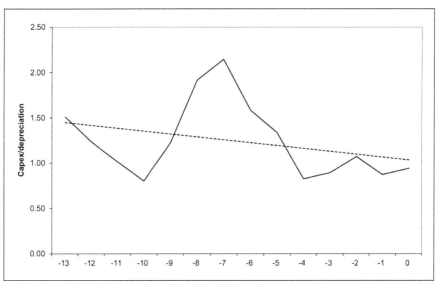

In this case the cycle matches our expectation reasonably well. Capital expenditure was slashed during the early years of the history, and only began to rise in a lagged response to demand several years later. It fell away after the recession of year −5, and remained rather low thereafter.

But the trend is again interesting. The ratio has fallen from about 1.5 at the start of the period. It was below 1.0 in year −1. Of course the former year reflected the high demand of a boom period, after which it was cut, and the latter reflects the poor environment of a period of lower growth. But still, the figures would deserve investigation.

To conclude, the drivers to a cyclical company are the same as those to Magna, but are likely to oscillate more wildly. We build the forecasts in the same way as we built Magna's, but the inputs for growth, margin and capital requirements need rather more careful thought, and an analysis of historical trends.

In the case of Swordfish, historical analysis might leave us fairly happy with our sense of underlying growth and of mid-cycle margins, but might leave us less happy with what we expect regarding capital requirements, and with whether or not the capital expenditures that we are seeing are consistent with the trend growth rate that we might expect. Whatever the outcome regarding working capital it is probably safe to conclude that either growth is going to slow considerably or capital expenditures will have to rise considerably.

4.3 'Asset light' companies

Companies that have small balance sheets and that appear to earn exceptionally high returns on equity and on capital are often referred to as being 'asset light'. This is in many ways a deeply misleading description, as it implies that they do indeed have very few assets and that they are extraordinarily profitable, neither of which are generally true of the larger ones. As with all companies, as they become large and mature, their economic returns drop towards their cost of capital.

So how do we reconcile the paradox? Companies such as Unilever, Novartis or Colgate Palmolive all look very profitable and look as if they do not employ very many assets, yet we are arguing that this cannot be true. It is not. The explanation is that for all of these companies their main assets are not capitalised, but this does not mean that they did not invest large sums to acquire them, or that the returns that they are making on these investments are particularly high.

The point is that, despite a shift towards valuing assets and liabilities at more realistic levels on balance sheets, it will still remain true for the foreseeable future that most of the intangible assets represented by brands, drug patents, television franchises, and other intangibles will only be recognised on balance sheets at fair value if they are acquired. The cost of building them, mainly R&D and marketing costs, has historically been almost all charged to the profit and loss account, and will continue to be except to the extent of development costs.

This is awkward for valuation, because as we have seen it is only practical to value companies, whatever the methodology used, if a sensible economic value can be put on their balance sheet assets and liabilities so that some reasonable measure can be made of what their returns on capital really are. Fortunately, many companies provide enough information about their costs incurred for it to be possible to derive a sensible guess as to what they have really invested to achieve their current position, and to estimate the return that they are really earning on it.

Before progressing to an example, let us consider one common objection to this line of argument. It runs as follows. Most of the money spent on R&D or marketing is wasted, therefore it should all be written off as it is imprudent to do anything else. This confuses two points. Firstly, it is true that most of the money spent on these activities is unsuccessful. Secondly, the successful bit has to carry the rest. It is no good a company saying that it spent €100m on R&D, and that it has made a great return on the €10m that it capitalised. It has to make an acceptable return on the lot.

So, having dismissed the objection, let us return to the more practical question of how we arrive at a fair measure of both the capital and the return on capital of 'asset light' companies.

We are going to use as an example the French company, under the name of Dandy, whose main businesses are the manufacture of yoghurts, mineral water and biscuits. Before we dive into its figures, we need to establish one point. In addition to its capitalised and uncapitalised intangible assets, Dandy also has a substantial amount of goodwill on its balance sheet. Goodwill is a very different type of intangible asset from a brand or a drug patent. In fact, one of the reasons that the goodwill paid in 'asset light' industries is so high is precisely that most of the assets are not on the balance sheet. If they were, the premium paid over the fair value of the net assets of the target company would be a fair reflection of the present value of its growth prospects, and would be a lot lower. We shall discuss goodwill at length in chapter seven, and will therefore defer further discussion of it here. Suffice it to say that here we shall strip the goodwill out of Danone's balance sheet and ignore it, as if the company had grown organically.

Exhibit 5.9 comprises three pages. The first is a simplified extract of figures from Dandy's latest report and accounts. The second is a set of four very different calculations of the company's capital employed, NOPAT and ROCE. The third is an exercise in rebuilding the company's balance sheet and amortisation charges as if it had capitalised its historical marketing and R&D costs. We shall explain them in turn.

Exhibit 5.9: Dandy ROCE calculations

Dandy accounting items	Euro Million
NOPAT calculation	
EBIT	1,604
Amortisation charge	84
EBITA	1,688
Tax rate	*35%*
Tax on EBITA	(591)
NOPAT (EBIT-tax)	**1,013**
NOPAT before amortisation	**1,097**
Opening operating capital employed including goodwill	
Net property, plant and equipment	2,992
Brand names	1,259
Other intangible assets	234
Goodwill	2,734
Fixed assets excluding financial assets	**7,219**
Inventories	592
Trade accounts and notes receivable	820
Other accounts receivable and prepaid expenses	775
Short term loans	128
Current assets excluding cash and marketable investments	2,315
Trade accounts and notes payable	(1,516)
Accrued expenses and other current liabilities	(1,541)
Current liabilities excluding short term debt	(3,057)
Non-cash working capital	**(742)**
Opening operating capital employed including goodwill	**6,477**
Opening operating capital employed excluding goodwill	**3,743**

Dandy return on capital employed

	Euro Million
Calc one:	
NOPAT after amortisation	1,013
Opening capital employed including goodwill	6,477
ROCE (stated accounts)	*16%*
Calc two:	
NOPAT before amortisation	1,097
Opening capital employed including goodwill	6,477
ROCE (excluding amortisation)	*17%*
Calc three:	
NOPAT before amortisation	1,097
Opening capital employed excluding goodwill	3,743
ROCE (ex-goodwill returns)	*29%*
Calc four:	
NOPAT before amortisation	1,097
Addition of annual spend on intangibles	1,013
Amortisation of capitalised intangibles	(775)
Adjusted NOPAT	**1,336**
Opening capital employed excluding goodwill	3,743
Capitalised intangibles	5,044
Adjusted operating capital	**8,787**
ROCE (economic return)	*15%*

Dandy intangible assets (Euro Million)

Year	-9	-8	-7	-6	-5
Advertising costs	659	678	699	720	741
R&D costs	102	106	109	112	115
Capitalised costs	761	784	807	832	857
Gross capitalised costs	**761**	**1,545**	**2,352**	**3,184**	**4,041**
Amortisation charge	0	(76)	(154)	(235)	(318)
Net capitalised costs	**761**	**1,469**	**2,122**	**2,718**	**3,256**

	-4	-3	-2	-1	0
Advertising costs	764	786	810	845	883
R&D costs	119	122	126	133	130
Gross intangibles ex-goodwill	882	909	936	978	1,013
Gross capitalised costs	**4,923**	**5,832**	**6,768**	**7,746**	**8,759**
Amortisation charge	(404)	(492)	(583)	(677)	(775)
Net intangibles ex-goodwill	**3,735**	**4,151**	**4,504**	**4,805**	**5,044**

The page containing accounting items should be fairly self-explanatory. The obvious and dramatic point is that capital employed excluding goodwill is less than 60% of capital employed including goodwill. If we are going to take seriously our own view that goodwill is irrelevant to the underlying profitability of the operations, then this is going to make the operations look very profitable.

Now turn to the second page, with the four calculations of NOPAT, capital employed and profit. It is notable that the effect of amortising intangibles is not very material, the reason being that it is only other intangible assets, not the brands, that are being amortised. What is material is that if we cut goodwill out of the balance sheet, its value falls by over 40% and the return on capital correspondingly rises by about 75% to what looks like an unsustainable number. It is unsustainable. In fact, it has never been sustained. To understand why, we need to turn to the next page, on Dandy's intangible assets.

The third page above shows a simple set of accounting adjustments. We need to start by assuming an amortisation period for the costs that we are going to capitalise. We use 10 years. A longer period, which may be justifiable, would increase the impact. As we saw in our discussion of retirements of fixed assets earlier in this chapter, after 10 years any new asset will have been retired out of gross assets and will have been fully depreciated out of net assets, so if we capitalise the run from year −9 to year 0 we have everything that we need.

The latest form 20F for Dandy gives its expenses on marketing and R&D for the last three years −2 to 0. Prior to that we have simply assumed a trend growth of 3% annually, which is unlikely to be fatally wrong. Amortisation each year is set at 10% of opening gross costs and net intangibles grow with expenditure and fall with amortisation. The point of the series is merely to derive reasonable estimates for the final year. If we wanted reasonable estimates for previous years, we should have to go back further so that there was a 10-year run into the first figures that we wanted to use.

In the fourth calculation of Dandy's NOPAT, capital employed and return on capital employed in the second page above we have used the capitalisation schedule to make the following adjustments.

1. We have added back into its profit Dandy's year 0 spend on marketing and R&D as if it had been capitalised.

2. We have subtracted out of its profit Dandy's year 0 amortisation of intangibles as if they had been capitalised and amortised.

3. We have added the net historical intangibles back into Dandy's capital employed.

The result is striking. First, Dandy emerges as making a return on capital of 15%, slightly less than the apparent return, but about half of the apparent return on capital excluding goodwill. The addition to income almost compensates for a near doubling of the balance sheet size, versus the simple calculation in version two.

But if the measure of profitability is the same, the implications for valuation are definitely not. A return on capital of 15% is probably slightly less than twice Dandy's cost of capital. If we take the capital base to be the figure in calculation four, including the capitalised intangibles, then this would justify an enterprise value of about €18bn for Dandy. At time of writing its enterprise value was €21bn. This would imply a low value being placed on its reinvestment opportunities, and perhaps concern over possible erosion of the profitability of its existing ones. Both of these would be consistent with worries at the time about the sustainability of profits from consumer companies owing to pressure from hypermarkets.

If we did the same exercise for calculation three, we would conclude that the company was indeed worth a big premium over the value of its tangible assets, but no amount of manipulation of the numbers would get us to a value of €21bn. This would require a fairly high value to be put on the value expected to be added from incremental investments, at a time when most industry experts do not believe this to be likely. The food manufacturing industry is mature. It is difficult to see why companies in this sector should have a high proportion of their value attributed to future investments. The same applies to pharmaceutical companies, and other mature 'asset light' industries.

> Practical proof is hard in the world of investment. We shall rest our case on a simple point. For many 'asset light' companies, it is relatively easy to justify their valuations and their profitability if we capitalise intangible assets, and it is almost impossible to do either if we do not.

4.4 Growth companies

Whereas the key to understanding cyclical companies lies in their past performance, the opposite is the case for growth companies. They often have no past and rather little to go on in the present. They are usually highly risky, equity financed, and will look very different if and when they become mature. Meanwhile, any sensible valuation will recognise the fact that their existing investors, who are generally venture capitalists, will require a very high return on their successful investments to carry the unsuccessful ones. CAPM and Betas are strictly for the mature. In addition, they are often in industries that are 'asset light', so they combine most of the issues that we have already addressed, and some more of their own.

We shall take as our example a small UK-listed biotechnology company for which one of the authors provided some consultancy work and which we shall examine under the name, Skylark. The model is shown in exhibit 5.10 below.

Perhaps the best introduction would be to point out that end year 0 shareholders' equity comprised £6.7m of subscribed capital, £5.5m of accumulated losses and net shareholders' funds of £1.2m. The company had only begun to generate sales in year −2, and was hoping to break even for the first time in year 2. A further remove from the companies that we have looked at so far in this chapter, it would be hard to imagine.

The business of Skylark was to act as a sub-contractor to much larger companies, and its service comprised screening of products in a research and development pipeline. The assets of the company were almost entirely intellectual property, with no balance sheet value.

In year 1, the company was still very closely held, essentially by venture capitalists, whose evident ambition was that it should be grown rapidly, and who expected to achieve high returns on equity during the intervening period, to compensate them for illiquidity and high risk of failure.

In practical terms, the difficulty with modelling the company was lack of transparency to future sales growth. Most costs were fixed, related to employee costs. In addition, after a long period in which it had been unable to borrow or to afford any significant capital expenditure, both items were changing. The company planned to borrow to buy the freehold of its head office, and it was beginning to spend again, mainly on information technology.

In modelling terms, the challenges included the fact that the company was carrying forward substantial tax losses, and had been applying for cash tax credits, rather than rolling forward the tax losses. In addition, as with Dandy, the company was 'asset light', and while its long-term returns on capital (essentially R&D) was likely to be high (in the event of success) it still required capitalising of intangibles if it was to be even remotely realistic or useable.

We reproduce the full detail of a model and valuation of Skylark below as exhibit 5.10. It is not our intention to describe it line by line, as we did with Magna. This should not be necessary. Instead, we shall concentrate on the features of the model that are importantly different, and relate to its then status as a very small growth stock. We have retained the same conventions as with Magna. Inputs are boxed and percentages are italicised.

One difference is entirely cosmetic. In this model the equity is valued by adding the present value of forecast economic profit to shareholders' funds, rather than adding it to capital and then subtracting debt. The result is clearly identical.

Exhibit 5.10: Skylark model

1. Skylark profit and loss account (£)

Year	-2	-1	0	1	2	3	4	5
US sales growth					10.0%	10.0%	10.0%	10.0%
Average $/£ rate				1.30	1.30	1.30	1.30	1.30
UK sales growth		556.9%	62.6%	80.5%	110.0%	30.0%	20.0%	10.0%
Gross margin	95.9%	90.3%	76.3%	84.0%	84.0%	84.0%	84.0%	84.0%
R&D growth		833.4%	5.3%	0.0%	0.0%	0.0%	0.0%	0.0%
R&D/sales	80.4%	114.3%	74.0%	41.0%	19.5%	15.0%	12.5%	11.4%
Other admin growth		650.1%	-31.0%	15.0%	5.0%	5.0%	5.0%	5.0%
Other admin/sales	403.3%	460.6%	195.5%	124.6%	62.3%	50.3%	44.0%	42.0%
Statutory tax rate	20.0%	20.0%	20.0%	20.0%	20.0%	20.0%	20.0%	20.0%
Effective tax rate	0.0%	4.4%	9.2%	10.1%	0.0%	0.0%	0.0%	1.0%
US sales ($)				100	110	121	133	146
US sales				77	85	93	102	113
UK sales	98,614	647,770	1,052,953	1,900,000	3,990,000	5,187,000	6,224,400	6,846,840
Turnover	98,614	647,770	1,052,953	1,900,077	3,990,085	5,187,093	6,224,502	6,846,953
Cost of sales	(4,029)	(62,836)	(249,852)	(304,012)	(638,414)	(829,935)	(995,920)	(1,095,512)
Gross profit	94,585	584,934	803,101	1,596,065	3,351,671	4,357,158	5,228,582	5,751,440
Research and development	(79,290)	(740,104)	(779,366)	(779,366)	(779,366)	(779,366)	(779,366)	(779,366)
Other administrative expenses	(397,723)	(2,983,325)	(2,058,857)	(2,367,686)	(2,486,070)	(2,610,373)	(2,740,892)	(2,877,937)
Exceptional admin exp	0	(425,712)	0	0	0	0	0	0
Total admin exp	(477,013)	(4,149,141)	(2,838,223)	(3,147,052)	(3,265,436)	(3,389,739)	(3,520,258)	(3,657,303)
Operating profit/(loss)	(382,428)	(3,564,207)	(2,035,122)	(1,550,987)	86,235	967,419	1,708,324	2,094,138
Interest receivable	146	111,522	38,875	89,192	83,984	97,782	155,439	242,917
Interest payable	(4,470)	(57,842)	(53,154)	(28,251)	(56,000)	(56,000)	(56,000)	(56,000)
Pre-tax profit	(386,752)	(3,510,527)	(2,049,401)	(1,490,045)	114,219	1,009,201	1,807,763	2,281,055
Taxation charge	0	153,345	189,256	150,000	0	0	0	(22,650)
Net profit	(386,752)	(3,357,182)	(1,860,145)	(1,340,045)	114,219	1,009,201	1,807,763	2,258,405
Dividends	0	0	0	0	0	0	0	0
EPS (p)	(0.83)	(3.96)	(2.05)	(1.07)	0.09	0.81	1.45	1.81
DPS (p)	0.00	0.00	0.00	0.00	0.00	0.00	0.00	0.00
Payout ratio	0.0%	0.0%	0.0%	0.0%	0.0%	0.0%	0.0%	0.0%
Average shares	46,696,000	84,836,652	90,623,382	124,913,793	124,913,793	124,913,793	124,913,793	124,913,793
End period shares		90,413,793	94,913,793	124,913,793	124,913,793	124,913,793	124,913,793	124,913,793
Net profit	(386,752)	(3,357,182)	(1,860,145)	(1,340,045)	114,219	1,009,201	1,807,763	2,258,405
FX gains/(losses)		6,898	52,649	0	0	0	0	0
Total recognised gains/(losses)	(386,752)	(3,350,284)	(1,807,496)	(1,340,045)	114,219	1,009,201	1,807,763	2,258,405
Tax losses brought forward				3,758,944	5,098,989	4,984,771	3,975,570	2,167,807
Pre-tax profit/(loss) for year				(1,490,045)	114,219	1,009,201	1,807,763	2,281,055
Tax charge				150,000	0	0	0	(22,650)
Cash tax credit			189,256	150,000	0	0	0	0
Tax loss brought forward				5,098,989	4,984,771	3,975,570	2,167,807	0

2. Skylark balance sheet (£)

Year	-2	-1	0	1	2	3	4	5
Inventory days	1129	344	99	99	99	99	99	99
Debtor days	198	266	141	141	141	141	141	141
Trade creditor days	3666	2209	40	40	40	40	40	40
Other creditor/sales	105.8%	2.7%	1.4%	1.4%	1.4%	1.4%	1.4%	1.4%
Accruals/sales	91.4%	55.4%	29.0%	30.0%	30.0%	30.0%	30.0%	30.0%
Fixed assets (tangible)	326,889	1,099,591	661,557	1,300,611	1,580,906	1,373,619	1,148,816	907,165
Stocks	21,250	50,783	67,766	82,456	173,153	225,099	270,118	297,130
Debtors	91,089	403,949	407,837	696,695	1,395,467	2,009,101	2,410,917	2,652,009
Cash	0	2,263,176	491,230	2,229,812	1,969,363	2,919,736	4,852,218	7,293,639
Current assets	112,339	2,717,908	966,833	3,008,962	3,537,984	5,153,935	7,533,254	10,242,778
Total assets	439,228	3,817,499	1,628,390	4,309,573	5,118,890	6,527,555	8,682,070	11,149,943
Trade creditors	69,021	325,893	27,429	33,375	70,086	91,111	109,333	120,266
Other creditors	177,999	14,848	14,375	25,940	54,473	70,815	84,977	93,475
Tax and social security	65,858	44,067	49,601	57,041	59,893	62,888	66,032	69,334
Deferrals & accruals	153,780	307,545	305,386	570,023	1,197,025	1,556,128	1,867,351	2,054,086
Short term debt	76,298	271,866	8,360	0	0	0	0	0
Current liabilities	542,956	964,219	405,151	686,379	1,381,477	1,780,941	2,127,694	2,337,161
Long term debt	86,954	392,045	0	800,000	800,000	800,000	800,000	800,000
Deferred tax	0	0	0	0	0	0	0	0
Other provisions	0	200,000	0	0	0	0	0	0
Long term liabilities	86,954	592,045	0	800,000	800,000	800,000	800,000	800,000
Share capital	68,000	90,414	94,914	124,914	124,914	124,914	124,914	124,914
Share premium account	0	5,779,787	6,544,787	9,454,787	9,454,787	9,454,787	9,454,787	9,454,787
Merger reserve	128,070	128,070	128,070	128,070	128,070	128,070	128,070	128,070
Profit and loss account	(386,752)	(3,737,036)	(5,544,532)	(6,884,577)	(6,770,359)	(5,761,158)	(3,953,395)	(1,694,989)
Shareholders' equity	(190,682)	2,261,235	1,223,239	2,823,194	2,937,412	3,946,613	5,754,376	8,012,782
Liabilitites and equity	439,228	3,817,499	1,628,390	4,309,573	5,118,890	6,527,555	8,682,070	11,149,943
Check	0.000	0.000	0.000	0.000	0.000	0.000	0.000	0.000
Capital employed	(27,430)	861,970	740,369	1,393,382	1,768,049	1,826,877	1,702,158	1,519,142
Net debt/(cash)	163,252	(1,599,265)	(482,870)	(1,429,812)	(1,169,363)	(2,119,736)	(4,052,218)	(6,493,639)
Net debt/equity	(85.6)%	(70.7)%	(39.5)%	(50.6)%	(39.8)%	(53.7)%	(70.4)%	(81.0)%

3. Skylark cash flow (£)

Year	1	2	3	4	5
Operating profit/(loss)	(1,550,987)	86,235	967,419	1,708,324	2,094,138
Depreciation	210,946	219,705	307,287	324,803	341,652
(Gain)/loss on disposal	0	0	0	0	0
Change in inventory	(14,690)	(90,698)	(51,945)	(45,019)	(27,012)
Change in debtors	(288,858)	(698,772)	(613,634)	(401,817)	(241,092)
Change in trade creditors	5,946	36,711	21,025	18,222	10,933
Change in other creditors	11,565	28,533	16,342	14,163	8,498
Change in tax and social security payable	7,440	2,852	2,995	3,144	3,302
Change in deferrals and accruals	264,637	627,002	359,103	311,223	186,735
Deferred taxation	0	0	0	0	0
Other provisions	0	0	0	0	0
Exchange rate differences	0	0	0	0	0
Cash flow from operations	(1,354,000)	211,568	1,008,591	1,933,043	2,377,154
Interest received	89,192	83,984	97,782	155,439	242,917
Interest paid	(28,251)	(56,000)	(56,000)	(56,000)	(56,000)
Net interest	60,942	27,984	41,782	99,439	186,917
Tax paid	150,000	0	0	0	(22,650)
Capital expenditure	(50,000)	(500,000)	(100,000)	(100,000)	(100,000)
Acquisition of building	(800,000)	0	0	0	0
Disposals	0	0	0	0	0
Cash flow to/from investments	(850,000)	(500,000)	(100,000)	(100,000)	(100,000)
Cash flow before financing	(1,993,058)	(260,448)	950,373	1,932,482	2,441,421
Dividends	0	0	0	0	0
Issue/buyback of equity	2,940,000	0	0	0	0
Change in short term debt	(8,360)	0	0	0	0
Change in long term debt	800,000	0	0	0	0
Cash flow to/from financing	3,731,640	0	0	0	0
Opening cash	491,230	2,229,812	1,969,363	2,919,736	4,852,218
Change in cash	1,738,582	(260,448)	950,373	1,932,482	2,441,421
Closing cash	2,229,812	1,969,363	2,919,736	4,852,218	7,293,639

4. Skylark fixed assets (£)

Year	-1	0	1	2	3	4	5
Fixed asset life	0.9	5.7	5.7	5.7	5.7	5.7	5.7
Fixed asset turn	1.5	1.0	3.3	6.2	7.7	13.5	30.0
Opening gross fixed assets	359,017	1,540,180	1,204,280	1,254,280	1,754,280	1,854,280	1,950,468
Additions	1,180,192	3,812	50,000	500,000	100,000	100,000	100,000
Retirements	0	0	0	0	0	(3,812)	(50,000)
Disposals	(14,690)	(367,449)	0	0	0	0	0
FX impact	15,661	27,737	0	0	0	0	0
Closing gross fixed assets	1,540,180	1,204,280	1,254,280	1,754,280	1,854,280	1,950,468	2,000,468
Opening cumulative depreciation	32,128	440,589	542,723	753,669	973,374	1,280,661	1,601,652
Depreciation	413,664	269,784	210,946	219,705	307,287	324,803	341,652
Retirements	0	0	0	0	0	(3,812)	(50,000)
Disposals	(6,701)	(153,929)	0	0	0	0	0
FX impact	1,498	(13,721)	0	0	0	0	0
Closing cumulative depreciation	440,589	542,723	753,669	973,374	1,280,661	1,601,652	1,893,303
Opening net fixed assets	326,889	1,099,591	661,557	500,611	780,906	573,619	348,816
Closing net fixed assets	1,099,591	661,557	500,611	780,906	573,619	348,816	107,165
Property			800,000	800,000	800,000	800,000	800,000

5. Skylark share issues/(buybacks)

Year	-1	0	1	2	3	4	5
Par value per share	0.1	0.1	0.1	0.1	0.1	0.1	0.1
Share price			9.8	13.0	13.0	13.0	13.0
Share premium	-0.1	-0.1	9.7	12.9	12.9	12.9	12.9
Share issue (£)			2,940,000	0	0	0	0
Shares issued			30,000,000	0	0	0	0
Share buyback (£)			0	0	0	0	0
Shares bought			0	0	0	0	0

6. Skylark debt and cash (£)

Year	-2	-1	0	1	2	3	4	5
Opening long term debt				0	800,000	800,000	800,000	800,000
Mandatory repayments				0	0	0	0	0
Discretionary issues/repayments				800,000	0	0	0	0
Closing long term debt	86,954	392,045	0	800,000	800,000	800,000	800,000	800,000
LTD/Operating capital	*-317.0%*	*45.5%*	*0.0%*	*57.4%*	*45.2%*	*43.8%*	*47.0%*	*52.7%*
Interest rate				*7.0%*	*7.0%*	*7.0%*	*7.0%*	*7.0%*
Interest paid			0	28,000	56,000	56,000	56,000	56,000
Opening short term debt				8,360	0	0	0	0
Change in short term debt				(8,360)	0	0	0	0
Closing short term debt	76,298	271,866	8,360	0	0	0	0	0
STD/Operating capital	*-278.2%*	*31.5%*	*1.1%*	*0.0%*	*0.0%*	*0.0%*	*0.0%*	*0.0%*
Interest rate			*6.0%*	*6.0%*	*6.0%*	*6.0%*	*6.0%*	*6.0%*
Interest paid			251	251	0	0	0	0
Opening cash				491,230	2,229,812	1,969,363	2,919,736	4,852,218
Change in cash				1,738,582	(260,448)	950,373	1,932,482	2,441,421
Closing cash		0	2,263,176	491,230	2,229,812	1,969,363	2,919,736	4,852,218	7,293,639
Interest rate				*4.0%*	*4.0%*	*4.0%*	*4.0%*	*4.0%*
Interest received				89,192	83,984	97,782	155,439	242,917
Net interest				60,942	27,984	41,782	99,439	186,917
Net debt				(482,870)	(1,429,812)	(1,169,363)	(2,119,736)	(4,052,218)
Interest rate (opening balance)				*12.6%*	*2.0%*	*3.6%*	*4.7%*	*4.6%*

7. Skylark capitalisation routine (£)

Year	-2	-1	0	1	2	3	4	5
Amortisation period	*5.0*	*5.0*	*5.0*	*5.0*	*5.0*	*5.0*	*5.0*	*5.0*
Opening gross intangibles	0	79,290	819,394	1,598,760	2,378,126	3,078,202	3,117,464	3,117,464
R&D spend	79,290	740,104	779,366	779,366	779,366	779,366	779,366	779,366
Retirement	0	0	0	0	(79,290)	(740,104)	(779,366)	(779,366)
Closing gross intangibles	79,290	819,394	1,598,760	2,378,126	3,078,202	3,117,464	3,117,464	3,117,464
Amortisation	0	15,858	163,879	319,752	475,625	615,640	623,493	623,493
Retirement	0	0	0	0	(79,290)	(740,104)	(779,366)	(779,366)
Cumulative amortisation	0	15,858	179,737	499,489	895,824	771,360	615,487	459,614
Closing net intangibles	79,290	803,536	1,419,023	1,878,637	2,182,378	2,346,104	2,501,977	2,657,850

8. Skylark return on capital (£)

Year	0	1	2	3	4	5
Stated operating profit	(2,035,122)	(1,550,987)	86,235	967,419	1,708,324	2,094,138
Plus R&D spend	779,366	779,366	779,366	779,366	779,366	779,366
Minus amortisation of R&D	(163,879)	(319,752)	(475,625)	(615,640)	(623,493)	(623,493)
Adjusted operating profit	(1,419,635)	(1,091,373)	389,976	1,131,144	1,864,197	2,250,011
Notional tax charge	0	150,000	0	0	0	0
Net operating profit after tax	(1,419,635)	(941,373)	389,976	1,131,144	1,864,197	2,250,011
Opening capital employed	861,970	740,369	1,393,382	1,768,049	1,826,877	1,702,158
Plus capitalised R&D	803,536	1,419,023	1,878,637	2,182,378	2,346,104	2,501,977
Adjusted opening capital employed	1,665,506	2,159,392	3,272,019	3,950,427	4,172,981	4,204,135
Adjusted ROCE	(85.2)%	(43.6)%	11.9%	28.6%	44.7%	53.5%
Tax losses brought forward		3,758,944	5,159,931	5,073,696	4,106,277	2,397,953
Stated operating profit		(1,550,987)	86,235	967,419	1,708,324	2,094,138
Tax charge		150,000	0	0	0	0
Cash tax credit		150,000	0	0	0	0
Tax loss brought forward		5,159,931	5,073,696	4,106,277	2,397,953	303,815

9. Skylark economic profit valuation (£)

Year	1	2	3	4	5	Terminus
Long term profit growth rate:	3.0%					
Return on incremental capital:	55.5%					
Net operating profit after tax	(941,373)	389,976	1,131,144	1,864,197	2,250,011	2,317,511
Adjusted opening capital employed	2,159,392	3,272,019	3,950,427	4,172,981	4,204,135	4,176,992
ROCE	-43.6%	11.9%	28.6%	44.7%	53.5%	55.5%
Cost of operating capital	25.0%	19.9%	15.8%	12.6%	10.0%	8.0%
Economic profit	(1,481,221)	(261,331)	505,044	1,337,603	1,827,598	1,983,352
PV economic profit	18,897,851	25,103,534	30,361,814	34,668,793	37,706,097	39,667,036
Stated shareholder's equity	1,223,239					
Net intangibles	1,419,023					
PV economic profit	18,897,851					
Market value	21,540,113					
Shares issued	124,913,793					
Value per share (p)	17.2					

The difficulties of forecasting sales in this situation are very obvious, and since there is a negligible cost of sales, operational gearing is very high (lots of fixed costs and very little variable costs, so the impact of a small change in sales is large). In modelling terms, the most difficult thing about the profit and loss account was the tax charge. It is usual that tax losses would roll forward to be utilised against future taxable profits. In this case, an additional line item was required, to model the cash tax credits.

Working capital items are forecast directly on the balance sheet page, with the differences from one year to the next carried to the cash flow. The other items on the balance sheet are derived from later pages of the model. The capital employed calculation includes provisions, as it effectively did for Magna, though in that case it was derived from the asset side of the balance sheet. Here we have aggregated shareholders' equity, net debt and provisions.

There is nothing notable to say about the cash flow page other than that the forecast items reflect a pick-up in capital expenditure and the purchase of the freehold referred to above.

On the fixed asset tab, the asset life sets the depreciation rate as a proportion of gross fixed assets as for Magna. It is low because the assets are largely related to laboratory equipment. More information is provided regarding the history, but forecasts are constructed in the same way as for Magna. Property is excluded from the main calculation as it is not depreciated or retired.

The shares page shows the calculations surrounding the early year 1 rights issue. There is nothing very notable about the debt page other than that forecast long-term debt entirely comprises the mortgage.

The intangibles page represents an attempt to capitalise assets that would otherwise be written off through the profit and loss account as R&D expenses, and works in the same fashion as for Dandy, except that here we can go back to inception, so all the historical numbers are an attempt at reality.

Most of the return on capital page will again be familiar from the Dandy calculations above. The tax calculations have to be redone, as a deleveraged company would utilise its tax losses less fast than one that receives interest. Our forecasts have a large cash accumulation by the end of the forecast period.

This leads to one of the interesting issues in the valuation calculation. Firstly, there was obviously the question about whether the forecast revenues would be achieved. Secondly, there was the question of what to do about discount rates. And, thirdly, there was the question of what to think about leverage. The forecasts seemed reasonable at the time. Let us take the other two separately.

As at the time of the valuation, the company's shares represented venture capital. But, clearly if it hit its targets, this would not be true in five years' time. The way to treat this is the same as the treatment for TVW where the variation come from balance sheet structure, except that here there is no need for iteration. We just assume that we want 25% now and shall only want a normal 8% when the company is mature.

But this is a capital-based valuation. It takes operating capital and the NOPAT that it is expected to generate. To make the capital base and the returns more reasonable, though they are still very extreme, because of the nature of the business, it capitalises intangibles, but it ignores the question of surplus cash altogether.

Go back and look at the projected year 5 balance sheet. It largely comprises cash! The problem with trying to distribute the cash is that there are no distributable retained earnings in shareholders' funds. This is why the tax loss brought forward falls faster in the forecast profit and loss account than in the restated ROCE calculation. Companies can usually find ways to reconstruct themselves so that surplus cash can be distributed. In practice, for this company, its ambitions were such that, at the time that the model was constructed, it seemed highly unlikely that the cash would not have been spent on some or other corporate deal, if all went well. So the question of the appropriate treatment of the inefficient projected balance sheet gearing, and the alternative of how the cash might be returned to the shareholder seemed rather academic. But readers are entitled to an explanation as to why we have not followed any of our own advice regarding the implications of leverage, and it was one of the many vulnerable points in the valuation. A proper valuation based on the assumption of the accumulation of a large pile of the cash in the company would have increased the discount rate (assuming that the base case was reasonable) and would have made a significant deduction from the value of the equity.

5. Three period models

In our discussions of terminal values we promised a comment on what to do in the event that we do not believe that existing capital will continue to generate stable returns into the long-term future. Moreover, Skylark, our growth company example, was assumed to mature within a five-year forecast. What should we do if we want to assume either that growth fades over a longish period, or that it is optimistic to assume even that existing installed capital can continue to generate its existing returns for ever, or both? After all, a more realistic assumption in many cases might be that both growth and profitability fall with maturity, and that the profitability of existing products as well as new ones might be reduced. The solution is a three period model.

In this section, we briefly discuss what a three period model is and how to create one, and then apply this to our valuation of Magna.

5.1 Fades

What we want is a series of individual annual forecasts for a period that exceeds our ability to extend the full detail of our company model sensibly. So instead we reduce the company to just a very few lines, at a minimum just Net Operating Profit After Tax (NOPAT), capital employed and free cash flow, and then run our valuations as usual. But the forecast period will now comprise our original estimates (in our case for five years), and an intermediate fade period, which can be as long as we like, which will then be followed by a terminal value, which works precisely as in our existing Magna valuation above.

The simplest form of fade gradually reduces growth in NOPAT year by year during the fade period. The slowdown may be linear, or may be compound (i.e., we reduce growth at a rate that over the fade period will take it down from its rate at the end of the forecast period to its rate in the Terminus). We also reduce the company's Return On Capital Employed (ROCE) annually over the same period, again using whatever system we find most realistic. For each year, if we know NOPAT and we know ROCE then the required capital drops out as a result. And if we know profit for a year and the opening and closing capital, then we know net investment and thereby free cash flow.

This argument should be familiar both from our discussion of growth and retentions in chapter one and of the value driver formula for terminal values above. It is yet another application of the principle that only two of growth, profitability and distribution can be independent. Set two and the third follows. This point implies that, if we wanted to, we could derive fades in a number of ways, not merely by changing the way in which annual rates fade, but by changing the lines of causation between the forecast items. So, for example, we could fade profit growth and payout, and derive capital. Or, and this is more common, we could apply growth to the capital base and use the returns to derive profit. We shall return to the implications of these choices when we have worked through a basic example.

5.1.1 Constructing a fade

The valuation routine of a three period model will tend to be cumbersomely long, since if there are five years of explicit forecast, followed by a 20-year fade, followed by a terminal value, the whole thing will extend to 26 columns. Fortunately, these need never be presented in any detail. All that is required is a specification of what is being faded, how, and to what rate. In exhibit 5.11 we have cut out a series which starts with the last forecast year and ends with the Terminus, with only a four-year intermediate, fade period. This should make the following explanation reasonably easy to understand. Having worked through this artificial example we shall then consider the application of a more realistic model to Magna.

Exhibit 5.11: Fade routine

Fade routine (£ million)						
Year	Final forecast	1	2	3	4	Terminus
NOPAT	100	106	111	115	118	122
Opening capital	1,000	1,050	1,185	1,327	1,476	1,520
NOPAT growth	7.0%	5.7%	4.6%	3.7%	3.0%	3.0%
ROCE	10.0%	10.1%	9.3%	8.6%	8.0%	8.0%
Free cash flow	50	-30	-31	-34	74	76

The boxed entries for the final forecast year reflect that these numbers are derived from our existing forecast. The boxed entries for growth and ROCE in the terminus are inputs, as they were in our earlier, two phase model. In between, NOPAT grows at an annual growth rate which varies year by year. ROCE trends down to its long-term rate. Opening capital is derived by dividing NOPAT for the year by the ROCE for the year. And free cash flow is NOPAT less the increase in capital during the year. It should be noted that opening capital in the first year of the fade is already known. It is ending capital at the close of the last forecast year. So, in this example, we have four years in which to fade our earnings growth, but only three years in which to fade our ROCE, since year one ROCE is set by NOPAT and opening capital. It is only in years two, three and four that ROCE is the driver and opening capital the result. Since we are using compound fade rates, each year's growth (and ROCE) is derived by multiplying the previous one by a factor. Taking growth for an example, the formula for the annual factor is as follows:

Factor = (gl/gf)^(1/t)

where gl is long-term growth, gf is growth in the last forecast year, and t is the number of years in the fade.

5.1.2 Types of fade

We mentioned above that as well as having a choice about the derivation of the annual fade rate (for example, linear or compound, as above), there is also choice as to what to grow and what to derive. One option would be to grow revenue, and then use the DuPont drivers of margin and capital turn to derive NOPAT, capital and thereby free cash flow. Another, which is quite common, is to apply the growth term to the capital, rather than to the profit, and to derive profit by applying ROCE to capital. It is important to realise that ostensibly the same long-term assumptions regarding growth rate and profitability may result in considerably different forecasts and valuations, depending on which choice gets taken regarding the construction of the fade routine, even if the number of years that the intermediate period extends over is fixed. This will be clearer if we take our Magna example and put a fade routine on it.

5.2 Three period Magna valuation model

Look back to page twelve of our Magna model, above. It comprised five years of forecast and a terminal value. We shall examine what happens to the value if we make exactly the same assumptions about the long term, incremental ROCE of 9% and growth of 2%, but instead of assuming that the €11,107m that is installed at end year 5 carries on producing a profit of €1,237m for ever (with only incremental capital earning the lower return of 9%) we instead assume that the return on all capital fades over a ten-year intermediate period, to 9%. Moreover, we shall fade annual growth during the intermediate period gradually down to 2%. But there will be two valuations using the three period model. The first will apply growth to NOPAT, and the second will apply growth to the capital base.

Before we look at the results, let us just consider, on the basis of the numbers on page 12 of the model, what one might expect to happen. In our two period base case from page 12 of the model, earnings growth slows from over 7% per annum in year 5, to 2% thereafter, a sharp drop. In the first fade, earnings growth fades slowly towards the 2% rate, which it hits in year 15. The company makes an 11% return on capital employed in year 5, almost 5% above its cost of capital. In the base case, incremental investment in the terminus only earns 9%, a reduction in the investment spread of some 40%, but the existing installed capital continues to earn its 11% rate. In the first fade, on the other hand, returns on all capital, including already installed capital, fades from year 5 onwards, and is 9% by year 15. There is clearly a trade-off here. Compared with the base case, the first fade valuation will benefit from a longer period of higher earnings growth, but will suffer from a faster decline in overall return on capital.

Turing to the second fade, growth will here be applied to the capital base, and, again, return on overall capital will fade down to 9 %. But if you look back at page 12 of the model, Magna's capital base shrinks through our forecasts, and only grows slightly during year 5, which is the base for our fade. So, decline in ROCE is not going to be offset by a longer period of higher growth, since growth starts at less than 2%, and slowly rises through our fade period. So we would expect our second fade valuation to be materially lower than the first. Let us look at the results in exhibit 5.12.

Exhibit 5.12: Three values for Magna

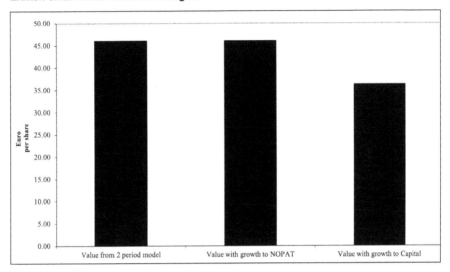

As expected, the value from the first fade routine is very similar to the value we derived from our base case, two period model. The second routine produces a valuation which is some €10 per share lower. This is a massive difference, and is entirely attributable to the fact that returns on capital that is installed by the end of the forecast period are projected to fall over the following decade, whereas in the two phase model it is explicitly assumed that profit is ongoing, and only new capital earns at a lower rate. Our first fade made the same assumption about ROCE, but offset it with relatively higher earnings growth throughout the ten-year fade period.

So which is right? As a very general rule we would be inclined to suggest that there are relatively few businesses in which it is sensible to assume that the capital that is installed in five years' time (or whenever) will continue to generate the same profit for ever, and only incremental capital will earn less. The principles underlying a fade seem more likely to be right for more businesses than those underlying a two phase model.

But when it comes to what to fade, how, and over what period, the choices are considerable, and it is important to realise how much they may matter. After all, we are making the same assumption about Magna's long-term growth rate and profitability in both fade routines, and one gives €46 and the other €36 as a target price. In this particular case it seems to us more logical to assume that growth should apply to earnings. This is a consumer goods company, in which profit growth is driven by revenue expansion, and in which balance sheets follow, as the necessary capacity is installed. The opposite might apply to a mineral resources company, in which reserves and fixed assets are closely related, and, for any given price assumption, profit and revenue is a function of installed capacity, not the other way round.

So, as so often, we would recommend making the decision on company or industry specific grounds, rather than universally applying a single approach to any of the key questions. Two period models or three period models? How long should the fade be? Will growth or profitability fall at a fixed rate per year or at a compound rate of deceleration? And, last but very much not least, does the growth apply to profit, to capital, or even to revenue?

5.3 Three period models in general

Since a three period model merely comprises a longer explicit forecast period, of which part is based on our full accounting model, and a longer fade period is based on only a few line items, followed by a terminal value as usual, it can be combined with all the other approaches to valuation that we have discussed above or in earlier chapters. So, the adjusted present value approach that we discussed in chapter two can also be used here, though we would need an assumed leverage and debt for each of the years in the fade period, and the same also applies to the time-varying WACC discussed above.

6. Conclusions regarding basic industrials

No company is that basic. Even Magna got us into difficulties regarding balance sheets and discount rates. But if the analysis above has any clear messages, we hope that they have come across as follows:

1. It is absolutely essential to understand the business that you are modelling. This often means pulling around the accounts, as for Dandy or Skylark, especially for 'asset light' companies.

2. Understanding cyclicals is largely a matter of close interpretation of history. Whereas growth stocks are gambles on the future, the efficient analysis of cyclical companies is crucially dependent on understanding when and why their volumes, margins and working capital behave as they do.

3. Although discount rates may represent the most intellectually challenging subject for investment analysts, they are unlikely to be the most rewarding. Simple, common-sense treatment is often better than arcane calculations based on an unlikely and unpredictable future.

Chapter Six

Special Cases

What makes them different?

The previous chapter showed how to apply investment theory and accounting practice to the building of forecasting models and the derivation of values. We also addressed some issues that arise frequently, such as companies with changing balance sheets, cyclical companies, growth companies, and 'asset light' companies. None of these required knowledge of additional accounting techniques, merely variants on our basic practice. This chapter addresses six types of companies for which completely different accounting, modelling and valuation issues apply: regulated utilities, resource extraction companies, banks and insurance companies, property companies, and lastly technology companies. In each case, the differences start with the fundamental economics of the business, extend through the accounting for and modelling of the business, and have implications for the valuation techniques used. We shall therefore be required to mix discussion of accounting issues with discussion of modelling and valuation issues on a case by case basis as we proceed.

The interested reader should gain a reasonable understanding of the accounting, fiscal, valuation and (where relevant) regulatory issues needed to model and value companies in these sectors. But depending on his or her interest and needs, further specialist reading is likely to be required on whichever of the businesses the reader wishes to specialise.

1. Utilities

1.1 What makes utilities difficult?

One might have thought that regulated utilities would be simple to model on the basis that demand is usually fairly predictable, and the fact that they are regulated should mean that the same applies to their cash flows and values, other than at times of regulatory uncertainty. In a way, they are, but complications arise for three main reasons, even in the case of companies that are 100% regulated monopolies.

- Firstly, their regulatory balance sheets are not necessarily the same as their accounting balance sheets.

- Secondly, regulation does not guarantee a specific outcome if it takes the form of, for example, price caps.

- Thirdly, in Europe (though not in the USA), most regulation applied to current cost accounts, rather than to historical cost accounts.

Where groups comprise a mix of regulated and unregulated businesses, there is the usual issue as to whether or not disclosure is adequate to permit separate modelling. If companies have assets that are either dedicated to unregulated businesses, or have been disallowed by the regulator on the ground that they should not be included in the base for calculations of permitted tariffs, then this may or may not be transparent. And it is clearly a matter of judgement whether or not a company will exceed or fail to match the regulator's expectations regarding, for example, achievable reductions in unit costs. All of these things inevitably have to be assessed on a case-by-case basis.

We shall concentrate on the third point, since if the connections between current cost accounting and historical cost accounting, and the issues that the former poses for valuation, are not understood then no amount of understanding of the business issues will result in accurate valuations.

1.2 The past is another country (L.P. Hartley)

In this chapter, we are going to refer to Historical Cost Accounting (what we have been using so far) as HCA and to Current Cost Accounting (which adjusts for inflation) as CCA. Readers should be aware that there are two possible approaches to CCA accounting.

The simplest, but one which is not use by utilities, is to adjust all historical figures upwards to bring them into line with current purchasing power. It is the equivalent of using year end exchange rates for translation of foreign balance sheets. In the same way that hyperinflation grows the accounts of a subsidiary in the relevant country, and they then shrink back again when we apply the new exchange rate, so apparently high growth rates shrink if we inflate historical numbers to reflect their then purchasing power. This approach is referred to, appropriately enough, as Current Purchasing Power (CPP) accounting.

The alternative, which is much more complicated, but which is generally used by European utilities, is to adjust accounting items into line with estimated replacement cost. Under Replacement Cost Accounting (RCA), fixed assets are carried at a value that reflects their depreciated replacement cost. In practice, it is the valuation and depreciation of the fixed assets that represent the main adjustment to replacement cost accounting, though there are two others. Firstly, the components of working capital should also be revalued at current cost. Other than at times of hyperinflation, the effect is likely to be small. Secondly, to the extent that the company has debt in its balance sheet, the real value of this is eroded by inflation, resulting in a profit.

In our discussion of CCA accounts we shall, for simplicity, concentrate only on fixed assets, and we shall ignore leverage and model a dummy company on an unleveraged basis. For real companies with complex balance sheets the reader would probably find our discussion hard to follow, though all of the same points would apply. Given the simplification, we shall refer to the increase in the replacement cost of fixed assets as 'inflation', though the reader should be aware that it need not equate to changes in the retail price index.

1.2.1 Why use CCA accounts?

Given that the EU member states, the USA and Japan at least have now enjoyed low levels of inflation (or, in the case of Japan, deflation) for many years, it is legitimate to ask why utilities are generally regulated using a real, rather than nominal, approach. The reason is that the fixed asset life of the relevant assets often extends to decades. Even at a rate of inflation of only 2–3%, the difference between the purchase cost and the eventual replacement cost of a gas pipeline with a life of perhaps 30 years is extremely high. It would be palpably unfair to shareholders to only permit them a fair return on the former, if they are to be expected to finance maintenance of the business out of internally generated funds. So, whatever the mode of regulation adopted, European regulators almost always structure their regulation with respect to a real, rather than a nominal, assumed cost of capital, and with regard to projected current cost, rather than historical cost, accounts.

1.3 How does regulation work?

In addition to the use of real or nominal returns, European and US regulators also differ in the model of regulation that they tend to adopt. In both cases, the modern convention is to attempt to separate what used to be vertically integrated monopolies between the elements that can be exposed to competition and those that cannot. So, in the power industry, generation of electricity is a business in which it is reasonable to attempt to establish competition and then to let market mechanisms determine prices, whereas the transmission and distribution of power comprises a series of natural monopolies, which will need to be regulated if they are not to exploit their pricing power.

We are really concerned here with the natural monopolists, the owners of wires, pipes and telephone lines, whose businesses are and are likely to remain monopolies, subject to price regulation. They may or may not be owned by groups that also operate in the competitive parts of the chain. In some cases this is precluded by regulation. In others, arm's length transactions within a vertically structured group are permitted.

Where the transatlantic difference comes is that in the USA regulatory boards have tended to specify a permitted return on the companies, whereas in Europe regulators have tended to adopt a price-cap of the form 'RPI-x'. The former explicitly determines profitability. The latter does not, in that if the company exceeds or fails to achieve expected operating costs, then it will earn more or less than the targeted return on capital.

There is a case to be made either way, but it is not one that we shall address in this book. Our model will jump straight to profits and cash flows, and will ignore revenues and operating costs, but it should be borne in mind when modelling that if a given price formula has been set with the intention of permitting a given target return on capital then the regulator is assuming that the combination of the price cap, expected volumes and expected cash operating costs will result in cash flows from operations and profits that will be consistent with the target return. The price has been set by starting at the bottom, with the implied level of profit, and then adding back assumed costs (which may require the company to restructure if they are to be achieved) to derive an implied revenue stream, which in turn determines the price cap.

1.4 Implications for models

In chapter three we addressed the difference between an accounting Return on Capital Employed (ROCE) and an economic Internal Rate of Return (IRR). We made the point that they will tend to be greatest for companies with assets that have a long life and a steadily rising stream of income through the asset life. We also pointed out that for many companies it is more or less acceptable to assume that with a portfolio of assets of varying age then the overall company ROCE more or less approximates to the IRR of its assets.

Unfortunately, utilities represent exactly the sort of company for which this assumption is least true. In addition, the relationship between accounting and economic returns may look rather different, depending on whether we are looking at nominal or real (HCA or CCA) numbers. Finally, given that they are stable and regulated industries it is important for us to be precise in exactly the area where up to now we have been content to accept some inconsistencies. So the rest of this section on utilities is aimed at ensuring that you are confident with the connection between HCA and CCA accounts, and that you know how to translate both into values.

1.4.1 Assets and cash flows

As with the discussion of the Magna model in the previous chapter, we reproduce altogether the full model that we shall be discussing, and then refer back to its individual pages in the text that follows. As with Magna, in exhibit 6.1 we have followed the convention of boxing the figures that are inputs, and of using italics for percentages. Key lines and totals have been emboldened.

Exhibit 6.1: Current cost accounts model

1. HCA accounts

Inflation	5.00%					
Asset life (years)	3.0					
Real cash on cash return	39.71%					

Year	0	1	2	3	4	
Cash flows						
Capital expenditure	(100.00)	(105.00)	(110.25)	(115.76)	(121.55)	5.0%
Cash flow from Year 0 capex	0.00	41.69	43.78	45.97	0.00	-100.0%
Cash flow from Year 1 capex	0.00	0.00	43.78	45.97	48.27	5.0%
Cash flow from Year 2 capex	0.00	0.00	0.00	45.97	48.27	5.0%
Cash flow from Year 3 capex	0.00	0.00	0.00	0.00	48.27	na
Total cash flow from operations	**0.00**	**41.69**	**87.56**	**137.90**	**144.80**	5.0%
Net cash flow	(100.00)	(63.31)	(22.69)	22.14	23.25	5.0%
HCA gross balance sheet						
Opening gross capital	0.00	100.00	205.00	315.25	331.01	5.0%
Capital expenditure	100.00	105.00	110.25	115.76	121.55	5.0%
Retirements	0.00	0.00	0.00	(100.00)	(105.00)	5.0%
Closing gross capital	**100.00**	**205.00**	**315.25**	**331.01**	**347.56**	**5.0%**
Cumulative depreciation	0.00	33.33	101.67	106.75	112.09	5.0%
Cum depr/gross closing capital	0.00%	16.26%	32.25%	32.25%	32.25%	
HCA net balance sheet						
Opening net capital	0.00	100.00	171.67	213.58	224.26	5.0%
Capital expenditure	100.00	105.00	110.25	115.76	121.55	5.0%
Depreciation	0.00	(33.33)	(68.33)	(105.08)	(110.34)	5.0%
Closing net capital	**100.00**	**171.67**	**213.58**	**224.26**	**235.48**	**5.0%**
HCA profit and loss account						
Cash flow from operations	0.00	41.69	87.56	137.90	144.80	5.0%
Depreciation	0.00	(33.33)	(68.33)	(105.08)	(110.34)	5.0%
Profit	**0.00**	**8.36**	**19.22**	**32.82**	**34.46**	**5.0%**
HCA ROCE						
Profit	0.00	8.36	19.22	32.82	34.46	5.0%
Opening capital	0.00	100.00	171.67	213.58	224.26	5.0%
ROCE	*0.00%*	*8.36%*	*11.20%*	*15.37%*	*15.37%*	

2. CCA accounts

Inflation	5.00%					
Asset life (years)	3.0					
Real cash on cash return	39.71%					

Year	0	1	2	3	4	
CCA gross balance sheet						
Opening gross capital	0.00	100.00	210.00	330.75	347.29	5.0%
Capital expenditure	100.00	105.00	110.25	115.76	121.55	5.0%
Retirements	0.00	0.00	0.00	(115.76)	(121.55)	5.0%
Cl gross cap before inflation adj	100.00	205.00	320.25	330.75	347.29	5.0%
Inflation adjustment	0.00	5.00	10.50	16.54	17.36	5.0%
Closing gross capital	**100.00**	**210.00**	**330.75**	**347.29**	**364.65**	**5.0%**
Cumulative depreciation	0.00	34.15	106.67	112.00	117.60	5.0%
Cum depr/gross closing capital	*0.00%*	*16.26%*	*32.25%*	*32.25%*	*32.25%*	
CCA net balance sheet						
Opening net capital	0.00	100.00	175.85	224.08	235.29	5.0%
Capital expenditure	100.00	105.00	110.25	115.76	121.55	5.0%
Depreciation	0.00	(34.15)	(72.52)	(121.10)	(127.15)	5.0%
Inflation adjustment	0.00	5.00	10.50	16.54	17.36	5.0%
Closing net capital	**100.00**	**175.85**	**224.08**	**235.29**	**247.05**	**5.0%**
CCA profit and loss account						
Cash flow from operations	0.00	41.69	87.56	137.90	144.80	5.0%
Depreciation	0.00	(34.15)	(72.52)	(121.10)	(127.15)	5.0%
Profit	**0.00**	**7.55**	**15.04**	**16.81**	**17.65**	**5.0%**
CCA ROCE						
Profit	0.00	7.55	15.04	16.81	17.65	5.0%
Opening capital	0.00	100.00	175.85	224.08	235.29	5.0%
ROCE	*0.00%*	*7.55%*	*8.55%*	*7.50%*	*7.50%*	
Reconciliation						
CCA profit	0.00	7.55	15.04	16.81	17.65	5.0%
Supplementary depreciation	0.00	0.81	4.19	16.01	16.81	5.0%
HCA profit	0.00	8.36	19.22	32.82	34.46	5.0%

3. Nominal cash flows

Year	0	1	2	3	4	5	6	7
Nominal								
Year 0 capex cash flows	(100.00)	41.69	43.78	45.97				
Opening NPV		100.00	73.06	40.06				
Closing NPV	100.00	73.06	40.06	0.00				
Impairment		(26.94)	(33.00)	(40.06)				
Profit		14.75	10.78	5.91				
Nominal IRR	*14.75%*	*14.75%*	*14.75%*	*14.75%*				
Year 1 capex cash flows		(105.00)	43.78	45.97	48.27			
Opening NPV			105.00	76.71	42.06			
Closing NPV		105.00	76.71	42.06	0.00			
Impairment			(28.29)	(34.65)	(42.06)			
Profit			15.49	11.32	6.20			
Nominal IRR		*14.75%*	*14.75%*	*14.75%*	*14.75%*			
Year 2 capex cash flows			(110.25)	45.97	48.27	50.68		
Opening NPV				110.25	80.55	44.16		
Closing NPV			110.25	80.55	44.16	0.00		
Impairment				(29.70)	(36.38)	(44.16)		
Profit				16.26	11.88	6.52		
Nominal IRR			*14.75%*	*14.75%*	*14.75%*	*14.75%*		
Year 3 capex cash flows				(115.76)	48.27	50.68	53.21	
Opening NPV					115.76	84.57	46.37	
Closing NPV				115.76	84.57	46.37	0.00	
Impairment					(31.19)	(38.20)	(46.37)	
Profit					17.08	12.48	6.84	
Nominal IRR				*14.75%*	*14.75%*	*14.75%*	*14.75%*	
Year 4 capex cash flows					(121.55)	50.68	53.21	55.87
Opening NPV						121.55	88.80	48.69
Closing NPV					121.55	88.80	48.69	0.00
Impairment						(32.75)	(40.11)	(48.69)
Profit						17.93	13.10	7.18
Nominal IRR					*14.75%*	*14.75%*	*14.75%*	*14.75%*

4. Adjusted HCA accounts

Year	0	1	2	3	4
Adjusted balance sheet					
Opening net capital	0.00	100.00	178.06	227.02	238.37
Capital expenditure	100.00	105.00	110.25	115.76	121.55
Impairment	0.00	(26.94)	(61.29)	(104.41)	(109.63)
Closing net capital	**100.00**	**178.06**	**227.02**	**238.37**	**250.29**
Cash flow from operations		41.69	87.56	137.90	144.80
Adjusted profit		14.75	26.27	33.49	35.17
Return on opening capital employed		*14.75%*	*14.75%*	*14.75%*	*14.75%*

5. Nominal valuation

				Terminus	
Year	1	2	3	4	5
Profit	8.36	19.22	32.82	34.46	36.18
Opening capital	100.00	171.67	213.58	224.26	235.48
Net cash flow	**(63.31)**	**(22.69)**	**22.14**	**23.25**	**24.41**
ROCE	*8.36%*	*11.20%*	*15.37%*	*15.37%*	*15.37%*
Discount rate	*14.75%*	*14.75%*	*14.75%*	*14.75%*	*14.75%*
Economic profit	**(6.39)**	**(6.10)**	**1.31**	**1.38**	**1.44**

DCF valuation

4 year net cash flow	(44.34)
Terminal value	144.34
Enterprise value	**100.00**

Economic profit valuation

Opening capital	100.00
4 year economic profit	(8.54)
Terminal value	8.54
Enterprise value	**100.00**

---

6. Real cash flows (Year 0 money)

Year	0	1	2	3	4	5	6	7
Year 0 capex cash flows	(100.00)	39.71	39.71	39.71				
Opening NPV		100.00	69.58	36.33				
Closing NPV	100.00	69.58	36.33	0.00				
Impairment		(30.42)	(33.25)	(36.33)				
Profit		9.29	6.46	3.37				
Nominal IRR	*9.29%*	*9.29%*	*9.29%*	*9.29%*				
Year 1 capex cash flows		(100.00)	39.71	39.71	39.71			
Opening NPV			100.00	69.58	36.33			
Closing NPV		100.00	69.58	36.33	0.00			
Impairment			(30.42)	(33.25)	(36.33)			
Profit			9.29	6.46	3.37			
Nominal IRR		*9.29%*	*9.29%*	*9.29%*	*9.29%*			
Year 2 capex cash flows			(100.00)	39.71	39.71	39.71		
Opening NPV				100.00	69.58	36.33		
Closing NPV			100.00	69.58	36.33	0.00		
Impairment				(30.42)	(33.25)	(36.33)		
Profit				9.29	6.46	3.37		
Nominal IRR			*9.29%*	*9.29%*	*9.29%*	*9.29%*		
Year 3 capex cash flows				(100.00)	39.71	39.71	39.71	
Opening NPV					100.00	69.58	36.33	
Closing NPV				100.00	69.58	36.33	0.00	
Impairment					(30.42)	(33.25)	(36.33)	
Profit					9.29	6.46	3.37	
Nominal IRR				*9.29%*	*9.29%*	*9.29%*	*9.29%*	
Year 4 capex cash flows					(100.00)	39.71	39.71	39.71
Opening NPV						100.00	69.58	36.33
Closing NPV					100.00	69.58	36.33	0.00
Impairment						(30.42)	(33.25)	(36.33)
Profit						9.29	6.46	3.37
Nominal IRR					*9.29%*	*9.29%*	*9.29%*	*9.29%*

```
7. Adjusted CCA accounts (Year 0 money)
```

Year	0	1	2	3	4
Adjusted balance sheet					
Opening net capital	0.00	100.00	169.58	205.91	205.91
Capital expenditure	100.00	100.00	100.00	100.00	100.00
Impairment	0.00	(30.42)	(63.67)	(100.00)	(100.00)
Closing net capital	**100.00**	**169.58**	**205.91**	**205.91**	**205.91**
Adjusted profit					
Cash flow from operations		39.71	79.42	119.13	119.13
Profit		9.29	15.75	19.13	19.13
Return on opening capital employed		*9.29%*	*9.29%*	*9.29%*	*9.29%*
Reconciliation					
Real IRR	*9.29%*				
Nominal IRR	*14.75%*				
Implied inflation	*5.00%*				

```
8. Real valuation
```

Year	1	2	3	Terminus 4	5
CCA profit	7.55	15.04	16.81	17.65	18.53
CCA inflation adjustment	5.00	10.50	16.54	17.36	18.23
CCA profit plus inflation adjustment	12.55	25.54	33.34	35.01	36.76
Opening capital	100.00	175.85	224.08	235.29	247.05
Net cash flow	**(63.31)**	**(22.69)**	**22.14**	**23.25**	**24.41**
ROCE	*12.55%*	*14.52%*	*14.88%*	*14.88%*	*14.88%*
Nominal discount rate	*14.75%*	*14.75%*	*14.75%*	*14.75%*	*14.75%*
Economic profit	**(2.20)**	**(0.40)**	**0.29**	**0.30**	**0.32**
DCF valuation					
4 year net cash flow	(44.34)				
Terminal value	144.34				
Enterprise value	**100.00**				
Economic profit valuation					
Opening capital	100.00				
4 year economic profit	(1.87)				
Terminal value	1.87				
Enterprise value	**100.00**				

The first page of this model derives projected historical cost accounts for a company which plans to make an investment of 100 at the end of year 0, and whose investments grow at 5% annually thereafter, this merely representing the inflation rate. (As this is an artificial calculation, not based on a real company, we have left the currency unspecified.) Of course 5% inflation is a high number but it has been chosen to make the figures relatively easy to interpret. So once the company is mature it will not grow but will merely maintain itself. To keep the spreadsheet manageable, the asset life is set at three years (it could be ten times that in reality), so by year 4 we have a mature company, which should simply be growing in line with inflation.

Each annual investment is permitted by the regulator to generate a stream of cash which begins at 39.71% of the original investment (we shall explain this odd figure below), and which grows annually with inflation. So the initial 100 investment in year 0 generates 39.71 * 1.05 = 41.69 in year 1, and 5% more in each subsequent year of its life. It is retired at the end of year 3. The cash flow calculations culminate with a calculation of cash flow from operations and of net cash flow (cash flow from operations minus capital expenditure). By year 4, the company is mature, and both are growing at 5% annually.

1.4.2 HCA accounts

Now, we need to convert these cash flows into balance sheets and profit and loss accounts. Starting with gross assets, these grow each year with capital expenditure, but in year 3, that year's expenditure is offset by the retirement of the investment made in year 0. So, by year 4, gross assets are also expanding at 5% annually, as one third of the balance sheet is uplifted by 15% (three years' worth of inflation). Net assets in the balance sheet also grow with capital expenditure, but are reduced by an annual depreciation charge, which is the opening gross asset figure, divided by the asset life, in this case by three. The cumulative depreciation charge is the difference between closing gross assets and closing net assets, and grows each year by the difference between depreciation and retirements (when an asset is retired it drops out of gross assets and cumulative depreciation). With a three-year asset life, after two years the proportion of gross assets that have been depreciated is a stable number. There will always be two partly depreciated assets and one un-depreciated asset in the balance sheet at the end of each future year.

Profit is simply cash flow from operations minus depreciation, and return on opening capital is profit divided by opening capital (which, in this model, merely comprises fixed assets as there is no working capital).

1.4.3 CCA accounts

The second page of exhibit 6.1 takes the same cash flows and converts them into current cost account. As with the HCA numbers, we capitalise capital expenditure. But when we calculate the closing balance sheet figure for gross fixed assets, we include an adjustment for inflation, to increase the opening figure by the rate of inflation. Then, when we retire assets, we retire them at the current equivalent of their purchase cost, so the 100 that we spent in year 0 is retired as $100 * 1.05^3 = 115.76$ when it drops out of the gross assets in year 3.

The net assets in CCA accounts are derived by looking at the ratio of net to gross assets in the HCA accounts and applying it to the gross replacement cost assets. Then since we know the opening value, the closing value and the capital expenditure, we can derive depreciation as a result. So, at end year 2, cumulative depreciation (from the HCA accounts) comprises 32.25% of gross assets, so in the CCA accounts if gross assets comprise 330.75 then cumulative depreciation must be 106.67. Closing net assets must be 330.75–106.67=224.08. Now, if we know that opening net assets were 175.85, closing net assets were 224.08 and capital expenditure was 110.25, then by deduction the annual depreciation charge for the year is 72.52.

As with HCA accounts, CCA profit is cash flow minus CCA depreciation and return on opening capital is CCA profit divided by opening CCA capital. Notice that the return on capital employed stabilises at exactly 7.5%. That is where our rather eccentric looking 'real cash on cash return' number comes from. It is the figure for real cash return on cash investment that would provide the company with a 7.5% CCA return on capital assuming a three-year asset life. In reality, the regulator would not set the cash flow directly, as we have discussed, but would set a price cap such as to generate expected cash flows that are consistent with the target return.

The reconciliation between the HCA and the CCA profit numbers is the difference between the two depreciation charges, the 'supplementary depreciation' in the CCA accounts. But there is an important difference between the two accounts to which we shall return. For the HCA accounts, clean value accounting holds. So, for example, in year 1, capital grows from 100.00 to 171.67, and the net investment of 71.67 equals capital expenditure of 105.00 minus depreciation of 33.33 (net investment), which in turn equals profit of 8.36 plus negative net cash flow (new capital) of 63.31. But these relationships do not hold in CCA accounts. The reason is the inflation adjustment.

> Capital grows each year by more than net investment or the sum of profit and negative cash flow. Clean value accounting does not hold. This will have strong implications for how our valuation methodology will have to work, if we are running off CCA accounts.

1.4.4 Economics HCA-style

The third page of exhibit 6.1 illustrates the individual cash flows generated by each of the four years' of capital expenditure in our forecasts. This exercise has two purposes. The first is to demonstrate what the economic rate of return is. The IRR of 14.75% compares with an apparent return of 15.37% from the first page. The second purpose is to work out what the impairment of value of the company's assets is each year. If we do this and aggregate the figures for each year, then we get a set of numbers that we can substitute for depreciation, to derive a more meaningful set of accounts. This is done on page four of the model.

In this calculation, adjusted net capital grows with investment and shrinks with impairment of value. Adjusted profit is cash flow from operations less impairment of value. Return on capital every year is 14.75%, so if we were to value this company using 14.75% as a discount rate it would generate zero economic profit each year, and be worth its opening balance sheet value of 100. As clean value accounting holds, a DCF would also arrive at the same result.

1.4.5 Valuing the HCA accounts

Suppose that we had only the consolidated HCA accounts to work from, and could not reconstruct individual cash flows by asset or by annual investment (which one would not normally be able to do from outside a company). Then we should be working from the consolidated cash flows, profits and balance sheets from page one in exhibit 6.1. Let us start with the cash flows. If we know that the company will be mature after four years and will then just grow its net cash flow in line with inflation of 5% annually, we have a simple stream of cash flow to discount.

Turning to the profits and balance sheets, we know that if clean value accounting applies, then we know from chapter one that we must always get the same answer out of an economic profit model and a DCF model, so a valuation based on the stated profits and balance sheets must yield the right same answer as the DCF.

Let us try it. On page five of exhibit 6.1 we have extracted the profits, balance sheets and net cash flows from page one. To begin with, let us assume that we knew that the IRR that the company was really making on its projects was 14.75%, as opposed to the 15.37% ROCE, and use 14.75 as the discount rate. The DCF value at start year 1 comes out at precisely 100, which is what one would expect if the company earns precisely its cost of capital. New investments do not add value and we are worth the 100 that we have already spent. The figures in the terminus are just the year 4 figures grown for inflation.

Let us try to value the company again using the economic profit model. The terminal value in the economic profit model can be calculated as just the economic profit from the terminus divided by 14.75%–5.00% (WACC minus growth, the Gordon Growth model) as we are assuming that returns on new capital will be the same as that on old capital (see chapter five on terminal values in economic profit models). There is no question of earning different returns on incremental capital. As with the DCF, the model has correctly derived a fair value of 100, and by implication it has correctly put a value of zero on the stream of future economic profit. All that is happening is that returns are underestimated in the first two years and overestimated after that. The two effects cancel out.

But the crucial point here was that we knew that the appropriate discount rate was 14.75%. Suppose instead that we were valuing a US utility where the regulator was using accounting returns as a proxy for economic returns (which it probably would) so that we were all using the assumption that the company was generating returns of 15.37% on its assets.

Substituting this discount rate results in a valuation of 88.50 (again, for both methodologies). The valuation is being understated if the valuer follows the regulator in taking the ROCE to be a proxy for the IRR. The valuation shows the company to be worth less than its regulatory asset base (the 100 of sunk investment at end Year 0), which would be perverse, if it were being permitted to earn its cost of capital.

1.4.6 Economics CCA-style

The easiest way to model real projected cash flows is to convert them all into year 0 money, so that the year 1 numbers are discounted for one year's worth of inflation, year 2 for two years' worth, and so on.

Page six of the model does this and allows us to make the same calculations as we did in page three for the nominal figures. Firstly, the calculations show us that the real IRR on our investments is 9.29%, which compares with the 7.5% real ROCE that we see in the CCA accounts. Thus in this case the accounts are seriously understating the actual profitability that we are achieving, rather than overstating it as in the HCA calculations.

Secondly, if we are prepared to stay in year 0 money then we can produce adjusted profits and balance sheets CCA, as we did on page four for the HCA accounts. These are shown on page seven of exhibit 6.1, and they illustrate the following points. Firstly, as with the HCA equivalents, the calculated CCA ROCE each year is 9.29%, which we know to be the correct IRR. Secondly, an economic profit model would therefore value the company at 100 as at start year 1. Thirdly, as clean value accounting applies, a DCF model would necessarily do the same.

Incidentally, to understand the reconciliation between the real and the nominal returns, you need to remember that returns compound, so that 1.0929 (real IRR) times 1.05 (inflation) equals 1.1475 (nominal IRR).

1.4.7 Valuing the CCA accounts

Now suppose that you are valuing a company for which the published accounts are the consolidated CCA figures from page two of exhibit 6.1. There are a couple of seductive but horribly wrong things that you could do, and we look first at the wrong and then at the right approaches below.

1. An obvious mistake would be to take the net cash flows, grow them in the terminus at 5% annually, and then discount them at a real discount rate. If we use the 7.5% target CCA return on capital we get a value for the enterprise of 687.77, which has the merit of being very obviously wrong!

2. Since how the company accounts cannot alter its cash flows, it follows that if we are going to value the company by discounting its net cash flows the discount rate that we should use is the nominal rate of 14.75%, even if we are applying it to cash flows derived from a CCA model in which the forecasts have been obtained by assuming a real rate of return on replacement cost assets.

3. Another superficially attractive way to value the company would be to use an economic profits model and to use a real discount rate. Unfortunately, as we have seen in page two, the projected returns on capital are in all years lower than the real discount rate of 9.29%. In fact, running an economic profit valuation on this basis gives a negative intrinsic value for the enterprise of −41.11, which again has the sole merit of being obviously wrong! The culprit is the breakdown in clean value accounting.

Clean value accounting implies that balance sheet growth must equal net investment, which must equal profit plus negative net cash flow (new capital). So we have to add back the inflation adjustment, which of course means that the returns on capital that we derive are again now nominal. Look at page eight. We are correctly deriving a value of 100 by applying a nominal discount rate of 14.75% to returns that include the inflation adjustment. The pattern of economic profit is, however, different from that calculated in page five, because the inflation adjustments are providing a better picture of value creation than the HCA accounts did, with their straight line depreciation. However, it is still not perfect. We still have a small negative value creation in the first four years perfectly offset by a positive terminal value of 1.87. To apply economic profit to CCA accounts you must include the inflation adjustment in the calculation of NOPAT, and then discount the resulting economic profit at the nominal cost of capital.

1.5 Conclusions for modelling utilities

To explain the accounting and modelling points that relate to CCA accounts, which are not intuitively obvious, we have had to take recourse to a rather simple company. It has no working capital and is entirely funded by equity. Its asset life is three years. It does not grow in real terms. And we were able to construct its accounts from underlying cash flows based on discrete annual investments, to ensure that we had the proper discount rate. We have ignored tax. None of this is likely to apply when you find yourself modelling a real utility.

But the principles are the same. If the company is regulated on the basis of a target real return on replacement cost capital, then it makes sense to model its forecast accounts on that basis, driving the forecasts off that accounting return, or something slightly higher or lower in the event that you believe the company can beat, or will not achieve, the required cost cutting. This will end up producing a set of forecast CCA accounts.

Your can then, as usual, either value the company by discounting its cash flow or by discounting its economic profit. The counterintuitive fact here is that either way you must use a nominal, not a real, discount rate. For an economic profit model the inflation adjustment (or adjustments, if there are working capital and gearing adjustments as well as inflation of the fixed assets) must be included in the NOPAT and ROCE calculations.

1.6 What discount rate to use?

Most regulation does not work on the basis of IRRs. Regulators estimate the real cost of capital (or nominal in the USA) and apply it as a target ROCE, even if this is in theory not quite right. Look back to page eight. If we use a real 7.5% and then convert that to a nominal return of $1.075 * 1.05 = 1.12875$, and then plug 12.875% into our valuation model, the resulting enterprise value is 146.77. This would be the correct valuation for the enterprise if we agreed with the regulator that its real cost of capital is 7.5%. We would go from the CCA forecasts on page two to the valuation including inflation adjustments on page eight, with a discount rate of 12.875%, instead of a discount rate of 14.75%. The company would be worth a 46% premium over its asset base because its

IRRs would represent a substantial spread over its WACC, even if this was not evident in its ROCE.

In practice, most utilities are valued using forecasting models that run off the regulatory regime and assumptions about volumes, cost-cutting, etc, but the valuation routines used generally derive their WACC from application of the standard CAPM methodology with measured Betas and an assumed equity risk premium. There is no obligation on the valuer to agree with the regulator's estimate of the cost of capital. And, ironically, one of the risks to a regulated utility is that the calculations on which its regulation is based will go out of date during the period of perhaps five years that the regulatory regime runs before a subsequent review. So, in practice, we should certainly not use a discount rate of 12.875%, but it is quite unlikely that we would use 14.75% either. A real company earns different and changing returns on different assets, so no attempt to calculate a corporate IRR (or, CFROI) will be perfect. And even if we knew the number there is no reason to assume that this is the discount rate that investors actually require as a cost of capital.

As a final note on regulators and costs of capital, we would also point out that European regulators tend to target a real, pre-tax return on capital. They derive a real, pre-tax cost of capital by calculating the nominal cost of debt and equity in the normal way, and then convert this to a real number. As usual, this is an after corporation tax figure, so it has to be 'grossed up' to derive a pre-tax number. But the marginal rate of tax does not in fact apply to current cost profits. It applies to taxable profits based on historical cost accounts. And, as we have seen in our discussions of deferred taxation, the economic tax wedge is usually quite different (often lower) from the statutory rate of corporation tax. This all means that the regulators' calculations of the real cost of capital are highly questionable, even before we get to the fact that targeting ROCEs is not the same as targeting IRRs.

1.7 IFRS and the utilities industry

In common with most industries, there is no specific IFRS standard for the utilities sector despite its somewhat unique nature. Nonetheless, there are a small number of technical areas that are worthy of mention in addition to the more mainstream aspects of IFRSs covered in chapters four and seven.

1.7.1 Asset capitalisation

The assets of a utility may be owned by the government or directly owned by the utility company for a period of time prior to being returned to the government. The recognition (or not) of these assets will reflect the detailed substance of the agreement between the government and the service provider. For example, if the asset is merely used by the utility company, and the key risks rest with the government, then it would appear highly likely that the asset would not be recognised on the company's balance sheet. If an asset were to be recognised then the depreciation period would be a function of the period over which the utility company is expected to use the asset.

1.7.2 Licences

If a utility corporation purchases the right to use the asset from the government then it will be recognised as an intangible asset.

1.7.3 Decommissioning costs

One of the key challenges for companies in these industries is to deal with future 'dismantling' costs. These costs are difficult to identify and are not required to be paid for a very long period. Under IFRS, the best estimate of the cost of decommissioning is added to the cost of the asset. The other entry is to establish a provision. The provision is thus established but not yet expensed. Instead the 'expense' is achieved by virtue of higher depreciation on the higher cost. The provision estimate is also discounted to present value.

In summary the entries that will flow through the financials will be:

- Estimate a provision for future asset retirement obligations and:

  - Increase the cost of fixed assets by the present value of this estimate.

  - Record the provision at the same amount.

- Depreciate the asset (including the decommissioning cost component) as normal over its useful life.

- Accrete the provision over its 'life' to the undiscounted amount. This is achieved by charging an annual interest cost.

1.7.4 Emission rights

Utility companies are often allocated (e.g., by a government) emission rights. These rights come with a target level (so called 'cap') and companies are allowed to trade the rights attached. (The schemes are often referred to as 'cap and trade').

Some of the key issues are:

- **Should an asset be recognised?**

An asset should be recognised when the rights were received, and it should be classified as an intangible asset.

- **What value should be ascribed to the asset?**

The asset should initially be recognised at cost where there was a cost or at fair value where there was no initial cost.

- **Should the asset be revalued?**

The IASB's IFRIC committee decided that emission rights and liabilities should be measured at fair value, with changes in value recognised in profit and loss.

- **If an asset is recorded what would the other entry be?**

When an asset is recognised, a liability should be recognised in the amount of the minimum obligation assumed by accepting the asset.

2. Resource extraction companies

2.1 Selling fixed assets: creative destruction

All resource extraction companies present the same accounting and valuation challenges. To be accurate, it is the upstream, exploration and production, end of resource extraction companies that represent the challenges. The downstream, metal processing or oil refining and marketing, businesses are very similar to other cyclical companies, so we shall largely ignore them here, and concentrate on the upstream.

Put in a nutshell, what is odd about resource extraction companies is that they sell their fixed assets. Most companies do not. They employ fixed assets to add value to raw materials, and what is sold is a finished product or service. But what a resource extraction company sells is barrels of oil, millions of cubic feet of gas, or tonnes of coal or some mineral. It is therefore constantly liquidating itself, and in the absence of development of additional reserves would simply liquidate itself into a large pile of cash. On the other hand, it will tend to be extremely cash generative, the question being how much of the cash flow from operations is really free and how much needs to be ploughed back to maintain the resource base.

Accounting for resource extraction companies explicitly reflects their oddity, in that they do not depreciate their reserves. They deplete them. The difference is that instead of applying straight line depreciation, reserves are depleted on a unit of production basis. The rate applied per unit is the total relevant capitalised cost divided by the recoverable reserve, and it may be calculated by asset or using wider cost-pools.

Because the asset life of a company's reserves may be large (10 to 15 years for oil companies, 20 to 30 years for mineral and mining companies are not uncommon), the accrued profit during a single year is a more than usually useless figure. Imagine a company that produced lots during the year but that found and developed no new reserves. It would look very profitable, but would merely have converted what started the year as a reserve base into an amount of cash. The profit would have been offset by a fall in the value of its remaining reserves. If one were to calculate value added as profit minus the fall in the value of the reserves then the resulting figure would merely reflect the unwinding of the discount rate for one year, not an impressive result.

On the other hand, suppose that a resource extraction company made a significant discovery of new reserves during a particular year. Development lead times are such that it would have no positive impact on the profit and loss account for several years after the discovery was made. But the value would have been added at the point of the discovery.

This second feature of resource extraction companies has strong implications for how we should measure their performance, and how we should value them. The difference between internal rates of return and accounting returns on capital is going to be particularly acute, and over quite long periods of time there may be little connection between accounting and actual profitability. In addition, the wasting value of the resource base may mean that it makes more sense to value them in terms of a division between the present value of their existing assets and the potential upside from exploration, than to run a 'going concern' value of the kind that we built for Magna in chapter five.

2.2 Reserves and resources

The first time that a mineral extraction company will know with absolute certainty how much it will extract from a mine or field will be when it shuts it down and abandons it. Up to that point, all reserve numbers are probabilistic. The absolute volume of reserves in place is generally known fairly accurately. The question is how much of it will be recoverable, using current technology and predicted sales prices. Higher prices permit the application of enhanced recovery techniques that increase recovery factors. So reserve estimates are not merely technical calculations. They are also commercial.

For both mining and oil companies, a distinction is drawn between reserves and resources. The former represent volumes that are estimated to be capable of commercial production. The latter may come in either one of two categories: accumulations that have not been sufficiently appraised to establish their commerciality, or accumulations that have been appraised but are not commercial under current conditions.

There are several definitions in use in both mineral extraction industries which are broadly comparable but, unlike the USGAAP, at time of writing there is no specified approach under IFRS. The two most prominent definitions used are, for minerals, the *International Reporting Template for the Public Reporting of Exploration Results, Mineral Resources and Mineral Reserves* (Committee for Mineral Reserves International Reporting Standards), and for oil and gas, the *Petroleum Resource Management System*, sponsored by the Society of Petroleum Engineers, the World Petroleum Council, the American Association of Petroleum Geologists and the Society of Petroleum Evaluation Engineers.

Exhibit 6.2: Reserves and resources

Petroleum				
		Probability		Note
	1P	2P	3P	
Reserves	Proved	Probable	Possible	Commercial
Contingent resources	1C	2C	3C	Marginal Sub-commercial
Prospective resources	Low estimate	Best estimate	High estimate	Possibly commercial

Minerals				
Mineral reserves	Proved	Probable		Commercial
Mineral resourses	Measured	Indicated	Inferred	Marginal Sub-commercial
		Discovered not economic		
		Exploration results		Possibly commercial

Exhibit 6.2 illustrates the mapping of the reserve and resource classifications under the two templates. Although there are differences between the techniques used by the two industries, the resulting classification between reserves and resources is similar as is the definition of proved reserves. In addition, what the mineral companies identify as mineral resources approximately equates to the marginal contingent element of the resource category for petroleum.

The probability distribution for commercial reserves of petroleum is conventionally cut at three points: that which is 90% likely to be exceeded (proven); that which is 50% likely to be exceeded (proven and probable); and that which is only 10% likely to be exceeded (proven, probable and possible). The three horizontal lines in exhibit 6.2 therefore represent cumulative values, as is the case for the three categories of contingent resources.

When petroleum companies make investment decisions or buy assets they will put a value on all three categories, and would typically value commercial reserves using proven and probable volumes. When companies account, they use proven reserves only in the calculation of fixed assets per barrel, and in the calculation of depletion charges.

Whereas petroleum proved and probable reserves are a cumulative total, the convention for mining companies is that probable reserves are an incremental addition over and above the proved reserves. As with petroleum companies, financial statements will deplete the mine on a unit of production basis using proved reserves, but commercial values will generally reflect proved and probable reserves (plus some upside for resources and exploration assets).

There are two ways to arrange the calculations for depreciation and depletion. The first is 'successful efforts' accounting. Under successful efforts, each asset is treated as a separate item, and is capitalised and depleted accordingly. The second is 'full cost' accounting. Under this method, costs are capitalised in geographical pools and depleted against production from the pool.

The former method involves the writing off of unsuccessful exploration expenditure as the company incurs it. The latter will involve the capitalisation of all expenditure so long as the overall cost pool is not impaired. The difference, in practical terms, is akin to a company capitalising or expensing most of its marketing costs, or its R&D costs. As we have seen, in our valuations we would do better to calculate returns on capital and invested capital using the full cost method. Most large companies use successful efforts, so there is some adjusting to do, in the same way that we capitalised Dandy's historical marketing costs in chapter five.

2.3 Oil company tax: productions sharing agreements

Only in a relatively small number of countries do oil companies have title to the oil that they produce, paying tax on the profit from extraction. These include the USA, Canada, the UK, Australia, New Zealand and Norway, but they remain a minority. Most oil production occurs under so-called Production Sharing Agreements (PSAs) or Production Sharing Contracts (PSCs).

Under these agreements, the oil company has a contract entitling it to develop the field. Early cash flows are used to reimburse its capital expenses and operating costs (cost oil) and the balance (profit oil) is split between the host state oil company and a smaller proportion that accrues to it. There are large numbers of variations on this basic theme.

Accounting for PSAs is complex. The company will book as its equity reserves the proportion of the gross recoverable barrels that it expects to accrue to it as cost or profit oil. Its turnover and profit will be high early in the life of the field, but once payback has been reached, both will drop into line with its percentage entitlement to recovery of operating costs and its share of profit oil, which will be much lower. Changes in oil prices will have the perverse effect of changing depletion charges because a higher price reduces the proportion of the oil that will accrue to the oil company as cost oil, increasing its depletion charge per barrel.

Measures of company reserves and of its replacement cost of reserves must therefore be constructed carefully to ensure that it is net entitlement barrels that are counted in both cases. Tax rates will look very odd, since most of the state tax-take is removed before the revenue line in the profit and loss account.

2.4 Valuing upstream assets

Oilfields and mines are discrete assets with finite lives. Their cash flow profiles take the form of an initial high level of capital expenditure, followed by a long tail of positive flows, with remediation costs when the asset is shut down. It is therefore natural to value the companies by modelling cash flows to individual assets, adding something for upside, to derive an enterprise value. This is usually the practice applied to mining companies, which typically have assets with very long lives, and which also often provide sufficient information for external analysts to produce fairly accurate asset by asset models.

Petroleum companies typically provide information in a more aggregated form, though they often also provide discounted cash flow valuations as well (see below). Moreover, they often have many more assets, which are generally of shorter duration than mines, though this varies considerably. The result is that it is sometimes practical to value the smaller exploration and production companies asset by asset, but this is not practical when it comes to the international oil majors. For these companies we need a method of appraisal and valuation which is not asset by asset but which does reflect, as far as is possible, fluctuations in the values of their upstream assets.

2.5 Oil company accounts: interpretation and modelling

For this section of the book we are going to break with our usual concentration on IFRS accounting, and will model an operation that reports under US GAAP. This is because all of the large international oil companies have their shares listed on the New York stock market. They all file form 20Fs every year. And it is to the form 20F that anyone who is interested in modelling them will go for detailed information on their upstream (exploration and production) businesses. We will however, refer to some IFRS driven accounting changes later in the chapter.

As discussed earlier, we shall concentrate merely on upstream operations, since the downstream is similar to any capital intensive, cyclical industry. The US GAAP requires that companies with upstream activities account for them separately, and provide the following information: a profit and loss account, a statement of capitalised costs, information about costs incurred during the year, a statement of reserves with the components of movements in reserves, a discounted net present value of the year end reserves, and a statement showing the drivers to annual change in the discounted net present value of the year end reserves.

This all sounds too good to be true, and it almost is. The reserves used for the discounted present value calculations are only the proven category. The discounted present values must use first-day-of-the-month average historical 12-month prices, year end cost and tax rates, do not allow for inflation, and are discounted at a high (because it is effectively real) rate of 10%. The net effect is generally to understate reserves, and to understate values. But it provides a much better indicator of value creation than unadjusted accounts, as we shall see.

Since upstream operations are separately accounted for it makes no difference whether we use as an example an independent company or the upstream business of an oil major. The latter is probably more indicative of industry trends, so we have taken an international major oil company, which we shall call Stanoil, as our case study.

Exhibit 6.3 shows Stanoil's upstream business modelled in three pages, and then a calculation of its ROCE and adjusted ROCE for year 0 (the last reported financial year) on page four.

Exhibit 6.3: Stanoil exploration and production model

1. Stanoil upstream financials ($ million)

Year	-2	-1	0	1	2	3	4	5
Profit and loss account								
Revenue	30,917	39,702	48,114	43,730	44,167	44,609	45,055	45,506
Production costs	(13,113)	(13,447)	(14,109)	(13,707)	(13,844)	(13,982)	(14,122)	(14,263)
Exploration expenses	(1,467)	(1,790)	(1,466)	(1,823)	(1,841)	(1,860)	(1,878)	(1,897)
Depreciation and depletion	(18,331)	(15,401)	(13,928)	(10,354)	(10,586)	(10,812)	(11,034)	(11,252)
Taxes other than income	(2,387)	(2,608)	(3,503)	(3,184)	(3,216)	(3,248)	(3,280)	(3,313)
Related income tax	900	2,154	(8,459)	(8,209)	(8,220)	(8,234)	(8,253)	(8,276)
Results of producing activities	**(3,481)**	**8,610**	**6,649**	**6,453**	**6,461**	**6,472**	**6,487**	**6,505**
Tax % of results before income tax	*21%*	*-33%*	*56%*	*56%*	*56%*	*56%*	*56%*	*56%*
Costs incurred								
Acquisition	270	10,603	2,679	0	0	0	0	0
Exploration	1,631	2,107	2,228	2,272	2,295	2,318	2,341	2,364
Development	9,474	6,934	11,421	14,405	14,549	14,695	14,842	14,990
Total	**11,375**	**19,644**	**16,328**	**16,677**	**16,844**	**17,013**	**17,183**	**17,355**
Exploration success	*10%*	*15%*	*34%*	*20%*	*20%*	*20%*	*20%*	*20%*
Capitalised costs								
Opening net capitalised costs		180,665	184,999	181,188	185,239	189,202	193,085	196,892
Development costs incurred		6,934	11,421	14,405	14,549	14,695	14,842	14,990
Depreciation and depletion		(15,401)	(13,928)	(10,354)	(10,586)	(10,812)	(11,034)	(11,252)
Acquisition costs/other		12,801	(1,304)	0	0	0	0	0
Closing net capitalised costs	**180,665**	**184,999**	**181,188**	**185,239**	**189,202**	**193,085**	**196,892**	**200,631**

2. Stanoil oil and gas reserves

Year	-2	-1	0	1	2	3	4	5
Oil reserves (million barrels)								
Opening	12,954	8,737	10,302					
Revisions	(3,823)	951	3,438					
Purchases	111	597	10					
Sales	(28)	(55)	(26)					
Improved recovery	0	8	36					
Extensions and discoveries	254	764	958					
Production	(731)	(700)	(698)					
Closing	**8,737**	**10,302**	**14,020**					
Of which developed	5,378	5,819	9,299					
Of which undeveloped	3,359	4,483	4,721					
Gas reserves (billion cubic feet)								
Opening	35,626	33,434	33,602					
Revisions	(943)	673	1,135					
Purchases	148	1,038	104					
Sales	(59)	(190)	(271)					
Improved recovery	0	1	0					
Extensions and discoveries	1,196	1,238	4,175					
Production	(2,534)	(2,592)	(2,395)					
Closing	**33,434**	**33,602**	**36,350**					
Of which developed	22,209	23,426	22,794					
Of which undeveloped	11,225	10,176	13,556					
Oil equivalent reserves (mmboe)								
Opening	18,892	14,309	15,902	20,078	20,279	20,482	20,687	20,894
Revisions	(3,980)	1,063	3,627	893	902	911	920	929
Purchases	136	770	27	0	0	0	0	0
Sales	(38)	(87)	(71)	0	0	0	0	0
Improved recovery	0	8	36	9	9	9	9	9
Extensions and discoveries	453	970	1,654	407	411	415	419	424
Production	(1,153)	(1,132)	(1,097)	(1,108)	(1,119)	(1,130)	(1,142)	(1,153)
Closing	**14,309**	**15,902**	**20,078**	**20,279**	**20,482**	**20,687**	**20,894**	**21,103**
Of which developed	9,080	9,723	13,098	13,229	13,361	13,495	13,630	13,766
Of which undeveloped	5,230	6,179	6,980	7,050	7,121	7,192	7,264	7,336
Developed percentage	*63%*	*61%*	*65%*	*65%*	*65%*	*65%*	*65%*	*65%*

3. Stanoil upstream performance

Year	-2	-1	0	1	2	3	4	5
Reserve replacement								
Production volume growth		*(2%)*	*(3%)*	*1%*	*1%*	*1%*	*1%*	*1%*
Reserve replacement ratio	*76%*	*111%*	*126%*	*101%*	*101%*	*101%*	*101%*	*101%*
Finding cost per barrel (excluding revisions)	3.60	2.15	1.32	1.74	1.74	1.74	1.74	1.74
Development cost per barrel (excluding revisions)		9.73	13.52	11.63	11.63	11.63	11.63	11.63
Opening reserve/production ratio	16.4	12.6	14.5	18.1	18.1	18.1	18.1	18.1
Per barrel numbers								
Revenue	26.81	35.07	43.85	39.46	39.46	39.46	39.46	39.46
Production costs	11.37	11.88	12.86	12.37	12.37	12.37	12.37	12.37
Depreciation and depletion	15.89	13.61	12.69	9.34	9.46	9.57	9.66	9.76
Taxes other than income	2.07	2.30	3.19	2.87	2.87	2.87	2.87	2.87
Taxes other than income/revenue	*8%*	*7%*	*7%*	*7%*	*7%*	*7%*	*7%*	*7%*
Capitalised costs per developed barrel	19.90	19.03	13.83	14.00	14.16	14.31	14.45	14.57
Depletion/opening capitalised costs		*68%*	*67%*	*68%*	*68%*	*68%*	*68%*	*68%*

---

4. ROCE ($ million)

Year	0
Accounting ROCE	
Stated income	6,649
Opening capitalised costs	184,999
ROCE	**4%**
Capitalised costs per boe	9.21
NPV adjustments	
Opening NPV of reserves	65,201
Closing NPV of reserves	106,104
Change in NPV of reserves	40,903
Capitalised costs	(14,862)
Unrealised profit	**26,041**
Closing NPV of reserves/boe	5.28
Adjusted ROCE	
Stated income	6,649
Unrealised profit	26,041
Adjusted income	**32,690**
Opening NPV of reserves	65,201
Adjusted ROCE	**50.1%**

We have followed our customary convention of boxing the input numbers and of showing percentage movements in italics. The entries for page one are the components of the historical profit and loss accounts, the history of costs incurred in exploration and production, and the closing year −3 net capitalised costs. Notice that there are two tax lines. The first relates to specifically upstream taxes that we shall discuss later. The second relates to income tax, and is calculated as a proportion of profit before income tax.

Stanoil uses successful efforts accounting. Each year, it writes off as an operating cost a proportion of its exploration expenditure: that which is not successful. The model calculates the proportion that has been successful for each of the last three years and carries the average forward as an assumption. The forecasts of future profits and of future expenditures will require us to look at the later pages in the model.

Page two of the model shows the history of Stanoil's upstream business in terms of opening and closing volumes, and the movements for the year split between categories. We need a single composite for oil and gas, so the third block of numbers converts gas to oil at 6,000 cubic feet of gas = 1 barrel of oil. For the forecasts we shall need the next page but while on page two just notice that the company provided information as to the amount of its reserves that are developed. Clearly, it is developed reserves that are produced and depleted. In effect, fixed assets comprises two pools: one of developed reserves, and one of undeveloped reserves (capitalised exploration). As most exploration costs are written off, the second pool is very small so most of Stanoil's capitalised costs are represented by the 65% of the barrels that are developed. And as it is a mature company it may be reasonable to assume that the ratio of developed to total reserves will remain stable. There should always be a 'pipeline' of projects under appraisal or development.

Page three of the model shows the drivers to our forecasts. Clearly, it is possible to set two out of three of volume growth, reserve replacement and reserve to production ratio, as any two will derive the third. We have set volume growth and reserve life as the inputs, and the reserve replacement ratio drops out as a result. Simply put, if we want to grow at 1% annually and maintain a constant reserve life then this is the amount of oil that we need to discover. Converting barrels of oil equivalent to financials, requires two further assumptions: finding costs per barrel and development costs per barrel.

Turning to the second block on page three, we are explicitly forecasting oil prices and production costs per barrel (we have maintained the average of the previous two years in both cases). Upstream taxes are forecast as a constant proportion of revenue, but depletion per barrel is more complicated.

Depletion is calculated on a field-by-field basis, which we cannot reproduce. In addition, it comprised depletion of reserves but also straight line depreciation of some other assets. So it is not going to be amenable to perfect modelling. Approximation will have to do. A starting point is to take the capitalised costs from page one and the developed reserves from page two, and calculate a cost per developed barrel. This can be compared with the depletion charge per barrel produced for the subsequent year. So our depletion and depreciation charge per barrel is simply forecast assuming that it will bear the same relation to the opening capitalised cost per developed barrel as was the average for the previous two historical years.

Returning to page two, since we now know what our reserve replacement ratio has to be we can forecast reserve additions. Clearly, production is driven off the assumed production growth, also from page three. Additions are split between discoveries, revisions and enhanced oil recovery for purely presentational reasons, using the allocation from year 0. Lumping them all together would make no difference to the model. Finally, once we have closing reserves for each year, we can calculate an assumed amount that is developed, so that we have a number to use to derive future depletion charges.

Finally, we can return to page one. Revenues, operating costs and depreciation and depletion are calculated as barrels times the figure from page three, as is upstream tax. Income tax is at the rate shown, held at the year 0 rate. Note that these earnings numbers will generally not equal what is shown as earnings from upstream operations in the group consolidated accounts. These include the activities that Stanoil treats as upstream but that are excluded from the SEC calculation (pipes, liquefied natural gas facilities, etc).

Costs incurred are a multiple of barrels replaced and assumed finding and development costs. Assets grow with expenditure and fall with depreciation and depletion. This closes the model since the ending net capitalised costs, divided by developed reserves, provide the figure for the following year's depletion charge.

Modelling reserve extraction companies is hard. This is because physical and financial entities have to be more closely related than for other industrial companies. It can get worse, since if the company is immature it stops being reasonable to assume that the proportion of reserves that are developed is a constant, in which case the transfer of reserves from undeveloped to developed, and the capitalisation of exploration and development, has to be modelled slightly more carefully. We assumed that the same proportionate volumes of oil would be found and developed each year, and this assumption may be unreasonable in some cases.

Remember also that it is a matter of taste, or of what the modeller can best estimate, which items to forecast out of production growth, reserve life, and reserve replacement. It may sometimes be sensible to forecast the latter two and let the production volumes drop out as a result.

2.6 Valuing major oil companies

Although the SEC values for discounted cash flows from reserves are artificial, they are clearly better than nothing, and if one is not in a position to value the assets oneself (hardly likely given the size of Stanoil, but very practicable for a smaller company with fewer assets) then the figure should be used and not ignored, as it frequently is.

Page four in the model calculates the company's ROCE in two ways. The first is simply to take net income (which excludes financial items) for year 0, and to divide by opening net capitalised costs. We find $184.999bn of capital earning a 4% return.

The problem with this is that the figure of $184.999bn is simply the partially depleted cost that Stanoil incurred in developing its oilfields, some of which will have been developed at times of very different oil prices. And even those that were developed in an era of more expensive oil, to the extent that they are largely depleted, will look very profitable. See our discussion of ROCE versus IRR in chapter three. The effect is very marked for oil companies, and they often refer to assets that are almost depreciated as 'legacy assets'.

If the denominator is not much use, sadly the same can be said for the numerator. If we produce lots of oil but do not find any then the profit we generate should be offset by a decline in the remaining value of the business. Netting off the profit with the fall in the value of the reserves should just leave us unwinding the discount rate and earning a 10% return on capital. (This effect is similar to the interest charge that attaches to the PBO of a pension scheme, discussed in chapter four, or the movement in the current value of a life insurance contract, to be discussed in a later section of this chapter.)

The solution is to adjust both numbers. We want our profit to reflect not merely that which has been realised but also the movement in the value of our reserves, adjusted for costs capitalised during the year. These comprise costs incurred minus exploration costs expensed directly. And we want our return to be calculated by dividing profit by the opportunity cost of our reserves at the start of the year, for which we shall take the SEC discounted value as a proxy. The point is that we could in theory sell our reserves at this value. If we keep them and run the company as a going concern, then it is presumably because we can earn an acceptable return on the fair value of the capital.

The adjustments are shown on page four, and the result is that our opening capital is now valued at \$65.201bn. Adjusted income includes unrealised profit calculated as \$40.903bn increase in the value of reserves, less \$14.862bn of capitalised costs, and that the return made during year 0 becomes 50%. Clearly, these calculations result in violent annual swings in adjusted returns, because they are highly influenced by changes in annual average oil prices. And remember that the SEC NPV can be lower than the book value of the assets without requiring any write down as it is based on highly restrictive assumptions that are not mirrored in the ceiling tests that the company is required to apply to its assets. That all said, returns adjusted in this way over a run of years produce averages that more closely reflect value added than simple historical cost accounts. Clearly, adjusted numbers using realistic appraised values would be a great improvement but are not practical to calculate for large companies with many assets.

Pursuing this analysis would require us to take a longer term view of Stanoil's historical performance over several years and to make explicit assumptions about future value added that go beyond the space that we can allocate here. For the reasons discussed earlier, the SEC valuation of Stanoil's reserves will usually be substantially below a fair market value, because of the restrictiveness of the reserve definition, and the high discount rate applied to forecast cash flows. The approach is therefore best regarded as a performance measure rather than a direct valuation.

2.7 Accounting issues in extractive and energy sectors

The accounting for extractive and energy sectors is derived mainly from the various accounting standards that constitute international GAAP under IFRS. However, in contrast to other sectors, there is a specific industry standard, IFRS 6 *Exploration for and Evaluation of Mineral Resources*. The main aspects of IFRS 6 are explained below, before proceeding to a brief summary of other areas for IFRSs more generally that are of particular relevance to these sectors.

2.7.1 Main requirements of IFRS 6

- IFRS 6 is very limited in scope in that it only applies to expenditures on the exploration and evaluation activities of companies in the oil and gas, mining and related industries.

- This limitation in scope means that expenditures on, for example, prospecting, development and decommissioning are excluded from the standard and the general IFRS model applies.

- IFRS 6 permits companies to capitalise certain expenditures on exploration and evaluation which would not otherwise meet the definitions and requirements in other accounting standards. For example, amounts capitalised within the scope of this standard would often not satisfy the strict definition of an asset found elsewhere in IFRSs.

- There is a broad range of costs that might be considered for capitalisation under the standard including:

  - acquisition of rights to explore;

  - topographical, geological, geochemical and geophysical studies;

  - exploratory drilling;

  - trenching;

  - sampling;

  - activities in relation to evaluating the technical feasibility and commercial viability of extracting a mineral resource.

- Companies can choose an accounting policy to capitalise all of these costs, none of these costs or a selection. Once chosen such an accounting policy must be applied consistently.

- Exploration and evaluation assets need to be assessed for impairment when facts and circumstances suggest that the carrying amount of capitalised expenditure exceeds its recoverable amount. However, the requirements for these impairment tests are considerably more relaxed than those for other assets outlined in IAS 36 *Impairments*. This relaxation is driven by the intrinsic uncertainty surrounding these assets during the exploration and evaluation phases. If the normal impairment model had been applied to these assets, it is likely to have resulted in significant volatility which would not, in all likelihood, have communicated economically useful information.

- The important disclosure requirements of IFRS 6 fall into two main areas. The first is the disclosure of the accounting policies adopted for exploration and evaluation assets. The second is the requirement to disclose the amounts of assets, liabilities, income and expense and cash flows arising from exploration and evaluation activities.

2.7.2 Other relevant parts of IFRS

- Decommissioning costs

In a similar vein to utilities, one of the key challenges for companies in these industries is to deal with future 'dismantling' costs. Over and above the points raised in the discussion of utilities above, the situation is often complicated for oil companies by the substantial tax credits that can be created through abandonment.

- Joint ventures

The nature of a joint venture is usually such that there are at least two parties to the venture, bound by a contractual arrangement, and that the agreement establishes joint control of an entity. The structure is commonplace in extractive and energy industries.

IFRS 11 *Joint Arrangements* requires the use of equity accounting for joint ventures (i.e., using the same approach as for associates). This is a relatively recent change as, until 2013, joint ventures could be accounted for using either equity accounting or proportionate consolidation. Full consolidation is not warranted on the basis that the investor has significant influence but not control. These forms of consolidation are explained fully in chapter seven.

- Oil reserve disclosure requirements

Unlike the US, there are no oil reserve disclosure requirements under IFRS.

3. Banks

3.1 Why do we analyse banks separately from industrial corporations?

Banks and related financial institutions form a large part of any index of equity prices. They tend to be large, complex organisations. But let us be more precise about what makes banks significantly different from other large organisations:

3.1.1 Banking business is very different

Banks are involved in taking a spread from the differential in interest rates that are charged to borrowers and paid to depositors. Therefore banks have no involvement in traditional operating activities such as the acquisition of inventory, equipment and fixed assets and production activities related to same. In addition banks have extended their core 'traditional' activities to encompass areas such as:

- investment banking
- structuring derivatives
- trading financial instruments
- undertaking financial research.

For these reasons banks are very different operationally from typical industrial corporations.

3.1.2 Financial items and operating items are not distinguishable

One of the fundamentals of valuation is that we often attempt to separate operating items and financial items. This allows us to focus on the operations as distinct from how they are financed. This is a continuation of the classical finance approach that views operating decisions as distinct from the financial decision. If financing items cannot be distinguished then our focus is on measures to equity rather than to the broader concept of capital. For example we talk of free cash flow to equity not free cash flow to the firm. This core element of bank valuation is covered later in the chapter.

3.1.3 Regulation of banks is very different

Given their preeminent role at the centre of the financial system, it is no surprise that banks are subject to much more stringent regulation than industrial corporations. This regulation can have a significant impact on financial analysis. In particular the concept of regulatory capital is important. This is based on minimum levels of capital required by regulators that act as a protector of investors and depositors. Some further details regarding regulatory capital are provided below.

3.2 Accounting issues when examining banks

3.2.1 The balance sheet

The first thing to remember is that the shape of the balance sheet is very different as can be seen in exhibit 6.4 below.

Exhibit 6.4: Bank balance sheet

Assets	Liabilities
Cash	Deposits
Loans and advances	Other financial liabilities (including derivatives)
Other financial assets (including investments and derivatives)	Subordinated debt
	Non-controlling ('minority') interests
	Equity

The rules governing bank accounting are arcane and detailed. In many cases the precise rules are a function of the precise nature of the transactions and it can be difficult to make generalisations. However, some of the key technical areas would include the fair valuing of investments, fair valuing of derivatives and provisioning. All of these are addressed in a general way in chapter four. Some further thoughts are included below about some of the key assets and liabilities of a bank.

Loans and advances

Naturally a significant asset of any bank will be its loan book. The book is typically recorded at amortised cost, which is consistent with the amount that is recognised by the borrower. This is generally calculated as:

Principal of the loan	X
+ Accrued Interest	X
– Repaid interest and principal	(X)
– Write-offs (and writebacks)	(X)
Gross loan balance	**X**
– Provision for credit losses	(X)
Net loan balance (amount on balance sheet)	**X**

The term amortised cost refers to the amortisation of any discounts/premiums when the loan is issued, if the coupon is below/above the market rate respectively. Therefore the accrued interest will be based on the internal rate of return on the transaction (i.e., the market rate) at inception of the loan. This internal rate of return will not change over time except in the case of loans with variable interest rates..

Banks can classify loans in many ways for management reporting purposes, as illustrated in exhibit 6.5 below, and banks frequently provide disclosure of these classifications in their financial statements, since they are useful in helping understand the underlying risks in the loan portfolio. A key classification is between those loans that are performing and those that are non-performing, since this provides information on the extent to which the credit risk of the loan portfolio has deteriorated (or improved) over time. Also, as explained below, this classification is particularly relevant for how credit provisions are calculated under IFRS.

Exhibit 6.5: Classification of bank loans

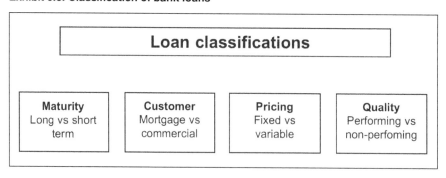

New accounting rules have recently been introduced under both IFRS and US GAAP which provide new guidance for how provisions for credit losses are calculated (note that provisions for credit losses are also referred to as 'impairment provisions').

Although the detailed approach within IFRS and US GAAP differs, the overall aim of the two frameworks is similar: to ensure that banks have sufficient provisions recorded to anticipate future credit losses ('expected credit losses'). Both frameworks therefore require a certain level of provisions to be recognised right from the moment the loan is originated, representing a significant conceptual change from the previous set of accounting rules (which allowed provisions only once there was evidence that the loan is non-performing). Under IFRS 9 provisions are recognised using a three-stage approach:

* Stage one is at origination of the loan. The bank recognises a provision for the credit losses that are expected if a 'loss event' occurs in the next 12 months.

* Stage two occurs when the loan is identified as 'underperforming'. The bank recognises a provision for all expected credit losses on the loan, but interest income continues to be calculated on the gross loan balance.

* Stage three occurs when the loan is identified as 'non-performing'. The bank continues to recognise a provision for all expected credit losses but interest income is now calculated on the net loan balance (so-called 'suspended interest').

US GAAP uses a one-step approach, requiring banks to recognise full expected credit losses right from origination of the loan.

Other financial assets

Banks use liquid and illiquid investments to manage liquidity demands and to invest surplus cash, and therefore have significant balances of 'other financial assets', which include investments in equities and bonds. In addition, they enter into derivatives for risk management purposes. Whilst the accounting for derivatives is addressed fully in chapter four, we provide further detail on the accounting for other types of financial assets below.

Under IFRS 9, financial assets must be accounted for as one of three of the following categories:

Exhibit 6.6: Financial asset categories under IFRS 9

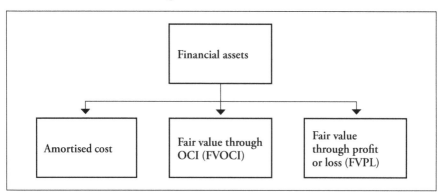

The names of the categories essentially describe the accounting treatment for the assets within these categories. However, there are strict criteria governing which assets are classified in each of the categories:

Amortised cost: Only debt instruments can be classified at amortised cost, and even then it is only where they satisfy the following two criteria:

- Payment test – The contractual cash flows give rise solely to 'payments of principal and interest on specific dates'.

- Business model test – the objective of the business model is to collect cash flows, rather than holding them for trading purposes.

FVOCI: Where debt securities satisfy the payment test but fail the business model test then they are classified as FVOCI. In addition, banks can make a permanent election to classify equity investments at FVOCI.

FVPL: Investments which fail the payments and business model test are automatically classified as FVPL. In addition, banks make an election to include any financial assets as FVPL.

As a general comment, the requirements of IFRS 9 provide a reasonably high hurdle for banking assets to be recorded at amortised cost or FVOCI (when compared with the previous accounting rules). This ensures that, for many banks, a sizeable proportion of assets are recorded at FVPL, also ensuring that the bank's profits reflect current market conditions.

Customer deposits

The major liability for many banks will be the deposits from customers. Accounting complications are rare for deposits as the coupon and effective yield will be the same and hence no discount or premium complication arises. Deposits are carried at their nominal value less any transaction costs. The only area of complexity that can arise is where banks enter into derivatives to hedge their exposure to interest rate fluctuations on deposits. Issues surrounding hedge accounting can become very important in this regard, and are addressed in chapter four.

Subordinated debt

Banks regularly issue bonds to help manage their longer-term financing needs. Although accounting rules allow for these financial liabilities to be accounted for at amortised cost, this creates a certain asymmetry in the accounting if a large proportion of the financial assets are recorded as FVPL. The accounting rules therefore permit companies to choose to record financial liabilities at FVPL (the 'fair value option'), if doing so helps reduce this asymmetry. This option is frequently utilised by banks for their subordinated debt and other issued debt securities.

However, recording financial liabilities at FVPL can create a perverse effect if a bank has a deteriorating credit rating, since this would result in profits being recognised in earnings (as the value of their debt reduces in the market). IFRS 9 has introduced a restriction which prevents companies from recognizing the effects of changes in own credit risk in earnings. Therefore, fair value changes relating to own credit risk are recognised in OCI (and referred to as the 'own credit adjustment') whilst the balance sheet still reflects the full fair value of the liabilities.

3.2.2 The income statement

The core principles of income statement construction continue to apply. However, a few specific items deserve attention. Exhibit 6.7 illustrates some of the key elements of a bank income statement.

Exhibit 6.7: Bank income statement

Revenues	Expenditure
Net interest income	Credit losses
Net commission income	Operating expenses
Net gains on financial instruments	

Net interest income

This is the difference between interest income on loans and securities recorded at amortised cost (primarily bonds and money market deposits) and interest expense on deposits, and any borrowings or issued debt recorded at amortised cost. Interest income is accounted for using the traditional accruals system; i.e., interest is accounted for when earned irrespective of whether it had been received or not. Amortised cost accounting is used which entails not only accounting for the coupon on a debt security but also for the unwinding discounts or premiums. For example interest income would be would be recorded each year by the holder of a zero coupon bond even though no coupon is received.

Net fees and commissions

This is the difference between fee and commission income and fee and commission expenses. Net fees and commissions are another important source of banking revenues. There is scope for a bank to recognise certain components of this category upfront (e.g., arrangement fee for a loan).

Net gains on financial instruments

In comparison to industrial companies banks are likely to have significant financial assets and liabilities, for investment and trading purposes. Since most of these investments and trading balances will be classified as FVPL, the fair value movements of these items are recognised immediately in the income statement; and this income stream can therefore be very volatile depending on changes in market conditions.

Credit losses

Credit losses represent the increase in credit loss provisions each period net of any provision utilisation/recoveries. As provisions for credit losses are such an important aspect of the balance sheet it is no surprise that they are a core expense in the income statement.

3.3 Regulatory issues

As mentioned before regulatory issues are extremely important in a banking context due to the size of the sector and its importance to the entire financial system. The list below summarises some of the key regulatory concepts.

Regulatory issues for banks

Banks are subject to strict requirements with regards to their capital position. There are several reasons why banks require adequate capital ratios:

- To get regulatory approval and a banking license when they are set up.

- To absorb financial and operating losses resulting from the risks inherent in banking activities, namely:

    1. Credit risk, i.e., risk of loss on loans or similar activities due to counterparty default. Credit risk increases in periods of economic downturns, making banking a highly cyclical business.

    2. Market risk, i.e., risk of loss on investments and trading activities due to adverse changes in financial asset prices. This includes interest rate risk and foreign exchange risk.

    3. Operational risk, i.e., risk of loss due to quality control failures and simple human error.

    4. Liquidity risk, i.e., risk of loss because a lack of market participants results in them trading or selling investments at distressed prices in order to meet obligations as they fall due.

    5. To maintain depositors' and creditors' confidence in the bank, by protecting their savings and interests from risks above.

    6. To support growth of banking activities. Regulators require bank capital to increase in line with risky assets.

    7. To achieve desired credit rating from rating agencies and thus keep their cost of funding on capital markets under control.

Regulatory framework for European banks

Bank regulation has traditionally been the remit of national governing authorities. However, growing internationalisation of financial markets has increased the risk that the impact of a major bank failure spreads beyond the national banking system. In addition, regulators have become increasingly keen to prevent banks moving to less prudent jurisdictions to reduce their cost of maintaining minimum capital ratios.

These factors contributed to a trend towards increasing standardisation of capital regulations.

In 1975, the Basel Committee on Banking Regulations and Supervisory Practices ('The Basel Committee') was established to create a unified approach to capital regulation. In July 1988, the Basel Committee published the 'International Convergence of Capital Measurement and Capital Standards' ('The Basel Capital Accord' or 'Basel I'), which provided a definition of capital (Tier I and Tier II) and minimum capital requirements in particular in relation to credit risk (measured rather crudely by risk weighted assets, see below). In January 2001, the Basel Committee proposed the development of regulations ('Basel II') recognising the effectiveness of sophisticated internal risk models developed by large banks to assess capital adequacy, and also exploring further capital requirements related to operational risk. Basel II was implemented in Europe in 2007. However, shortly after this, the financial crisis of 2008/09 occurred, revealing significant shortfalls in the regulatory system with respect to the liquidity risk of banks. In response to this, further changes were proposed in 2009 ("Basel III") which included the introduction of leverage ratios and liquidity requirements, and which are discussed further in the 'Regulatory Ratios' section below. Basel III implementation commenced in 2013, with full implementation by 2022 (as the implementation process is phased). However, this is not the end of regulatory changes for the sector, with further refinements currently being proposed by the Basel Committee (although these refinements don't officially represent a new regulatory regime, they are widely referred to as "Basel IV").

Basel III uses a three pillar approach to regulation:

- Pillar 1 requires banks to hold a minimum amount of regulatory capital that reflects the riskiness of banks' assets;

- Pillar 2 provides supervisors with the authority to evaluate risk management practices and impose more stringent capital requirements if they deem the current level of capitalisation to be inadequate; and

- Pillar 3 focuses on market discipline, requiring transparent reporting.

Definition of regulatory capital

Capital essentially represents a margin of net assets which is available to absorb losses. Although capital calculations are based on accounting numbers, certain adjustments are made ('prudential filters') to ensure that the regulatory capital is adequately prudent.

A bank's regulatory capital can be broadly described as net tangible asset value, i.e., the value of realisable assets (less goodwill and intangibles) in excess of expected commitments or liabilities. The precise calculation of regulatory capital is described in the next section.

However, there is also a continuum of hybrid capital instruments between debt and equity, with varying degree of ability to absorb losses and preserve creditors' and depositors' interests. For this reason, regulators have decided to define capital according to a tier structure, recognising that there might be different layers of capital ranging from higher quality (Common Equity Tier 1, essentially pure shareholders' equity) to poorer quality (Tier 2, hybrid instruments and long term subordinated debt). Certain forms of capital are also eligible as 'Additional Tier 1 Capital'.

The EU is also in the process of introducing an additional requirement for loss absorbing capital ('Minimum Requirement for own funds and Eligible Liabilities' or 'MREL') to provide an extra layer of stability in the financial system.

Tier 1

Tier 1 capital consists of Common Equity Tier 1 capital (CET 1) and Additional Tier 1 capital. They are calculated as:

+	Permanent shareholders capital, including: Fully paid common stock Retained earnings Accumulated other comprehensive income and other disclosed reserves
+	Minority interests (i.e., non-controlling interest)
–	Goodwill and other intangible assets
-	Deferred tax assets and defined benefit pension assets
–	Shortfall on provision stock against expected losses
-	Cumulative reserves relating to cash flow hedges
-/+	Gains or losses on liabilities at fair value resulting from changes in own credit
=	Common Equity Tier 1
+	Perpetual instruments (e.g., non-cumulative preferred stock)
+	Contingent convertible securities
=	Additional Tier 1

Some comments on the calculation of CET 1:

- Disclosed reserves from cumulated retained earnings are part of CET 1, whereas cash flow hedge reserves are explicitly excluded, though they are part of shareholders' funds.

- Including minority interests in CET 1 recognises that minority interests represent equity invested by third parties in subsidiaries belonging to the group which can absorb part of the losses.

- Deducting goodwill (and other intangibles) reflects the fact that these assets could not be easily liquidated in case of losses and therefore do not help to protect depositors and creditors.

- Retained earnings will include credit losses calculated using accounting standards (IFRS 9). Prudence requires a further adjustment for any shortfall in the accounting credit loss provisions (the 'provision stock') against the expected losses calculated using the regulatory methodology (i.e., using either the standardised approach or the internal ratings-based approach).

Additional tier 1 consists of hybrid instruments with more 'equity-like' characteristics (e.g., non-cumulative preferred stock).

Tier 2

Tier 2 is calculated as follows:

+	Undisclosed reserves
+	Perpetual, cumulative preferred stock
+	Perpetual subordinated debt
+	Term subordinated debt (maturity > 5 years)
+	Surplus on provision stock against expected losses
=	Tier 2

Some comments on the calculation of Tier 2 capital:

- Tier 2 capital tends to include hybrid instruments with more 'debt-like' characteristics (e.g., cumulative preferred shares and perpetual debt). Also long term subordinated debt can qualify provided it has a long enough maturity.

- Tier 2 also allows as an adjustment where there is a surplus in the accounting credit loss provisions (the 'provision stock') against the expected losses calculated using the regulatory methodology (i.e., using either the standardised approach or the internal ratings based approach). However, this adjustment is subject to certain limits.

Banks are obliged to publish their Tier 1, Tier 2 and Total Capital but they do not have to disclose a reconciliation of their calculation with the information contained in the balance sheet. However, many banks show a breakdown of the calculation of capital in the directors' report.

Regulatory ratios

We outline below the four key regulatory ratios: the capital ratio, the leverage ratio, the liquidity coverage ratio and the net stable funding ratio.

Capital Adequacy Ratio

The capital adequacy ratio is considered the key regulatory ratio for banks. Although minimum levels are set for both CET 1 and Total Capital (see next section for details), Basel III has increased the focus on CET1 capital ratios.

The capital ratio is calculated as:

Capital ratio = Regulatory Capital / Risk Weighted Assets

The minimum CET 1 ratio is set at 4.5% under Basel III, though various countercyclical buffers can be added to this by national authorities resulting in a minimum CET 1 ratio of up to 9.5% including all buffers. In reality, banks will target capital ratios in excess of the regulatory minimum values.

In the above calculation:

The regulatory capital is calculated as described in the previous section, for CET 1 or Total Capital.

The calculation of Risk Weighted Assets (RWAs) uses the 'Standardised Approach' for most banks. For credit risk and market risk, this involves applying certain risk weightings (as detailed in the Basel III documentation) to certain categories of asset, depending on how 'risky' each of those asset categories are considered to be; the credit risk categories are broadly aligned with the credit ratings provided by the rating agencies whilst the market risk groups assets by 'risk class' (e.g., interest rate risk, fx risk, commodity risk, credit spread risk etc.). For operational risk, the standardised measurement approach involves applying risk weightings based on the size of certain items of income and expenditure alongside information on historic operational losses.

However as an alternative to this, for credit risk and market risk, banks can use internal credit ratings ('Internal Ratings Based Approach') and valuation models ('Internal Models Approach'). Since these alternative approaches rely on the bank applying its own judgements and estimation techniques, their use is allowed only where approval of the national regulator has been obtained. In order to approve these internal ratings and models, the regulator will review the robustness of the banks' models and the judgements and criteria that they rely upon.

Leverage Ratio

The aim of the leverage ratio is to prevent the build up of excessive leverage in the banking system and uses a relatively simple (non-risk based) formula:

Leverage Ratio = Capital Measure /Exposure Measure

The minimum leverage ratio is set at 3% under Basel III, though global systematically important banks are subject to higher leverage ratio requirements.

The capital measure is Tier 1 capital whilst the exposure measure incorporates exposures from: 1) on-balance sheet liabilities 2) derivative liabilities 3) securities financing transactions and 4) off-balance sheet items. Various prescriptive formulae (detailed in the Basel III rules) are used to calculate these exposures, though as we mention above, these are non-risk based. The leverage ratio therefore acts as a leverage backstop against the risk-based capital adequacy model, with the benefits that it is not dependent on in-house risk models to determine the outputs.

Liquidity Coverage Ratio (LCR)

The LCR is designed to ensure that banks hold sufficient liquid assets to survive a 30-day stress period. It is calculated as:

LCR= High Quality Liquid Assets / Net Cash Outflow Over 30 days

Various limits are in place for the composition of high-quality liquid assets, and they are sub-classified by quality: Level 1 assets include cash, central bank holdings and bond with a zero-risk weight whilst Level 2 assets include claims on sovereigns, central banks and public-sector entities.

The total net cash outflow is calculated as the outflow less the inflow, but the inflow is restricted to 75% of the outflow (thus acting as a floor).

Net Stable Funding Ratio (NSFR)

The NSFR's purpose is to ensure that banks maintain a stable level of funding in relation to the composition of their assets and off-balance sheet activities. It is calculated as:

NSFR = Total Available Stable Funding/ Total Required Stable Funding

The numerator and the denominator are calculated by applying pre-defined available stable funding factors and required stable funding factors to the bank's liabilities and assets respectively, as follows:

Available stable funding (ASF)	ASF Factor	Required stable funding (RSF)	RSF Factor
Regulatory capital and liabilities maturing > 1 yr	100%	Cash and central bank reserves	0%
Stable retail deposits <1 yr	95%	Highly quality liquid assets	5-50%
Less stable retail deposits <1 yr	90%	Residential mortgages and loans > 1yr and RW<35%	65%
Funding from NFC and sovereigns < 1 yr	50%	Other performing loans > 1yr and RW>35%	85%
All other liabilities	0%	Net derivative receivables, deferred tax assets and pension assets	100%

The above section on regulatory matters is mainly adapted from chapter sixteen of Financial Statement Analysis Under IFRS, Kenneth Lee and Deborah Taylor, 6th Edition, 2018, Financial Edge publication.

3.4 Start with the balance sheet

When modelling an industrial company it is almost always sensible to start with the profit and loss account, then project investments in fixed assets and working capital, and then derive the resulting balance sheets. The financing decisions such as whether or not to issue or buy-back equity capital come last, and financial leverage may quite reasonably be assumed to vary considerably as the company matures or goes through economic cycles.

All of this is reversed with financial companies. The starting point is the balance sheet. Changes in the level of demand for a bank's services are exemplified by an increase or a decrease in the volume of its loans outstanding or its customer deposits. If we imagine a very simple bank, with no activities other than the extension of loans and mortgages, and the taking of deposits, then its loan portfolio will generate interest income, and its customer deposits will pay some interest, and the bank will also incur the costs associated with the provision of other banking services. Margins relate to the spread between interest received on loans and interest paid on deposits, and to the proportion of income that is absorbed by operating costs. Forecasting the profit and loss account is therefore best done by starting with the balance sheet and then estimating interest rates and operating costs.

There are clearly operations on both sides of a bank's balance sheet. On the asset side, loans are extended at rates that are higher than the risk-free rate (and that should be higher than the risk adjusted cost of capital), and on the liabilities side interest costs and operating expenses are incurred to raise capital more cheaply than could be achieved by issuing bonds. The interface between the two sides of a bank is its treasury, and the management of the bank will regard the three functions as being separate profit centres, with transfer prices between them and capital allocated to each activity. But from outside the bank it is usually impossible to be so sophisticated, and we are left modelling a stream of returns to equity capital.

Banks are very highly leveraged, though the concept of leverage is clearly different from that of an industrial company. Assets are not mainly financed by equity and debt that the bank has issued. They are mainly financed by customer deposits, with capital representing a fairly small proportion of the total balance sheet (subject to the regulatory requirements). The Basel requirements for capital adequacy, discussed earlier, imply that something akin to equity capital (CET 1 capital) can be leveraged by 22 times, this being the inverse of (one divided by) a 4.5% capital requirement. Small changes in capital ratios are therefore important to the risk and return characteristics of the equity of a bank, as we shall see shortly.

For a bank, there is no equivalent to the acquisition of fixed assets and their depreciation, which plays such a large part in the cash flow of industrial companies. Instead, cash flows result from profit and the increase or decrease in loans and deposits. Since we are in any case starting with projected balance sheets, most external models of banks therefore do not model cash flows, but simply project the balance sheet and the profit and loss account.

Bank valuation models use the same techniques of discounted cash flow and discounted economic profit that we used for industrial companies, but it is cash flow to equity and residual income to equity that are discounted, and the discount rate is therefore a cost of equity, and not a cost of capital. It should be noted that none of this is true if one is able to model the separate operations of the bank independently of one another.

3.4.1 Duration and derivatives

Remaining with our simple bank for a moment, it is evident that there is likely to be a mismatch between the duration of the loan portfolio and the duration of customer deposits. Mortgages and commercial loans have durations that run to many years. Many deposits are overnight, and terms are often between one month and one year. Therefore one of the functions of the bank's treasury is to manage the duration risk associated with a business that would otherwise be acutely vulnerable to changes in the shape of the yield curve. It is possible for a bank to look very profitable by lending long and borrowing short, but as we move forward through time if annual rates rise to the levels implied by the initial yield curve then the high profits of the yearly years will be offset by some horrible losses later on! Clearly, this would be no way to run a highly leveraged business.

The implication of all this is that banks must be avid consumers of derivative products, because these offer the simplest way to hedge what would otherwise be a highly asymmetrical exposure to interest rate risks. This is another important element of a bank that it is unlikely to be possible to value correctly from outside. A clue to how effectively a bank is hedged against duration risk should be offered by the robustness of its historical performance to past shifts in the yield curve (and net interest margins have proven rather stable over time), but in the real world it is likely to be very hard to establish this given other drivers to bank profitability through economic cycles, and given that in reality banks have other businesses, such as investment banking and asset management, that cannot hedge their exposure to asset prices.

3.4.2 Provisions and loan losses

The purpose of bank regulation is to ensure the continued solvency of banks. One item that we ignored in the discussion of our simple bank was the fact that some of its customers will default and fail to service and repay their loans. As we have seen, this is a key driver of the capital adequacy requirements discussed earlier, since each asset is risk weighted to derive the total of risk weighted assets (RWA) to which the minimum capital ratios are applied. The corollary to a high credit risk, and a high risk weighting, is likely to be a high interest margin and a high loan loss provision. In addition, like demand for loans and deposits, and the structure of interest rates, loan losses will tend to be cyclical.

3.4.3 Drivers to profitability and value

The drivers to profitability are therefore complex, even for a simple bank. Margin structures have to be seen in terms of yield curves, not just spot rates. Operational gearing is high, since operating costs often represent a large proportion of operating income (the cost/income ratio). And superimposed on all this is the cycle of loan losses. In general, it could be said that the ideal environment for a bank is one of a high level of economic activity, because of demand and low loan losses, and a flattening yield curve, because in practice across all of their businesses they tend to be net holders of long duration financial assets, despite hedging. But this is a generalisation, will vary between banks, and is extremely hard to model from the outside.

Bank shares tend to be high Beta for two reasons. The first is the cyclicality of the business, as already described. The second is just a function of leverage. However well hedged, any business whose assets represent a multiple of 20 times its equity is likely to be high Beta. One complication with banks is that there is no real equivalent to an unleveraged cost of equity for the business, as there is for an industrial company. The business is inherently highly leveraged, before we start to consider the allocation of capital between equity, preference shares, subordinated debt, and so on.

This creates a valuation conundrum to which we shall return. What do we do with a bank that has a significant surplus of capital over and above its regulatory requirements, or even that of its peers? One answer is to assume that it is distributed, and value the stream of cash flow to equity including these distributions. But, surely, if the balance sheet of the bank is materially altered by large buy-backs then this would result in an increase in its cost of equity? We shall return to this question after looking at a model of a real bank.

3.5 An example bank model and valuation

We have produced a bank model for a fictional commercial bank ('Bank plc') to demonstrate the modelling and valuation of traditional banking activities.

As with other models of companies, we reproduce in exhibit 6.8 below the full nine pages of the model, and shall then talk through them in the paragraphs that follow. The nine pages comprise the balance sheet, profit and loss account, drivers to forecast balance sheets, drivers to forecast profit and loss accounts, capital ratio analysis, modelling of equity, key ratio analysis, calculation of discount rate and valuation tabs. As usual, the figures that have been input are boxed, and all percentages, whether drivers or results, are italicised.

Exhibit 6.8: Bank plc accounting and valuation model

1. Bank plc Balance Sheet (Euro million)

Year	-1	0	1	2	3	4	5
Assets							
Cash in hand and on demand	36,206	55,733	56,290	56,853	57,422	57,996	58,576
Loans and debt securities at amortised cost (gross)	280,306	268,235	270,542	272,694	275,733	278,609	283,256
Loss provisions on loans and advances	(3,729)	(2,523)	(2,976)	(3,136)	(3,171)	(3,204)	(3,257)
Loans and debt securities - private clients	82,636	93,476	97,215	100,131	103,135	105,198	107,302
Loans and debt securities - corporates	97,590	94,267	92,382	91,458	91,458	91,458	92,372
Loans and debt securities - other	96,351	77,969	77,969	77,969	77,969	78,749	80,324
Loans and debt securities at amortised cost (net)	**276,577**	**265,712**	**267,566**	**269,558**	**272,562**	**275,405**	**279,998**
Interest earning assets	**312,783**	**321,445**	**323,856**	**326,412**	**329,984**	**333,401**	**338,574**
Financial assets at FV through OCI	39,634	31,155	31,155	31,155	31,155	31,155	31,155
Financial assets -FV through P&L	24,797	23,745	23,745	23,745	23,745	23,993	24,393
Financial assets -held for trading	88,862	63,666	63,666	63,666	63,666	63,666	63,666
Positive fair values from derivative hedging instruments	2,385	1,617	1,631	1,644	1,662	1,680	1,708
Equity accounted investments	180	181	190	200	210	221	232
Goodwill	1,484	1,507	1,507	1,507	1,507	1,507	1,507
Other intangible assets	1,563	1,806	1,806	1,806	1,806	1,806	1,806
Fixed assets	1,723	1,600	1,600	1,600	1,600	1,600	1,600
Tax assets	3,664	3,717	3,717	3,717	3,717	3,717	3,717
Other assets	2,172	1,977	2,870	4,066	5,435	6,960	8,509
Assets held for sale	1,188	78	0	0	0	0	0
Total assets	**480,435**	**452,494**	**455,743**	**459,518**	**464,487**	**469,705**	**476,867**
Liabilities							
			0	0	0	0	0
Deposits - private clients	105,815	114,087	118,650	122,210	125,876	128,394	130,962
Deposits - corporates	83,672	86,297	84,571	83,725	83,725	83,725	84,563
Deposits - other	108,565	97,506	97,506	97,506	97,506	98,481	100,451
Deposits at amortised cost	**298,052**	**297,890**	**300,728**	**303,441**	**307,108**	**310,600**	**315,975**
Money market instruments	5,566	4,428	4,472	4,517	4,607	4,699	4,793
Covered bonds	17,060	17,237	17,237	17,409	17,583	17,935	18,294
Subordinated debt instruments	10,969	9,900	9,999	10,099	10,301	10,507	10,717
Other debt securities issued	12,152	11,804	11,922	12,041	12,282	12,528	12,778
Debt securities at amortised cost	**45,747**	**43,369**	**43,630**	**44,067**	**44,774**	**45,669**	**46,583**
Interest bearing liabilities	**343,799**	**341,259**	**344,358**	**347,508**	**351,882**	**356,270**	**362,558**
Financial liabilities - FV option	18,084	14,940	15,089	15,391	15,853	16,329	16,818
Financial liabilities - held for trading	77,772	56,484	56,484	56,484	56,484	56,484	56,484
Negative fair values from derivative hedging instruments	4,081	2,746	2,770	2,792	2,823	2,852	2,900
Provisions	3,436	3,291	3,291	3,291	3,291	3,291	3,291
Tax liabilities	721	707	707	707	707	707	707
Other liabilities	2,970	3,024	3,024	3,024	3,024	3,024	3,024
Minority interests	1,027	1,164	1,182	1,216	1,253	1,296	1,344
Total liabilities	**451,890**	**423,615**	**426,905**	**430,413**	**435,316**	**440,252**	**447,125**
Subscribed capital	1,252	1,252	1,252	1,252	1,252	1,252	1,252
Capital reserve	17,192	17,192	17,192	17,192	17,192	17,192	17,192
Retained earnings	11,117	11,249	11,211	11,478	11,544	11,826	12,114
Revaluation reserve	(781)	(571)	(571)	(571)	(571)	(571)	(571)
Measurement of cash flow hedges	(97)	(54)	(54)	(54)	(54)	(54)	(54)
Reserve from currency translation	(137)	(192)	(192)	(192)	(192)	(192)	(192)
Shareholders funds	**28,546**	**28,876**	**28,838**	**29,105**	**29,171**	**29,453**	**29,741**
Total liabilities and shareholders funds	**480,436**	**452,491**	**455,743**	**459,518**	**464,487**	**469,705**	**476,867**
Loan loss provisions and analysis							
Opening provision for loan losses - loans and advances		2,300	2,523	2,976	3,136	3,171	3,204
Provision for year - loans and advances	900	781	1,082	1,363	1,103	836	850
Amounts utilised and other changes		(558)	(629)	(1,203)	(1,068)	(803)	(796)
Closing provision for loan losses - loans and advances	**3,729**	**2,523**	**2,976**	**3,136**	**3,171**	**3,204**	**3,257**
NPL ratio	*2.72%*	*2.08%*	*2.20%*	*2.30%*	*2.30%*	*2.30%*	*2.30%*
Coverage ratio	*48.90%*	*45.30%*	*50.00%*	*50.00%*	*50.00%*	*50.00%*	*50.00%*
Impairment charge (%)	*0.32%*	*0.29%*	*0.40%*	*0.50%*	*0.40%*	*0.30%*	*0.30%*
Total impaired assets	*7,626*	*5,569*					

2. Bank plc Income Statement (Euro million)

Year	-1	0	1	2	3	4	5
Net interest income - private clients	2,281	2,353	3,814	4,046	4,167	4,271	4,356
Net interest income - corporates	1,924	1,730	1,680	1,655	1,646	1,646	1,654
Net interest income - other	(40)	117	67	0	0	0	0
Net interest income	**4,165**	**4,200**	**5,561**	**5,700**	**5,813**	**5,917**	**6,011**
Risk result (impairment losses)	(900)	(781)	(1,082)	(1,363)	(1,103)	(836)	(850)
Net interest income after provisioning	**3,265**	**3,419**	**4,478**	**4,337**	**4,710**	**5,081**	**5,161**
Commission income	3,837	3,923	3,923	3,962	4,002	4,042	4,082
Commission expenses	(626)	(745)	(775)	(790)	(806)	(814)	(822)
Net commission income	**3,211**	**3,178**	**3,148**	**3,172**	**3,196**	**3,228**	**3,260**
Net income from hedge accounting	(37)	(86)	(86)	(86)	(86)	(86)	(86)
Net income from trading	1,019	1,092	1,092	1,092	1,092	1,092	1,092
Other income from financial assets	557	365	312	312	312	312	312
Net income from equity accounted investments	150	23	9	10	10	11	11
Other income	333	389	379	382	385	390	395
Staff costs	(3,724)	(3,600)	(4,118)	(3,980)	(4,111)	(4,238)	(4,210)
Other operating expenses	(3,376)	(3,479)	(3,890)	(3,754)	(3,874)	(3,988)	(3,958)
Operating profit	**1,398**	**1,301**	**1,324**	**1,484**	**1,634**	**1,801**	**1,976**
Exceptional items	(627)	0	0	0	0	0	0
Restructuring expenses	(128)	(808)	(500)	0	0	0	0
Profit before taxation	**643**	**493**	**824**	**1,484**	**1,634**	**1,801**	**1,976**
Taxation	(261)	(245)	(371)	(668)	(735)	(810)	(889)
Taxation rate (%)	40.6%	49.7%	45.0%	45.0%	45.0%	45.0%	45.0%
Consolidated profit/loss	**382**	**248**	**453**	**816**	**899**	**991**	**1,087**
Profit attributable to non-controlling interests	(103)	(94)	(18)	(33)	(38)	(43)	(48)
Profit attributable to ordinary shares	**279**	**154**	**435**	**783**	**861**	**948**	**1,039**
Other comprehensive income	(683)	290	0	0	0	0	0
Attributable to non-controlling interests	71	(62)	0	0	0	0	0
Total comprehensive income attributable to ordinary shares	**(333)**	**382**	**435**	**783**	**861**	**948**	**1,039**
Ordinary dividends payable	**(250)**	0	(218)	(391)	(431)	(474)	(520)
Payout ratio	89.6%	0.0%	50.0%	50.0%	50.0%	50.0%	50.0%
Year end shares outstanding	1,252.4	1,252.4	1,177.7	1,130.7	1,066.8	1,029.6	985.8
Weighted average shares outstanding	1,252.4	1,252.4	1,215.0	1,154.2	1,098.7	1,048.2	1,007.7
Earnings per share	0.22	0.12	0.36	0.68	0.78	0.90	1.03
Dividends per share	0.20	0.00	0.18	0.35	0.40	0.46	0.53

3. Bank plc Balance Sheet Drivers

Year	-1	0	1	2	3	4	5
Assets							
Cash in hand and on demand	53.9%	1.0%	1.0%	1.0%	1.0%	1.0%	1.0%
Loans and debt securities at amortised cost (gross)	-4.3%	0.9%	0.8%	1.1%	1.0%	1.7%
Loss provisions on loans and advances	-32.3%	18.0%	5.4%	1.1%	1.0%	1.7%
Loans and debt securities - private clients	13.1%	4.0%	3.0%	3.0%	2.0%	2.0%
Loans and debt securities - corporates	-3.4%	-2.0%	-1.0%	0.0%	0.0%	1.0%
Loans and debt securities - other	-19.1%	0.0%	0.0%	0.0%	1.0%	2.0%
Loans and debt securities at amortised cost (net)	-3.9%	0.7%	0.7%	1.1%	1.0%	1.7%
Interest earning assets	2.8%	0.8%	0.8%	1.1%	1.0%	1.6%
Financial assets at FV through OCI	-21.4%	0.0%	0.0%	0.0%	0.0%	0.0%
Financial assets -FV through P&L	-4.2%	0.0%	0.0%	0.0%	1.0%	1.7%
Financial assets -held for trading	-28.4%	0.0%	0.0%	0.0%	0.0%	0.0%
Positive fair values from derivative hedging instruments	-32.2%	0.9%	0.8%	1.1%	1.0%	1.7%
Equity accounted investments	0.6%	5.1%	5.1%	5.1%	5.1%	5.1%
Goodwill	1.5%	0.0%	0.0%	0.0%	0.0%	0.0%
Other intangible assets	15.5%	0.0%	0.0%	0.0%	0.0%	0.0%
Fixed assets	-7.1%	0.0%	0.0%	0.0%	0.0%	0.0%
Tax assets	1.4%	0.0%	0.0%	0.0%	0.0%	0.0%
Other assets	-9.0%	45.2%	41.7%	33.7%	28.1%	22.2%
Assets held for sale	-93.4%	-100.0%	0.0%	0.0%	0.0%	0.0%
Total assets	-5.8%	0.7%	0.8%	1.1%	1.1%	1.5%
Liabilities							
Deposits - private clients	7.8%	4.00%	3.00%	3.00%	2.00%	2.00%
Deposits - corporates	3.1%	-2.00%	-1.00%	0.00%	0.00%	1.00%
Deposits - other	-10.2%	0.00%	0.00%	0.00%	1.00%	2.00%
Deposits at amortised cost	-0.1%	1.0%	0.9%	1.2%	1.1%	1.7%
Money market instruments	-0.1%	1.00%	1.00%	2.00%	2.00%	2.00%
Covered bonds	-20.4%	0.00%	1.00%	1.00%	2.00%	2.00%
Subordinated debt instruments	1.0%	1.00%	1.00%	2.00%	2.00%	2.00%
Other debt securities issued	1.0%	1.00%	1.00%	2.00%	2.00%	2.00%
Debt securities at amortised cost	-2.9%	1.0%	1.0%	2.0%	2.0%	2.0%
Interest bearing liabilities	-5.2%	0.6%	1.0%	1.6%	2.0%	2.0%
Financial liabilities - FV option	-17.4%	1.00%	2.00%	3.00%	3.00%	3.00%
Financial liabilities - held for trading	-27.4%	0.00%	0.00%	0.00%	0.00%	0.00%
Negative fair values from derivative hedging instruments	-32.7%	0.86%	0.80%	1.11%	1.04%	1.67%
Provisions	-4.2%	0.0%	0.00%	0.00%	0.00%	0.00%
Tax liabilities	-1.9%	0.0%	0.00%	0.00%	0.00%	0.00%
Other liabilities	1.8%	0.0%	0.00%	0.00%	0.00%	0.00%
Minority interests	13.3%	1.6%	2.8%	3.1%	3.4%	3.7%
Total liabilities	-6.3%	0.8%	0.8%	1.1%	1.1%	1.6%
Subscribed capital	0.0%	0.0%	0.0%	0.0%	0.0%	0.0%
Capital reserve	0.0%	0.0%	0.0%	0.0%	0.0%	0.0%
Retained earnings	1.2%	-0.3%	2.4%	0.6%	2.4%	2.4%
Revaluation reserve	-26.9%	0.0%	0.0%	0.0%	0.0%	0.0%
Measurement of cash flow hedges	-44.3%	0.0%	0.0%	0.0%	0.0%	0.0%
Reserve from currency translation	40.1%	0.0%	0.0%	0.0%	0.0%	0.0%
Shareholders funds	1.2%	-0.1%	0.9%	0.2%	1.0%	1.0%
Total liabilities and shareholders funds	-5.8%	0.7%	0.8%	1.1%	1.1%	1.5%

4. Bank plc Profit and Loss Drivers

Year	0	1	2	3	4	5
Net interest margin - private clients	2.67%	4.00%	4.10%	4.10%	4.10%	4.10%
Net interest margin - corporates	1.80%	1.80%	1.80%	1.80%	1.80%	1.80%
Net interest margin - other	0.09%	0.05%	0.00%	0.00%	0.00%	0.00%
Net interest margin (NII/average interest earning assets)	1.32%	1.72%	1.75%	1.77%	1.78%	1.79%
Interest earning assets/interest bearing liabilities	94.19%	94.05%	93.93%	93.78%	93.58%	93.38%
Growth in commissions received	2.24%	0.00%	1.00%	1.00%	1.00%	1.00%
Growth in commissions paid	19.01%	4.00%	2.00%	2.00%	1.00%	1.00%
Growth in income from trading assets (FVTPL)	7.16%	0.00%	0.00%	0.00%	0.00%	0.00%
Realised gains on OCI investments	1.03%	1.00%	1.00%	1.00%	1.00%	1.00%
Returns on associates	12.74%	5.00%	5.00%	5.00%	5.00%	5.00%
Staff costs/interest and commission income	54.57%	54.00%	53.00%	52.00%	51.00%	50.00%
Other operating expenses/interest and commission income	52.74%	51.00%	50.00%	49.00%	48.00%	47.00%
Other operating result/total assets	0.08%	0.08%	0.08%	0.08%	0.08%	0.08%
Profit attributable to non-controlling interests	-37.90%	4.03%	4.10%	4.18%	4.30%	4.40%

5. Bank plc Capital Ratios (Euro million)

Year	-1	0	1	2	3	4	5
Risk weighted assets (RWA)							
Assets - Private Clients		128,214	133,343	137,343	141,463	144,292	147,178
Risk weighted assets - Private Clients		39,000	40,560	41,777	43,030	43,891	44,769
RWA/total assets - Private Clients		**30%**	**30%**	**30%**	**30%**	**30%**	**30%**
Assets -Corporates		173,095	169,633	167,937	167,937	167,937	169,616
RWA - Corporates		88,000	84,817	83,968	83,968	83,968	84,808
RWA/total assets -Corporates		**51%**	**50%**	**50%**	**50%**	**50%**	**50%**
Assets - Other		151,185	152,767	154,238	155,088	157,476	160,072
RWA - Other		44,019	45,830	46,272	46,526	47,243	48,022
RWA/assets - Other		**29%**	**30%**	**30%**	**30%**	**30%**	**30%**
Total book assets	480,435	452,494	455,743	459,518	464,487	469,705	476,867
Total risk weighted assets (RWA)	160,190	171,019	171,207	172,017	173,525	175,102	177,598
Risk weighted assets/total assets	33.34%	37.79%	37.57%	37.43%	37.36%	37.28%	37.24%
Target CET 1 ratio (>8.5% reg min)	13.00%	13.00%	13.00%	13.50%	13.50%	14.00%	14.00%
Target total capital ratio (>13 % reg min)	15.00%	15.00%	15.00%	16.00%	16.00%	17.00%	17.00%
Target leverage ratio (>3% reg min)	5.00%	5.00%	5.00%	5.00%	5.00%	5.00%	5.00%
CET 1 capital							
Equity capital in balance sheet	29,573	30,040	30,020	30,321	30,424	30,749	31,085
Minority interests	1,027	1,164	1,182	1,216	1,253	1,296	1,344
Goodwill and intangible assets	(3,047)	(3,313)	(3,313)	(3,313)	(3,313)	(3,313)	(3,313)
Adjustments	(4,158)	(3,852)	(3,852)	(3,852)	(3,852)	(3,852)	(3,852)
Core Tier I capital	**23,395**	**24,039**	**24,037**	**24,372**	**24,513**	**24,880**	**25,263**
Core capital ratio	14.60%	14.06%	14.04%	14.17%	14.13%	14.21%	14.23%
Target capital		22,232	22,257	23,222	23,426	24,514	24,864
Surplus capital		1,807	1,781	1,150	1,087	365	400
Supplementary capital							
CET 1	23,395	24,039	24,037	24,372	24,513	24,880	25,263
Additional Tier 1 capital	0	0	0	0	0	0	0
Tier II capital	5,691	5,808	5,866	5,925	6,043	6,164	6,287
Total capital	**29,086**	**29,847**	**29,904**	**30,297**	**30,556**	**31,044**	**31,551**
Total capital ratio	18.16%	17.45%	17.47%	17.61%	17.61%	17.73%	17.77%
Target capital	24,029	25,653	25,681	27,523	27,764	29,767	30,192
Surplus capital	5,058	4,194	4,222	2,774	2,792	1,276	1,359
Leverage ratio							
Total assets in balance sheet		452,494	455,743	459,518	464,487	469,705	476,867
Adjustment for derivatives		(33,141)	(33,426)	(33,692)	(34,067)	(34,423)	(34,997)
Adjustment for off-balance sheet items		51,721	52,238	53,283	54,881	56,528	58,224
Other adjustments		243	243	243	243	243	243
Leverage exposure measure		**471,317**	**474,798**	**479,352**	**485,545**	**492,053**	**500,337**
Leverage ratio		5.10%	5.06%	5.08%	5.05%	5.06%	5.05%
Target capital		23,566	23,740	23,968	24,277	24,603	25,017
Surplus capital		473	298	404	235	277	247

6. Bank plc Equity (Euro million)

Year	0	1	2	3	4	5
Share price (Euro)	6.33					
Par value (Euro)	1.00					
Equity issued		0	0	0	0	0
Equity bought back		(473)	(298)	(404)	(235)	(277)
Shares issued		0	0	0	0	0
Shares bought back		(75)	(47)	(64)	(37)	(44)

7. Bank plc Key Ratios

Year	-1	0	1	2	3	4	5
Net interest margin		1.32%	1.72%	1.75%	1.77%	1.78%	1.79%
Cost/income ratio	96.26%	95.95%	91.95%	87.17%	88.63%	89.95%	88.11%
Closing tangible NAV	25,498	25,566	25,525	25,792	25,858	26,140	26,428
Closing tangible NAV per share	20.36	20.41	21.01	22.35	23.53	24.94	26.23
Return on opening tangible equity		0.97%	1.77%	3.20%	3.48%	3.83%	4.16%
Return on total opening equity		0.87%	1.57%	2.83%	3.09%	3.40%	3.69%
Loan to deposit ratio		89.20%	88.97%	88.83%	88.75%	88.67%	88.61%

8. Bank plc cost of equity

Current cost of equity:		
Risk free rate	2.50%	
Equity risk premium	5.00%	
Beta	1.2	
Current cost of equity	**8.50%**	
Market capitalisation	7,928	
Surplus capital	(1,807)	-22.79%
Target capitalisation	6,121	77.21%
Proforma Beta	1.55	
Proforma cost of equity	**10.27%**	

9. Bank plc Valuation (Euro million)

Year	1	2	3	4	5	Terminus
Terminus assumptions:						
Assumed long term growth rate	2.00%					
Assumed long term ROE	10.27%					
Inputs from forecasts:						
Profit after taxation	435	783	861	948	1,039	1,060
Cash flow from equity	**473**	**515**	**796**	**666**	**751**	**853**
Retained earnings	(38)	268	66	282	288	
Opening shareholders' funds	28,876	28,838	29,105	29,171	29,453	29,741
Return on opening shareholders' funds	1.51%	2.71%	2.96%	3.25%	3.53%	10.27%
Cost of equity	10.27%	10.27%	10.27%	10.27%	10.27%	10.27%
Implied residual income	**(2,531)**	**(2,179)**	**(2,128)**	**(2,048)**	**(1,986)**	**(1,995)**
Discounted cash to equity value:						
NPV five year free cash flow	2,357	27.1%				
NPV terminal value	6,329	72.9%				
Value of shareholders' funds	**8,686**	100.0%				
Shares issued (million)	1,252					
Value per share (Eur)	**6.94**					
Share price	6.33					
Premium/(discount)	-8.73%					
Residual income valuation:						
Opening shareholders' funds	28,876	332.4%				
PV five year residual income	(8,278)	-95.3%				
PV terminal value (ex incremental investment)	(11,912)	-137.1%				
PV terminal value (incremental investment)	0	0.0%				
Value of shareholders' funds	**8,686**	100.0%				
Shares issued (million)	1,252					
Value per share (Eur)	**6.94**					
Share price	6.33					
Premium/(discount)	-8.73%					

3.5.1 Historic balance sheet

The balance sheet items are fairly self-explanatory, and we shall restrict our comments to a few details on how we have presented the information, which differs slightly to how information is presented on the face of the primary statements:

- On the asset side of the balance sheet, we include detail for loans and debt securities on both a gross basis and net basis (i.e., gross and net of loan loss provisions), since this detail is useful when analysing loan performance and provisions.

- We have disaggregated loans, debt securities and deposits between the major categories of counterparty: private clients, corporates and other. This disaggregation helps us both analyse historic performance and forecast future performance as the different business segments are likely to have different levels of profitability.

- We have disaggregated debt securities on the liabilities side of the balance sheet by type and specifically separate out subordinated debt instruments. Since subordinated debt is generally classified as Tier II capital, including this as a separate line item is useful when calculating capital ratios.

3.5.2 Historic income statement

Turning to the income statement, we note the following:

- Net interest income has been disaggregated by business segment, following the classification used in the balance sheet (note that banks may also provide some disaggregation by class of financial asset on the face of the balance sheet and income statement, though this is generally less useful for valuation purposes).

- Impairment losses are low relative to gross loan balances (c0.3%) reflecting the fact that, in this example, counterparties are assumed to be of a high credit quality. Impairment losses would be expected to be higher for a bank with a large retail customer base, particularly if there is a large unsecured lending portfolio.

- Operating expenses are significant, resulting in a cost/income ratio of c95%. Although this is higher than average for US and European banks, this ratio will usually be at least 50%, reflecting the high level of staff costs and IT costs that they operate with.

3.5.3 Forecast balance sheets

Turning to the forecasts, page three shows the balance sheet drivers, i.e., balance sheet items growth rates. The main drivers to the balance sheet are the claims on banks and customers and the liabilities to banks and customers, and it seems reasonable to suppose that hedges and securitised liabilities will grow with the business. Most other items, such as provisions and tax assets and liabilities, have been assumed to remain unchanged, though in some cases it may be possible to model them more accurately.

The balance sheet items which we are not forecasting here are loan loss provisions (to which we shall return) and the components of equity, including minority interests (which are a result of other items) and other assets (which are used as a balancing item). Other assets therefore needs to be monitored carefully as a sanity check.

Turning back to the analysis of provisioning on page two, banks carry provisions against the possibility of non-recovery of loans. Each year they make additional provisions, and each year they utilise some of the provisions, when writing off unpaid debts. We have forecast:

- the closing balance sheet provisions, based on forecast gross loan balances combined with our assumptions for the loan coverage ratio (loan provision balances as a percentage of non-performing loans) and the non-performing loan ratio (non-performing loans as a percentage of total gross loan balances). Both these metrics are key ratios reported by banks; and

- the impairment losses as a percentage of gross loans outstanding.

Which leaves amounts utilised and other changes backed out as a result. Clearly, it is only possible to forecast two of these three items, and the third is an implied result.

3.5.4 Forecast profit and loss account

The key drivers to the profit and loss account are: the net interest margin generated on interest earning assets (loans and debt securities) in each of the business segments, the rate of growth in commission income, and the forecast of operating expenses to net interest and net commission income (the cost/income ratio).

Note that by forecasting net interest margin based only on interest earning assets, we are implicitly assuming a stable level of leverage within each segment, since a change in the ratio of interest earnings assets to interest bearing liabilities would impact on the interest margin, regardless of changes in the business mix or economic outlook. Whilst this is generally a reasonable assumption (since regulatory restrictions generally result in stable leverage levels for banks) it is important to keep a sense check on this, and it is for this reason that we include the 'loan to deposit ratio' in the key ratios page (page seven of the model).

We have modelled the minority interests by assuming that their share of net profit will be commensurate with their share of net assets, and have assumed that all of the profit attributable to minorities accrues to the balance sheet (no dividends paid to minorities).

3.5.5 Capital ratios

Banks manage their businesses with reference to the capital ratios that are required to support their business, treading a careful line between meeting the regulatory capital requirements whilst also maintaining a certain level of capital efficiency.

In our analysis, we have assumed that the key limiting factors for a bank's capital structure are the capital adequacy ratios (CET 1 ratio and total capital ratio) as well as the leverage ratio.

Helpfully, the bank's annual reports provide some detail on the above calculations including:

- the calculation of available capital, reconciled to balance sheet amounts

- the allocation of Risk Weighted Assets (RWA) by business line

- the calculation of the leverage exposure measure based on balance sheet assets and adjustments for derivatives and off balance sheet amounts

- the target capital ratios for the business (which will exceed regulatory minimum levels).

This information is usually sufficient to be able to 'flex' existing calculations for (i) available capital (based on forecast changes to equity and subordinated debt) and (ii) RWA and leverage exposure measure (based on changes in balance sheet assets for each business line/asset type). This can then be compared to target capital ratios to identify the level of surplus capital at each balance sheet date.

3.5.6 Equity issues and buy-backs

There is no difference between the accounting treatment of equity issues and buy-backs in this bank model – starting on page six and then playing back into the forecasts of balance sheets and shares outstanding – and the treatment in the Magna model in chapter five.

The modelling difference here is that the regulatory capital targets set by management will determine the size of any buy-backs. In our calculations we have calculated the size of the buy-backs in page six as the lowest value of the prior year surplus from each of the key capital ratios from page five: CET 1 ratio, total capital ratio and leverage ratio (so the €473m buy-back in FY1 reflects the €473m surplus capital in the FY0 leverage ratio calculation, which in turn represents the smallest surplus capital balance in FY0). This mechanism ensures that the target capital ratios explicitly determine the size of the buy-backs (or issues, in the opposite case of a bank whose projected capital was inadequate) to ensure a certain level of capital efficiency.

3.5.7 Performance ratios

Page seven of our model shows the simplest useful analysis of performance ratios for a bank.

The first metric is the net interest margin which is calculated as:

$$\frac{\text{Net interest income}}{\text{Interest earning assets}}$$

It's important to note that this margin calculation is different to a margin calculation for an industrial company (which compares profits to revenues).

The second metric is the cost/income ratio, which is a key measure of operating performance/cost control and is calculated as:

$$\frac{\text{Total operating costs}}{\text{Total income}}$$

where total income refers to net interest income and net fee and commission income.

Between the net interest margin and the cost/income ratio, these two metrics are an important way of understanding the profitability drivers for a bank.

The third and fourth metrics are balance sheet measures, tangible NAV and tangible NAV per share, which are based on net asset values after deducting goodwill and other intangible assets. As discussed in the 'Regulatory issues' section above, regulatory capital calculations exclude intangible assets, and therefore banks analysis tends to focus on tangible net asset values when tracking balance sheet values for equity capital.

Following on from the earnings and balance sheet metrics above are two key return measures: return on tangible NAV and return on equity. These measures are similar to the return metrics used for industrial companies and, in a similar way, we can use

'DuPont analysis' as a useful way to understand drivers for return on equity and to link in with the profitability ratios referred to above. Applying the DuPont formula in a banking context gives:

$$ROE = \frac{\text{Net Income}}{\text{Equity}} = \frac{\text{Net Income}}{\text{Total Income}} \times \frac{\text{Total Income}}{\text{Total Assets}} \times \frac{\text{Total Assets}}{\text{Equity}}$$

where Total Income refers to net interest income plus net fee and commission income.

Finally, we include loan-to-deposit ratios as our last key ratio. As highlighted in our discussion on P&L forecasting, the net interest margin is forecast based only on interest earning assets, and therefore this ratio acts to flag any material changes in leverage over our forecast period which might impact on forecasts of net interest margin.

3.5.8 Discount rates

We mentioned above that banks are inherently leveraged. Even a bank whose capital entirely comprised equity would have a balance sheet for which the larger part of the liabilities represented creditors representing customer deposits. The corollary is that assets will never be fully backed by equity capital, as can happen for industrial companies. We have seen that one approach is to identify the amount of regulatory capital that the bank is targeting, and to assume that it distributes any surplus over and above that amount. But distributing a surplus has the effect of increasing the cost of equity.

Our recommended approach to this is to assume that the CET 1 capital in a bank can be valued as having two components. The first is the target capitalisation and the second is the surplus capital. The cost of capital to the latter is the risk free rate, since it is not being allocated as risk capital, and the cost of capital to the former can be derived by adjusting the measured Beta, in exactly the same way that one would deleverage the Beta of an industrial company with net cash in its balance sheet. Instead of the leveraged Beta being divided by (1+D/E) to derive an unleveraged Beta it is divided by (1–Cash/Equity), to derive an unleveraged Beta. In our case we are just treating surplus capital as if it were cash.

3.5.9 Valuation

Our valuation on page seven is an absolutely standard DCF/residual income to equity model, and should require no explanation, since it is structurally identical to the model used for Magna in chapter five, other than that it values equity directly, rather than debt.

As usual, most of the DCF value lies in the terminus, which represents about 70% of the value derived. Much more interesting is the allocation of value in the residual income model. Even assuming that incremental investments after the forecast period earn exactly their cost of capital, and add or subtract nothing from the value of the business, it turns out that the current book value represents more than the appraised value of the equity. Forecast residual income is negative throughout the projected period and into the long-term future.

3.5.10 Sum-of-parts

Where adequate information is provided it may be possible to value the bank business by business. In that instance we would again recommend modelling returns (cash flow or profit) to projections of target capital by business, and then adding on the value of the surplus capital as a separate item. In this instance, the discount rates used would be determined separately on a business by business basis, and would again apply only to risk capital, with surplus capital treated as risk free cash.

4. Insurance companies

4.1 What's unique about insurance companies?

In a similar vein to banks, insurance companies are very different from industrial concerns. In many ways they share significant characteristics with banks in that they are subject to strict regulatory control, they are sophisticated managers of risk and they are heavily involved in investment and trading of securities. Indeed given these similarities many banks have insurance businesses leading to the term 'bancassurers'.

However, even given this overlap between the business of insurance companies and banks, there are a number of aspects of their business which are unique, as discussed below.

4.1.1. Specific nature of insurance business

Insurance companies are a specialised group of financial institutions that sell life and non-life insurance policies. When an insurance policy is sold, the customer undertakes a contractual obligation to pay either a lump-sum or regular premiums for a pre-determined period of time in exchange for the promise by the insurer for payment under pre-determined circumstances. In the case of life insurance policies, the payment is related either to the death of the policyholder, or simply to the contract reaching maturity. In the case of non-life insurance policies (also called general insurance policies or 'Property & Casualty' policies), the payment is related to an accidental event, such as a car accident, a theft, or the policyholder's disease, in the case of car, property and health insurance, respectively.

This promise by the insurer is one key aspect of why the insurance business is so unique; the exact cost of goods sold is not known when they 'sell' the policy. Therefore, insurance business (and in turn the accounting) is heavily reliant on the use of estimates. Insurance companies have access to detailed statistical tables which allow them to calculate the risk associated with each policy and charge a premium sufficient to cover the risk of claims, insurance expenses, and a profit margin for shareholders. Insurers make money thanks to asymmetry of information which allows them to price the risk undertaken.

4.1.2 Long-term nature of life business

There are additional factors which make life insurance accounting in particular, very specific. The main factor is the very long-term nature of life business; some life insurance products will last decades, whereas published accounts reflect only the flow of revenues and profits generated over a single year, making it difficult to have visibility on life business profitability.

Secondly, there is the range of different life insurance products offered globally providing different coverage risks, and with different profitability profiles. For example, some policies cover only underwriting risk (e.g., annuity products, which are common in the UK), whilst others will cover both underwriting risk and investment risk (e.g., unit-linked policies, which are common in continental Europe), making it even more difficult to track business profitability.

In other words, published accounts of insurance companies are specifically difficult to interpret, because they show only a snapshot of a multi-year business and often cover a range of different 'businesses'.

4.1.3 Regulation of insurance industry

Similarly to banks, insurance companies receive policyholders' funds in their custody and have to manage them to protect their customers' right to be compensated and/or rewarded according to the contracted terms of the policy. For this reason, insurance companies are also subject to strict regulation, aimed at preventing insurers from managing customers' funds unwisely, failing to deliver on their promises and becoming insolvent. This regulation has undergone change in recent years in an effort to achieve a greater level of international standardisation, and to bring the solvency regime up to date with current views on assessing risk. The most significant of these changes was the introduction of the Solvency II regime across Europe in 2017, and which is discussed in more detail in section 4.3.

4.2 Insurance company accounting

Insurance accounting has presented a particularly significant challenge for the accounting standard setters; the long term nature of insurance business, its heavy reliance on the use of estimates and the variety of different types of insurance contracts written globally have provided a number of hurdles to the IASB's attempts to develop a single comprehensive accounting standard for insurance contracts over the last two decades.

These efforts finally came to fruition in 2017, with the publication of IFRS 17 *Insurance Contracts*, which provides a single set of principles to determine the accounting for all insurance contracts. However, this standard is not expected to take effect until 2022, in order to allow the insurance industry sufficient time to implement such a major accounting change. A summary of this new standard is provided in section 4.2.4 below.

In the meantime, insurance companies are relying on an interim IFRS standard (IFRS 4 *Insurance Contracts*) which effectively ratifies local GAAP accounting for insurance contracts and liabilities. Some companies also choose to provide disclosures using 'embedded value' accounting (which provides an estimate of the net present value of future cash flows generated by life insurance business). However, embedded value accounting is not accepted in many European countries since there is no official standard prescribing the methodology.

It is also important to note that the insurance industry will adopt IFRS 9 financial instruments, in relation to their investment balances, at the same time as IFRS 17. This is because the insurance industry was granted a 'carve out' from adopting IFRS 9 in 2018 (when it was adopted by all other industries) so that it could adopt IFRS 9 at the same time as IFRS 17. Until then the insurance industry will continue to use the 'old' IAS 39 accounting rules for financial instruments for their investment balances.

4.2.1 Fundamental aspects of insurance accounting

Essentially insurance companies receive policyholder funds in advance of providing the risk coverage. Therefore it is obvious that premium recognition will be a major accounting issue, even if not especially complex. In order to obtain this business insurance companies incur quite substantial costs. Therefore the recognition of these costs is a substantial issue. Once the monies have been received the insurance company will invest these so the treatment of investment income is significant. Finally the insurance company will have to estimate the amount of expected future claims. It will often develop sophisticated models for establishing provisions. Therefore provisioning is a major component of insurance company accounting.

In summary therefore the key accounting issues can be distilled into four areas:

- **Premium recognition**: At what point can premium income received from clients be recognised?

- **Customer acquisition costs**: At what point are these expensed? Can they be capitalised? If capitalised they are referred to as deferred acquisition costs.

- **Investments**: How are they valued and when does investment income flow through the income statement?

- **Provisions**: How are provisions estimated and recognised in an insurance context?

Each of these issues are addressed as we discuss an insurance company's financial statements below.

4.2.2 Insurance company financial statements

As with banks, an insurer's balance sheet and income statement are very different to that of an industrial company, as well as containing certain terminology which is specific to the insurance industry. Exhibit 6.9 provides an overview of the balance sheet and income statement structure and we provide a summary below of the key line items.

Exhibit 6.9: Accounts for typical insurance company

Income statement of typical insurance company	€
Net earned premiums	70
Benefits and claims	-65
Commissions	-2
Underwriting profit (sometimes referred to as 'technical margin')	**3**
Investment income	15
Operating expenses	-13
Pre-tax profit	**5**

Balance sheet of typical insurance company	€
Intangible assets	10
Investments	500
Amounts ceded to reinsurers	10
Other assets	30
Insurance provisions - non-life *	-50
Insurance provisions - life *	-400
Other liabilities	-50
=Equity	**50**

* Insurance provisions are sometimes referred to as 'technical reserves'

Net earned premiums

As stated above, premium recognition is a core issue for insurance company accounting, and this issue arises because of two key aspects of insurance business:

• Reinsurance activities

In order to reduce underwriting risk, an insurance company will transfer some of its risk to a reinsurance company, which is referred to as 'ceding risk'. As a result, the insurer also transfers a proportion of the total premiums received from customers (the 'gross written premium') to the reinsurance company. The amount retained by the insurance company after reinsurance activities is referred to as the net written premium.

• Premiums earned

Insurance premiums are frequently received well before some (or all) of the risk coverage is provided. Accounting principles allow revenue to be recognised only to the extent that they are 'earned' i.e., to the extent that the underlying insurance services have been provided. For an insurance company, any premiums received may reflect a policy which lasts from 12 months (e.g., most non-life insurance) or many years (e.g., life insurance). Either way, the amount of premium actually recognised each period ('the net earned premium') must reflect only premiums where the insurance risk coverage has been provided in that period.

The net earned premium is therefore calculated by adjusting the amount of net premium actually received from customers in the period (the 'net written premium') for changes in the unearned premium provision. The changes in this provision reflect (i) premiums due from customers in the year which must be deferred as they are not yet earned and (ii) net written premium deferred from previous years which has been earned in the current year.

Exhibit 6.10 below illustrates the calculation of net earned premiums:

Exhibit 6.10: Calculation of net earned premiums

Calculation of net earned premiums	€
Gross written premiums	220
- Reinsured premiums	-120
= Net written premiums	100
- Change in provision for unearned premiums	-30
Net earned premiums	**70**

The unearned premium provision is similar in nature to deferred income – monies received from customers that have not yet been earned. It is a liability as the insurance company 'owes' the coverage to the customer. This liability will sit on the balance sheet and is included within technical reserves.

Benefits and claims

Benefits and claims represent amounts paid out to policyholders during the period, including any related expenses (e.g., legal costs). There are two key components to this line in the income statement:

• Reinsurers share

If the insurance company has ceded a proportion of the policy risk to a reinsurer, then an adjustment is required to ensure that the claims expense recognised by the insurance company reflects only its own 'share' of the claims.

The reinsurers share of amounts paid out to policy holders is therefore deducted from gross claims, when calculating net claims paid.

• Change in provision for claims outstanding

In this case a provision for claims outstanding is established. Like all provisions, it is the movement in the provision that is included in the claims expense in the period. The balance of the claim will be included in the balance sheet within technical reserves.

Technical reserves therefore include both provisions for claims outstanding and provisions for unearned premium. Although the calculation of technical reserves is one of the key areas where the current accounting rules lack detail (and is therefore one of the areas where local GAAP still prevails) an overarching requirement of IFRS is that provisions for claims outstanding may not include 'possible' future claims (prior to IFRS these were referred to as catastrophe or equalisation provisions). However, the provisions should include claims that have not yet been reported but where it is probable that the claims have been incurred, based on historical evidence and statistical analysis. These are often referred to as 'incurred but not reported' or 'IBNR' provisions.

The calculation of technical provisions for life business is particularly significant given the duration of the policies, and therefore this is addressed in more detail in the next section.

Exhibit 6.11 illustrates the calculation of the benefits and claims expense.

Exhibit 6.11: Calculation of benefits and claims

Calculation of benefits and claims expense	€
Gross claims paid	215
- Reinsurers share	-120
= Net claims paid	95
- Change in provision for claims outstanding	-30
Net insurance benefits and claims	**65**

Commissions

As mentioned previously, insurance companies often incur upfront costs – in the form of commission payments to insurance brokers – in order to acquire customers. If we apply the matching principle then there is an argument for deferring some of these costs as the benefit will also be recognised (earned premiums) in future years. This approach will therefore give rise to deferred acquisition costs (or 'DAC') whereby they are capitalised as an intangible asset and amortised over the duration of the policy.

Accounting standards have tried to standardise this practice as there were widely divergent approaches in the industry. Both US GAAP and IFRS provide that DAC can only be capitalised if:

1. They are costs that relate directly to the acquisition of insurance premiums, such as commissions to agents and brokers, are deferred and amortised over the related policy period.

2. If the future policy revenues on existing policies are not sufficient to cover the DAC, then the costs are written off to earnings.

3. Investment income is NOT considered in determining whether such a deficiency does exist.

DAC are classified as an intangible asset on the balance sheet, with the amortisation period disclosed in the financials.

Investments

As highlighted previously, insurance companies are still relying on the accounting rules contained within IAS 39 for their investment balances. Under IAS 39 investments are classified as either:

- Held to maturity (debt instruments only) – investments are valued in the balance sheet at amortised cost with only interest income included in earnings.

- Available for sale (equity and debt instruments) - investments are valued in the balance sheet at fair value, with fair value gains and losses being recorded in equity.

- Held for trading (equity and debt instruments) – investments are valued in the balance sheet at fair value, with fair value gains and losses being recorded in equity.

In general, a large proportion of an insurer's investment portfolio will be classified as held to maturity or available for sale, minimising the amount of fair value gains and losses that are recorded in earnings. Therefore the future adoption of IFRS 9 – which increases the proportion of assets recorded at fair value through profit and loss – will represent a significant change for the insurance industry.

It should be noted that the IAS 39 investment categories highlighted above are broadly consistent with those under US GAAP.

Amounts ceded to reinsurers

When an insurance company cedes part of its underwriting risk to a reinsurance company, it has the ability to claim back a proportion of any future claims from the reinsurer, giving rise to an insurance asset which is equal and opposite to the amount included in the technical provisions in relation to this portion of the risk.

Accounting rules prevent insurance companies from netting off of reinsurance assets against the underlying technical provisions, and therefore these reinsurance assets are recorded separately in the balance sheet. Accounting rules also require that these reinsurance assets are valued consistently with the underlying technical reserves.

4.2.3 Life insurance contracts

Life insurance contracts tend to be more complex than general insurance contracts. This is also reflected in the accounting and we therefore provide some additional commentary on two key areas for life insurers: technical reserves and premium recognition for life insurers.

Technical reserves for life insurance:

These reserves are derived from three distinct sources;

1. **Reserves for claims outstanding**: these are the same as the provisions referred to above.

2. **Mathematical reserves:** these are reserves that are calculated using sophisticated data. They are not a provision against a specific certain event, instead they are the necessary cover for the insurer's expected (mathematically calculated) future commitments towards policyholders. They are built over time as premiums flow in, the maturity of the contract approaches and the probability of claims increase. The calculation of mathematical reserves is a complex task and involves consideration such factors as:

   • mortality rates

   • acquisition and administrative expenses

   • minimum guaranteed returns promised to customers.

   As mentioned previously, insurance contract accounting under IFRS currently relies on an interim standard (IFRS 4). This standard does not provide detailed guidance on the calculation of reserves, instead ratifying previous local GAAP. However there is an overarching principle of prudence.

   Under US GAAP there is a detailed suite of rules regarding the calculation of mathematical reserves.

3. **Reserves relating to unit-linked business and pensions business:** unit-linked and pensions policies tend to include an investment component where the investment risk is 'shared' between the insurance company and the policy holder. The investment risk on these policies is usually based on the performance of a pre-defined pool of assets.

   The technical reserves – and the related claims expense included in the income statement – include amounts 'accruing' to policyholders under these policies even though the risk is being borne by the policy holder. Therefore, the reserves relating to these policies are separately disclosed in the balance sheet or the notes to the accounts.

   It should also be noted that the policyholders' share of the pool of assets which back these policies are also included – though again separately disclosed – within the investments balance in the balance sheet, with returns on these assets included in investment returns. These policies in effect result in a 'grossing up' of balance sheet investments and reserves, and of the related investment returns and claims expense.

Gross written premiums for Life business

From an insurer's point of view the premium is composed of three distinct parts as shown in exhibit 6.12:

Exhibit 6.12: Calculation of premium for life cover

Fair premium	Safety margin	Loading
PV of insurance compensation X probability of claim (death)	Premium charged slightly exceeds the fair premium as protection for insurer	This covers the insurance company's costs – commission and administrative costs

Pure premium

There is also some government tax paid on top of this. Given that life insurance premiums can be single (one-off lump) or regular (e.g., monthly), short cuts are often used when looking at revenues. One approach is to take annual premiums and add to it a portion for the single premium policies. It is common practice to assume that the average maturity of a single premium policy is 10 years: then the annual premium equivalent or APE would simply be the annual premiums + single premiums X 1/10.

Another approach is to just look at the new business written thereby ignoring business sold (but not earned) that has been included in revenues in the financials.

4.2.4 Future accounting developments

The insurance industry will soon be undergoing a major overhaul of its accounting, with a new accounting standard, *IFRS 17 Insurance Contracts*, expected to become effective in 2022.

IFRS 17 represents an enormous accounting change for insurance companies – particularly for life insurance business. It is the first comprehensive accounting for all insurance contracts and will result in insurance contracts being recorded on balance sheet at 'current value' (essentially at fair value) which is a significant shift away from the current approach of accrual accounting for insurance premiums, claims and costs.

IFRS 17 building blocks approach

IFRS 17 uses a 'building blocks approach' to calculate the current value of an insurance contract, with this amount being recorded on the balance sheet.

Exhibit 6.13 below demonstrates how the calculation of current value is derived under IFRS 17:

Exhibit 6.13: Building blocks approach under IFRS 17

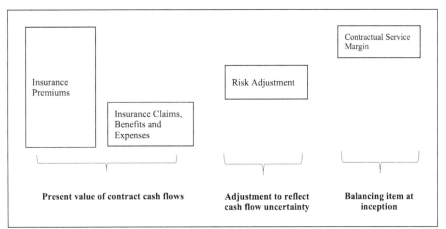

Key points to note from above are:

- The 'contractual service margin' is new terminology introduced by IFRS 17. It reflects the expected future profit from the insurance contract as part of the balance sheet value, ensuring that the contract has zero balance sheet value at inception. Therefore on day one of the contract no profit is recognised (though a loss would be recognised if the contract was deemed onerous).

- The present value of future cash flows is based on 'best estimates' of cash inflows (premiums) and cash outflows (claims, benefits and expenses). Where these estimates change, the contractual services margin is adjusted in the balance sheet so the estimates change doesn't give rise to any immediate gain or loss in earnings.

- The discount rate for calculating the net present values of the insurance premiums, claims and expenses reflects the risk characteristics of the insurance contract (e.g., duration, currency and liquidity - though it shouldn't reflect the insurer's own credit risk). The discount rate must be consistent with observable market prices and updated at each balance sheet date.

- The risk adjustment reflects the uncertainty in the expected cash flows.

IFRS 17 income statement

The IFRS 17 income statement will look very different to that under the current accounting; for a start there will be no gross or written premiums, claims expense or acquisition costs since the contract cash flows will be calculated on a net basis.

Instead, the income statement will include the following key elements:

Insurance service result

The insurance service result aims to show the profit generated from the insurance business each period. It will include:

- Contractual service margin recognised (or 'released') each period. The amount recognised is based on the proportion of claims paid out each period, relative to the total expected claims. Therefore the profit profile over the whole contract will match the profile of cash outflows (profits are recognised earlier for annuity contracts than for life insurance contracts).

- Release of risk. This is released to earnings based on the confidence level for contract cash flows.

Financial result

The investment result aims to show the financing expenses and income of the business each period. It will include:

- Interest cost on insurance liabilities. Each year, the present value of the insurance liabilities will increase as the effect of discounting the cash flows partially unwinds. This gives rise to an interest cost which is included in the investment result.

- Investment income. This will include the returns generated on all investments (e.g., equities, fixed income instruments and investment property). As highlighted previously, the returns generated from investments in equities and fixed income instruments will be accounted for under IFRS 9, once IFRS 17 is adopted.

One further item which hasn't been mentioned previously is gains or losses arising from changes in discount rates (since IFRS 17 requires discount rates to be updated each balance sheet date). Insurance companies will be able to choose whether to present these gains or losses in the investment result or in 'other comprehensive income'. This choice helps insurers manage earnings volatility.

4.3 Regulation

Insurance companies are subject to extensive regulation aimed at ensuring that they can fulfil their commitments to policyholders and that in case of poor operating performance there are sufficient funds to absorb losses without endangering policyholders' rights. For EU insurers, the key regulatory framework is Solvency II.

Solvency II is divided into three thematic areas known as 'pillars':

Pillar 1 addresses adequacy of assets, technical provisions and capital of a firm. It specifies two sets of capital requirements: the Solvency Capital Requirements (SCR) and the Minimum Capital Requirement (MCR).

Pillar 2 addresses more qualitative areas such as risk management and governance.

Pillar 3 addresses transparency by requiring certain disclosures to be provided to regulators and in public reports.

It is worth noting the similarities in this 'three pillar' approach to the regulatory framework for banks under Basel III.

The capital requirements included in Pillar 1 are particularly important as they are designed to provide regulators with a so-called 'supervisory ladder of intervention': the Solvency Capital Ratio is a higher ratio and – if breached – results in intervention by the regulator to ensure remedial action is taken (e.g., suspending further dividend payments), whilst a breach of the Minimum Capital Ratio can ultimately result in an insurance company having its authorisation withdrawn.

The calculation of the capital requirements is addressed further in the following sections, but at this point it is important to note that they are based on using 'the economic balance sheet' approach to valuing the company's assets and liabilities, as demonstrated in exhibit 6.14 below:

Exhibit 6.14: The economic balance sheet approach under Solvency II

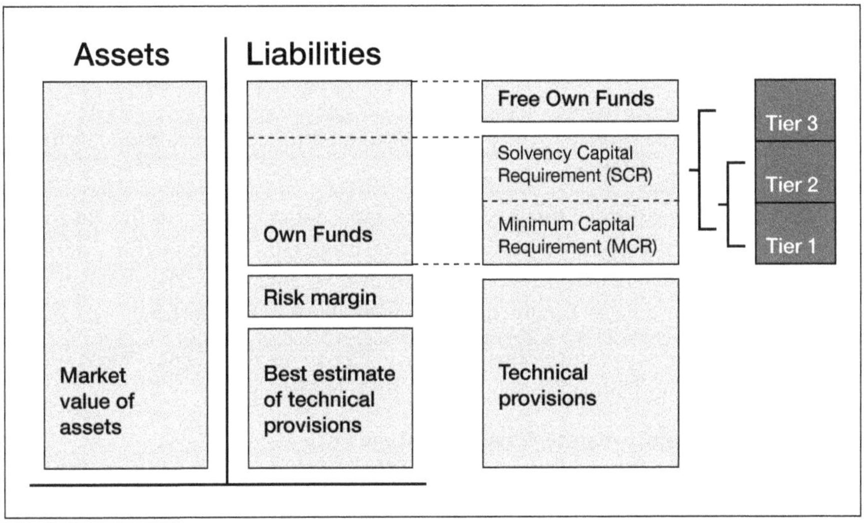

The key elements of this approach are:

- Assets are valued at market value. However, goodwill and most intangible assets are assigned a nil value.

- Insurance liabilities are calculated using the 'best estimate' of the future liability cash flows (i.e., insurance claims and benefit payments) calculated on a probability-weighted average basis. This calculation uses a risk-free discount rate, but is adjusted to the extent that there is matching between the assets and liabilities, to avoid unnecessary volatility in the difference between the asset and liability values.

- A risk margin is applied to cover the uncertainty in the future cash flows; this risk margin is essentially the difference between the best estimate of the future liability cash flows and the transfer value of the liabilities if they were to be transferred to a third party.

- Own funds are defined as assets in excess of technical provisions. They are split into three tiers, with Tier 1 being the highest quality and most permanent forms of capital (e.g., ordinary share capital, non-cumulative preference shares and long term subordinated liabilities) and Tier 2 being lower quality (e.g., cumulative preference shares and shorter-term subordinated liabilities. Tier 3 includes any own funds which do not satisfy the Tier 1 and Tier 2 requirements.

Solvency capital requirement

Under Solvency II, insurance companies are expected to maintain their own funds at more than 100% of the solvency capital requirement (SCR).

This requirement is often expressed as a solvency ratio:

$$\text{Solvency ratio} = \frac{\text{Own Funds}}{\text{Solvency Capital Requirement}} \geq 100\%$$

The SCR is a risk-based assessment and is calculated on the business assets, technical provisions and other liabilities.

The calculation covers operational risk, market risk, underwriting risk (life and non-life), health risk and credit risk and is calculated using either a standardised formula or an internal model (where supervisory approval is obtained). The calculation is calibrated to assume a 99.5% confidence level on a one-year time horizon.

For the solvency ratio, own funds include Tier 1, Tier 2 and Tier 3 capital but there are various constraints and limits for the different tiers. For example:

- Tier 1 capital must cover more than 50% of the SCR

- Tier 3 capital cannot be used to cover more than 15% of the SCR

Minimum capital requirement

The minimum capital requirement (MCR) is designed to be the minimum solvency threshold for the business, and therefore insurance companies must maintain own funds at more than 100% of the MCR.

$$\text{Minimum capital ratio} = \frac{\text{Own Funds}}{\text{Minimum Capital Requirement}} \geq 100\%$$

Similar to above, the MCR is also a risk-based assessment. The calculation is standardised and applies specific factors (as detailed in the regulations) to technical provisions and written premiums for different lines of business. The calculation is calibrated to assume an 85% confidence level on a one-year time horizon.

For assessing the own funds against the minimum capital requirement, additional constraints are placed on the composition of own funds including:

- Only Tier 1 and Tier 2 capital can be used to cover MCR

- Tier 1 capital must cover more than 80% of the MCR

The above section on regulatory matters is mainly adapted from chapter sixteen of *Financial Statement Analysis Under IFRS*, Kenneth Lee and Deborah Taylor, 6th Edition, 2018, Financial Edge publications.

4.4 Valuing insurance companies

4.4.1 What is the problem?

Insurance companies are complicated. Of all the sectors of the market, they are the hardest to value, particularly in their life businesses. The reasons for this are merely extensions of issues that we have already met. As with banks, it is not meaningful to distinguish between the operating business and financial items. As with banks, there are operations on both sides of the balance sheet, so it is generally necessary to model flows to equity. For life businesses, to a far greater degree than with banks, the duration of the cash flows is such that statutory accounts do not present a fair reflection of the businesses. This is recognised explicitly by those companies that publish so-called embedded value numbers. Unlike either banks or oil companies, the biggest problem with insurance companies is establishing the present value of their liabilities. This is similar to the difficulty in addressing a PBO for a funded pension scheme, and it is not coincidental that both tasks are performed by actuaries. As with pensions, much of what happens in the accounts of a life business reflects treatment of changes in expectation, either of longevity or of investment returns.

In this section we shall divide our treatment of insurance companies between two separate approaches reflecting the two key different types of insurance business: general insurance and life insurance.

4.4.2 General insurance businesses

We have produced a model for a fictional general insurance business ('General Insurance plc'), for which we have left the currency unspecified. It makes no difference whatsoever to the analysis, in any case.

The business has four main divisions, for private, commercial, industrial, and marine and energy, in addition to which it has business lines that it is not maintaining, which are modelled as a separate 'run-off'. Since each of the business lines is modelled in the same way, we shall discuss only the first of the four pages, and the run-off.

The remaining forecasting pages relate to the consolidated profit and loss account, the consolidated balance sheet, forecasts of technical provisions, forecasts of investments, debtors and creditors, and projections of cash flow. The latter differs from profits to the extent that the company has tax losses accounted for as deferred tax assets, so while these are utilised it will not pay tax as charged to the profit and loss account. There is nothing new about the valuation routine, as this is consistent with the approach that we used in our bank model in section 3.

Exhibit 6.15 below is our full 12-page model, and we shall comment on it in subsequent paragraphs.

Exhibit 6.15: Model of general insurance business

1. General Insurance plc - Private business

Year	-2	-1	0	1	2	3	4
Gross written premiums	7,553	8,091	8,604	9,023	9,499	9,944	10,398
Reinsured premiums	(270)	(223)	(314)	(280)	(294)	(308)	(322)
Net written premiums	7,283	7,868	8,290	8,743	9,205	9,635	10,075
Net earned premiums	7,089	7,593	7,837	8,446	9,020	9,443	9,874
Net claims	(6,145)	(6,531)	(7,266)	(7,426)	(7,740)	(7,988)	(8,156)
Net operating expenses	(1,660)	(1,701)	(1,800)	(2,086)	(2,264)	(2,361)	(2,409)
Underwriting result	(716)	(639)	(1,229)	(1,066)	(983)	(906)	(691)
Growth in written premiums		7.1%	6.3%	4.9%	5.3%	4.7%	4.6%
Retention ratio	96.4%	97.2%	96.4%	96.9%	96.9%	96.9%	96.9%
Earned/net written premiums	97.3%	96.5%	94.5%	96.6%	98.0%	98.0%	98.0%
Loss ratio	86.7%	86.0%	92.7%	87.9%	85.8%	84.6%	82.6%
Expense ratio	23.4%	22.4%	23.0%	24.7%	25.1%	25.0%	24.4%
Combined ratio	110.1%	108.4%	115.7%	112.6%	110.9%	109.6%	107.0%
Reserves	11,750	12,065	13,625	13,925	14,513	14,980	15,293
Reserves/Net earned premiums	165.7%	158.9%	173.9%	164.9%	160.9%	158.6%	154.9%

Year	5	6	7	8	9	10	11
Gross written premiums	10,858	11,325	11,751	12,209	12,631	13,078	13,554
Reinsured premiums	(337)	(351)	(364)	(378)	(392)	(405)	(420)
Net written premiums	10,522	10,974	11,387	11,831	12,239	12,673	13,134
Net earned premiums	10,311	10,755	11,159	11,594	11,995	12,420	12,871
Net claims	(8,548)	(8,937)	(9,050)	(9,380)	(9,895)	(10,432)	(10,735)
Net operating expenses	(2,413)	(2,409)	(2,388)	(2,423)	(2,567)	(2,658)	(2,729)
Underwriting result	(650)	(592)	(279)	(209)	(468)	(671)	(592)
Growth in written premiums	4.4%	4.3%	3.8%	3.9%	3.5%	3.5%	3.6%
Retention ratio	96.9%	96.9%	96.9%	96.9%	96.9%	96.9%	96.9%
Earned/net written premiums	98.0%	98.0%	98.0%	98.0%	98.0%	98.0%	98.0%
Loss ratio	82.9%	83.1%	81.1%	80.9%	82.5%	84.0%	83.4%
Expense ratio	23.4%	22.4%	21.4%	20.9%	21.4%	21.4%	21.2%
Combined ratio	106.3%	105.5%	102.5%	101.8%	103.9%	105.4%	104.6%
Reserves	16,029	16,758	16,970	17,588	18,556	19,563	20,129
Reserves/Net earned premiums	155.5%	155.8%	152.1%	151.7%	154.7%	157.5%	156.4%

2. General Insurance plc - Commercial business

Year	-2	-1	0	1	2	3	4
Gross written premiums	5,907	6,093	6,023	6,529	6,820	7,093	7,365
Reinsured premiums	(427)	(627)	(603)	(276)	(284)	(293)	(305)
Net written premiums	**5,480**	**5,466**	**5,420**	**6,253**	**6,537**	**6,800**	**7,060**
Net earned premiums	5,397	5,419	5,404	6,125	6,406	6,664	6,919
Net claims	(5,000)	(4,373)	(5,241)	(5,408)	(5,530)	(5,582)	(5,598)
Net operating expenses	(1,392)	(1,399)	(1,360)	(1,525)	(1,630)	(1,639)	(1,634)
Underwriting result	**(995)**	**(353)**	**(1,197)**	**(808)**	**(755)**	**(556)**	**(313)**
Growth in written premiums		3.1%	-1.1%	8.4%	4.5%	4.0%	3.8%
Retention ratio	92.8%	89.7%	90.0%	95.8%	95.8%	95.9%	95.9%
Earned/net written premiums	98.5%	99.1%	99.7%	98.0%	98.0%	98.0%	98.0%
Loss ratio	92.6%	80.7%	97.0%	88.3%	86.3%	83.8%	80.9%
Expense ratio	25.8%	25.8%	25.2%	24.9%	25.5%	24.6%	23.6%
Combined ratio	118.4%	106.5%	122.2%	113.2%	111.8%	108.3%	104.5%
Reserves	**10,370**	**9,258**	**9,939**	**10,256**	**10,488**	**10,585**	**10,616**
Reserves/Net earned premiums	192.1%	170.8%	183.9%	167.5%	163.7%	158.8%	153.4%

Year	5	6	7	8	9	10	11
Gross written premiums	7,633	7,896	8,142	8,413	8,681	8,974	9,295
Reinsured premiums	(318)	(335)	(352)	(368)	(382)	(394)	(403)
Net written premiums	**7,314**	**7,561**	**7,790**	**8,045**	**8,300**	**8,581**	**8,892**
Net earned premiums	7,168	7,410	7,634	7,884	8,134	8,409	8,714
Net claims	(5,947)	(6,291)	(6,291)	(6,344)	(6,758)	(7,139)	(7,244)
Net operating expenses	(1,698)	(1,759)	(1,736)	(1,723)	(1,830)	(1,911)	(1,973)
Underwriting result	**(476)**	**(641)**	**(392)**	**(182)**	**(455)**	**(642)**	**(503)**
Growth in written premiums	3.6%	3.4%	3.1%	3.3%	3.2%	3.4%	3.6%
Retention ratio	95.8%	95.8%	95.7%	95.6%	95.6%	95.6%	95.7%
Earned/net written premiums	98.0%	98.0%	98.0%	98.0%	98.0%	98.0%	98.0%
Loss ratio	83.0%	84.9%	82.4%	80.5%	83.1%	84.9%	83.1%
Expense ratio	23.7%	23.7%	22.7%	21.9%	22.5%	22.7%	22.6%
Combined ratio	106.6%	108.6%	105.1%	102.3%	105.6%	107.6%	105.8%
Reserves	**11,277**	**11,931**	**11,930**	**12,030**	**12,817**	**13,539**	**13,737**
Reserves/Net earned premiums	157.3%	161.0%	156.3%	152.6%	157.6%	161.0%	157.6%

3. General Insurance plc - Industrial business

Year	-2	-1	0	1	2	3	4
Gross written premiums	2,957	3,004	2,923	3,081	3,189	3,300	3,418
Reinsured premiums	(1,506)	(1,602)	(1,579)	(1,157)	(1,192)	(1,230)	(1,270)
Net written premiums	**1,451**	**1,402**	**1,344**	**1,924**	**1,996**	**2,070**	**2,147**
Net earned premiums	1,469	1,352	1,375	1,797	1,956	2,029	2,104
Net claims	(1,253)	(1,147)	(1,311)	(1,797)	(1,701)	(1,713)	(1,714)
Net operating expenses	(338)	(352)	(395)	(410)	(490)	(492)	(489)
Underwriting result	**(122)**	**(147)**	**(331)**	**(410)**	**(235)**	**(176)**	**(99)**
Growth in written premiums		1.6%	-2.7%	5.4%	3.5%	3.5%	3.6%
Retention ratio	49.1%	46.7%	46.0%	62.4%	62.6%	62.7%	62.8%
Earned/net written premiums	101.2%	96.4%	102.3%	93.4%	98.0%	98.0%	98.0%
Loss ratio	85.3%	84.8%	95.3%	100.0%	87.0%	84.4%	81.5%
Expense ratio	23.0%	26.0%	28.7%	22.8%	25.0%	24.2%	23.2%
Combined ratio	108.3%	110.9%	124.1%	122.8%	112.0%	108.7%	104.7%
Reserves	**3,264**	**3,360**	**3,187**	**4,368**	**4,136**	**4,164**	**4,168**
Reserves/Net earned premiums	222.2%	248.5%	231.8%	243.1%	211.4%	205.3%	198.0%

Year	5	6	7	8	9	10	11
Gross written premiums	3,541	3,672	3,804	3,939	4,073	4,210	4,349
Reinsured premiums	(1,313)	(1,358)	(1,405)	(1,452)	(1,500)	(1,548)	(1,597)
Net written premiums	**2,229**	**2,314**	**2,399**	**2,487**	**2,574**	**2,662**	**2,752**
Net earned premiums	2,184	2,268	2,351	2,437	2,522	2,609	2,697
Net claims	(1,813)	(1,914)	(1,930)	(1,966)	(2,101)	(2,200)	(2,246)
Net operating expenses	(514)	(540)	(536)	(536)	(576)	(596)	(617)
Underwriting result	**(143)**	**(187)**	**(115)**	**(64)**	**(154)**	**(187)**	**(166)**
Growth in written premiums	3.6%	3.7%	3.6%	3.6%	3.4%	3.4%	3.3%
Retention ratio	62.9%	63.0%	63.1%	63.1%	63.2%	63.2%	63.3%
Earned/net written premiums	98.0%	98.0%	98.0%	98.0%	98.0%	98.0%	98.0%
Loss ratio	83.0%	84.4%	82.1%	80.6%	83.3%	84.3%	83.3%
Expense ratio	23.5%	23.8%	22.8%	22.0%	22.8%	22.9%	22.9%
Combined ratio	106.5%	108.2%	104.9%	102.6%	106.1%	107.2%	106.2%
Reserves	**4,408**	**4,653**	**4,693**	**4,778**	**5,107**	**5,348**	**5,460**
Reserves/Net earned premiums	201.8%	205.2%	199.6%	196.0%	202.5%	205.0%	202.5%

4. General Insurance plc - Marine & Energy business

Year	-2	-1	0	1	2	3	4
Gross written premiums	1,365	1,214	1,180	1,043	1,080	1,117	1,157
Reinsured premiums	(580)	(403)	(490)	(279)	(289)	(299)	(309)
Net written premiums	**785**	**811**	**690**	**764**	**791**	**819**	**847**
Net earned premiums	795	869	719	755	775	802	830
Net claims	(438)	(494)	(803)	(702)	(651)	(674)	(689)
Net operating expenses	(205)	(207)	(220)	(268)	(186)	(184)	(183)
Underwriting result	**152**	**168**	**(304)**	**(215)**	**(62)**	**(56)**	**(42)**
Growth in written premiums		*-11.1%*	*-2.8%*	*-11.6%*	*3.5%*	*3.5%*	*3.5%*
Retention ratio	*57.5%*	*66.8%*	*58.5%*	*73.3%*	*73.3%*	*73.3%*	*73.3%*
Earned/net written premiums	*101.3%*	*107.2%*	*104.2%*	*98.8%*	*98.0%*	*98.0%*	*98.0%*
Loss ratio	*55.1%*	*56.8%*	*111.7%*	*93.0%*	*84.0%*	*84.0%*	*83.0%*
Expense ratio	*25.8%*	*23.8%*	*30.6%*	*35.5%*	*24.0%*	*23.0%*	*22.0%*
Combined ratio	*80.9%*	*80.7%*	*142.3%*	*128.5%*	*108.0%*	*107.0%*	*105.0%*
Reserves	**1,718**	**2,805**	**2,059**	**1,800**	**1,669**	**1,728**	**1,767**
Reserves/Net earned premiums	*216.1%*	*322.8%*	*286.4%*	*238.5%*	*215.4%*	*215.4%*	*212.8%*

Year	5	6	7	8	9	10	11
Gross written premiums	1,197	1,239	1,282	1,327	1,374	1,422	1,471
Reinsured premiums	(320)	(331)	(343)	(355)	(367)	(380)	(394)
Net written premiums	**877**	**907**	**939**	**972**	**1,006**	**1,041**	**1,078**
Net earned premiums	859	889	920	953	986	1,021	1,056
Net claims	(713)	(729)	(755)	(800)	(828)	(837)	(887)
Net operating expenses	(198)	(213)	(212)	(210)	(227)	(245)	(246)
Underwriting result	**(52)**	**(53)**	**(46)**	**(57)**	**(69)**	**(61)**	**(77)**
Growth in written premiums	*3.5%*	*3.5%*	*3.5%*	*3.5%*	*3.5%*	*3.5%*	*3.5%*
Retention ratio	*73.3%*	*73.3%*	*73.3%*	*73.3%*	*73.3%*	*73.3%*	*73.3%*
Earned/net written premiums	*98.0%*	*98.0%*	*98.0%*	*98.0%*	*98.0%*	*98.0%*	*98.0%*
Loss ratio	*83.0%*	*82.0%*	*82.0%*	*84.0%*	*84.0%*	*82.0%*	*84.0%*
Expense ratio	*23.0%*	*24.0%*	*23.0%*	*22.0%*	*23.0%*	*24.0%*	*23.3%*
Combined ratio	*106.0%*	*106.0%*	*105.0%*	*106.0%*	*107.0%*	*106.0%*	*107.3%*
Reserves	**1,829**	**1,870**	**1,935**	**2,052**	**2,124**	**2,146**	**2,275**
Reserves/Net earned premiums	*212.8%*	*210.3%*	*210.3%*	*215.4%*	*215.4%*	*210.3%*	*215.4%*

5. General Insurance plc - Runoff business

Year	-2	-1	0	1	2	3	4
Gross written premiums	122	163	3	3	3	3	3
Reinsured premiums	(100)	(132)	2	(2)	(2)	(2)	(2)
Net written premiums	**22**	**31**	**5**	**1**	**1**	**1**	**1**
Net earned premiums	210	75	339	1	1	1	1
Net claims	(216)	(164)	(367)	(73)	(73)	(73)	(73)
Net operating expenses	(92)	(24)	(59)	(58)	(47)	(55)	(53)
Underwriting result	**(98)**	**(113)**	**(87)**	**(130)**	**(119)**	**(127)**	**(125)**
Growth in written premiums		33.6%	-98.2%	0.0%	0.0%	0.0%	0.0%
Retention ratio	18.0%	19.0%	166.7%	33.3%	33.3%	33.3%	33.3%
Earned/net written premiums	954.5%	241.9%	6780.0%	100.0%	100.0%	100.0%	100.0%
Loss ratio	102.9%	218.7%	108.3%	5833.3%	4711.1%	5481.5%	5342.0%
Expense ratio	43.8%	32.0%	17.4%	5833.3%	4711.1%	5481.5%	5342.0%
Combined ratio	146.7%	250.7%	125.7%	13133.3%	12011.1%	12781.5%	12642.0%
Reserves	**1,629**	**1,603**	**1,848**	**2,300**	**2,300**	**2,300**	**2,300**

Year	5	6	7	8	9	10	11
Gross written premiums	3	3	3	3	3	3	3
Reinsured premiums	(2)	(2)	(2)	(2)	(2)	(2)	(2)
Net written premiums	**1**	**1**	**1**	**1**	**1**	**1**	**1**
Net earned premiums	1	1	1	1	1	1	1
Net claims	(73)	(73)	(73)	(73)	(73)	(73)	(73)
Net operating expenses	(52)	(54)	(53)	(53)	(54)	(53)	(53)
Underwriting result	**(124)**	**(126)**	**(125)**	**(125)**	**(126)**	**(125)**	**(125)**
Growth in written premiums	0.0%	0.0%	0.0%	0.0%	0.0%	0.0%	0.0%
Retention ratio	33.3%	33.3%	33.3%	33.3%	33.3%	33.3%	33.3%
Earned/net written premiums	100.0%	100.0%	100.0%	100.0%	100.0%	100.0%	100.0%
Loss ratio	5178.2%	5411.7%	5342.0%	5310.6%	5354.8%	5335.8%	5333.7%
Expense ratio	5178.2%	5411.7%	5342.0%	5310.6%	5354.8%	5335.8%	5333.7%
Combined ratio	12478.2%	12711.7%	12642.0%	12610.6%	12654.8%	12635.8%	12633.7%
Reserves	**2,300**	**2,300**	**2,300**	**2,300**	**2,300**	**2,300**	**2,300**

6. General Insurance plc - Profit and loss account

Year	-2	-1	0	1	2	3	4
Gross written premiums	17,904	18,565	18,733	19,679	20,591	21,457	22,340
Reinsured premiums	(2,883)	(2,987)	(2,984)	(1,994)	(2,061)	(2,132)	(2,208)
Net written premiums	**15,021**	**15,578**	**15,749**	**17,685**	**18,529**	**19,325**	**20,131**
Net earned premiums	14,960	15,308	15,674	17,124	18,159	18,939	19,729
Net claims	(13,052)	(12,709)	(14,988)	(15,406)	(15,695)	(16,030)	(16,230)
Net operating expenses	(3,687)	(3,683)	(3,834)	(4,347)	(4,618)	(4,731)	(4,768)
Underwriting result	**(1,779)**	**(1,084)**	**(3,148)**	**(2,630)**	**(2,154)**	**(1,822)**	**(1,270)**
Allocated investment return	1,535	1,380	1,239	1,229	1,287	1,320	1,357
Technical result	**(244)**	**296**	**(1,909)**	**(1,401)**	**(867)**	**(502)**	**87**
Total investment result	2,907	3,450	2,376	2,074	2,143	2,172	2,208
Investment expenses	(203)	(202)	(197)	(203)	(210)	(213)	(216)
Net investment result	**2,704**	**3,248**	**2,179**	**1,871**	**1,933**	**1,959**	**1,992**
less:allocated investment return	(1,535)	(1,380)	(1,239)	(1,229)	(1,287)	(1,320)	(1,357)
Profit/(loss) before tax	**925**	**2,164**	**(969)**	**(759)**	**(221)**	**137**	**722**
Tax charge/credit	(259)	(606)	0	212	62	(38)	(202)
Profits/(loss) after tax	**666**	**1,558**	**(969)**	**(546)**	**(159)**	**99**	**520**
Growth in written premiums		*3.7%*	*0.9%*	*5.0%*	*4.6%*	*4.2%*	*4.1%*
Retention ratio	*83.9%*	*83.9%*	*84.1%*	*89.9%*	*90.0%*	*90.1%*	*90.1%*
Earned/net written premiums	*99.6%*	*98.3%*	*99.5%*	*96.8%*	*98.0%*	*98.0%*	*98.0%*
Loss ratio	*87.2%*	*83.0%*	*95.6%*	*90.0%*	*86.4%*	*84.6%*	*82.3%*
Expense ratio	*24.6%*	*24.1%*	*24.5%*	*25.4%*	*25.4%*	*25.0%*	*24.2%*
Combined ratio	*111.9%*	*107.1%*	*120.1%*	*115.4%*	*111.9%*	*109.6%*	*106.4%*
Investment return	*8.7%*	*10.4%*	*7.2%*	*6.1%*	*6.1%*	*6.1%*	*6.1%*
Investment expenses	*0.6%*	*0.6%*	*0.6%*	*0.6%*	*0.6%*	*0.6%*	*0.6%*
Tax rate	*28.0%*	*28.0%*	*0.0%*	*28.0%*	*28.0%*	*28.0%*	*28.0%*

Year	5	6	7	8	9	10	11
Gross written premiums	23,232	24,134	24,982	25,891	26,762	27,688	28,672
Reinsured premiums	(2,290)	(2,377)	(2,466)	(2,555)	(2,643)	(2,730)	(2,816)
Net written premiums	**20,943**	**21,757**	**22,516**	**23,336**	**24,120**	**24,958**	**25,856**
Net earned premiums	20,524	21,322	22,066	22,869	23,637	24,459	25,339
Net claims	(17,094)	(17,945)	(18,099)	(18,562)	(19,656)	(20,681)	(21,185)
Net operating expenses	(4,874)	(4,976)	(4,925)	(4,945)	(5,253)	(5,464)	(5,618)
Underwriting result	**(1,444)**	**(1,598)**	**(958)**	**(638)**	**(1,272)**	**(1,686)**	**(1,464)**
Allocated investment return	1,745	1,864	1,950	1,644	1,729	1,833	1,910
Technical result	**301**	**266**	**992**	**1,006**	**457**	**146**	**446**
Total investment result	2,760	2,921	3,031	2,581	2,692	2,832	2,931
Investment expenses	(225)	(238)	(247)	(253)	(264)	(277)	(287)
Net investment result	**2,535**	**2,683**	**2,784**	**2,328**	**2,428**	**2,555**	**2,644**
less:allocated investment return	(1,745)	(1,864)	(1,950)	(1,644)	(1,729)	(1,833)	(1,910)
Profit/(loss) before tax	**1,091**	**1,085**	**1,826**	**1,690**	**1,157**	**868**	**1,180**
Tax charge/credit	(306)	(304)	(511)	(473)	(324)	(243)	(330)
Profits/(loss) after tax	**786**	**781**	**1,315**	**1,217**	**833**	**625**	**850**
Growth in written premiums	*4.0%*	*3.9%*	*3.5%*	*3.6%*	*3.4%*	*3.5%*	*3.6%*
Retention ratio	*90.1%*	*90.2%*	*90.1%*	*90.1%*	*90.1%*	*90.1%*	*90.2%*
Earned/net written premiums	*98.0%*	*98.0%*	*98.0%*	*98.0%*	*98.0%*	*98.0%*	*98.0%*
Loss ratio	*83.3%*	*84.2%*	*82.0%*	*81.2%*	*83.2%*	*84.6%*	*83.6%*
Expense ratio	*23.7%*	*23.3%*	*22.3%*	*21.6%*	*22.2%*	*22.3%*	*22.2%*
Combined ratio	*107.0%*	*107.5%*	*104.3%*	*102.8%*	*105.4%*	*106.9%*	*105.8%*
Investment return	*7.4%*	*7.4%*	*7.4%*	*6.1%*	*6.1%*	*6.1%*	*6.1%*
Investment expenses	*0.6%*	*0.6%*	*0.6%*	*0.6%*	*0.6%*	*0.6%*	*0.6%*
Tax rate	*28.0%*	*28.0%*	*28.0%*	*28.0%*	*28.0%*	*28.0%*	*28.0%*

7. General Insurance plc - Balance sheet

Year	-2	-1	0	1	2	3	4
Assets							
Investments:							
Fixed Income	25,735	25,681	25,396	26,140	26,345	26,837	27,238
Equities	7,583	7,567	7,483	8,713	8,782	8,946	9,079
Total investment assets	33,318	33,248	32,879	34,854	35,126	35,783	36,317
Reinsurers' share of technical prov.	5,250	6,263	7,573	7,462	6,999	6,609	6,196
Debtors:							
Arising out of direct insurance operations	na	na	2,162	2,361	2,471	2,575	2,681
Arising out of reinsurance operations	na	na	910	984	1,030	1,073	1,117
Total debtors	3,039	3,885	3,072	3,345	3,500	3,648	3,798
Deferred tax	na	na	1,370	1,582	1,644	1,606	1,404
Other assets	1,788	2,799	2,941	3,089	3,094	3,120	3,125
Deferred acquisition costs	808	819	912	869	924	946	954
Total assets	44,203	47,014	48,747	51,203	51,288	51,711	51,793
Liabilities							
Provisions for unearned premiums	7,311	7,598	7,837	6,244	4,956	3,917	3,093
Provisions for claims outstanding	26,691	27,757	30,351	33,868	35,149	36,449	37,247
Technical reserves-gross	34,002	35,355	38,188	40,112	40,105	40,366	40,340
Creditors:							
Arising from direct insurance operations	na	na	1,126	1,181	1,235	1,287	1,340
Arising out of reinsurance operations	na	na	240	256	268	279	290
Total creditors	1,427	1,330	1,366	1,437	1,503	1,566	1,631
Reinsurer's share of def. acq. costs	62	59	58	52	55	57	57
Shareholders' Funds	8,712	10,270	9,135	9,602	9,625	9,722	9,765
Total liabilities	44,203	47,014	48,747	51,203	51,288	51,711	51,793
Deferred acq costs/net operating expenses	21.9%	22.2%	23.8%	20.0%	20.0%	20.0%	20.0%
Reinsurers' share of Def. acq. costs	7.7%	7.2%	6.4%	6.0%	6.0%	6.0%	6.0%
NAV/NPE	58.2%	67.1%	58.3%	56.1%	53.0%	51.3%	49.5%
Solvency Ratio							
Financial and credit risk			1,560	1,654	1,667	1,698	1,723
Financial and credit risk % investments			4.7%	4.7%	4.7%	4.7%	4.7%
Insurance risk			3,140	3,298	3,298	3,319	3,317
Insurance risk % reserves			8.2%	8.2%	8.2%	8.2%	8.2%
Operational risk			790	790	790	790	790
Diversification benefit			(560)	(560)	(560)	(560)	(560)
Total SCR			4,930	5,182	5,194	5,247	5,270
Solvency Capital Ratio			185%	185%	185%	185%	185%

Year	5	6	7	8	9	10	11
Assets							
Investments:							
Fixed Income	28,890	30,515	31,124	32,075	33,856	35,502	36,271
Equities	9,630	10,172	10,375	10,692	11,285	11,834	12,090
Total investment assets	38,520	40,686	41,499	42,767	45,141	47,336	48,362
Reinsurers' share of technical prov.	6,034	5,863	5,493	5,232	5,138	5,016	4,781
Debtors:							
Arising out of direct insurance operations	2,788	2,896	2,998	3,107	3,211	3,323	3,441
Arising out of reinsurance operations	1,162	1,207	1,249	1,295	1,338	1,384	1,434
Total debtors	3,949	4,103	4,247	4,402	4,550	4,707	4,874
Deferred tax	1,098	795	283	0	0	0	0
Other assets	3,247	3,367	3,371	3,428	3,588	3,734	3,797
Deferred acquisition costs	975	995	985	989	1,051	1,093	1,124
Total assets	53,824	55,809	55,879	56,817	59,467	61,885	62,938
Liabilities							
Provisions for unearned premiums	2,440	1,923	1,510	1,187	930	730	573
Provisions for claims outstanding	39,436	41,453	41,812	42,794	45,110	47,181	48,109
Technical reserves-gross	41,876	43,376	43,321	43,981	46,041	47,911	48,682
Creditors:							
Arising from direct insurance operations	1,394	1,448	1,499	1,553	1,606	1,661	1,720
Arising out of reinsurance operations	302	314	325	337	348	360	373
Total creditors	1,696	1,762	1,824	1,890	1,954	2,021	2,093
Reinsurer's share of def. acq. costs	58	60	59	59	63	66	67
Shareholders' Funds	10,193	10,612	10,675	10,887	11,409	11,887	12,095
Total liabilities	53,824	55,809	55,879	56,817	59,467	61,885	62,938
Deferred acq costs/net operating expenses	20.0%	20.0%	20.0%	20.0%	20.0%	20.0%	20.0%
Reinsurers' share of Def. acq. costs	6.0%	6.0%	6.0%	6.0%	6.0%	6.0%	6.0%
NAV/NPE	49.7%	49.8%	48.4%	47.6%	48.3%	48.6%	47.7%
Solvency Ratio							
Financial and credit risk	1,828	1,930	1,969	2,029	2,142	2,246	2,295
Financial and credit risk % investments	4.7%	4.7%	4.7%	4.7%	4.7%	4.7%	4.7%
Insurance risk	3,443	3,567	3,562	3,616	3,786	3,939	4,003
Insurance risk % reserves	8.2%	8.2%	8.2%	8.2%	8.2%	8.2%	8.2%
Operational risk	790	790	790	790	790	790	790
Diversification benefit	(560)	(560)	(560)	(560)	(560)	(560)	(560)
Total SCR	5,501	5,727	5,761	5,875	6,157	6,415	6,528
Solvency Capital Ratio	185%	185%	185%	185%	185%	185%	185%

8. General Insurance plc - Reserves

Year	-2	-1	0	1	2	3	4
Total net technical reserves	28,731	29,091	30,658	32,650	33,105	33,757	34,144
Adjustment	21	1	(43)	0	0	0	0
Reinsurers' share	5,250	6,263	7,573	7,462	6,999	6,609	6,196
Total gross reserves	**34,002**	**35,355**	**38,188**	**40,112**	**40,105**	**40,366**	**40,340**
Provisions for unearned premiums	7,311	7,598	7,837	6,244	4,956	3,917	3,093
Claims reserves	**26,691**	**27,757**	**30,351**	**33,868**	**35,149**	**36,449**	**37,247**
Reinsurers' share of technical reserves	*15.4%*	*17.7%*	*19.8%*	*18.6%*	*17.5%*	*16.4%*	*15.4%*
Provisions for unearned premiums	*40.8%*	*40.9%*	*41.8%*	*31.7%*	*24.1%*	*18.3%*	*13.8%*

Year	5	6	7	8	9	10	11
Total net technical reserves	35,843	37,513	37,828	38,749	40,903	42,895	43,901
Adjustment	0	0	0	0	0	0	0
Reinsurers' share	6,034	5,863	5,493	5,232	5,138	5,016	4,781
Total gross reserves	**41,876**	**43,376**	**43,321**	**43,981**	**46,041**	**47,911**	**48,682**
Provisions for unearned premiums	2,440	1,923	1,510	1,187	930	730	573
Claims reserves	**39,436**	**41,453**	**41,812**	**42,794**	**45,110**	**47,181**	**48,109**
Reinsurers' share of technical reserves	*14.4%*	*13.5%*	*12.7%*	*11.9%*	*11.2%*	*10.5%*	*9.8%*
Provisions for unearned premiums	*10.5%*	*8.0%*	*6.0%*	*4.6%*	*3.5%*	*2.6%*	*2.0%*

9. General Insurance plc - Investments

Year	-2	-1	0	1	2	3	4
Fixed Income	25,735	25,681	25,396	26,140	26,345	26,837	27,238
Equities	7,583	7,567	7,483	8,713	8,782	8,946	9,079
Total investment assets	**33,318**	**33,248**	**32,879**	**34,854**	**35,126**	**35,783**	**36,317**
Total investment result	2,907	3,450	2,376	2,074	2,143	2,172	2,208
Fixed income securities/total investments	*77.2%*	*77.2%*	*77.2%*	*75.0%*	*75.0%*	*75.0%*	*75.0%*
Equities/total investments	*22.8%*	*22.8%*	*22.8%*	*25.0%*	*25.0%*	*25.0%*	*25.0%*
Bond yield				*5.5%*	*5.5%*	*5.5%*	*5.5%*
Equity return				*8.0%*	*8.0%*	*8.0%*	*8.0%*
Investment return	*8.7%*	*10.4%*	*7.2%*	*6.1%*	*6.1%*	*6.1%*	*6.1%*
Investment expenses	*0.6%*	*0.6%*	*0.6%*	*0.6%*	*0.6%*	*0.6%*	*0.6%*

Year	5	6	7	8	9	10	11
Fixed Income	28,890	30,515	31,124	32,075	33,856	35,502	36,271
Equities	9,630	10,172	10,375	10,692	11,285	11,834	12,090
Total investment assets	**38,520**	**40,686**	**41,499**	**42,767**	**45,141**	**47,336**	**48,362**
Total investment result	2,760	2,921	3,031	2,581	2,692	2,832	2,931
Fixed income securities/total investments	*75.0%*	*75.0%*	*75.0%*	*75.0%*	*75.0%*	*75.0%*	*75.0%*
Equities/total investments	*25.0%*	*25.0%*	*25.0%*	*25.0%*	*25.0%*	*25.0%*	*25.0%*
Bond yield	*6.5%*	*6.5%*	*6.5%*	*5.5%*	*5.5%*	*5.5%*	*5.5%*
Equity return	*10.0%*	*10.0%*	*10.0%*	*8.0%*	*8.0%*	*8.0%*	*8.0%*
Investment return	*7.4%*	*7.4%*	*7.4%*	*6.1%*	*6.1%*	*6.1%*	*6.1%*
Investment expenses	*0.6%*	*0.6%*	*0.6%*	*0.6%*	*0.6%*	*0.6%*	*0.6%*

10. General Insurance plc - Debtors and creditors

Year	-2	-1	0	1	2	3	4
Debtors:							
Arising out of direct insurance operations	na	na	2,162	2,361	2,471	2,575	2,681
Arising out of reinsurance operations	na	na	910	984	1,030	1,073	1,117
Total debtors	**3,039**	**3,885**	**3,072**	**3,345**	**3,500**	**3,648**	**3,798**
Creditors:							
Arising from direct insurance operations	na	na	1,126	1,181	1,235	1,287	1,340
Arising out of reinsurance operations	na	na	240	256	268	279	290
Total creditors	**1,427**	**1,330**	**1,366**	**1,437**	**1,503**	**1,566**	**1,631**
Debtors							
Direct insurers/gross premiums written			*11.5%*	*12.0%*	*12.0%*	*12.0%*	*12.0%*
Reinsurers/gross premiums written			*4.9%*	*5.0%*	*5.0%*	*5.0%*	*5.0%*
Creditors							
Direct insurers/gross premiums written			*6.0%*	*6.0%*	*6.0%*	*6.0%*	*6.0%*
Reinsurers/gross premiums written			*1.3%*	*1.3%*	*1.3%*	*1.3%*	*1.3%*

Year	5	6	7	8	9	10	11
Debtors:							
Arising out of direct insurance operations	2,788	2,896	2,998	3,107	3,211	3,323	3,441
Arising out of reinsurance operations	1,162	1,207	1,249	1,295	1,338	1,384	1,434
Total debtors	**3,949**	**4,103**	**4,247**	**4,402**	**4,550**	**4,707**	**4,874**
Creditors:							
Arising from direct insurance operations	1,394	1,448	1,499	1,553	1,606	1,661	1,720
Arising out of reinsurance operations	302	314	325	337	348	360	373
Total creditors	**1,696**	**1,762**	**1,824**	**1,890**	**1,954**	**2,021**	**2,093**
Debtors							
Direct insurers/gross premiums written	*12.0%*	*12.0%*	*12.0%*	*12.0%*	*12.0%*	*12.0%*	*12.0%*
Reinsurers/gross premiums written	*5.0%*	*5.0%*	*5.0%*	*5.0%*	*5.0%*	*5.0%*	*5.0%*
Creditors							
Direct insurers/gross premiums written	*6.0%*	*6.0%*	*6.0%*	*6.0%*	*6.0%*	*6.0%*	*6.0%*
Reinsurers/gross premiums written	*1.3%*	*1.3%*	*1.3%*	*1.3%*	*1.3%*	*1.3%*	*1.3%*

11. General Insurance plc - Cash flow

Year	0	1	2	3	4	5
Deferred tax asset - opening balance	1,370	1,582	1,644	1,606	1,404	1,098
Tax credit/charge	212	62	(38)	(202)	(306)	(304)
Deferred tax-closing balance	1,582	1,644	1,606	1,404	1,098	795
Tax paid	**0**	**0**	**0**	**0**	**0**	**0**
Deferred tax	(212)	(62)	38	202	306	304
Profit after tax	(546)	(159)	99	520	786	781
Cash flow	**(759)**	**(221)**	**137**	**722**	**1,091**	**1,085**

Year	6	7	8	9	10	
Deferred tax asset - opening balance	795	283	0	0	0	
Tax credit/charge	(511)	(473)	(324)	(243)	(330)	
Deferred tax-closing balance	283	0	0	0	0	
Tax paid	**0**	**(190)**	**(324)**	**(243)**	**(330)**	
Deferred tax	511	283	0	0	0	
Profit after tax	1,315	1,217	833	625	850	
Cash flow	**1,826**	**1,500**	**833**	**625**	**850**	

12. General Insurance plc - Valuation

Cost of equity:

Risk free rate	2.50%
Equity risk premium	5.00%
Beta	0.8
Cost of equity	**6.50%**
Assumed long term growth rate	2.50%
Assumed long term ROE	7.50%

Year	0	1	2	3	4	5
Inputs from forecasts:						
Profit after taxation	(546)	(159)	99	520	786	781
Deferred tax	(212)	(62)	38	202	306	304
Adjusted profit after tax	**(759)**	**(221)**	**137**	**722**	**1,091**	**1,085**
Opening shareholders' funds	9,135	9,602	9,625	9,722	9,765	10,193
Implied free cash flow	**(1,226)**	**(243)**	**39**	**679**	**663**	**666**
Acc. Return on opening shareholders' funds	-5.98%	-1.65%	1.02%	5.35%	8.05%	7.66%
Adj. return on opening shareholders' funds	-8.31%	-2.30%	1.42%	7.42%	11.17%	10.64%
Investment spread	-14.81%	-8.80%	-5.08%	0.92%	4.67%	4.14%
Implied residual income	**(1,353)**	**(845)**	**(489)**	**90**	**456**	**422**

Year	6	7	8	9	10	Terminus
Inputs from forecasts:						
Profit after taxation	1,315	1,217	833	625	850	
Deferred tax	511	283	0	0	0	
Adjusted profit after tax	**1,826**	**1,500**	**833**	**625**	**850**	**907**
Opening shareholders' funds	10,612	10,675	10,887	11,409	11,887	12,095
Implied free cash flow	**1,763**	**1,288**	**310**	**147**	**642**	**605**
Acc. Return on opening shareholders' funds	12.39%	11.40%	7.65%	5.48%	7.15%	
Adj. return on opening shareholders' funds	17.21%	14.05%	7.65%	5.48%	7.15%	
Investment spread	10.71%	7.55%	1.15%	-1.02%	0.65%	
Implied residual income	**1,136**	**806**	**125**	**(116)**	**77**	**121**

Discounted cash to equity value:

PV eleven year free cash flow	2,624	25.8%
PV terminal value	7,563	74.2%
Value of shareholders' funds	**10,187**	**100.0%**

Residual income valuation:

Adjusted opening shareholders' funds	9,135	89.7%
PV eleven year residual income	(461)	-4.5%
PV of terminal value (no growth)	931	9.1%
PV terminal value (future growth)	582	5.7%
Value of shareholders' funds	**10,187**	**100.0%**

4.4.2.1 Underwriting results

To understand page one, which relates to the private business, it is necessary to understand that re-insurance activities are a key part of risk management for general insurance. As a reminder from earlier in this section, net premiums earned is the accrued income after reinsurance activities, whereas gross premiums written are as the total premiums due from customers before reinsurance activities. There are two costs to be set against earned income. The first is the cost of paying out against claims, and the second is the operating cost of running the business. The total of these costs, as a proportion of earned income, is known as the combined ratio, and is often more than 100%. Claims drive the loss ratio and expenses the expenses ratio.

How can a business be profitable if it has negative margins? Because there is a timing difference between when it receives income and when it pays out against claims. The other side of the insurance business is its investment activity, and when investment returns are taken into account the overall business should (under normal circumstances) generate a profit. Not for nothing have insurance companies been named 'investment trusts with an expensive hobby', though this is unfair. The underwriting business generates cash on which the investment business aims to earn a return.

Although we have not yet looked at the balance sheet, it is evident that the balance sheet of an insurance company is dominated by two items. The first is investment assets, and the second is the provision for the payments ('technical reserves') that it is likely to have to pay out in future against claims. Estimating the required reserves is clearly an actuarial matter, but it is notable that in this business reserves represent more than 100% of net earned premiums. The reason for this is that many contracts have a life of more than one year. General insurance contracts will vary in length, and it is not surprising that reserves in the industrial and marine and energy businesses represent a larger multiple of annual net earned premiums. The contracts cover longer periods. Establishing the appropriate level of reserves is clearly the most complex task for the management of an insurance company and its actuaries.

We shall pass over the subsequent three pages of this model without comment, since these work in exactly the fashion just described. But we need to pause at page five, the run-off business. This represents a long-tailed exposure to a business that the company is discontinuing (imagine insurance against asbestos-related health claims as a possible example) and against which the company believes that it will be required to place considerable reserves, despite enjoying no operating income from the business.

4.4.2.2 Consolidated profit and loss account

Most of the profit and loss account on page six of the model represents an aggregation of the businesses that we have already modelled. The main item requiring explanation is the investment return. We shall look at how this is forecast later, but at this stage will merely concentrate on the allocation of investment income. Insurance company investments comprise two separate sources of funds. The larger part represents the provisions that have been made against future expected claims. The smaller part represents the equity shareholders' interests. Unlike an industrial company, or even a bank, for an insurance company equity does not finance the operations of the business. For an industrial company, we finance invested capital with debt and equity. With a bank we finance the assets with capital and deposits. But with an insurance company the act of underwriting generates cash. The equity does not, in that sense, finance anything, other than at the start of the company's life, when it is required to fund the acquisition cost of the first new business. Once the company is mature, equity is just there to provide a cushion, which is why part of our profit is the return that we make on the equity capital. Underwriting operations relate to the liabilities side of the balance sheet. The asset side of an insurance company's balance sheet is dominated by financial investments, and these are allocated between those that relate to the underwriting business and those that relate to the equity shareholder.

4.4.2.3 Balance sheet

Within the balance sheet (page seven) the dominant items are, as expected, investments, technical reserves and shareholders' funds. We shall discuss investments and shareholders' funds in more detail below and address technical reserves in the next section. We also find:

- the reinsurer's share of the technical provisions (on the asset side) which we will model alongside gross technical reserves;

- debtor and creditor items, which grow in line with gross premiums written;

- deferred tax assets, which are a result of the business having previously generated substantial tax losses. These get utilised in forecast profitable years, and will be modelled separately;

- deferred acquisition costs represent prepayments relating to business not yet earned, which are modelled as a percentage of operating expenses; and

- other assets, which are assumed to grow in line with total assets.

We will now concentrate on investments and shareholders' funds.

Firstly, we shall turn to investments. As with modelling a bank, we will need a balancing item on the asset side of the balance sheet. For our general insurance business, we use the investment balance as the balancing item, since we assume that management will invest any surplus capital in the short term. This line item therefore needs to be monitored carefully as a sanity check.

Secondly, we turn to shareholders' funds. As discussed earlier in this chapter, insurance companies are required to manage their capital structure with reference to a solvency capital ratio. We have therefore assumed that the driver for shareholders' funds is the company's target solvency ratio, since any excess capital is likely to be distributed to shareholders. The target ratio is either based on the company's own disclosure, or targets disclosed by similar insurance companies. In any case, the solvency capital ratio will need to exceed the regulatory minimum level of 100%.

However, in order to forecast shareholder's funds in this way, we have to forecast the Solvency Capital Requirement (SCR) throughout the forecast period, as demonstrated at the foot of the balance sheet. Our SCR forecasts have been calculated by flexing each component of the company's latest capital requirement for changes in the relevant line items; i.e., financial and credit risk is assumed to grow with the investments balance and underwriting risk is assumed to grow with technical reserves. The components of the solvency capital requirement can usually be obtained from company annual reports.

One final point to add before we move on from shareholders' funds is that, for simplicity, we have assumed here that shareholders' funds in the balance sheet are equivalent to 'own funds' in our solvency capital ratio. In reality, the two numbers will differ – remember that Solvency II uses the market values of assets, 'best estimate' values of technical reserves and excludes goodwill and intangible assets. This simplification is unlikely to matter if the business and balance sheet structure is broadly stable over time, however we provide an alternative approach later in this section, when we model a life insurance company.

4.4.2.4 Modelling reserves

As we have seen, quantifying the appropriate level of reserves from inside the company is both crucial and extremely complex. From the outside it is essentially impossible. What we can do, and have done, is to model technical reserves by business, so that differential growth rates will result in changes in the ratio of reserves to net earned premiums.

The reserves that we modelled by business were net (excluding those relating to reinsured businesses). The two main additions to get from this figure to the gross technical reserves in the balance sheet are to add back the reinsurers' share and to include a provision for that part of gross written premiums that relates to as yet unearned income. This is modelled on page eight as a proportion of gross written premiums.

4.4.2.5 Investments

Investment balances, and the returns on these, are shown on page nine of the model. As a reminder, we have assumed that the total investment balance is a balancing item. However, within this, we need to determine the asset allocation between fixed income investments and equities, as well as the expected returns on each of these. Given their need for predictable cash flows from their investments, insurance companies tend to maintain a fairly high proportion of their investments in bonds, rather than equities. But the allocation, and the expected returns from each asset class, again represent an important actuarial assumption and management decision.

4.4.2.6 Debtors and creditors

As already mentioned, when we discussed the balance sheet, the debtor and creditor items on page ten of the model are derived as a proportion of gross written premiums.

4.4.2.7 Cash flow and taxation

As a general rule the statutory accounts of an insurance company reflect cash flows. As we have seen, earned premium income is a cash item as are claims and expenses. In the case of General Insurance plc, however, we are carrying large deferred tax assets in the balance sheet that it is expected will be relieved against future tax liabilities. This is modelled on page eleven; the technique used is as described in chapter four, section 3.6 and is identical to that which would apply for an industrial company in the same situation.

To the extent that the company creates losses, these add to the deferred tax asset, and to the extent that it makes profits these reduce it. The opening balance for each year is relieved against tax charges until it is exhausted, at which point the company starts to pay tax. The consequence is that there may be a run of years, as in this case, where there are tax charges in the profit and loss account, but no tax payments made, to the benefit of the cash flow.

The cash flow figure derived here is prior to retentions, which represent that proportion of earnings that are not distributable if the company is to maintain its required solvency ratio.

4.4.2.8 Valuation

After a lot of comment on the forecasting of the accounting items we have nothing to say about the mechanics of the valuation on page 12. The cost of equity is derived in the usual fashion, and the cash flows to equity and residual income to equity are discounted in the normal way. It should be noted that free cash flow is cash flow from operations minus the retentions required to maintain the solvency ratio.

The valuation conclusion in this instance is that the 11 years of specific forecast represents less than 30% of its cash flow valuation with over 70% in the terminus. The forecast cash flow for the first year is negative, though cash flows start to improve by the second year.

The residual income value suggests that the company is worth a very small premium over its book net asset value. This premium is more than 100% attributable to the terminal value, with an expected small value destruction over the 11 years of the forecast period.

4.4.3 Valuing a life insurance business

The main difference between life business and general insurance business is that the life business is much longer term and therefore even more reliant on actuarial inputs. However, a further difference is that the products on offer tend to be much more varied – and often linked to the geography of the business – with products ranging from those containing a significant investment component (e.g., unit linked policies) to those with only an insurance component (e.g., annuity business) and a variety of other products in between. Also, given the longer-term nature of life insurance, the regulatory capital constraints become more important and therefore require similar levels of analysis to that conducted when valuing a bank.

To illustrate these issues we have produced a model for a fictional life insurance business ('Life Insurance plc'), for which we have also included a small amount of non-life business, since it is typical for a life insurance company to also have some non-life activities.

As with other models of companies, we reproduce in exhibit 6.16 below the full nine pages of the model, and shall then talk through them in the paragraphs that follow.

Exhibit 6.16:

1. Life Insurance plc Balance Sheet (Euro million)

Year	-1	0	1	2	3	4	5
Assets							
Goodwill	6,664	6,679	6,679	6,679	6,679	6,679	6,679
Other intangible assets	2,202	2,105	2,105	2,105	2,105	2,105	2,105
Tangible assets	4,476	4,075	4,075	4,075	4,075	4,075	4,075
Amounts ceded to reinsurers	3,933	4,294	4,337	4,380	4,424	4,468	4,513
Investment properties	12,584	12,993	13,374	13,767	14,096	14,384	14,674
Associates / JVs	1,194	1,171	1,205	1,241	1,270	1,296	1,323
Held to maturity	2,168	2,267	2,333	2,402	2,459	2,510	2,560
Loans and receivables	44,178	40,262	41,443	42,660	43,680	44,574	45,471
Available for sale	313,933	320,641	41,443	42,660	43,680	44,574	45,471
Investments at FVTPL	95,114	93,897	96,650	99,489	101,869	103,952	106,046
Investments	469,171	471,231	485,049	499,293	511,239	521,695	532,203
Life	413,430	426,789	436,544	449,364	460,115	469,526	478,983
P&C	39,183	38,639	38,804	39,943	40,899	41,736	42,576
Other	16,558	5,803	9,701	9,986	10,225	10,434	10,644
Receivables	11,790	11,676	12,007	12,349	12,636	12,887	13,139
Other assets	15,414	30,170	31,026	31,909	32,650	33,298	33,950
Cash and cash equivalents	7,533	6,849	7,043	7,244	7,412	7,559	7,707
Total assets	**521,183**	**537,079**	**552,322**	**568,034**	**581,219**	**592,767**	**604,371**
Liabilities							
Share capital	1,560	1,562	1,562	1,562	1,562	1,562	1,562
Capital reserve	7,098	7,098	7,098	7,098	7,098	7,098	7,098
Retained earnings	10,685	11,319	11,876	12,224	12,938	13,380	13,641
Unrealised gains and AFS	5,166	5,224	5,224	5,224	5,224	5,224	5,224
Other reserves	35	(123)	(123)	(123)	(123)	(123)	(123)
Shareholders equity	24,544	25,080	25,637	25,985	26,699	27,141	27,402
Minority interests	1,123	1,098	1,194	1,304	1,431	1,572	1,726
Other provisions	1,804	1,950	1,970	1,989	2,029	2,070	2,111
Insurance provisions - life	388,128	397,588	409,620	422,218	432,249	440,894	449,712
Of which borne by policyholder	*60,799*	*67,997*	*73,437*	*79,312*	*82,484*	*84,134*	*85,817*
Insurance provisions -P&C	33,349	32,902	33,231	33,563	33,899	34,238	34,580
Insurance provisions	421,477	430,490	442,851	455,782	466,148	475,132	484,292
Financial liabilities - operating activities	38,747	30,501	31,377	32,293	33,027	33,853	34,699
Financial liabilities - subordinated debt	9,126	8,379	8,588	8,803	9,032	9,267	9,508
Financial liabilities - other financing activities	3,543	3,436	3,522	3,610	3,704	3,800	3,899
Financial liabilities	51,416	42,316	43,487	44,706	45,763	46,920	48,106
Payables	9,550	10,494	10,795	11,110	11,365	11,593	11,826
Other liabilities	11,269	25,653	26,389	27,158	27,783	28,340	28,908
Total liabilities	**496,639**	**512,001**	**526,685**	**542,049**	**554,520**	**565,626**	**576,969**
Total liabilities and shareholders funds	**521,183**	**537,081**	**552,322**	**568,034**	**581,219**	**592,767**	**604,371**

2. Life Insurance plc Income Statement (Euro million)

Year	-1	0	1	2	3	4	5
Life segment							
Technical margin	5,895	5,867	5,893	6,072	6,152	6,287	6,412
Investment result	2,080	2,209	2,158	2,215	2,501	2,557	2,608
Expenses	(4,890)	(4,936)	(5,043)	(5,143)	(5,246)	(5,351)	(5,458)
Life segment operating profit	3,085	3,140	3,008	3,144	3,407	3,492	3,562
P&C segment							
Net premium earned	19,446	19,661	19,909	20,108	20,309	20,512	20,717
Benefits and claims	(12,640)	(12,784)	(13,140)	(13,271)	(13,404)	(13,538)	(13,673)
Acquisition and admin costs	(5,403)	(5,580)	(5,674)	(5,731)	(5,788)	(5,846)	(5,904)
Technical margin	1,403	1,297	1,095	1,106	1,117	1,128	1,139
Investment result	968	940	929	945	990	1,012	1,033
Expenses	(297)	(264)	(267)	(269)	(272)	(275)	(277)
P&C segment operating profit	2,074	1,973	1,758	1,782	1,835	1,866	1,895
Holding and other businesses							
Financial result	384	513	349	443	460	470	480
Expenses	(458)	(454)	(454)	(454)	(454)	(454)	(454)
Holding and other businesses operating profit	(74)	59	(105)	(11)	6	16	26
Consolidation adjustments	(300)	(278)	(278)	(278)	(278)	(278)	(278)
Total operating profit	**4,785**	**4,894**	**4,383**	**4,636**	**4,970**	**5,096**	**5,205**
Non operating income -other investment gains	(214)	86	95	98	100	103	105
Non-operating expense - interest on financial liabilities	(794)	(756)	(754)	(772)	(798)	(819)	(841)
Other non-operating expenses	(518)	(432)	(444)	(457)	(468)	(477)	(486)
Profit before taxation	**3,259**	**3,792**	**3,280**	**3,504**	**3,804**	**3,902**	**3,983**
Taxation	(1,059)	(1,280)	(1,082)	(1,156)	(1,255)	(1,288)	(1,314)
Taxation rate (%)	32.5%	33.8%	33.0%	33.0%	33.0%	33.0%	33.0%
Discontinued operations	40	(217)	0	0	0	0	0
Consolidated profit/loss	**2,240**	**2,295**	**2,197**	**2,348**	**2,549**	**2,614**	**2,669**
Profit attributable to non-controlling interests	(158)	(185)	(96)	(109)	(128)	(140)	(155)
Profit attributable to ordinary shares	**2,082**	**2,110**	**2,101**	**2,238**	**2,421**	**2,474**	**2,514**
Other comprehensive income	(69)	(189)	0	0	0	0	0
Attributable to non-controlling interests	79	88	0	0	0	0	0
Total comprehensive income attributable to ordinary shares	**2,092**	**2,009**	**2,101**	**2,238**	**2,421**	**2,474**	**2,514**
Ordinary dividends payable	(1,249)	(1,330)	(1,261)	(1,343)	(1,574)	(1,608)	(1,634)
Payout ratio	60%	63%	60.0%	60.0%	65.0%	65.0%	65.0%
Year end shares outstanding	1,562	1,562	1,548	1,508	1,485	1,456	1,415
Weighted average shares outstanding	1,559	1,561	1,555	1,528	1,497	1,471	1,436
Earnings per share	1.34	1.35	1.35	1.46	1.62	1.68	1.75
Dividends per share	0.80	0.85	0.81	0.89	1.06	1.10	1.15

Premiums analysis

	-1	0	1	2	3	4	5
Life segment							
Gross written premiums	48,400	47,788	48,744	49,719	50,713	51,727	52,762
Premium growth rate		-1.3%	2.0%	2.0%	2.0%	2.0%	2.0%
Net premiums earned	45,498	44,943	45,842	46,759	47,694	48,648	49,621
NPE / GWP	94.0%	94.0%	94.0%	94.0%	94.0%	94.0%	94.0%
NPE / Reserves		11.4%	11.4%	11.2%	11.2%	11.1%	11.1%
P&C segment							
Gross written premiums	20,507	20,749	20,956	21,166	21,378	21,591	21,807
Premium growth rate		1.2%	1.0%	1.0%	1.0%	1.0%	1.0%
Net premiums earned	19,446	19,661	19,909	20,108	20,309	20,512	20,717
NPE / GWP	94.8%	94.8%	95.0%	95.0%	95.0%	95.0%	95.0%
NPE / Reserves		59.4%	60.2%	60.2%	60.2%	60.2%	60.2%

3. Life Insurance plc Balance Sheet Drivers

Year	-1	0	1	2	3	4	5
Assets							
Goodwill	0.23%	0.00%	0.00%	0.00%	0.00%	0.00%
Other intangible assets	-4.41%	0.00%	0.00%	0.00%	0.00%	0.00%
Tangible assets	-8.96%	0.00%	0.00%	0.00%	0.00%	0.00%
Amounts ceded to reinsurers % insurance provisions	1.00%	1.00%	1.00%	1.00%	1.00%	1.00%
Investment properties % investments	2.76%	2.76%	2.76%	2.76%	2.76%	2.76%
Associates / JVs % investments	0.25%	0.25%	0.25%	0.25%	0.25%	0.25%
Held to maturity % investments	0.48%	0.48%	0.48%	0.48%	0.48%	0.48%
Loans and receivables % investments	8.54%	8.54%	8.54%	8.54%	8.54%	8.54%
Available for sale % investments	68.04%	68.04%	68.04%	68.04%	68.04%	68.04%
Investments at FVTPL % investments	19.93%	19.93%	19.93%	19.93%	19.93%	19.93%
Investments	0.44%	2.93%	2.94%	2.39%	2.05%	2.01%
Life investments % total investments	90.57%	90.00%	90.00%	90.00%	90.00%	90.00%
P&C investments % total investments	8.20%	8.00%	8.00%	8.00%	8.00%	8.00%
Other investments % total investments	1.23%	2.00%	2.00%	2.00%	2.00%	2.00%
Receivables	-0.97%	2.84%	2.84%	2.32%	1.99%	1.96%
Other assets	95.73%	2.84%	2.84%	2.32%	1.99%	1.96%
Cash and cash equivalents	-9.08%	2.84%	2.84%	2.32%	1.99%	1.96%
Total assets	3.05%	2.84%	2.84%	2.32%	1.99%	1.96%
Liabilities							
Share capital	0.13%	4.00%	3.00%	3.00%	2.00%	2.00%
Capital reserve	0.00%	-2.00%	-1.00%	0.00%	0.00%	1.00%
Retained earnings	5.93%	0.00%	0.00%	0.00%	1.00%	2.00%
Unrealised gains and AFS	1.12%	2.87%	2.92%	2.27%	1.93%	1.93%
Other reserves	-451.43%	1.00%	1.00%	2.00%	2.00%	2.00%
Minority interests	-2.23%	0.00%	1.00%	1.00%	2.00%	2.00%
Shareholders equity	2.18%	1.00%	1.00%	2.00%	2.00%	2.00%
Other provisions	8.09%	1.00%	1.00%	2.00%	2.00%	2.00%
Insurance provisions - traditional life	2.44%	2.00%	2.00%	2.00%	2.00%	2.00%
Insurance provisions - unit linked	11.84%	8.00%	8.00%	4.00%	2.00%	2.00%
Insurance provisions - P&C	-1.34%	1.00%	1.00%	1.00%	1.00%	1.00%
Insurance provisions	2.14%	2.87%	2.92%	2.27%	1.93%	1.93%
Financial liabilities - operating activities	-21.28%	2.87%	2.92%	2.27%	2.50%	2.50%
Financial liabilities -financing activities	-3.02%	2.50%	2.50%	2.60%	2.60%	2.60%
Financial liabilities	-17.70%	2.77%	2.80%	2.36%	2.53%	2.53%
Payables	9.88%	2.87%	2.92%	2.30%	2.00%	2.01%
Other liabilities	127.64%	2.87%	2.92%	2.30%	2.00%	2.01%
Total liabilities	3.09%	2.87%	2.92%	2.30%	2.00%	2.01%
Total liabilities and shareholders funds	3.05%	2.84%	2.84%	2.32%	1.99%	1.96%

4. Life Insurance plc Profit and Loss Drivers

Year	0	1	2	3	4	5
Life segment						
Technical margin % of ave insurance provisions	1.49%	1.46%	1.46%	1.44%	1.44%	1.44%
Investment margin % of ave investments	0.53%	0.50%	0.50%	0.55%	0.55%	0.55%
Expenses % NPE	10.98%	11.00%	11.00%	11.00%	11.00%	11.00%
P&C segment						
Loss ratio	65.02%	66.00%	66.00%	66.00%	66.00%	66.00%
Expense ratio	28.38%	28.50%	28.50%	28.50%	28.50%	28.50%
Investment margin % of ave investments	2.42%	2.40%	2.40%	2.45%	2.45%	2.45%
Financial and other segment						
Investment margin % of ave investments	4.59%	4.50%	4.50%	4.55%	4.55%	4.55%
Other						
Returns on associates and JVs	10.15%	8.00%	8.00%	8.00%	8.00%	8.00%
Interest expense on financial liabilities	6.18%	6.30%	6.30%	6.35%	6.35%	6.35%

5. Life Insurance plc Ratios (Euro million)

Year	-1	0	1	2	3	4	5
Solvency Capital Requirement (SCR)							
Financial and credit risk		23,214	23,895	24,596	25,185	25,700	26,218
Financial and credit risk % investments		**4.9%**	**4.9%**	**4.9%**	**4.9%**	**4.9%**	**4.9%**
Life underwriting risk		4,017	4,139	4,266	4,367	4,455	4,544
Life underwriting risk % provisions		**1.0%**	**1.0%**	**1.0%**	**1.0%**	**1.0%**	**1.0%**
Non life underwriting risk		5,011	5,061	5,112	5,163	5,214	5,267
Non life underwriting risk % provisions		**15.2%**	**15.2%**	**15.2%**	**15.2%**	**15.2%**	**15.2%**
Operational risk		2,286	2,351	2,418	2,474	2,523	2,572
Diversification benefit	-	7,465 -	7,465 -	7,465 -	7,465 -	7,465 -	7,465
SCR after diversification		27,063	27,980	28,927	29,724	30,427	31,135
Tax absorption	-	6,001 -	6,363 -	6,578 -	6,760 -	6,920 -	7,081
Other regimes		1,162	1,162	1,162	1,162	1,162	1,162
Total SCR		**22,224**	**22,779**	**23,510**	**24,126**	**24,669**	**25,217**
Target Own Funds / SCR (>100% reg min)	*178.00%*	*200.00%*	*200.00%*	*200.00%*	*200.00%*	*200.00%*	*200.00%*
Target Tier 1 capital % of SCR (>50% reg min)		*100.00%*	*100.00%*	*100.00%*	*100.00%*	*100.00%*	*100.00%*
Group Own Funds							
Equity capital in balance sheet		25,080	25,637	25,985	26,699	27,141	27,402
Goodwill and intangible assets (inc deferred tax assets)		(10,767)	(10,767)	(10,767)	(10,767)	(10,767)	(10,767)
MtM Assets (Inv Property and HTM Bonds)		9,884	10,174	10,473	10,723	10,942	11,163
MtM Liabilities		21,807	22,411	23,039	23,584	24,180	24,791
Net of deferred taxes		(7,207)	(7,410)	(7,621)	(7,802)	(7,987)	(8,176)
Subordinated liabilities		8,379	8,588	8,803	9,032	9,267	9,508
Proposed dividend		(1,330)	(1,261)	(1,343)	(1,574)	(1,608)	(1,634)
Other deductions and unrealized gains		(1,184)	(1,184)	(1,184)	(1,184)	(1,184)	(1,184)
Group own funds		**44,662**	**46,188**	**47,385**	**48,711**	**49,983**	**51,102**
Of which Tier 1		**37,279**	**37,600**	**38,581**	**39,679**	**40,716**	**41,594**
Capital ratio		*200.96%*	*203%*	*202%*	*202%*	*203%*	*203%*
Target capital		44,448	45,558	47,021	48,252	49,339	50,433
Surplus capital		214	630	364	459	644	669
Of which Tier 1 surplus		15,055	14,821	15,071	15,553	16,047	16,378

6. Life Insurance plc Equity (Euro million)

Year	0	1	2	3	4	5
Share price (Euro)	15.77					
Par value (Euro)	1.00					
Equity issued		0	0	0	0	0
Equity bought back		(214)	(630)	(364)	(459)	(644)
Shares issued		0	0	0	0	0
Shares bought back		(14)	(40)	(23)	(29)	(41)

7. Life Insurance plc Key Ratios

Year	-1	0	1	2	3	4	5
Life business							
Operating profit / insurance provisions		*0.80%*	*0.75%*	*0.76%*	*0.80%*	*0.80%*	*0.80%*
Growth in insurance provisions		*2.44%*	*3.03%*	*3.08%*	*2.38%*	*2.00%*	*2.00%*
P&C business							
Operating profit / insurance provisions		*5.96%*	*5.32%*	*5.33%*	*5.44%*	*5.48%*	*5.51%*
Premium growth		*1.2%*	*1.0%*	*1.0%*	*1.0%*	*1.0%*	*1.0%*
Combined ratio		*93.4%*	*94.5%*	*94.5%*	*94.5%*	*94.5%*	*94.5%*
Balance sheet							
Tangible NAV per share	*10.06*	*10.44*	*10.84*	*11.25*	*11.97*	*12.48*	*12.97*
Return on opening tangible equity		*13.4%*	*12.9%*	*13.5%*	*14.4%*	*14.1%*	*14.0%*
Return on total opening equity		*9.35%*	*8.76%*	*9.16%*	*9.81%*	*9.79%*	*9.83%*
Financial liabilities / shareholders equity		*169%*	*170%*	*172%*	*171%*	*173%*	*176%*

8. Life Insurance plc cost of equity

Current cost of equity:

Risk free rate	2.50%
Equity risk premium	5.00%
Beta	1.40
Current cost of equity	**9.50%**

Market capitalisation	24,633	
Surplus capital	(214)	-0.87%
Target capitalisation	24,419	99.13%

Proforma Beta	1.41	
Proforma cost of equity	**9.56%**	

---

9. Life Insurance plc Valuation (Euro million)

Year	1	2	3	4	5	Terminus
Terminus assumptions:						
Assumed long term growth rate	2.00%					
Assumed long term ROE	9.56%					
Inputs from forecasts:						
Profit after taxation	2,101	2,238	2,421	2,474	2,514	2,564
Cash flow from equity	**1,544**	**1,891**	**1,707**	**2,033**	**2,253**	**2,028**
Retained earnings	557	348	714	442	262	
Opening shareholders' funds	25,080	25,637	25,985	26,699	27,141	27,402
Return on opening shareholders' funds	8.38%	8.73%	9.32%	9.27%	9.26%	9.56%
Cost of equity	9.56%	9.56%	9.56%	9.56%	9.56%	9.56%
Implied residual income	**(297)**	**(213)**	**(64)**	**(78)**	**(81)**	**(56)**
Discounted cash to equity value:						
NPV five year free cash flow	7,120	29.5%				
NPV terminal value	16,989	70.5%				
Value of shareholders' funds	**24,109**	100.0%				
Shares issued (million)	1,562					
Value per share (Eur)	**15.43**					
Share price	15.77					
Premium/(discount)	2.17%					
Residual income valuation:						
Opening shareholders' funds	25,080	104.0%				
PV five year residual income	(602)	-2.5%				
PV terminal value (ex incremental investment)	(369)	-1.5%				
PV terminal value (incremental investment)	0	0.0%				
Value of shareholders' funds	**24,109**	100.0%				
Shares issued (million)	1,562					
Value per share (Eur)	**15.43**					
Share price	15.77					
Premium/(discount)	2.17%					

4.4.3.1 Historical balance sheet

Page one of the model shows the balance sheet for Life Insurance plc, which includes some additional detail compared with that usually provided on the face of the balance sheet, most notably:

- We have disaggregated investments and insurance provisions by business segment: life, non-life and other. Within insurance provisions we have further disaggregated life insurance provisions attributable to policyholders (i.e., unit linked business). This disaggregation is important for understanding the profitability of the different lines of insurance business; particularly for unit-linked vs other life business. This disaggregation will also help with our forecasting, since we will use different approaches for modelling life vs non-life business.

- When disaggregating our investment balances above, we have not concerned ourselves with the proportion of life business investment balances which are attributable to policy holders for unit-linked policies, since the returns on these are included within our investment returns on a gross basis. As discussed earlier in this section, these returns are offset by an equal and opposite amount in the 'claims expense' within the underwriting profit, to ensure that total profits reflect only those attributable to shareholders.

- On the asset side of the balance sheet we have also disaggregated investments by different categories of investment (e.g., investment properties vs financial assets), since this will be useful when analysing and forecasting investment returns. As evident in this balance sheet, the largest asset category for a life insurance company tends to be 'available for sale' investments; most of this balance relates to portfolios of liquid fixed income investments. These investments don't qualify as 'held to maturity' as it allows management flexibility to dispose of them before maturity.

- On the liabilities side of the balance sheet we disaggregated financial liabilities to show subordinated debt and financial liabilities used for financing purposes separately from financial liabilities used for operating activities. This has two benefits: firstly, since subordinated debt is generally excluded from Tier 1 capital, including this as a separate line item is useful when calculating capital ratios. Secondly, this will help us to identify which financing costs are absorbed into operating profits at the segment level verses those which are treated as a 'financing' expense.

4.4.3.2 Historic income statement

The income statement of life insurance companies usually provides scarce detail for analyzing and forecasting insurance company performance, since it can be highly aggregated and vary significantly in how it is presented. Therefore investors and analysts tend to rely heavily on the non-GAAP disclosures that insurance companies usually provide. Although this disclosure can vary somewhat by company, we have based the line items on our income statement on the typical disclosures provided by life insurance companies, most notably:

- The segment analysis shows operating profits by business line separately from 'non-operating' items. Operating profits relate to profits from underwriting activities and their related investment activities, whilst non-operating items include returns on 'company' investments, interest expenses on financial liabilities and central business costs.

- We have further disaggregated operating profits to show, for each business segment, the profits generated from underwriting activities (the 'technical margin') separately from investment returns and operating expenses. The technical margin essentially represents the difference between net premiums earned and the claims expense (remember this includes claims on unit-linked policies). The investment returns include returns on all investments related to underwriting activities; this includes investment of premium income as well investments for unit-linked policies. Operating expenses primarily relate to the amortisation of acquisition costs and other administration costs, such as payroll costs.

- At the foot of the income statement we have included a section on premiums analysis, where we analyse the growth rate for gross written premiums as well as the levels net premium earned relative to gross written premiums. This analysis will be important when forecasting the income statement, since net premiums earned will be used as a driver for other income statement items.

4.4.3.3 Forecast balance sheets

Page three shows the balance sheet drivers and the growth rates associated with each of the line items.

On the asset side, it is important to note that the investment balance is being used as a balancing item, since we assume that management will invest any surplus capital in the short term. This is consistent with the approach used for our general insurance model above. Our forecasts of investment balances are therefore limited to flexing the investment allocation by investment type (investment properties vs financial assets) and by business segment (life business vs P&C). Also, in this instance, we haven't separately modelled current assets (receivables and cash) and have instead assumed that they grow in line with total assets.

On the liabilities side is one of the main drivers for our model: the growth in insurance provisions by business line. This driver is important since it essentially drives most of the balance sheet growth and, in turn, much of the operating profits. The other driver on the liabilities side is the growth in financial liabilities. As with current assets, current liabilities are assumed to grow in line with total liabilities.

The routine for the components of equity and minority interests, should be familiar by now, with reserves movements reflecting retained earnings plus any anticipated equity issuance or share repurchase, whilst increases in minorities reflect the share of profits forecast in the income statement.

4.4.3.4 Forecast income statement

Page four shows the income statement drivers for our model. It is important to note that we have modelled the profits from the life business differently to that of the non-life business. However, the approach for modelling gross and net premium income is consistent across both businesses, and we discuss this first, followed by discussion on modelling the life and non-life business.

For both business segments we have modelled net premium earned for each business segment on page two of the model (see the Premium analysis section at the foot of the income statement). This has been done by forecasting (i) the growth rate for gross written premiums and (ii) premiums earned as a percentage of growth written premiums for each business line. The latter of these would not be expected to change significantly year on year, unless there was a material change in business mix. To ensure that our forecasts of net premium earned are consistent with (or at least appropriate compared with) the growth in insurance provisions, we have included a 'check ratio' here to show net premium earned divided by insurance provisions.

For the life business, we have started by forecasting the technical margin generated by average life insurance provisions. Although forecast as a single assumption here, in reality the forecasts will need to take into account the different profitability levels for the different streams of life business (e.g., by region and product). The next step is to forecast the investment margin generated by average life insurance investments, with this forecast taking into account the allocation of investments in the balance sheet. Finally, the operating expenses have been forecast as a percentage of net premium earned.

For the non-life (P&C) business, we have started by including our forecasts for net premium earned on P&C business. This is followed by forecasting the claims expense relative to net premium earned (the 'loss ratio') and the acquisition costs as a percentage of net premium earned (the 'expense ratio'). Finally, we forecast the investment margin generated on average P&C investments, again taking into account the allocation of investments in the balance sheet.

In relation to the other operating and non-operating items, we have separately forecast the investment margin on other investments, the returns on associates and JVs and the interest expense on financial liabilities.

4.4.3.5 Capital ratios

As highlighted previously, insurance companies are required to manage their capital structure with reference to capital ratios whilst also ensuring capital efficiency. Page five of our model incorporates analysis of the solvency capital ratio which, as explained in section 4.3, must exceed 100% using group own funds and of which more than 50% must be covered by Tier 1 capital.

Insurance companies are required to provide some disclosure of the calculation of the calculation of the Solvency Capital Requirement (SCR) and available capital. This information should be sufficient to flex the historic calculations for our forecast balance sheet numbers by (i) forecasting group own funds and Tier 1 capital using balance sheet line items and (ii) using the relevant balance sheet line items (investments and life/non-life insurance provisions) and assuming risk weighting for each of these to calculate the SCR during our forecast period.

In our analysis we have assumed that target capital ratios are well in excess of the minimum capital requirements and, in practice, insurance companies tend to disclose their capital targets. We have used this analysis to identify the level of surplus capital each year.

4.4.3.6 Equity issues and buy-backs

The modelling on page six of the model is identical to that of our bank model in section 3 in that we have assumed that the amount of surplus regulatory capital will determine the size of buy-backs in any given year (or a deficiency will give rise to additional equity issuance).

We have calculated the size of the buy-backs in page six as the lowest value of the prior year surplus from the two key solvency capital ratios from page five: the group own funds ratio and the Tier 1 ratio (so the €214m buy-back in FY1 reflects the €214m surplus capital in the FY0 group own funds capital ratio calculation, which in turn represents the smallest surplus capital balance in FY0).

This mechanism ensures that the target capital ratios explicitly determine the size of the buy-backs (or equity issuance, in the case of an insurance company whose projected capital was inadequate) to ensure a certain level of capital efficiency.

4.4.3.7 Key ratios

Page seven of our model shows the simplest useful analysis of performance ratios for an insurance company and, consistent with how we have approached the forecasting of this business, we have separated the performance metrics into life business and non-life business.

For the life business, we focus on two key metrics: operating profit/insurance provisions and the growth in insurance provisions. The former allows us to see the overall profitability being generated by the life insurance business, relative to the related insurance liabilities, whilst the latter allows us to track the overall growth of this segment.

For the non-life business, we focus instead on three key metrics: operating profit/insurance provisions, premium growth rate and the combined ratio (which is the sum of the claims expense and acquisition costs divided by the net premium earned). The first two have the same aims as above – tracking profitability and growth – whilst the combined ratio is useful in providing further visibility on profitability and is one of the key metrics used in the general insurance industry.

The next set of ratios focus on balance sheet metrics and returns: tangible NAV per share, return on tangible NAV and return on equity, which are consistent with the metrics we used for banks. The focus on tangible net asset values for the insurance industry is again a consequence of the exclusion of intangible assets from regulatory capital calculations.

Finally, we include financial liabilities to shareholders equity as our last key ratio. Although regulatory capital requirements should prevent significant changes in this metric from one year to another, it is useful to keep an eye on this leverage measure. In particular, the investment result calculated for the life and non-life businesses is after deducting financing costs of 'operating' financial liabilities and therefore any change in leverage which also impacts on operating financial liabilities may also need to be reflected in increased or decreased investment margins.

4.4.3.8 Discount rates

Our calculation of an insurance company discount rate is identical to that for a bank, having assumed that the group own funds consists of target capital and surplus capital, and that the cost of capital to the former can be derived by adjusting the measured Beta, in exactly the same way that one would deleverage the Beta of an industrial company with net cash in its balance sheet. Instead of the leveraged Beta being divided by (1+D/E) to derive an unleveraged Beta it is divided by (1-Cash/Equity), to derive an unleveraged Beta. In our case we are just treating surplus capital as if it were cash.

4.4.3.9 Valuation

Our valuation on page nine is a standard DCF/residual income to equity model, and should require no explanation, since it is identical to the model used for Magna in chapter five, other than that it values equity directly, rather than capital.

As usual, most of the DCF value lies in the terminus, which represents about 70% of the value derived. Interestingly, the residual income model calculations show a similar result to that for our bank model, in that forecast residual income is negative throughout the projected period and into the long-term future, giving an overall valuation which is below opening shareholders funds.

5. Property companies

5.1 Accounting for property companies

Most of the core IFRS standards are as relevant to property companies, otherwise known as real estate companies, as they are to other sectors. The crucial aspect of accounting in a real estate context is how the property portfolio is reflected in the financial statements. In this regard the key standard is IAS 40 *Investment Property*. If the company is constructing its own fixed assets then IAS 16 *Property, Plant and Equipment* is also relevant. In terms of revenue recognition on constructed real estate assets IFRS 15 *Revenues Under Contracts* is the key standard and has been addressed in detail in chapter four. Here we shall concentrate on the accounting requirements of IAS 40.

IAS 40 key standard and has

What is investment property?

Investment property is land and/or buildings a company holds to earn rentals or for capital appreciation. If a company uses the asset for its own operations then the part used cannot be an investment property and must be separated out.

How are investment properties valued?

For financial statement purposes the initial recognition shall be at cost, including incidental costs of acquiring the property.

Subsequently, two different models exist within IAS 40 to determine the ongoing valuation.

Model 1: Cost model

The cost model requires the investment property to be valued at cost less depreciation/impairments. If this model is chosen the fair values for investment properties must be disclosed.

Model 2: Fair value model

This model requires valuations of property at the balance sheet date are up-to-date with movements going through the income statement. Fair value should be based on sales comparisons or future cash flows in less liquid markets.

The valuation should be based on properties in their current condition.

Note that where the fair value model is adopted the carrying value of an asset will deviate from its tax base (typically cost) and so deferred tax liabilities/assets will arise.

How are disposal profits/losses calculated?

The calculation will be based on the disposal proceeds less carrying amount.

5.2 Valuing property companies

The profit and loss account of a property company can be divided into two basic components: that which relates to rental income and operating costs, and that which relates to capital gains or losses, whether realised or unrealised. Much of the content of this book has been concerned with treatment of different types of accrual, and property companies represent an extreme case of the problem. The operating profit that results from rental income and operating costs does not, on average, produce a return that matches the company's cost of capital. The balance is made up by capital gains on the existing portfolio, whether realised or unrealised, and value added resulting from new developments.

This all suggests that the most appropriate approach to valuing property companies will be to use an economic profit model, for two reasons. First, it clearly makes sense to think of the enterprise value of the company as being the current fair market value of its portfolio, and then to adjust for expected value added or subtracted in future years. And, secondly, much of the value creation or destruction that occurs in any one year will have little to do with cash flows for the year. The value of properties is traditionally represented as a function of rental income and a yield. This makes it relatively straightforward to assess the impact on values of expected changes in market yields, for example, and means that the value of a new development can be derived from its expected rental and an assumed future yield.

5.2.1 The modelling approach

Since the principles of economic profit valuation have been well rehearsed in earlier sections, we shall concentrate here on the components of the forecasting process, and shall take the valuation routine as read. The key drivers to a property company model will comprise the following:

At the operating level, we have rental income which may be modelled on an asset-by-asset basis, complete with rent reviews, void period, etc. At the pre-financing, operating level, the main deductions will be administrative costs.

Clearly, often the largest and almost always the most volatile component of the profit and loss account will relate to revaluation gains and losses on the portfolio. This can be approximated as a function of two items: rental income growth and change in rental yield. In other words, if we have a portfolio of property which at the start of the year has a value of £10m and a rental income of £500,000 then it follows that the rental yield is 5%. If it is expected that rental income will rise year on year by 2%, to £510,000, but that property yields are likely to increase to 5.2%, then the resulting projected valuation is approximately £9.8m (£510,000/0.052). We have suffered a capital loss of some £200,000 on our portfolio during the year, which offsets 40% of our rental income.

In addition to operating profit and capital gains or losses on the existing portfolio, we also have the impact of new developments. Development costs are capitalised as incurred. Expected values on completion are derived from expected rental income and the appropriate rental yield. To the extent that this value exceeds the development cost, a surplus is created which is allocated proportionately to the profit and loss account over the life of the development.

So, if we exclude financing, which we should need to build into a set of financial forecasts, but which will be irrelevant to a valuation routine that values returns to capital, we now have three streams of return to capital: the operating profit, which largely comprises rental income less administrative costs; the gain or loss on the existing portfolio, which is a function of rental income growth and market yields; and profits on new developments, which are a function of costs, expected rental and expected market yield.

5.2.2 Fades in property valuation models

Once capital gains or losses are taken into account, property company returns are extremely volatile, and may range from –20 to +30%. This clearly means that from the top, or the bottom, of a cycle, trends in yields and values are likely to result in large positive or negative economic profit over a run of years as the market returns to trend rates. But most property company models are very detailed, with rentals forecast asset by asset and committed developments modelled year by year. So we have a tension between the need for a long-term forecast and the impossibility of realistically extending our model for the required period.

The solution is the sort of fade routine described at the end of chapter five. In this case it clearly makes sense for profit to be run off the opening capital base, rather than the other way round. And it also makes sense to divide the stream of NOPAT in the valuation model between an operating return, which may be very stable, and a capital return, which may be the volatile component that corrects violently, and then reverts to a mean.

What is different for property companies is that it makes sense, even in the fade period, to assume a stable operating profit, and separately to forecast a trend in capital gains. Since property companies distribute most of their operating profits (Real Estate Investment Trusts, known as REITs, must, for example, distribute at least 90% of operating income), it is reasonable in the fade to assume zero retentions, so the capital base simply grows with capital gains.

Since this all sounds more complicated than it really is, we illustrate it with an example in exhibit 6.21.

Exhibit 6.17 Property company fade routine

Property company fade routine (£ million)							
Year	Final forecast	1	2	3	4	5	*LT average*
Opening capital	10,000	8,100	8,973	9,846	10,720	11,593	*3.0%*
Operating return	5.0%	5.0%	5.0%	5.0%	5.0%	5.0%	*5.0%*
Capital return	-20.0%	10.8%	9.7%	8.9%	8.1%	3.0%	*3.0%*
ROCE	-15.0%	15.8%	14.7%	13.9%	13.1%	8.0%	*8.0%*
WACC	8.0%	8.0%	8.0%	8.0%	8.0%	8.0%	*8.0%*
Investment spread	-23.0%	7.8%	6.7%	5.9%	5.1%	0.0%	*0.0%*
Economic profit	-2,300	630	604	578	552	0	

What is illustrated here is merely figures from the last year of the forecast period, in year zero, and a very short fade period of five years. The company has a cost of capital of 8%, and this is the rate of return on capital to which it fades, so there is no terminal value. It is assumed to earn a stable 5% operating return on its capital, so the volatility all comes from the capital gains or losses. The last forecast year is clearly a recession, since there is a 20% capital loss on the portfolio, but note that the opening year one value of the capital is £100m higher than implied by the capital loss, indicating that there was some net investment forecast in this year. Both the opening capital numbers for year

0 and year 1 are imported from the underlying forecasts. During the fade itself, capital movements will simply be the result of capital gains or losses, in this case all gains.

The mechanics of the fade are that we assume a trend rate of growth in the value of the portfolio through time. In this simplified case, we are assuming that start year 5 capital will be equivalent to start year 0 capital after a 3% underlying capital growth. The figure of 3%, added to a 5% operating return, ensures that the overall return on capital is the same as the discount rate by the end of the fade, and is derived accordingly. The capital values for the intervening years are a linear interpolation, so the resulting percentage gains are high early in the recovery, and then slow down.

The resulting economic profit numbers would be discounted back to the base year, at the start of the forecast, as usual. It is notable here that although the fade contains a sharp recovery from the recession of year 0, the overall impact of the period on value would be negative. Clearly the opposite would happen if the forecast period were expected to include large capital gains, with a reversion to the normal following on.

The important point here is not the basis for the assumptions, which are clearly artificial, given only one year of explicit forecast, no history and a very short fade, but the points that are specific to property companies: that it is reasonable to fade to a zero value added, that returns can usefully be split between stable operating returns and widely fluctuating capital returns, and that the long end of forecasts can assume no retention of operating profits.

5.2.3 Adjusting for financial liabilities

In chapter five it was made clear that when bridging the gap between a calculated fair value of the enterprise value of a company and that of its equity, deductions for the financial liabilities should be at fair value, rather than at book value. This is particularly important for property companies, since movements in the value of the property portfolio will be accompanied by changes in deferred tax liabilities, and probably also by changes in the fair value of the company's debt, and possibly also of derivatives associated with the debt. This should be clearer after reading the glossary below, but the general point is that where accounts do not record balance sheet items at fair value then fair value number (debt, for example) should be substituted for balance sheet numbers.

5.2.4 Real estate terminology

There are two areas of terminology that relate to property companies that are unique to the sector. The first relates to yield which, as we have seen, is a key determinant of valuation for real estate. And the second relates to the definition of Net Asset Value (NAV). While our proposed approach to modelling property companies is, as with industrials, to model returns to capital, and to deduct financial liabilities at the end, to derive a fair value of equity, property company reports and accounts place heavy emphasis on various measures of net asset value, the point being that this is a proxy for the fair value of the equity based on the current portfolio of assets. The definitions that follow are taken from a glossary produced by the European Public Real Estate Association (EPRA).

Initial yield: Annualised rental income based on the cash rents passing at the balance sheet date, less non-recoverable property operating expenses, divided by the market value of the property, increased with (estimated) purchasers' costs.

Estimated Rental Value (ERV): The value at which space would be let in the market conditions prevailing at the date of valuation (normally the balance sheet date).

Estimated reversionary yield: The ERV of the property or portfolio less property operating expenses, expressed as a percentage of the market value of the property increased with (estimated) purchaser's transaction costs.

Equivalent yield: The theoretical IRR of the cash flows from a particular property or portfolio, assuming the property becomes fully occupied and that all rents revert to the current market level (ERV) at the next rent review date or lease expiry. No future rental growth is allowed for. The equivalent yield is sometimes described as the weighted average yield between the initial and the reversionary yield.

EPRA Net Asset Value: Net Asset Value adjusted to include properties and other investment interests at fair value and to exclude certain items not expected to crystallise in a long-term investment property business model.

EPRA NNNAV: EPRA NAV adjusted to include the fair values of (i) financial instruments, (ii) debt and (iii) deferred taxes.

6. Technology companies

6.1 Issues when modelling and valuing technology companies

Technology companies are modelled as are other industrial companies, but they combine certain characteristics that we have discussed in chapters two and five. Specifically, they typically have high levels of research and marketing costs, which are treated in their accounts as operating costs while having many of the economic characteristics of capital expenditure, and they may be fast growing over quite long periods of time, with additional implications for their financial structure and cost of capital. They may be predominantly equity financed until they come to maturity, with significant net cash generation.

Since the mechanics of the modelling processes required have already been addressed we shall concentrate here on the drivers to the life cycle of technology companies, and issues that would determine the assumptions one might make about their future prospects, such as where their products might be in their life cycle, the degree to which the company has established barriers to entry that protect it from having its market share undermined, and its ability to renew its market strength through the introduction of new products. Finally, we shall discuss an additional variant on corporate valuation, namely scenario analysis.

6.2 Product life cycle

Although there are variants on the theme, the prevailing theory of product life cycle is that it undertakes four periods: introduction, growth, maturity and decline. Each of these periods has implications for growth, profitability, cash generation and market competition and concentration. The starting point is an 'S' shaped curve, delineating the volumes of the product sold.

During the introductory phase, the product experiences a slow take up, while low volumes and high levels of investment, including investment in further research and marketing, result in low levels of profitability and probably in negative net cash flows requiring further injections of equity capital. The outlook for cash generation at that point is too uncertain for the business to sustain much debt finance.

During the growth phase, volumes and revenues rise sharply, as the product rapidly increases its market penetration. Product quality, reliability and economies of scale are all likely to improve, as will margins. From the competitive viewpoint, there are likely to be two main issues: the first is whether the new product is a 'disrupter', displacing demand for an established but less sophisticated product, as when the Blackberry was effectively displaced by smartphones; or whether the product opens up an entirely new area of demand. The second relates to the success or otherwise with which the first mover, or first movers, establish barriers to entry, permitting an element of monopolistic pricing. Net cash flows are likely to remain negative during the growth phase.

At some point there will be a transition from growth to maturity. At this point competition is likely to become more intense, as the emphasis shifts from innovation to cost control and product quality. Net cash flows will tend to become significantly positive, and the business can be increasingly financed by debt.

With decline, there is likely to be increasing pressure on businesses to return equity capital to shareholders and for consolidation in the industry, as elimination of costs through restructuring becomes the dominant driver to value addition.

Of course, it is possible for one company to introduce new product lines, though the risks in an industry with rapid innovative change are high. Apple managed to transfer its success in the computer industry to becoming a market leader in smartphones; Microsoft did not. At time of writing it remains to be seen whether Alphabet (the parent company of Google) will succeed with any of its wide-ranging diversifications.

6.3 Market structures

The discussion above made clear likely trends in horizontal market structures – the degree of competition. But in considering industry economics there is also the vertical structure to consider, namely the degree or otherwise of vertical integration. Here, the stem work was produced by Ronald Coase in his 1937 paper, 'The nature of the firm'. Coase addressed the question of why some markets were internalised, with transactions taking place within a firm, rather than via a price mechanism. His conclusion hinged on an analysis of transaction costs. His point was that although there are advantages to market transactions there are also costs. There has to be a process of price discovery;

contracts have to be agreed, possibly quite complex if the transaction is ongoing or has elements of service as well as provision of goods, and so on. Subsequent work has suggested that in the early stages of an industry, high transaction costs tend to favour vertical integration, whereas industry maturity, which is likely to involve more competitors and also more suppliers, may facilitate market-based vertical transactions, and therefore reduce the benefit of vertical integration. An example from the technology sector is the computer industry, which was dominated by vertically integrated structures in 1980, with the dominant players being IBM, DEC, Sperry Univac and Wang, but which by 2000 had fragmented into horizontal layers of competition in five largely discrete industries: chips, hardware, operating systems, software, and sales and distribution. Incidentally, the originator of this analysis was Andrew Grove, in his wonderfully named 'Only the paranoid survive' (1996). He should have known his subject as he was CEO of Intel from 1987 to 1998, having been with the company since its inception in 1968.

6.4 Barriers to entry

The alleged monopoly power of some technology companies was starkly illustrated in July 2018 when the European Commission fined Google €4.34bn for breaching European Anti-Trust rules. The charge against Google was that it:

- 'Has required manufacturers to pre-install the Google search app and browser app (Chrome) as a condition for licensing Google's app store (the Play Store);

- made payments to certain large manufacturers and mobile network operators on condition that they exclusively pre-installed the Google search app on their devices; and

- has prevented manufacturers wishing to pre-install Google apps from selling even a single smart mobile device running on alternative versions of Android that were not approved by Google (so-called "Android forks").'

As against this, it has been argued that the market power of many technology companies is much more fragile than it appears. They operate in an industry that is subject to regular disruptive innovation, which can eliminate or weaken hitherto strong companies, as in the case of Blackberry referred to above. And by virtue of their not being capital intensive, their activities are inherently more open to new entrants than industries in which the established players have a large base of infrastructure which it would be difficult to replicate.

Perhaps the most obvious conclusion is that the life cycle of products in the technology industry is likely to be much shorter than that for most other industries, which of course has implications for modelling and valuation, since the presumption of a constant growth terminal value is even less realistic than usual.

6.5 Scenario analysis

In chapter two we discussed the way in which, according to the Capital Asset Pricing Model (CAPM), risk is taken care of in valuations through increases in the discount rate applied. This approach works well for large, liquid, well capitalised companies. Venture capitalists who provide equity finance for seed-corn companies require significantly higher rates of return than those implied by CAPM. This is to compensate them for undertaking considerable risk of failure through illiquid investments.

An alternative approach to handling risk, which is particularly appropriate to cases that are bivariate (it either works or it does not), or which have scenarios for the future that are clearly very highly differentiated (what the ultimate market size turns out to be, for example), is to run alternative valuations using different scenarios, and then to probability weight the different values that drop out of each run. In an extreme case it may be possible to produce so-called Monte-Carlo analyses, but these generally require more information about the relevant probability distributions than would apply to technology companies. One example of an industry that makes extensive use of probability weighted scenarios is the pharmaceuticals industry, where clinical trials make for a clear bivariate outcome at each stage: failure or continuation, with various possible revenue streams in the event of eventual success.

In principle, applying probability-weighted valuations is not complex; the complexity lies in the choice of outcomes and probabilities. Exhibit 6.18 below shows an example of the calculation, in which each probability-weighted outcome is derived by multiplying the value by the probability of each case, and the resulting probability-weighted value is the sum of the probability-weighted outcomes.

Exhibit 6.18: Scenario analysis

Scenario analysis (£ million)

Case	Probability	Value	Weighted value
Best	10%	35,000	3,500
Good	25%	25,000	6,250
Base	30%	15,000	4,500
Low	25%	5,000	1,250
Worst	10%	-	-
	100%		15,500

It is extremely important not to combine the two approaches: a high initial discount rate to reflect early stage risk, or weighted probabilities to reflect early stage risk. If it is possible to derive sensible scenarios and probability weightings, the latter approach is very much more transparent.

But when analysing technology companies that are in the growth, maturity, or decline stages, it probably also makes sense to run scenarios and to apply probabilities to them. The entire thrust of the analysis above suggests that these companies supply products that are likely to be subject to relatively short life cycles, where disruption is likely to be violent, and where the ability to renew the product range is demonstrably hazardous.

6.6 Conclusions

Most of the industries whose analysis we have addressed in this chapter require fundamentally different treatment from that traditionally applied to industrial companies, because the way in which they account and the nature of their business is entirely different from that of normal industrial companies. That is not quite the case with technology companies, but they do represent extreme cases of short product lives, frequent disruptive technology, high dependence on research, and uncertainties that are not well handled by the traditional methodologies for portfolio risk. In this section we have provided a product life cycle taxonomy and discussed some of the factors that might protect, or leave vulnerable, a market leader in a technology industry. We have also introduced one additional valuation approach, that of scenario analysis.

Chapter Seven

Modelling Mergers and Acquisitions

1. Introduction

Although there may be occasions where an analyst might wish to analyse the financial statements of individual companies, it is more typical to find analysts facing interpretation issues related to group or consolidated financials. Consolidated financials are an amalgam of the individual financials of the corporate entities that constitute the group. There is a particular methodology for preparing these financial statements. Analysts need to understand this in order to deal with the output from the consolidation process. This chapter examines the techniques used to prepare consolidated financial statements and the various related analysis points. The final part of the chapter considers the modelling issues raised by groups.

2. Treatment of investments

2.1 Introduction

IFRS 9 *Financial Instruments* is quite explicit about fair valuing equity investments. However, IFRS 9 focuses on the accounting treatment in the 'investor' individual corporate accounts. In certain circumstances further accounting issues arise which require the application of consolidation principles. A useful starting point is exhibit 7.1. The table shows the three classifications of investments for the purpose of preparing consolidated financials. The classification is driven by the degree of influence the investing company has over the investee. Note that these percentages are merely indicative and IFRS 3 *Business Combinations* makes it clear that it is the substance of the scenario that is important not merely the percentage holding. However, for the purposes of this discussion the percentages form useful guidelines.

Exhibit 7.1: Classifications of investment

	Holding 0 < 20%	Holding 20% < 50%	Holding >50%
Extent of influence over investment	None	Significant	Control
Accounting term	Investment	Associated undertaking	Subsidiary undertaking
Accounting treatment	Financial asset	Equity method	Purchase method in consolidated financial statements

3. Methods of consolidation

Historically there have been two methods of consolidation: pooling and purchase. IFRS 3 *Business Combinations* has prohibited the use of the pooling method for many years.

Therefore, the only consolidation technique available is where control is attained is the purchase method. This method is explored in the remaining parts of this chapter. The exception is section 5 which addresses the form of investments that drop into the middle column of exhibit 7.1, where significant influence rather than control is achieved. These forms of investment are referred to as associated undertakings.

In the sections below we explore the building blocks of consolidation under the purchase method. It is important to understand these fundamentals prior to considering analytical matters related to the reported numbers.

3.1 Core aspects of consolidation

In a consolidated set of financial statements the central concept is 'aggregation'. In other words combining the financial statements of two or more entities into a single set of financial statements. The fundamental features of consolidation are as follows

- There is no 'IFRS 9' **investments in subsidiaries** line in the consolidated accounts. This is because the carrying value of the investments has been replaced by the underlying net assets of each subsidiary. Such line by line reporting is much more useful than a single investment asset.

- Following on from this, the **net assets** represent the line by line aggregation of each of the subsidiary's assets (current and non-current) and liabilities (current and non-current). Users are then provided with detailed information allowing them to assess the detailed operations of the group.

- The net asset aggregation brings together 100% of the assets and liabilities of all subsidiaries even if less than 100% is owned. This is designed to provide users with all assets under control.

- **Non-controlling interests** exist because many subsidiaries are not wholly owned.

Yet, as we see above, 100% of all net assets are consolidated. Non-controlling interests represent the outside interest in the net assets of the subsidiary that have been consolidated by the holding company. So 100% of the net assets of the subsidiary will have been added to the group's net assets to reflect control, but the holding company may only own 75%. Therefore, a 25% non-controlling interest must be recognised. It is normally disclosed under shareholders' funds and is calculated as:

Net assets of subsidiary x % owned by minorities

- **Common stock and preferred stock** relate to the holding company only. This is a fundamental aspect of consolidation. The group financials are prepared for the shareholders of the holding company only and therefore only reflect their shares.

- The **retained earnings** equal the holding company's retained earnings plus a share of the subsidiary's post-acquisition retained earnings. This is to reflect the change in ownership of the subsidiary and the ownership of earnings.

These key mechanical building blocks are reviewed in the following computational example (exhibit 7.2).

Exhibit 7.2: Acquisition without goodwill

Great S.A. acquired 100% of Notes S.A. on 1 January Year 1 for €40,000. Immediately after the acquisition, the balance sheets looked as follows:

	Great SA	Notes SA
	€	€
Investment in Notes SA	40,000	-
Other assets	130,000	40,000
	170,000	40,000
Common stock	38,000	10,000
Retained earnings	132,000	30,000
	170,000	40,000

Required

Prepare the consolidated balance sheet of Great S.A. Group.

Solution

Consolidated Balance Sheet as at 1 January Year 1

	€
Assets	170,000
Common stock	38,000
Retained earnings	132,000
	170,000

Points to Note

- Assets are those controlled by Great S.A.
- No non-controlling interest due to 100% acquisition.
- Common stock is only that of Great S.A.
- Common stock and earnings of Notes S.A. are cancelled with the cost of investment. No goodwill arises.

	€	€
Cost of investment		40,000
Net assets acquired as represented by:		
Common stock	10,000	
Retained earnings	30,000	
	40,000	
	× 100%	(40,000)
Goodwill		-

- Retained earnings are only those of Great S.A. We cannot consolidate earnings of Notes S.A. as these arise pre-acquisition and as a result were not controlled by the group.

3.2 Goodwill – premium on acquisition

The rules governing the recognition of goodwill are covered in IFRS 3. A revised IFRS 3 was issued in January 2008. It provided for two ways of calculating goodwill. Below we explain the partial goodwill method, and in the notes after the calculation in 7.4 we show the alternative 'full' method. Goodwill is a very significant part of the consolidation process although its valuation significance is less clear. In summary IFRS 3 requires that:

1. **A premium** is calculated as the difference between the value of the consideration paid and the value of separable assets acquired. This is then allocated to separable intangibles with the unidentifiable (residual) portion being goodwill.

2. **Fair values** will be used for both the consideration given in an acquisition and the assets acquired. Fair values would normally approximate to market values.

3. There is a **prohibition on the amortisation of goodwill**. Instead it is reviewed annually for impairment. The impairment test must be applied annually or more often, if changing circumstances indicate that the asset might be impaired. Impairments are recognised in the income statement as expenses.

4. If a business combination involves entities under **common control** (i.e., all controlled by the same party) then the combination is outside the scope of this standard.

5. When estimating the **fair value of the assets acquired** the acquirer shall not recognise liabilities for future losses or other costs expected to be incurred as a result of the business combination. Restructuring provisions (e.g., for redundancy) shall only be recognised if the aquiree had an existing liability at the balance sheet date.

6. Given that **intangibles** form an increasingly important component of the assets acquired in a transaction, the IASB have now put much more emphasis on companies separately identifying intangibles. Therefore, from now on there will be an obligation on companies to split out separable intangibles rather than to leave them 'blended' within goodwill.

A computational example is given in exhibit 7.3.

Exhibit 7.3: Acquisition with goodwill creation

MD S.A. acquired all of the common stock of Sublime S.A. on 1 January Year 1 for €10,000. The balance sheets immediately after acquisition were as follows:

	MD SA	Sublime SA
	€	€
Investment in Sublime S.A.	10,000	-
Other assets	20,000	10,000
	30,000	10,000
Common stock	16,000	10,000
Retained earnings	14,000	-
	30,000	10,000

Requirement

Prepare the consolidated balance sheet of the MD Group as at 1 January Year 1.

Approach

Cancel the Investment in MD's books with the Common Stock in Sublime

Aggregate the balance sheets

Solution

MD S.A. Consolidated Balance Sheet 1 January Year 1

	€
Other assets	30,000
Common stock	16,000
Retained earnings	14,000
	30,000

Points to Note

- No non-controlling interest as MD acquired 100% of Sublime.
- Other assets reflect the assets over which MD has control.
- Common stock is only that of MD.
- Common stock of Sublime is cancelled with the cost of investment. No goodwill arises on this cancellation since MD acquired Sublime for book value.

	€	€
Consideration		10,000
Net assets acquired as represented by:		
Stock	10,000	
Earnings	-	
100% x	10,000	(10,000)
		-

- Retained earnings are only those of MD. The next section considers the issue of the subsidiary's reserves/retained earnings at the date of acquisition.

Notes

The goodwill adjustment only happens on consolidation. It does not appear in the individual company financial statements. It needs to be accounted for each year.

1. Goodwill is recognised in the group balance sheet as an intangible asset.

2. The retained earnings of the group only include the post-acquisition earnings of Sublime.

3. No non-controlling interest due to 100% acquisition of Sublime.

Now we have seen all the key ingredients that make up a consolidated balance sheet it is useful to examine another computational example. Exhibit 7.4 illustrates an acquisition of 80% of the equity in a company.

Exhibit 7.4: Acquisition of 80% of a company

The balance sheets of Kane GmbH and Able GmbH immediately before an 80% acquisition by Kane GmbH of Able GmbH were as follows:

Pre-Acquisition Balance Sheets – Dec. 31, Year 1

	Kane GmbH	Able GmbH
	€	€
Current assets	96,000	32,000
Other assets	64,000	16,000
Total	160,000	48,000
Current liabilities	80,000	28,000
Common stock	56,000	12,000
Retained earnings	24,000	8,000
Total	160,000	48,000

Kane GmbH paid €80,000 cash for Able GmbH.

Required: Prepare the consolidated balance sheet immediately after the acquisition, assuming that the non-controlling interest is valued based on the proportionate share of net assets.

Solution: Kane Group Consolidated GmbH Balance Sheet

	€
Assets	
Current assets (96 + 32 − 80)	48,000
Goodwill (W1)	64,000
Other assets	80,000
	192,000
Liabilities	
Current liabilities	108,000
Non-controlling interests (W2)	4,000
Common stock	56,000
Retained earnings	24,000
	192,000

Workings

(W1) Goodwill	€
Cost of Investment	80,000
Value of non-controlling interest (W2)	4,000
Net assets/equity acquired	(20,000)
	64,000

(W2) Non-Controlling Interest	€	
Net assets consolidated as represented by:		
Stock	12,000	
Earnings	8,000	
	20,000	× 20% = €4,000

Points to Note

- Control is obtained via 80% stockholding. Kane GmbH only owns 80%, so there is a 20% non-controlling interest;
- Current assets are reduced to reflect the payment to acquire stock in Able GmbH:
  - ↑ investment €80,000
  - ↓ cash €80,000
- Cost of investment cancels with net assets acquired to produce goodwill of €64,000. This is reflected as an intangible asset in the consolidated balance sheet;
- Non-controlling interest are allocated their share of net assets of Able GmbH consolidated by the group;
- Common stock is just that of Kane GmbH;
- No post-acquisition reserves of Able GmbH as consolidation takes place at the same date as acquisition.
- As mentioned above, a new revised IFRS 3 on business combinations actually allows an alternative goodwill calculation where less than 100% of the shares are acquired. This is referred to as the full goodwill method. In the example above an estimate would be made for the cost of purchasing 100% of the shares rather than 80%. For ease of calculation let us assume this would be a straight line extrapolation of our 80% cost. In other words, if €80,000 was paid for 80% then €100,000 would be paid for 100%. We would then compare this €100,000 with all of the assets at fair value (here assumed to be €16,000) producing a 'full' goodwill of €84,000. The extra €20,000 added to assets is balanced by an increase of €20,000 in minority interests. This is their share of the goodwill.

3.3 Analysis implications of goodwill

Returns on capital

In the past goodwill was amortised and so the issue of how to treat the amortisation was an important analytical issue. However, as there is no goodwill amortisation under US GAAP, nor under IFRS, this issue is no longer relevant. Instead we should consider whether impairments are relevant for assessing underlying profitability. The problem of including impairments in an analysis of profits is their lumpy, uneven nature. Impairments are often very large and represent the financial statements 'catching up' with what markets may have already priced in. Additionally, if our objective is to forecast the future then impairments may not be likely to reoccur and so become less important analytically. On the other hand, we do wish to hold management accountable for the often vast amounts spent on acquisitions. Furthermore, impairments are calculated based on future cash flows and so there may be important and interesting perspectives revealed by the assumptions management are using to make these calculations. These will all be disclosed in the extensive impairment sections of the annual report. This is a section often ignored by users and something we think is very worthwhile reviewing.

Now let us think about the balance sheet rather than measures of income. When calculating returns on capital, what do we do with goodwill? What about the balance sheet? Well, when the company builds a new plant it is not going to build goodwill as well, so when forecasting we would be tempted to compute returns on capital excluding goodwill unless management indicated that further acquisitions where planned. In that case we could enviage further goodwill arising and so including good in the returns calculations would be sensible. Additionally, if we want to assess the

---

performance of a management team that has pursued a strategy of growth by acquisition then the inclusion of goodwill in measures of return would be essential. So where are we left? Like many of the more interesting questions facing analysts there is no clear answer! We would often suggest running both approaches (returns with goodwill in and returns with goodwill omitted) and judging which is most appropriate based on qualitative factors such as the strategic direction of the business especially as it pertains to acquisitions.

4. Further issues in consolidation

There are many issues of complexity when undertaking a consolidation. Although the technical issues are important, for modelling purposes the key task is to deal with the output reflected in the financials. Exhibit 7.5 addresses some other areas of consolidation that may be useful for analysts.

Exhibit 7.5: Further issues in consolidation

Issue	Accounting treatment/commentary
Preference stock shares	If the holding company owns both common stock and preferred then, unless it holds the same percentage of both, this has an impact on our calculations in a similar way to the calculation of minority interest on the consolidated balance sheet. Therefore, the company must disaggregate balance sheet and income statement numbers into those 'owned' by the preference shareholders and the balance 'residual' amounts owned by the common stockholders.
Mid-year acquisitions	A fundamental principle of consolidation is that only post acquisition profits are reflected in the group financials. Therefore, an income statement drawn up after a mid-year acquisition will only include those sales, costs and other items that have happened since consolidation. This often requires modellers to produce pro-forma adjustments to improve the comparability of information over time. For example, the year after an acquisition will include the full effect of the target's revenues, costs and profits. Therefore, we could choose to restate the prior year, during which we would only recognise post acquisition revenues, costs and profits to include the full amount. This would enhance the comparability of the numbers over time.
Inter-company transactions	The process of consolidation involves preparing an additional set of financial statements that reflects the economic position that would exist if the holding and subsidiary companies constituted a single economic entity. This, quite obviously, does not reflect legal reality. Each entity is typically a separate legal entity. Such companies trade with each other and this is reflected in their financial statements. However, if we are assuming a single economic entity then it no longer makes sense to reflect such transactions in the consolidated accounts.
Inter-company balances	If a holding company and its subsidiaries trade then such transactions will normally be on credit. Therefore, in each set of financials there will be offsetting balances. For example, if a parent company sold goods on credit to a subsidiary then there would be a receivable in the parent balance sheet and an equal payable in the financials of the subsidiary. As we are making the one entity assumption, both of these numbers will be dropped out of the asset aggregation exercise on consolidation.

Income statements	Consolidated income statements are prepared on a similar basis to balance sheets in that all profits under the control of management are consolidated. Also, in a similar manner to balance sheet consolidations, income statements are consolidated based on the single entity assumption. Therefore, the sales of subsidiaries are aggregated with the sales of the holding company in order to calculate group sales. An income statement consolidation example is included in exhibit 7.6.

Exhibit 7.6: Consolidating income from a subsidiary

Home purchased 75% of Time S.A. many years ago.

	Home S.A.	Time S.A.
	€	€
Revenues	49,000	31,200
Cost of goods sold	(28,000)	(20,000)
Operating income	21,000	11,2000
Dividend from Time S.A.	3,000	-
Income from continuing operations before taxes	24,000	11,200
Income taxes	(10,000)	(3,200)
Income from continuing operations	14,000	8,000
Dividends	(8,000)	(4,000)
	6,000	4,000

Required

Prepare the consolidated income statement of the Home S.A. group.

Solution

Home S.A. Consolidated Income Statement	€
Revenues (49,000 + 31,200)	80,200
Cost of goods sold (28,000 + 20,000)	(48,000)
Operating Income	32,200
Dividend from Time Inc.	-
Income from continuing operations before taxes	32,200
Income taxes (10,000 +3,200)	(13,200)
Income from continuing operations	19,000
Non-controlling interests (25% × 8,000)	(2,000)
	17,000

Points to Note

- 100% of the results of the subsidiary are consolidated from Revenue to Profit after tax.
- Dividend income from Time S.A. is not reflected in the consolidated income statement. Dividend income has been replaced by earnings. To include dividend income would be to double count.
- The group tax figure is just an amalgamation of the individual company tax expenses. Group accounts are tax neutral, i.e. have no impact on tax. Tax is levied at the individual company level.
- Non-controlling interest is the share of earnings after tax of the subsidiary.

5. Accounting for associates and joint ventures

We saw in the introductory parts of this chapter that investments fall into one of three categories. Those that afford the investor no significant influence are fair valued and accounted for in accordance with IFRS 9. The next category we looked at was those shareholdings that afford the investor control and result in the consolidation of subsidiaries. It is these forms of investment that result in the application of the purchase method and the calculations and mechanics that we have been exploring to this point. The last category includes those investments which fall somewhere in-between in that they offer neither passive investment nor control. We call this level of influence 'significant' and there is a completely different set of rules that govern how these type of investments are reflected in the financials as we shall describe below.

5.1 The nature of associates

The need for the preparation of consolidated financial statements is driven by the need of users to understand the full amount of resources and earnings over which the parent company has control. There is a similar need for understanding the resources and earnings over which the parent company has significant influence. These investments are referred to as associates. Associates are a form of inter-corporate investment. Such investments possess the following characteristics:

- Long-term investment.

- Investing company exercises significant influence.

- Typically involves at least 20% ownership.

In determining whether or not significant influence exists, IAS 28 *Investments in Associates and Joint Ventures* states that the following may be indicative:

1. Representation on the board of directors.

2. Participation in policy-making process.

3. Material transactions between investor and investee.

4. Interchange of managerial personnel.

5. Provision of essential technical information.

By way of contrast, the following may be indicative of a lack of significant influence:

1. Opposition by other shareholders.

2. Majority ownership by a small group of investors.

3. Inability to achieve representation on the board or to obtain information on the operations of the investee.

Given that an associate is influenced but not controlled by the investing company the purchase method is not appropriate. Instead a technique called equity accounting is employed. Equity accounting is only required in the consolidated financial statements of the investor. Therefore, equity accounting is not required where the investor does not prepare consolidated accounts, for example because the investor has no subsidiaries.

5.2 Equity accounting mechanics

Whereas consolidation under the purchase method requires a line-by-line consolidation of the individual balance sheet and income statement of the subsidiary, the equity method is simpler. Under IFRS, the equity method requires accounting for the group share of resources and earnings and is reflected as a one-line entity in the consolidated income statement and balance sheet. In the income statement the single line is 'share of profits' and in the balance sheet it is a non-current asset 'Investment in associate undertakings'. The precise mechanics of how these items are calculated is addressed in the two examples below.

Exhibit 7.7: Accounting for associated interests – the income statement

Stypen S.A. has a 40% holding in Standard S.A., which was acquired many years ago.

The group income statement of Stypen S.A., and its other subsidiaries, and the income statement of Standard S.A. for the year ended 31 January Year 1 are as follows:

	Stypen SA €	Standard SA €
Revenues	2,200	1,200
Operating costs	(660)	(600)
	1,540	600
Finance charges	(200)	(40)
Income taxes	(340)	(100)
Net income	1,000	460

Required

Prepare the consolidated income statement for Stypen S.A. and its subsidiaries, for the year ended 31 January Year 1.

Solution

Stypen S.A. Consolidated Income Statement for 31 January Year 1

	€
Revenues	2,200
Operating costs	(660)
Income before interest and taxes	1,540
Finance charges	(200)
Income before taxes	1,340
Income taxes	(340)
Net income	1,000
Share of associate net income	184
	1,184

Points to Note

- The basic principle is to account for the share of associates' net income. The actual methodology of how this is achieved can vary from jurisdiction to jurisdiction and IFRS is not particularly clear on this matter
- No minority interest arises in this situation as the group has only accounted for its share of income

The following example illustrates the key mechanics.

Exhibit 7.8: Accounting for associated interests – the balance sheet

The balance sheets of Home and Away many years after Home acquired Away are as follows:

	Home	Away
	€	€
Current assets	1,000	550
Plant, property and equipment	3,250	160
Investment in Away	500	-
Total assets	4,750	710
Current liabilities	750	200
Debt	1,000	120
Common stock	2,500	240
Retained earnings	500	150
	4,750	710

Home acquired 40% of Away for €500 when retained earnings were €200.

Required

Show the balance sheet if the investment is accounted for under the equity method.

Solution

Home Consolidated Balance Sheet

	€
Current assets	1,000
Plant, property and equipment	3,250
Investment in Associate (W1)	480
Total assets	4,730
Current liabilities	750
Debt	1,000
Common stock	2,500
Retained earnings (W2)	480
	4,730

Working

W1 Associates

	€
Cost of investment	500
Share of net assets at acquisition	
(240 + 200) × 40%	(176)
Share of net assets at asset at balance sheet date	
(240 + 150) × 40%	156
	480

W2 Retained Earnings

		€
Home		500
Away (post-acquisition)	$(150 - 200) \times 40\%$	(20)
		480

Points to Note

- The equity accounted investment in Away is incorporated in the group balance sheet and replace the cost of the investment.
- Net assets of Away at the date of the investment are calculated by reference to stockholder's equity at that date.
- Share of post-acquisition earnings are incorporated into group retained earnings.

Joint Ventures

IFRS 11 *Joint Arrangements* requires the use of equity accounting for joint ventures (i.e., using the same approach as for associates). This is a relatively recent change as, until 2013, joint ventures could be accounted for using either equity accounting or what is called proportionate consolidation.

Full consolidation is not warranted on the basis that the investor has significant influence but not control. The nature of a joint venture is usually such that there are at least two ventures bound by a contractual arrangement and that the agreement establishes joint control of the entity.

Associates throw up some interesting analysis and valuation implications for users.

How to value an associate?

The valuation of associates presents interesting problems for investors. If an analyst is forecasting profits based on accounting numbers then should he blend the associate with the core company or look at it separately? The problem is that valuing the associate separately requires a lot of detailed information. Therefore, a pragmatic approach is to blend small associates and/or those in similar businesses into the core earnings-based valuation. Larger and/or more unusual associates often represent non-core assets and should be valued separately. Sometimes this could be done by something as simple as applying a price to book multiple to their balance sheet carrying value. For substantial associates further, more detailed valuation work might be warranted.

But what about cash flow models?

From the text it is clear that the equity (rather than proportionate, see below) method of consolidation creates a strange outcome in group consolidated amounts. Profit includes the share of profits from associates, but assets and liabilities are netted off in the group balance sheet, which just shows a share of net assets. The cash flow statement is even more unusual in that it excludes the associate, except to the extent of dividends received from it. This means that analysts, when building cash flow models of companies with associates, must often exclude the associate completely from the analysis, and value the interest separately.

6. Foreign subsidiaries

Foreign subsidiaries need to be consolidated into the home group financials. As these will be prepared in a foreign currency, the accounting numbers will need to be translated into what is commonly called the reporting currency. This presents us with a number of mechanical issues relating to the translation of accounting numbers. In essence this boils down to a few questions:

1. What rate should be used?

2. Should accounting assets and liabilities be retranslated each year?

3. Where will translation gains/losses be shown?

In addition there are a number of interesting valuation issues:

- Should foreign currency forecasts be made and then translated or should models focus on the reporting currency *ab initio*?

- What cost of capital should be used to discount whatever currency flows are modelled?

The straightforward aspect is the accounting mechanics although in practice these can present auditors and accountants with huge practical, if not intellectual, problems. Let us take each of the three accounting issues in turn:

What rate should be used? Typically, balance sheets should be translated using closing rates and income statements using average rates.

Should all accounting captions be translated each year? All income statement items are translated every year. Furthermore, all assets and liabilities are translated at the closing rate, irrespective of their nature. This is merely a mechanical response to the requirement that we need everything in the same currency prior to consolidation, so we might as well use the most recent rate. At the very least it introduces consistency and clarity into the process.

When will translation gains or losses be shown? Translation differences in the consolidation process go straight to equity and are reported in the statement of other comprehensive income. As a reminder this is a catch all statement presented with the intention of disclosing those gains and losses that bypass the income statement. Therefore, they are a commonplace example of a violation of clean surplus accounting.

The valuation points can be made very simply. It is perfectly legitimate to value the local subsidiary of an international company using local currency forecasts and a local discount rate, or by using forecasts that have been exchanged at a reasonable projected exchange rate into the group's reporting currency, and then discounting these at the group's cost of capital. But it is clearly not acceptable to apply a discount rate based on one rate of inflation and interest rates to a set of cash flows denominated in a different currency, whichever way round the mistake is made.

Moreover, where there are currency gains or losses taken straight to equity then these 'dirty surpluses' (or 'dirty charges') should be taken through the NOPAT numbers in our intrinsic value models. As usual, we want to see the accrual of value reflected in what we are discounting, for all the reasons discussed in chapter one.

7. Accounting for disposals

The nature of accounting disposals and derecognition

A significant number of quite complex accounting issues arise in relation to disposals. Again, if a valuer is to appropriately model and conduct meaningful analysis then an appreciation of these is essential. Remember that the fundamental premise of disposal accounting relates to derecognition. In an accounting context derecognition means the removal of an asset (or liability) from the balance sheet. In most cases identifying the need for a derecognition is straightforward – the sale of an asset or the disposal of an entire shareholding are obvious examples. But there can be other more subtle instances such as when a subsidiary issues shares to a party other than the parent. In this case there is a 'deemed' disposal due to the dilution in the effective holding at the group level.

Assets or shares?

The first distinction to make is between asset and share disposals. In a similar way to purchasing decisions, business activities can be sold either by selling an interest in an entity's assets and liabilities, as represented by shares, or by selling some assets directly. This distinction is crucial for a number of reasons. Firstly, the accounting differs dramatically. Secondly, the purchase of an asset will often come with no other obligations whereas, if the shares are purchased, then there are control issues and a whole plethora of accounting follow on. Lastly, the distinction can be very important for tax purposes. If you want to benefit from another entity's tax losses then, under normal circumstances, there is little point in purchasing an asset – the shares are the only route to follow. Even then there can be strict tax rules around change of ownership that restrict the use of losses.

The accounting treatment of asset sales is straightforward so let us deal with that first.

Asset disposals

The key questions regarding the accounting treatment of asset sales are:

1. **Derecognition of the asset**: from the date of sale the asset will be derecognised from the balance sheet and, from that point, no depreciation will be charged through the income statement. Note that under IFRS this is not a legal ownership issue. Derecognition will occur when the economic risks and rewards of an asset pass to another party. This is very much a judgement call by the directors, subsequently examined by the auditor, decided on a case by case basis.

2. **Recognition of the proceeds of sale**: this will either be in the form of cash (straightforward) or an exchange of assets (use fair value of assets received).

3. **Recognition of a profit/loss on disposal**.

  - The calculation of a profit/loss on disposal is required unless an asset is sold for precisely its book value. Given that assets are valued at cost (or revalued amount) less cumulative depreciation, which is based on judgemental decisions and estimates, it would be most unusual if disposal proceeds equated precisely with selling at book value. It is important to remember that the objective of depreciation is not to establish an accurate valuation of an asset on the balance sheet. Instead, it is to charge the entity for the opportunity cost of using the asset, rather than disposing of it and to allocate this cost over the life of the asset. The extensive use of historical cost accounting limits the efficacy of the implementation but does not detract from the soundness of the principle.

  - Typically a profit or loss on disposal is treated as a non-recurring item in the income statement by those analysing the financial performance of the entity. Again, we must be careful here. If we see a continuous stream of profits/ losses on disposals could it be argued that these are a recurrent feature of the business? There is some validity to this argument, especially if disposals are of operating assets such as aircraft or retail stores. The management of a large pool of operating assets via judicious sub-leasing, disposal and exchange is an important aspect of the on-going activities in many industries. On the other hand, the disposal of a head office building in central Paris is unlikely to be followed by similar transactions in the future. Therefore, consideration should be given to treating the disposal of operating assets as recurring items to some degree. However, careful analysis of these numbers would be necessary to make informed decisions.

  - Disposals may also offer an insight into the adequacy, or otherwise, of a company's depreciation policy. A company with consistently high profits on disposals may be over-depreciating its assets whereas one reporting losses may not be charging a sufficient level. It is up to the analyst to consider whether the deviations from an appropriate 'economic' depreciation charge are sufficient to warrant adjustments to a more normalised number.

4. **Any accumulated depreciation on the derecognised asset must be reversed out.** The asset has been derecognised from the balance sheet and so the related accumulated depreciation must also be derecognised. Some complications arise where the asset has been revalued. Note that while revaluations are permitted under IFRS, this is not the case under US GAAP. If revaluations have been undertaken then the profit on disposal is based on a comparison between the sales proceeds and the depreciated revalued amount. This means that, *ceteris paribus,* assets that have been subject to revaluations will produce lower profits on disposals. A further adjustment is required for revalued assets as the balance in the revaluation reserve must be transferred to retained earnings as this amount has now been realised.

Example

Value place Inc. has disposed of two fixed assets. Asset 1 has not been revalued and the the relevant information together with profit on disposal and required adjustments is given below. The same information is given for Asset 2 but it has been revalued upward by 26,000 some years ago.

Note that:

- It incurs a loss on disposal. If assets have been revalued then there will be systematically lower profits on disposal or higher losses compared with assets that remain at historical cost.

- A transfer must be made of the balance on the revaluation reserve that relates to Asset 2. This amount is now realised and would be available to distribute, etc.

Exhibit 7.9: Accounting for asset disposals

	Asset 1	Asset 2
Cost/revalued amount	124,590	178,435
Accumulated dep'n	-45,876	-34,999
Net book value	**78,714**	**143,436**
Disposal proceeds	234,000	139,000
Profit/(loss)	155,286	-4,436
Adjustments		
Accumulated dep'n	-45,876	-34,999
Revaluation reserve		-26,000
Retained earnings		
Profit on disposal	155,286	-4,436
Revaluation transfer		26,000

Disposal of shares

The treatment of share disposals is more complex and diverse as it depends on the accounting treatment of the underlying investment. In turn this depends on the relationship between the investor and investee companies.

We shall look at three possibilities:

1. There is still a subsidiary after the disposal.

2. There is an associate after disposal having previously been a subsidiary.

3. It is a complete disposal and nothing is left.

The exhibit that follows (exhibit 7.10) addresses the first two scenarios. The third is much more straightforward so we merely describe the income statement and balance sheet treatment below.

Profit on disposal

A profit on disposal will be recognised in the income statement. In a similar way to the disposal of assets, a comparison is made between the proceeds and the value of the underlying assets. The numbers in the model are explained below:

Exhibit 7.10: Accounting for disposal of minority

Deconsolidation terms: original stake		Deconsolidation terms: original stake	
Per cent sold/floated	40%	Per cent sold/floated	55%
Per cent retained	60%	Per cent retained	45%
Gross consideration	400	Gross consideration	400
NAV sold	80	NAV sold	100
Book profit	320	Book profit	290
Tax rate	30%	Tax rate	30%
Capital Gains Tax	(96)	Capital Gains Tax	(87)
Net profit on disposal	224	Net profit on disposal	203
Net cash receipt	304	Net cash receipt	313
Goodwill sold	(80)	Goodwill sold	(110)
Adjustment to equity	144	Adjustment to equity	93

Notes

1. The percentage sold and retained is based on the assumption that we owned 100% to begin with. Here we assume that a disposal of 40% is made in the first case (exhibit 7.10, left hand side), and of 55% in the second (exhibit 7.10, right hand side);

2. The proceeds in each scenario are given as €400m.

3. The existing net assets are taken from the subsidiary balance sheet and multiplied by the percentage sold.

4. Book profit is calculated as the difference between the sales proceeds and the net assets disposed of.

5. We then apply a tax rate. Note that as these are disposals of fixed assets, it is the capital gains tax rate that applies although in some jurisdictions this is the same rate as that applied to income.

6. The net receipts is simply the consideration received less the tax that will have to be paid.

7. The goodwill disposed means that we have lost another asset. In the income statement this would also be deducted from the profit on disposal to be recognised;

8. The above calculations would be identical in the case of a complete disposal, i.e., there would be a profit on disposal and it would be based on the proceeds received less the entire NAV of the subsidiary now disposed.

Balance sheet		
Scenario	Implications	Model numbers
Disposal of 40% so a subsidiary (Exhibit 7.11)	The balance sheet is a statement at a point in time so after the disposal it merely reflects the fact that a 60% subsidiary is now in existence. So there is still full consolidation of the subsidiary	The net proceeds are added to the cash balance. Goodwill is adjusted for the portion disposed of. The adjustment to shareholder funds is the net proceeds and the adjustment for the goodwill disposed of. Non-controlling interests is based on the new minority number of 40%. There is no time apportionment as the balance sheet merely reflects the position at a point in time.
2. Disposal of 55% so it is now an associate (Exhibit 7.12)	There will no longer be full consolidation. Instead a proportion of the assets will be recognised and no minorities	No assets are consolidated on a line by line basis. Instead a financial asset equal to the share of the other entity's assets (and the remaining goodwill) is recognised. No non-controlling interests are recognised as the investing company is only including the share that it actually owns.
3. Complete disposal	In this case there is complete derecognition of the subsidiary and no consolidation	There is recognition of the net proceeds of the disposal in cash and the profit in equity in addition to the adjustment for goodwill disposed of.

Exhibit 7.11 shows the balance sheet calculations for the disposal of a minority stake.

Exhibit 7.11: Disposal of minority stake (balance sheet)

Balance sheet	Parent	Subsidiary	*Adjustments*	Proforma
Cash	100	25	*304*	404
Inventories	200	120	*0*	200
Trade receivables	150	50	*0*	150
Other current assets	50	30	*0*	50
Total current assets	500	225	*304*	804
P,P&E	750	300	*0*	750
Financial assets	50	25	*0*	50
Goodwill (all relates to subsidiary)	200	0	*(80)*	120
Total fixed assets	1,000	325	*(80)*	920
Total assets	**1,500**	**550**	**224**	**1,724**
Short term debt	150	45	*0*	150
Trade payables	100	45	*0*	100
Other current liabilities	150	75	*0*	150
Total current liabilities	400	165	*0*	400
Long term debt	350	120	*0*	350
Provisions	150	65	*0*	150
Minority interest	100	0	*80*	180
Shareholders' funds	500	200	*144*	644
Long term liabilities and equity	1,100	385	*224*	1,324
Total liabilities and equity	**1,500**	**550**	**224**	**1,724**

Exhibit 7.12 shows the balance sheet calculations for the disposal of a majority stake.

Exhibit 7.12: Disposal of a majority stake (balance sheet)

Balance sheet	Parent	Subsidiary	*Adjustments*	Proforma
Cash	100	25	*288*	388
Inventories	200	120	*(120)*	80
Trade receivables	150	50	*(50)*	100
Other current assets	50	30	*(30)*	20
Total current assets	500	225	*88*	588
P,P&E	750	300	*(300)*	450
Financial assets	50	25	*155*	205
Goodwill (all relates to subsidiary)	200	0	*(200)*	0
Total fixed assets	1,000	325	*(345)*	655
Total assets	**1,500**	**550**	**(257)**	**1,243**
Short term debt	150	45	*(45)*	105
Trade payables	100	45	*(45)*	55
Other current liabilities	150	75	*(75)*	75
Total current liabilities	400	165	*(165)*	235
Long term debt	350	120	*(120)*	230
Provisions	150	65	*(65)*	85
Minority interest	100	0	*0*	100
Shareholders' funds	500	200	*93*	593
Long term liabilities and equity	1,100	385	*(92)*	1,008
Total liabilities and equity	**1,500**	**550**	**(257)**	**1,243**

8. Modelling mergers and acquisitions

What is special about modelling and valuing mergers and acquisitions?

Most models of companies assume that they are going concerns, and that they will not undergo corporate changes in the form of acquisitions or disposals of assets, or spin-offs of subsidiaries. Inside companies, much, though not all, planning is undertaken on this basis, and investors generally assume that the entity in which they are investing will grow organically.

Naturally, there are times when this approach is wholly inappropriate. Companies, when they contemplate an acquisition, need to be able to value it and, quite separately, to assess the impact of the acquisition on their consolidated financial statements. Investors in companies that have been bid for need to make up their minds whether or not to accept the bid. And investors in companies that have made or are making acquisitions need to be able to assess them.

As with general company modelling and valuation, it is important to have both an understanding of the accounting issues involved, and to be able to make reasonable inferences regarding valuation. This chapter began with an explanation of the accounting treatment under IFRS of the consolidation and deconsolidation of the elements of a group. We shall now discuss in some detail the valuation and accounting implications of corporate acquisitions, since these represent the most dramatic and complex issues from the perspective of valuation, and they arise quite regularly.

8.1 Valuing an acquisition

Generally, one models a company first and values it afterwards. With mergers it is the other way round. The starting point is whether or not a bid is a good idea, and how much it would be worth paying, if you are acting for the bidder. If you are an investor and a bid has been announced, again, the key question is whether or not it will add value after taking the consideration into account.

But consolidated accounts do matter. There are proforma balance sheet structures that are quite simply unworkable. Whatever the theoretical arguments about how impact on earnings per share is unimportant, the reality is that a severe negative impact will at least have to be sold carefully to shareholders, and possibly also to the Board of the bidding company, whether or not it makes purely economic sense.

So our starting point is the value of the target, but there are two possible differences with respect to this exercise and the ones that we undertook in chapters five and six. The first is that acquisitions are generally motivated at least in part by the prospect of synergies. And the second is that the financing of the acquisition may mean that the capital structure of the target will be transformed by the acquisition. An extreme example of the latter point is the leveraged buy-out, where much of the upside from the deal may lie in the creation of large tax shelters.

Starting with synergies, these generally come in one of three types: enhancement of revenue; reduction in operating cost; or reduction in capital costs. Revenue enhancement might most likely result from cross-selling opportunities, either because of the ability to sell products in different geographical locations, or because of the ability to cross-sell products to existing customers of two different businesses. Pharmaceutical mergers offered the former synergy. Bancassurance mergers offer the latter. Pricing power may also result from mergers but for anti-trust reasons is never cited as a motive.

Cost reduction is most obviously achievable at the level of head office costs and layers of management, but may also extend to procurement, and to a general fall in fixed costs relative to the overall size of the business. Mergers in businesses including retail, downstream oil, utilities, and many others have been primarily motivated by these expectations.

Capital requirements are less often commented upon, in the same way that when analysing companies the financial press tends to concentrate more on margins that on capital requirements, but in fact the ability to reduce inventory requirements, for example, or to use fixed assets more efficiently, might well represent a significant driver to forecast synergies.

Turning to the second source of upside from mergers, a reduction in the cost of capital, our general approach to this would be to be very cautious. It is always important to separate out investment from financing decisions, and many bad acquisitions have been justified by arguments relating to tax shelters that could have been created by the bidder quite independently, merely by repurchasing its own shares. This argument is in addition to that expressed in chapter two, that for technical reasons related to discount rates tax shelters are often overestimated in any case. Probably the most appropriate basis for valuing acquisition targets in most cases is to assume that, however the bidder really funds the acquisition, the appropriate discount rate should be based on what would be a sensible balance sheet structure for the business if it were independently financed.

An extreme example, to prove the point, is the following:

> If a large well-capitalised company borrows money to fund a small cash acquisition, is the appropriate discount rate for the acquisition its net of tax cost of borrowing? Obviously not, because its cost of borrowing is only low because it is a big company with a strong balance sheet. The real question is how much equity it would have to put behind the assets if they were to be funded on a stand-alone basis.

Whether or not the bidder takes a possible alteration of the cost of capital into account in their assessment of a target, it is highly desirable to segment the valuation into two or three components. The first is the stand-alone value of the target as a going concern. This is what we have been doing throughout the last two chapters of this book. The second component is the value that includes synergies, whether attributable to revenue, cost or capital requirements. The third is, possibly, the value added through more efficient financing.

8.2 The exchange rate delusion

It is often argued (particularly by investment bankers) that the absolute value of the target is the key factor when assessing a cash acquisition, but it is the relative value of the shares that counts when assessing an acquisition for which the consideration will be new shares in the acquirer. This is a seductive argument. Surely, if my shares are trading at three times fair value, and those of the target are trading at two times fair value, then if I can swap my shares for his, the deal is a good one, irrespective of the fact that I shall probably have to write off half of the acquisition cost as impaired goodwill?

Well, actually, the answer is no. To see why, it is necessary to split the acquisition into its component parts: an investment decision and a financing decision. Taking the second one first, is it a good idea, if your share price is high, to use shares to buy things, or even to use the opportunity to accumulate some cash? Answer, yes. Taking the first one, is it a good idea, as a result of your being able to raise equity capital on good terms, to throw away half of this benefit by purchasing something at twice its fair value? Answer, no. Countless managements have made bad acquisitions through confusing investment with financing decisions, and this is a similar argument to the one we have already addressed regarding the appropriate discount rate for appraising targets.

It is always essential to separate investment from financing decisions and it is usually wrong to make a bad investment decision merely on the basis of arguments about financing. The gain created by tax shelters, for example, should also not be used to justify otherwise expensive acquisitions.

8.3 Bidding for Magna

Magna is the company that we have modelled in greatest detail, and we shall analyse it as a potential acquisition target for the US giant, Add-Brand. As already discussed, detailed consolidations come later. The first question for Add-Brand would be, 'What would we be prepared to pay?'

Our earlier valuation of Magna in exhibit 5.2 generated a value per share of €46.06, on the important assumption that we held market gearing stable into the future. Let us return to it and begin with some assumptions about what the change of ownership could plausibly do to the Magna business.

Cross-selling opportunities would be limited in this case, so we would be reduced to an estimate of what a possibly more aggressive management could achieve with the existing business. We shall assume that an uplift to projected revenues of 1% is projected.

More might plausibly be done with costs, especially fixed costs. In reality, there are three lines of fixed cost that could be attacked, but to keep the modelling down we shall ascribe all the benefits to general administrative expenses, and shall assume that these could be halved. We assume no change to cost of goods sold through lower procurement costs.

Exhibit 7.13 contains two additional pages of Magna model. The first (page 15) shows the effect of the synergies described above on after-tax profits and cash flows. The second (page 16) shows a reworking of the valuation table from exhibit 5.2, but this time with NOPAT reflecting the synergies from the merger. Our value per share has risen by 50% from €46.06 to €68.90.

Exhibit 7.13: Magna valuation with synergies

15. Magna synergies (Euro million)

Year	1	2	3	4	5
Restructuring costs	(1,049)				
Stand-alone revenues	54,900	56,378	58,060	59,990	62,221
Percentage uplift from merger	*0.0%*	*1.0%*	*1.0%*	*1.0%*	*1.0%*
Additional revenues	0	564	581	600	622
Gross margin	*22.7%*	*22.7%*	*22.7%*	*22.6%*	*22.5%*
Synergy benefit from revenue	**0**	**128**	**132**	**136**	**140**
General administrative expenses	(1,049)	(1,068)	(1,087)	(1,106)	(1,126)
Percentage reduction from merger	*0.0%*	*50.0%*	*50.0%*	*50.0%*	*50.0%*
Synergy benefit from cost reduction	**0**	**534**	**543**	**553**	**563**
Pre-tax synergies	(1,049)	662	675	689	703
Tax rate	*35.0%*	*35.0%*	*35.0%*	*35.0%*	*35.0%*
Net of tax synergies	**(682)**	**430**	**439**	**448**	**457**

16. Magna target valuation (Euro million)

Year	1	2	3	4	5	Terminus
WACC	*6.1%*					
Incremental ROCE	*9.0%*					
Long term growth	*2.0%*					
NOPAT	**953**	**1,005**	**1,064**	**1,133**	**1,213**	**1,237**
Net synergy benefits	(682)	430	439	448	457	
NOPAT including synergies	**271**	**1,435**	**1,503**	**1,581**	**1,670**	**1,703**
Depreciation & amortisation	1,521	1,551	1,587	1,628	1,674	
Capital expenditure	(1,500)	(1,600)	(1,700)	(1,800)	(1,900)	
Change in working capital	63	99	115	135	160	
Free cash flow	**356**	**1,485**	**1,506**	**1,544**	**1,604**	**1,325**
Opening capital employed	**11,140**	**11,055**	**11,006**	**11,003**	**11,040**	**11,107**
Earnings growth	*(67.7%)*	*429.5%*	*4.7%*	*5.1%*	*5.6%*	*2.0%*
Return on opening capital employed	*2.4%*	*13.0%*	*13.7%*	*14.4%*	*15.1%*	*9.0%*
Cost of capital	*6.05%*	*6.05%*	*6.05%*	*6.05%*	*6.05%*	*6.05%*
Investment spread	*(3.6%)*	*6.9%*	*7.6%*	*8.3%*	*9.1%*	*2.9%*
Economic profit	**(403)**	**766**	**837**	**915**	**1,002**	**1,031**

DCF valuation

+ PV 5 year cash flow	5,334	18.0%
+ PV terminal value	24,355	82.0%
= Enterprise value	**29,688**	**100.0%**
+ Financial assets	238	
- Non-controlling interests	(188)	
- Pension provisions	(1,012)	
- Net debt	(6,209)	
= Equity value	**22,517**	
Value per share	68.90	

Economic profit valuation

+ Opening balance sheet (excl. financial assets)	11,140	37.5%
+ PV 5 year economic profit	2,472	8.3%
+ PV terminal value (ex incremental investment)	12,691	42.7%
+ PV terminal value (incremental investments)	3,385	11.4%
= Enterprise value	**29,688**	**100.0%**
+ Financial assets	238	
- Non-controlling interests	(188)	
- Pension provisions	(1,012)	
- Net debt	(6,209)	
= Equity value	**22,517**	
Value per share	68.90	

Had Magna been holding a large pile of cash in its balance sheet, and suffered from a clearly inflated weighted average cost of capital then it would have been appropriate to run a third valuation, using the synergies as in exhibit 7.13 and a reduced WACC, based on a more efficient balance sheet. In that instance, we end up with three values: stand-alone, stand-alone plus synergies, and post-synergies plus lower WACC. (We should be unlikely to value the company on the basis of its balance sheet becoming steadily less efficient through time, as we did in the stand-alone model in chapter five. In fact, in addition to the synergies discussed above, a complimentary shape to stand-alone cash flows is another desirable when assessing the suitability of a target for acquisition.)

8.4 Consolidation of projections

The earlier part of this chapter addressed IFRS accounting treatment for consolidation of acquisitions, when producing a post-merger balance sheet. We need to do more than that, since we shall presumably start with integrated forecasts for both companies, and want to be able to project integrated forecasts for the post-merger consolidated group. For this purpose we shall assume the acquisition of Magna by the US company Add-Brand.

To keep the modelling under control, we have simplified our forecast of Magna (and converted them into dollar figures); produced an equally simplified forecast of Add-Brand, and consolidated them. Exhibit 7.14 shows on separate pages the stand-alone forecasts for each company, the mechanics of a merger for cash undertaken at fair value, the synergies, and a consolidated five-year forecast for the group assuming completion of the deal on 31 December year 1, so the forecasts have been extended for one year to provide a five year consolidation. Naturally, the value acquired should be slightly higher than that at start year 1, on which our valuation was based. Clearly, deals do not generally complete on balance sheet dates, and it is therefore necessary to consolidate balance sheets on the date of completion, with the result that there will be two part years (one for each company) ahead of the consolidation balance sheet and one part year after it (for the consolidated entity), which makes the models larger but does not fundamentally alter the difficulties of the process.

Exhibit 7.14: Add-Brand/Magna merger model

	Add-Brand ($ million)						
Year	0	1	2	3	4	5	6
Input ratios							
Sales growth		*4.0%*	*4.0%*	*4.0%*	*4.0%*	*4.0%*	*4.0%*
EBITDA margin	*7.0%*	*7.0%*	*7.0%*	*7.0%*	*7.0%*	*7.0%*	*7.0%*
Net interest rate	*4.1%*	*4.1%*	*4.1%*	*4.1%*	*4.1%*	*4.1%*	*4.1%*
Taxation rate	*35.3%*	*25.7%*	*25.7%*	*25.7%*	*25.7%*	*25.7%*	*25.7%*
Fixed asset turn	*4.5*	*4.5*	*4.5*	*4.5*	*4.5*	*4.5*	*4.5*
Working capital turn	*271.4*	*271.4*	*271.4*	*271.4*	*271.4*	*271.4*	*271.4*
Net debt/equity	*55.6%*	*55.6%*	*55.6%*	*55.6%*	*55.6%*	*55.6%*	*55.6%*
Depreciation (years)	*15.9*	*15.9*	*15.9*	*15.9*	*15.9*	*15.9*	*15.9*
Pension provisions/Operating costs	*0.0%*	*0.0%*	*0.0%*	*0.0%*	*0.0%*	*0.0%*	*0.0%*
Other provisions/sales	*0.7%*	*0.0%*	*0.0%*	*0.0%*	*0.0%*	*0.0%*	*0.0%*
Earning from associates/Recurring net profit	*0.0%*	*0.0%*	*0.0%*	*0.0%*	*0.0%*	*0.0%*	*0.0%*
Minority/Net profit	*2.4%*	*2.4%*	*2.4%*	*2.4%*	*2.4%*	*2.4%*	*2.4%*
Profit and loss account							
Sales	244,524	254,305	264,477	275,056	286,058	297,501	309,401
EBITDA	17,076	17,759	18,469	19,208	19,977	20,776	21,607
Depreciation	(3,432)	(3,569)	(3,712)	(3,861)	(4,015)	(4,176)	(4,343)
Amortisation of intangible assets	0	0	0	0	0	0	0
EBIT	**13,644**	**14,190**	**14,757**	**15,348**	**15,962**	**16,600**	**17,264**
Non recurring items	0	0	0	0	0	0	0
Net interest	(925)	(941)	(974)	(1,009)	(1,045)	(1,082)	(1,121)
Pre-tax profit	**12,719**	**13,249**	**13,783**	**14,339**	**14,917**	**15,518**	**16,143**
Taxation	(4,487)	(3,405)	(3,542)	(3,685)	(3,834)	(3,988)	(4,149)
Net profit	8,232	9,844	10,241	10,654	11,083	11,530	11,995
Earnings from associates	0	0	0	0	0	0	0
Minority interest	(193)	(236)	(246)	(256)	(266)	(277)	(288)
Attributable profit	**8,039**	**9,607**	**9,995**	**10,398**	**10,817**	**11,253**	**11,707**
Closing balance sheet							
Financial assets and other long term assets	0	0	0	0	0	0	0
Goodwill	9,521	9,521	9,521	9,521	9,521	9,521	9,521
Tangible and intangibles assets	54,681	56,868	59,143	61,509	63,969	66,528	69,189
Total fixed assets	**64,202**	**66,389**	**68,664**	**71,030**	**73,490**	**76,049**	**78,710**
Non-cash working capital	901	937	975	1,014	1,054	1,096	1,140
Capital employed	**65,103**	**67,326**	**69,638**	**72,043**	**74,544**	**77,145**	**79,850**
Net debt	22,643	23,438	24,264	25,124	26,018	26,948	27,915
Pension liabilities	0	0	0	0	0	0	0
Other deferred LT liabilities	1,761	1,761	1,761	1,761	1,761	1,761	1,761
Minority interest	1,362	1,598	1,844	2,100	2,366	2,643	2,931
Shareholders' funds	39,337	40,529	41,769	43,058	44,399	45,793	47,244
Capital employed	**65,103**	**67,326**	**69,638**	**72,043**	**74,544**	**77,145**	**79,850**
Check	*0.0*	*(0.0)*	*0.0*	*0.0*	*(0.0)*	*0.0*	*0.0*
Cash flow							
Attributable profit	8,039	9,607	9,995	10,398	10,817	11,253	11,707
Minority interest	193	236	246	256	266	277	288
Dividends - earnings from associates	0	0	0	0	0	0	0
Pension provisions	0	0	0	0	0	0	0
Other provisions	1,758	0	0	0	0	0	0
Depreciation	3,432	3,569	3,712	3,861	4,015	4,176	4,343
Goodwill amortisation	0	0	0	0	0	0	0
Change in working capital	(890)	(36)	(37)	(39)	(41)	(42)	(44)
Cash flow from operations	**12,532**	**13,377**	**13,915**	**14,475**	**15,058**	**15,663**	**16,293**
Capital expenditure	(9,709)	(5,757)	(5,987)	(6,226)	(6,475)	(6,734)	(7,004)
Dividends paid/shares repurchased	(4,560)	(8,415)	(8,755)	(9,109)	(9,476)	(9,859)	(10,257)
Change in net cash/net debt	**(1,737)**	**(795)**	**(827)**	**(860)**	**(894)**	**(930)**	**(967)**
Per share statistics							
Shares issued (million)	4,395.0	4,395.0	4,395.0	4,395.0	4,395.0	4,395.0	4,395.0
EPS after goodwill amortization	1.83	2.19	2.27	2.37	2.46	2.56	2.66
DPS	0.30	1.91	1.99	2.07	2.16	2.24	2.33
Share price	39.6						

Magna ($ million at Euro 1.00 = $1.1404)

Year	0	1	2	3	4	5	6
Input ratios							
Sales growth		*2.4%*	*2.7%*	*3.0%*	*3.3%*	*3.7%*	*3.7%*
EBITDA margin	*5.4%*	*6.2%*	*6.2%*	*6.3%*	*6.3%*	*6.4%*	*6.4%*
Net interest rate	*8.1%*	*7.2%*	*6.3%*	*5.5%*	*4.7%*	*4.0%*	*4.0%*
Taxation rate	*30.1%*	*34.5%*	*34.5%*	*34.6%*	*34.6%*	*34.6%*	*34.6%*
Fixed asset turn	4.3	4.1	4.1	4.0	4.0	3.9	3.9
Working capital turn	(14.6)	(14.2)	(14.2)	(14.2)	(14.2)	(14.2)	(14.2)
Net debt/equity	*142.8%*	*142.8%*	*142.8%*	*142.8%*	*142.8%*	*142.8%*	*142.8%*
Depreciation (years)	9.6	8.7	8.9	9.1	9.3	9.5	9.5
Pension provisions/Operating costs	*(0.0%)*	*0.1%*	*0.1%*	*0.1%*	*0.1%*	*0.1%*	*0.1%*
Other provisions/sales	*0.8%*	*(0.2%)*	*(0.2%)*	*(0.2%)*	*(0.2%)*	*(0.2%)*	*(0.2%)*
Earning from associates/Recurring net profit	*0.0%*	*0.0%*	*0.0%*	*0.0%*	*0.0%*	*0.0%*	*0.0%*
Minority/Net profit	*11.5%*	*12.8%*	*14.3%*	*16.0%*	*17.8%*	*19.8%*	*22.1%*
Profit and loss account							
Sales	61,120	62,608	64,293	66,212	68,412	70,957	73,597
EBITDA	3,292	3,884	4,010	4,154	4,321	4,514	4,682
Depreciation	(1,479)	(1,735)	(1,769)	(1,810)	(1,856)	(1,909)	(2,005)
Amortisation of intangible assets	(310)	(310)	(310)	(310)	(310)	(310)	(310)
EBIT	1,503	1,839	1,930	2,034	2,155	2,295	2,367
Non recurring items	0	0	0	0	0	0	0
Net interest	(571)	(544)	(495)	(450)	(406)	(359)	(368)
Pre-tax profit	932	1,296	1,435	1,584	1,749	1,936	1,999
Taxation	(281)	(447)	(496)	(548)	(605)	(671)	(800)
Net profit	651	849	940	1,036	1,144	1,265	1,199
Earnings from associates	0	0	0	0	0	0	0
Minority interest	(67)	(67)	(67)	(67)	(67)	(67)	(67)
Attributable profit	584	782	872	969	1,076	1,198	1,132
Closing balance sheet							
Financial assets	271	271	271	271	271	271	271
Goodwill	4,547	4,547	4,547	4,547	4,547	4,547	4,547
Tangible and intangible assets	14,165	15,159	15,765	16,442	17,204	18,071	18,982
Total fixed assets	18,983	19,978	20,583	21,260	22,023	22,889	23,800
Non-cash working capital	(4,177)	(4,414)	(4,533)	(4,669)	(4,824)	(5,003)	(5,189)
Capital employed	14,806	15,563	16,050	16,592	17,199	17,886	18,611
Net debt	7,081	7,550	7,859	8,199	8,577	9,001	9,439
Pension liabilities	1,154	1,222	1,292	1,364	1,437	1,512	1,601
Other deferred LT liabilities	1,611	1,503	1,394	1,286	1,177	1,069	960
Minority interest	214	282	349	416	484	551	618
Shareholders' funds	4,745	5,007	5,156	5,327	5,524	5,754	5,993
Capital employed	14,806	15,563	16,050	16,592	17,199	17,886	18,611
Check	*0.0*	*(0.0)*	*0.0*	*0.0*	*(0.0)*	*(0.0)*	*0.0*
Cash flow							
Attributable profit	584	782	872	969	1,076	1,198	1,132
Minority interest	67	67	67	67	67	67	67
Dividends - earnings from associates	0	0	0	0	0	0	0
Pension provisions	(7)	68	70	71	73	75	89
Other provisions	460	(109)	(109)	(109)	(109)	(109)	(109)
Depreciation	1,479	1,735	1,769	1,810	1,856	1,909	2,005
Amortisation of intangible assets	310	310	310	310	310	310	310
Change in working capital	376	237	119	135	155	179	186
Cash flow from operations	3,270	3,091	3,099	3,255	3,430	3,630	3,680
Capital expenditure	(1,391)	(3,039)	(2,685)	(2,797)	(2,929)	(3,086)	(3,225)
Dividends paid	(481)	(520)	(723)	(798)	(879)	(968)	(892)
Change in net cash/net debt	1,397	(469)	(309)	(340)	(378)	(424)	(438)
Per share statistics							
Shares issued (million)	326.8	326.8	326.8	326.8	326.8	326.8	326.8
EPS after goodwill amortization	1.79	2.39	2.67	2.97	3.29	3.67	3.46
DPS	1.47	1.59	2.21	2.44	2.69	2.96	2.73
Share price	41.92						

Acquisition arithmetic ($ million)

Date of acquisition	End Year 1
Share price ($)	41.92
Offer premium	*20.0%*
Offer price per share	50.31
Valuation of target equity	16,439
% paid in shares	*100.0%*
% paid in cash	*0.0%*
New shares issued (m)	415
Equity created on acquisition	16,439
Debt created on acquisition	0
Debt assumed on acquisition	7,550
Minority assumed on acquisition	282
Acquisition enterprise value	**24,271**
Goodwill created on acquisition	15,979
Prior goodwill	9,521
Proforma goodwill	**25,500**
Proforma acquiror net debt	**30,988**

Synergies ($ million)

Year	0	1	2	3	4	5	6
Addition to target sales			*0.0%*	*1.0%*	*1.0%*	*1.0%*	*1.0%*
Reduction in target costs			*0.0%*	*0.1%*	*0.1%*	*0.1%*	*0.1%*
Restructuring cost			(641)	0	0	0	0
Addition to target revenue			0	662	684	710	736
Reduction in target cost			0	62	64	66	69
Change to EBITDA			**(641)**	**724**	**748**	**776**	**805**
Change to tax charge			221	(250)	(259)	(269)	(279)
Change to Net Profit			**(420)**	**474**	**489**	**507**	**526**

Consolidation ($ million)

Year	Add-Brand				Add-Brand plus Magna				
	0	1	Adj	Proforma	2	3	4	5	6
Interest rate (Acquiror)	*4.1%*	*4.1%*			*4.1%*	*4.1%*	*4.1%*	*4.1%*	*4.1%*
Tax rate (Acquiror)	*35.3%*	*25.7%*			*25.7%*	*25.7%*	*25.7%*	*25.7%*	*25.7%*
Profit and loss account									
Acquiror sales	244,524	254,305			264,477	275,056	286,058	297,501	309,401
Target sales	0	0			64,293	66,212	68,412	70,957	73,597
Synergy revenues	0	0			0	662	684	710	736
Sales	**244,524**	**254,305**			**328,770**	**341,930**	**355,155**	**369,168**	**383,734**
Acquiror EBITDA	17,076	17,759			18,469	19,208	19,977	20,776	21,607
Target EBITDA	0	0			4,010	4,154	4,321	4,514	4,682
Synergy EBITDA	0	0			(641)	724	748	776	805
EBITDA	**17,076**	**17,759**			**21,838**	**24,087**	**25,046**	**26,066**	**27,093**
Acquiror depreciation	(3,432)	(3,569)			(3,712)	(3,861)	(4,015)	(4,176)	(4,343)
Target depreciation	0	0			(1,769)	(1,810)	(1,856)	(1,909)	(2,005)
Depreciation	(3,432)	(3,569)			(5,481)	(5,670)	(5,871)	(6,084)	(6,347)
Acquiror amortisation	0	0			0	0	0	0	0
Target amortisation	0	0			(310)	(310)	(310)	(310)	(310)
Amortisation	0	0			(310)	(310)	(310)	(310)	(310)
EBIT	**13,644**	**14,190**			**16,047**	**18,106**	**18,865**	**19,671**	**20,436**
Non recurring items	0	0			0	0	0	0	0
Net interest	(925)	(941)			(1,294)	(1,330)	(1,348)	(1,370)	(1,390)
Pre-tax profit	**12,719**	**13,249**			**14,753**	**16,776**	**17,516**	**18,302**	**19,046**
Taxation	(4,487)	(3,405)			(3,792)	(4,312)	(4,502)	(4,704)	(4,895)
Net profit	**8,232**	**9,844**			**10,962**	**12,465**	**13,014**	**13,598**	**14,151**
Acquiror earnings from associates	0	0			0	0	0	0	0
Target earnings from associates	0	0			0	0	0	0	0
Earnings from associates	0	0			0	0	0	0	0
Acquiror minority	(193)	(236)			(246)	(256)	(266)	(277)	(288)
Target minority	0	0			(67)	(67)	(67)	(67)	(67)
Minority interest	(193)	(236)			(313)	(323)	(333)	(344)	(355)
Attributable profit	**8,039**	**9,607**			**10,648**	**12,142**	**12,681**	**13,254**	**13,796**

Consolidation ($ million)

Year	Add-Brand				Add-Brand plus Magna				
	0	1	Adj	Proforma	2	3	4	5	6
Closing balance sheet									
Acquiror financial assets	0	0	0	0	0	0	0	0	0
Target financial assets	0	0	271	271	271	271	271	271	271
Other financial assets	0	0	271	271	271	271	271	271	271
Goodwill	9,521	9,521	15,979	25,500	25,500	25,500	25,500	25,500	25,500
Acquiror tangible and intangibles assets	54,681	56,868	0	56,868	59,143	61,509	63,969	66,528	69,189
Target tangible and intangibles assets	0	0	15,159	15,159	15,765	16,442	17,204	18,071	18,982
Other tangible and intangibles assets	54,681	56,868	15,159	72,028	74,908	77,951	81,173	84,599	88,171
Total fixed assets	**64,202**	**66,389**	**31,410**	**97,799**	**100,680**	**103,723**	**106,945**	**110,371**	**113,942**
Acquiror non-cash working capital	901	937	0	937	975	1,014	1,054	1,096	1,140
Target non-cash working capital	0	0	(4,414)	(4,414)	(4,533)	(4,669)	(4,824)	(5,003)	(5,189)
Non-cash working capital	901	937	(4,414)	(3,477)	(3,559)	(3,655)	(3,770)	(3,907)	(4,049)
Capital employed	**65,103**	**67,326**	**26,996**	**94,322**	**97,121**	**100,067**	**103,176**	**106,464**	**109,893**
Net debt	22,643	23,438	7,550	30,988	32,342	32,767	33,252	33,803	34,250
Acquiror pension liabilities	0	0	0	0	0	0	0	0	0
Target pension liabilities	0	0	1,222	1,222	1,292	1,364	1,437	1,512	1,601
Pension liabilities	0	0	1,222	1,222	1,292	1,364	1,437	1,512	1,601
Acquiror other deferred LT liabilities	1,761	1,761	0	1,761	1,761	1,761	1,761	1,761	1,761
Target other deferred LT liabilities	0	0	1,503	1,503	1,394	1,286	1,177	1,069	960
Other deferred LT liabilities	1,761	1,761	1,503	3,264	3,155	3,047	2,938	2,830	2,721
Acquiror minority	1,362	1,598	0	1,598	1,844	2,100	2,366	2,643	2,931
Target minority	0	0	282	282	349	416	484	551	618
Minority interest	1,362	1,598	282	1,880	2,193	2,516	2,850	3,194	3,549
Shareholders' funds	39,337	40,529	16,439	56,968	58,139	60,374	62,699	65,126	67,773
Capital employed	**65,103**	**67,326**	**26,996**	**94,322**	**97,121**	**100,067**	**103,176**	**106,464**	**109,893**
Net debt/equity	55.6%	55.6%		52.7%	53.6%	52.1%	50.7%	49.5%	48.0%
Check	0.0	0.0		0.0	0.0	0.0	0.0	0.0	0.0

Consolidation ($ million)

	Add-Brand				Add-Brand plus Magna				
Year	0	1	Adj	Proforma	2	3	4	5	6
Cash flow									
Attributable profit	8,039	9,607			10,648	12,142	12,681	13,254	13,796
Minority interest	193	236			313	323	333	344	355
Dividends - earnings from associates	0	0			0	0	0	0	0
Acquiror pension provisions	0	0			0	0	0	0	0
Target pension provisions	0	0			70	71	73	75	89
Pension provisions	0	0			70	71	73	75	89
Acquiror other provisions	1,758	0			0	0	0	0	0
Target other provisions	0	0			(109)	(109)	(109)	(109)	(109)
Other provisions	1,758	0			(109)	(109)	(109)	(109)	(109)
Depreciation	3,432	3,569			5,481	5,670	5,871	6,084	6,347
Amortisation	0	0			310	310	310	310	310
Acquiror change in working capital	(890)	(36)			(37)	(39)	(41)	(42)	(44)
Target change in working capital	0	0			119	135	155	179	186
Change in working capital	(890)	(36)			81	96	115	137	142
Cash flow from operations	**12,532**	**13,377**			**16,795**	**18,505**	**19,275**	**20,096**	**20,931**
Acquiror capital expenditure	(9,709)	(5,757)			(5,987)	(6,226)	(6,475)	(6,734)	(7,004)
Target capital expenditure	0	0			(2,685)	(2,797)	(2,929)	(3,086)	(3,225)
Capital expenditure	(9,709)	(5,757)			(8,672)	(9,023)	(9,404)	(9,820)	(10,229)
Acquirer dividends paid	(4,560)	(8,415)			(8,755)	(9,109)	(9,476)	(9,859)	(10,257)
Target dividends paid	0	0			(723)	(798)	(879)	(968)	(892)
Dividends paid/shares repurchased	(4,560)	(8,415)			(9,478)	(9,907)	(10,355)	(10,827)	(11,149)
Change in net cash/net debt	**(1,737)**	**(795)**			**(1,355)**	**(425)**	**(484)**	**(551)**	**(447)**
Per share statistics									
Shares issued (million)	4,395.0	4,395.0			4,810.1	4,810.1	4,810.1	4,810.1	4,810.1
EPS	1.83	2.19			2.21	2.52	2.64	2.76	2.87
(Dilution)/enhancement	*0.0%*	*0.0%*			*(2.7%)*	*6.7%*	*7.1%*	*7.6%*	*7.7%*

As with the initial valuation, a key objective should be to make as transparent as possible from where the forecasts are derived. If it is possible to split out the sources of the operating projections between the two underlying company models and the assumed synergies, then this is very helpful. Because we are not assuming any changes in capital requirements, in our case there are only really two lines of the forecasts that need to be split out: revenue and fixed costs.

What will be very different, post-merger, is the financial items, since the level of debt and the shape of the cash flows will be quite different, as, quite possibly, will be the level of dividends paid out, though for simplicity in this model we have retained the combined payout previously forecast. In addition, as we have seen, the equity of the target company disappears on consolidation. So our projections of debt and equity will need to be recalculated, although, because we have not altered our assumptions regarding capital expenditure and working capital requirements (and have not written any assets up to fair value on the acquisition), the asset side of our consolidated balance sheet has remained unchanged, other than through the capitalisation of goodwill. In reality, much of what we have capitalised as goodwill would probably be treated as intangible assets capitalised on consolidation. As discussed in chapter five, if these were then amortised this would depress profits but have no impact on cash flows.

In addition, forecast levels of consolidated capital requirements might differ from those assumed previously for the separate companies. But these are not difficult additional modelling adjustments to make.

8.4.1 What to do with consolidated forecasts

Companies have to plan, and it is obvious why the management of the bidder will need to have proforma estimates of its projected consolidated accounts. But investors will react to published proforma figures. They may or may not possess information that would permit them to undertake the kind of valuation that the bidding company would have undertaken. In addition, banks will often have extended loans with covenants attached to them that may be triggered by acquisitions. In some cases, loans may automatically become repayable in the case of a change of ownership. In others, there may be restrictions on the level of balance sheet leverage that a company may undertake before triggering repayment.

Credit analysis often becomes a fascinating business when bids occur as the position of different categories of creditor may be very different. Owners of bonds tend to be less well protected than bank creditors, and in extreme cases where the bidder risks becoming over-stretched by a cash transaction, it is quite possible for the value of bank debt in the target to rise (because it is secured against assets and will have to be repaid) while the value of bonds fall (because the consolidated balance sheet that represents their only security will be weaker than that of the target currently).

So, if we assume that we are outside the company, rather than in its corporate planning or treasury departments, then we shall primarily use the forecasts in exhibit 7.14 to calculate the impact of the deal on projected earnings per share and leverage ratios. If these are such as to result in unacceptable effects on either, then this may result in a forced decision regarding financing.

Cash or debt funded acquisitions generally enhance earnings per share, because the return on the investment is often higher than the cost of borrowing (though this clearly does not necessarily make it a good deal), and equity funded acquisitions will be either earnings enhancing or diluting depending on the multiple to earnings of the two companies. They will enhance earnings per share if the target's shares are acquired on a lower multiple to earnings than those of the bidder, and dilute earnings per share if the target's shares are acquired on a higher multiple to earnings than those of the bidder. So if earnings per share are the priority, use cash or debt. Again, the impact on earnings per share says nothing about whether or not value has been added by the acquisition.

On the other hand, borrowing to fund a cash acquisition will inevitably raise leverage, unless the target is under-leveraged, in which case the projected consolidated balance sheet may be acceptable. If a company buys another company which is close to it in size and not hugely underleveraged, then it is improbable that a cash acquisition will work without putting undue strain on the balance sheet. Such deals are customarily financed with new shares. In our case an all-share acquisition somewhat enhances prospective EPS, but results in gently declining book gearing. If the aim were to maintain leverage for the combined group then there would be scope for some increase in projected dividend payments.

8.5 A history of growth by acquisition

Some companies grow organically, others by acquisition. They will end up with very different looking balance sheets, even if they now comprise similar bundles of assets. So we need not merely to be able to analyse proposed deals but also to analyse companies whose accounts reflect a legacy of growth through acquisition.

8.5.1 Accounting for Goodwill

Both IFRS and US GAAP prohibit the amortisation of goodwill. Under normal circumstances it therefore remains permanently in the balance sheet at historical cost. It is however subject to annual impairment tests, and in the event of its value being deemed to be lower than its book carrying value, the surplus will have to be written off. But as we have seen much of what would once have been capitalised as goodwill is now represented by capitalised intangible assets, which may or may not be amortised depending on whether their value is assumed to be impaired over time, or not.

8.5.2 What should we do?

From the valuation perspective, the key questions are why or whether we should have worried about earnings after amortisation, and what balance sheet figure for goodwill we should be using to determine the company's profitability.

Our answer to these questions is as follows:

1. Amortisation of intangible assets may result in double counting of costs, if the combined group both charges it and the cost of replacing the assets (such as research or marketing) to the income statement. In that case the amortisation charge should be added back when assessing profitability.

2. In assessing the operating performance of a company, and in forecasting its profits, returns on capital excluding goodwill and capitalised intangibles are the key driver, since the company will not build a pile of goodwill on its new investments (unless it is a serial acquirer). Capitalised intangibles could be handled in one of two ways: either add back the amortisation relating to them, or capitalise the assets that have been and continue to be generated organically. Either way, avoid double counting.

3. It is important that the full value that is capitalised, however it is capitalised, is justified in the end, otherwise value has been eroded (this is not a contradiction to the sentences above).

4. For many companies, balance sheets understate economic capital, because much of what was really an investment is treated as if it were an operating cost.

8.5.3 Other intangibles do matter

Let us just kill off the last statement first. Imagine that a consumer goods company had grown entirely organically. All of the cost of building its brand would have been written off as operating costs. So the balance sheet would be hugely understated. Now imagine that a competitor, with an identical set of products, had built its business partly organically and partly by acquisition, which would imply capitalising those acquired either as intangible assets or as goodwill. The solution here is to remove the goodwill and to adjust the balance sheets of both companies to reflect the investments that they have made in building their brands, including investment made by companies that have been absorbed into the acquirer. Clearly, there are limits to what is practically feasible here, but this is the direction in which we believe that equity valuation should move.

8.5.4 Why treat goodwill as we suggest

Returning to the statements that relate directly to goodwill, the reason why it has always been inappropriate to consider amortisation is that goodwill is not an asset that will have to be replaced. We depreciate plant and amortise some intangible assets because they are wasting assets, and there is a cost to depleting them. But this does not apply to goodwill, which is actually a capitalisation of future value creation. For that reason, goodwill write-offs do matter, despite being non-cash costs. They illustrate the degree to which overpayment was based on excessively optimistic expectations.

8.5.5 Be careful with forecasts!

Turning to forecasts and valuation, it makes no difference whether we value a company with respect to economic profit generated on the balance sheet including goodwill or excluding goodwill. If we include goodwill, we shall have a large balance sheet on which we are making low returns. If we exclude goodwill, we shall have a small balance sheet, on which we are making higher returns. It makes no difference whether we discover that the net present value of the economic profit in the first case is a small positive, or whether we discover in the second case that it is a large positive, which just exceeds the goodwill that we have acquired. What is crucial is that when forecasting, returns on new investments are based on the underlying profitability of the assets in the balance sheet excluding goodwill. Failure to do this will result in undervaluation, but the problem will then lie not with the treatment of goodwill, but with the forecasts.

8.5.6 A worked example

Let us illustrate the point with a simple example. Suppose that an acquirer were to bid for a target for which the key statistics are that it has book value of 1,000, earns a 15% return on capital, and grows at 5% annually. The appropriate discount rate is 10%. Then fair value (if we assume that there are no synergies) is as follows (see chapter one for the explanation):

$$1000 \times (0.15-0.05) / (0.10-0.05) = 1000 \times 2 = 2000$$

Now, suppose the acquisition is completed, the balance sheet of the acquirer will include 1,000 of new tangible assets and 1,000 of goodwill. Its profit will be 1000 x 15% = 150, and it will therefore, in its first year, earn a return on capital of 150/2000, or 7.5%. Much bad analysis will be produced at this point, claiming that it has not earned its cost of capital on the transaction!

The truth, of course, is that the existing business justifies a value of 1,500. The balancing 500 is the net present value that will be created by the future investment stream.

What is happening is that we have a growing pile of prospective new capital on which we are earning 15% against a WACC of 10%, and this adds value to the existing capital which earns 7.5% on 2,000, or 15% on 1,000, depending on whether or not we capitalise the goodwill.

Starting with the existing capital, in the first case (capitalise goodwill) we have a PV for the negative economic profit of:

$$2000*(0.075-0.10)/0.10 = -500$$

so the value of the existing capital is 2000-500 = 1500.

And in the second case (do not capitalise goodwill) we have a PV for the positive economic profit of:

$$1000*(0.15-0.10)/0.10 = 500$$

so the value of the existing capital is 1000+500 = 1500.

This makes quite clear that the question of what to capitalise and what not to capitalise matters not so much to our value for the existing capital, which is worth 1,500 either way, but to our value of the future growth opportunities, where it is vital that we assume returns of 15%, and not 7.5%. The (rather unpleasant) formula is as follows (see Mathematical Appendix for the proof):

$$PVGO = NOPAT*g/ROCE*(ROCE-WACC)/[WACC*(WACC-g)]$$

Or:

$$150*0.05/0.15*(0.15-0.10)/[0.10*(0.10-0.05)] = 500$$

so the business is, as we thought, worth 1500+500 = 2000.

Goodwill capitalises expected economic profit

Our recommendation would be to show the calculation with goodwill capitalised, and with the probable result that the existing capital will appear not to be earning its cost of capital. The new capital should earn a stream of economic profit, or the deal really was a disaster! The net effect will be that as the forecasts extend into the future, the total amount of economic profit generated turns positive. The key question then becomes: 'Is the PV of the future stream of economic profit positive?' If yes, then it was a good deal, and if no then it was a bad one, and the negative figure is the measure of the impairment charge that should be taken in the company's accounts. In our worked example the PV of the future economic profit is -500 (on the existing capital) and +500 (on the new capital) so the total is zero (fair value).

An alternative, but less transparent approach, is to project and value the economic profit using capital excluding goodwill, and then to check that the PV of the future economic profit exceeds the goodwill in the balance sheet. In our worked example the PV of the future economic profit is +500 (on the existing capital) and +500 (on the new capital) so the total exactly matches the 1,000 of goodwill paid (fair value). The same point is being made either way: goodwill represents the capitalised value of the stream of economic profit expected to be generated by the transaction.

Analytical steps

You may remember our analysis of Dandy's return on capital employed in chapter five. There, exhibit 5.9 showed four different calculations for profitability. We argued in that chapter that if one were valuing Dandy it would, when capitalising future growth opportunities, be crucial to use the figure that excludes goodwill from measures of capital (because new assets will not have a pile of goodwill put on top of them). But if a deal is to be justified we must, over time, justify the goodwill created on the acquisition. The analytical steps when modelling and valuing a company with goodwill in its balance sheet are therefore as follows:

1. When projecting returns on new investments, assume that new capital earns a return that relates to the profitability of the business excluding goodwill (and with other intangible assets capitalised). In Dandy's case, this gave us a figure of 15%.

2. When projecting consolidated accounts, leave the goodwill in the balance sheet. This is how it will appear when published, and it is a reminder that the company's management has only added value if the fair value of the company's assets exceeds the book value, including goodwill.

3. Make sure that the valuation methodology that you use explicitly differentiates between the return that is being generated by currently installed capital and the return that is assumed from newly invested incremental capital.

Chapter Eight

Conclusions and Continuations

1. Conclusions

It has been a consistent theme of this book that while there are a number of techniques to estimate the intrinsic value of a company, the assumptions that inform them will almost always be driven off an interpretation of the company's historical financial statements. Our aim is to enable the reader to transfer from an analysis of historical performance to a projection of consolidated accounts to the derivation of a value.

In this process, there is much information provided by financial statements over and above that which may be extracted from the cash flow statement. Specifically, balance sheets increasingly reflect fair values of assets and liabilities (but not all assets and liabilities), and profit and loss accounts reflect accruals that contain useful information about future cash flows. Whatever the mechanics of the model used, ignoring this information will merely result in poorer valuations.

The European adoption of IFRS more than a decade ago – which brought more information onto the balance sheet and increased the use of fair value accounting – created both advantages and disadvantages for those using financial statements for company valuation. The advantages being that balance sheets became better indicators of the fair value of the existing business, and that income statements became better indicators of accrued value creation, whether or not they reflect cash transactions. The disadvantages were a greater dislocation between reported earnings and cash flows, as well as much greater subjectivity in calculating balance sheet values. It was the last of these concerns that was brought into sharp focus during the subsequent financial crisis, with questions raised as to whether fair value accounting allowed companies to overstate balance sheet values and 'hide' their risk exposure.

Whilst the financial crisis has not entirely dimmed appetites for fair value accounting, it appears that the more recent accounting standards provide some improvement on their predecessor standards in two key areas.

The first of these is the importance of robust disclosure, particularly disclosures which provide qualitative information regarding contractual arrangements and quantitative disclosures concerning the sensitivities and key assumptions in fair value calculations.

Using fair values in accounting is only half the answer – the disclosures supporting them are essential to understanding whether these are appropriate for use in valuations.

The second of these – particularly for industrial companies – is the importance of being able to adequately understand the assets, liabilities and flows related to operating activities separately from the assets and liabilities used to finance them. We view the new revenue recognition and lease accounting standards as helpful in supporting this separation since they explicitly require the financing component of certain contractual arrangements to be presented separately from 'operational' revenues and expenses.

While regarding the latest IFRS developments as an improvement in terms of the quality of the information that they provide, we would not wish to imply that it is perfect or the end of a process. In economic terms, what we want to know is the accrual of value that was achieved during a year, with profit fully reflecting all accruals of value during the year. Bringing more onto the balance sheet, marking more to fair value and ensuring appropriate disclosure and presentation of these items is clearly a step in this direction. In addition, our emphasis would always be on comprehensive income, not merely on the accruals that are reflected in the profit and loss account.

Where companies do provide information about fair values, this should always be substituted for book values, and the accruals included in comprehensive income. But where fair values are not provided, there will always be a choice as to whether to use book values, to try to build them up to reflect actual historical investment, or to estimate their fair values. And, just as balance sheet information does not reflect economic value, so depreciation does not reflect impairment. It is again a matter of choice whether to stick with straight line depreciation, or whether to try to estimate what the actual impairment of value has been.

For this reason, we have tried hard not to be excessively dogmatic about methodology. What is an almost essential adjustment for one company may be relatively trivial for another. We believe that it is more practical to bring an approach to modelling and valuation than it is to bring a standardised template which may be inappropriate to the company being analysed. And our approach would be to retain as far as possible the structure of profit and loss account and balance sheet, with such adjustments as are necessary to approximate to economic reality. How far to go is often a matter of judgement and of available resources.

2. Continuations

2.1 Discount rates

As we discussed in chapter two, there is something rather unsatisfactory about the assumption that the only risk that matters is market risk, and it is an assumption that we completely ignore when looking at illiquid investments, such as venture capital, or when we explain the risk premium of corporate debt in terms of default risk, rather than in terms of its market Beta. In this book we have largely retained the CAPM framework for the pragmatic reason that it is the most widely used, and that the advantages to be derived from alternatives, other than for illiquid investments, are questionable. In particular, Arbitrage Pricing Theory (APT) seems to be better able to explain returns after the event, but there is little evidence for its offering an improved prediction of returns.

One radical alternative to standard CAPM is to assume that the appropriate discount rate is always the risk-free rate, and then to deduct the cost of insuring against all other risks. Clearly, there are not market prices for all risks, but there are for many of them. Corporate risk may be broken down into the following five categories:

1. Market risk

2. Operational risk

3. Credit risk

4. Liquidity risk

5. Political risk

Many of these can be hedged, depending on the industry in which the company operates. So an alternative approach to valuation would be to discount expected cash flows at the risk free rate and separately to deduct a cost for each category of risk, in the same way that when using an APV to value a company we valued its assets and its tax shelter by discounting at the unleveraged cost of equity and then deducted a default risk. Clearly, in the present case we would have to make numerous deductions, and there is a problem with duration. For an asset, its cash flows are finite, and the associated risks are more easily quantifiable than for a going concern.

There is a connection between the direction in which this line of thinking takes us and our next suggestion for continuations, namely contingent claims theory. Because option models, on which contingent claims theory is based, discount future values at the risk-free rate and then calculate the appropriate 'certainty equivalent probabilities' with which to put weights on different outcomes. This is the equivalent of putting a cost on insurance against unwelcome outcomes.

2.2 Contingent claims

This book has concerned itself entirely with the derivation of intrinsic value, and has largely ignored the contingent claims approach to company analysis and valuation. The latter approach represents an extension of options pricing theory to the valuation of companies. It sees the value of the shares in a company as being largely derived from underlying factors, with the result that it can be seen as a bundle of options on the underlying factors. The classic example is the undeveloped oilfield, which has a negative net present value using current oil price expectations, but which clearly has a market value based on the probability that oil price expectations will rise.

Other real options are the scrap value of existing plant (a put option), the ability to expand a project cheaply (a call option) and the ability to discontinue a research and production programme at any one of a series of decision points (a series of embedded call options). Once one starts to think in these terms it is tempting to see real options almost everywhere.

So why have we not focused more on option pricing, other than in the very specific area of companies that are almost insolvent, where the equity can be seen as a call on the value of the underlying assets with the par value of the debt as the exercise price?

The first reason is that just as the value of equity approximates quite closely to its intrinsic value when the market value of a company's assets is well above the value of its debt, so the value of most assets is quite well approximated by intrinsic valuation, unless they have a negative or very small intrinsic value. Real options tend to be most important in certain quite extreme situations. For a large, mature, financially stable company, they may be useful tools when management values individual investment decisions, but they may not be that important to an overall valuation of the company.

The second reason is scepticism as to the applicability of option pricing models, which were designed to value financial options, to real assets. This does not in any way invalidate the principles of contingent claims. It merely suggests that rather more work may need to be done before the approach yields generally satisfactory results.

To see why, let us return to the example of the out-of-the-money oilfield. The value of an option depends on five factors: the exercise price; the market value of the asset; the volatility of the market value of the asset; the length of the option; and the risk-free rate of return. Textbooks on real options generally imply that the volatility of the asset that is being valued is the same as the volatility of the price from which the asset value is derived, but this is clearly not true. Even if it is true that the annual volatility of the oil price is, say, 20%, and that we can therefore propagate forward a series of possible oil prices in future years, which can be used to value our option, it is not the case that the resulting volatility of the oilfield will be 20%, or that it will even be symmetrical to rises or falls in the oil price. Lower prices will have a progressively bigger impact on value, as the impact of price on margin becomes progressively greater. In addition, if the oil price spikes up to a high level or down to a low one, future price expectations do not react proportionately, so it is a forward price curve that we should be using to value the asset at each node in our projections, not a spot price.

The volatility point is even harder for embedded call options such as those implied by drug pipelines. One approach to the problem is to use the volatility of shares in small quoted biotech companies as a proxy for the volatility of the value of the asset, but there is no reason to assume that this will be similar for different stages in the progress of the drug towards clinical approval, each of which has to be valued as an option-on-an-option.

Putting a clear time limit on the option is also often very difficult. This is not the case if the company owns or has an option on a licence, a patent or a franchise with a set life, but this is often not the case. Finally, if the contingent claims approach is to be taken seriously then values will often be derived from options on a variety of underlying factors, which will probably be correlated with one another. The skills required to value this kind of derivative are of a high order even in the financial markets for which the options were derived, let alone in the more opaque asset markets to which contingent claims theory would have to apply them.

We do not wish to imply any scepticism about the validity of real options pricing theory, or to doubt that there is considerable scope for advances that would make it generally useable in company valuation. But we would cast doubt on some of the more optimistic claims that have already been made for the approach. It is more work-in-progress than tried and tested methodology.

Further Reading

Introduction

This book has consciously attempted to span gaps between the interpretation of accounts, company modelling, and valuation theory and practice. Rather than offer the reader a lengthy list of academic sources, we shall instead suggest a list of books that are in print and readily available, to which the reader may be interested to refer for either additional information, or for a fuller representation of ideas covered in this book.

Corporate finance theory

The two texts that we would recommend in this area are the following:

- *Financial Theory and Corporate Policy*, Copeland, Weston and Kuldeep, Pearson New International Edition, 2013

- *Principles of Corporate Finance*, Brealey, Marcus, and Myers, McGraw-Hill Education, 2014

The two books cover much the same ground, introducing all of the key theoretical elements of modern finance theory. They differ in emphasis, with Brealey et al offering more practical applications and intuitive explanation, and Copeland et al being the more theoretical and mathematically rigorous. Both offer extensive bibliographies for the underlying academic articles.

Interpretation of accounts

Again, we recommend two books on this topic:

- *Financial Accounting: An Introduction*, Weetman, Pearson, 2016

- *Financial Statement Analysis under IFRS*, Lee and Taylor, Financial Edge Publication, 6 Edition, 2018

The first book is an excellent and detailed run through the basics of accounting. This would be useful for filling in some gaps in knowledge. It adopts a preparers perspective rather than being directly targeted at those who use financial statements for valuation and analysis. The second book, by two of the authors of this book, takes a deliberately international perspective, and focuses more on how financial statements are constructed as the basis for understanding and interpretation. As the title suggests, it focuses very much on how users of financial statements can extract information for, amongst other things, investment analysis and valuation. It has been published very recently and so is up to date for recent changes such as IFRS 16 *Leases* and IFRS 15 *Revenue from Contracts with Customers.*

Practical forecasting and valuation

Some of the books listed below cover both forecasting and valuation, though they mainly focus on valuation. We recommend five books that take rather different approaches from one another.

- *Cash Flow Return on Investment: CFROI Valuation, A Total System Approach to Valuing the Firm*, B.J. Madden, Butterworth-Heinemann, 1999

- *Creating Shareholder Value: A Guide for Managers and Investors*, A. Rappaport, Simon and Schuster, 1998

- *Valuation: Measuring and Managing the Value of Companies*, Koller, Goedhart, Wessels. John Wiley, 2015.

- *Financial Statement Analysis and Security Valuation*, S.H. Penman, McGraw Hill, 2012

- *Investment Valuation: Tools and Techniques for Determining the Value of Any Asset*, A. Damodaran, John Wiley, 2012

The first two books are based on one particular valuation approach and can be recommended as detailed expositions of the chosen methodology. The other books are more balanced in their approach. Koller et al concentrates on techniques of performance appraisal, forecasting and valuation, and continues into the realm of applying real options theory to company valuation. It also has sections on the analysis of financial companies. Penman's book is avowedly aimed at 'going with the grain' of accounting information, and puts great emphasis on the importance of accruals and the interpretation of accounts. Finally, although Damodaran's book does cover the valuation of all assets it is predominantly a discussion of approaches to valuation models, including a very useful discussion of the use of multiples and their relationship to intrinsic value methodologies.

Appendices

IAS and IFRS in, or coming into, force

IFRS 1   First time adoption of International Financial Reporting Standards

IFRS 2   Share Based Payment

IFRS 3   Business Combinations

IFRS 4   Insurance Contracts

IFRS 5   Non-current assets Held for Sale and Discontinued Operations

IFRS 6   Exploration for and Evaluation of Mineral Assets

IFRS 7   Financial Instruments: Disclosures

IFRS 8   Operating Segments

IFRS 9   Financial Instruments

IFRS 10   Consolidated Financial Statements

IFRS 11   Joint Arrangements

IFRS 12   Disclosure of Interests in Other Entities

IFRS 13   Fair Value Measurement

IFRS 14   Regulatory Deferral Accounts

IFRS 15   Revenue from Contracts with Customers

IFRS 16   Leases

IFRS 17   Insurance Contracts

IAS 1   Presentation of Financial Statements

IAS 2   Inventories

IAS 7   Statement of Cash Flows

IAS 8   Accounting Policies, Changes in Accounting Estimates and Errors.

IAS 10   Events after the Reporting period

IAS 12   Income Taxes

IAS 16   Property, Plant and Equipment

IAS 19   Employee Benefits

IAS 20   Accounting for Government Grants and Disclosure of Government Assistance

IAS 21   The Effects of Changes in Foreign Exchange Rates

IAS 23   Borrowing Costs

IAS 24   Related Party Disclosures

IAS 26   Accounting and Reporting by Retirement Benefit Plans

IAS 27   Separate Financial Statements

IAS 28   Investments in Associates and Joint Ventures

IAS 29   Financial Reporting in Hyperinflationary Economies

IAS 32   Financial Instruments: Presentation

IAS 33   Earnings Per Share

IAS 34   Interim Financial Reporting

IAS 36   Impairment of Assets

IAS 37   Provisions, Contingent Liabilities and Contingent Assets

IAS 38   Intangible Assets

IAS 39   Financial Instruments: Recognition and Measurement[1]

IAS 40   Investment Property

IAS 41   Agriculture

---

1   IAS 39 was largely superseded by IFRS 9 on 1 Jan 2018, except for insurance companies which may choose to continue applying IAS 39 until the adoption of IFRS 17 on 1 Jan 2022.

Analysis Formulae

1. Gordon Growth Model

$P=D(1+g)/(1+r)+D(1+g)^2/(1+r)^2+...D(1+g)^n/(1+g)^n$

$U=(1+g)/(1+r)$

$P=DU+DU^2+ ...DU^n$

$PU = DU^2 + DU^3 +...DU^{n+1}$

$P-PU=DU-DU^{n+1}$

[As n tends to infinity, U^{n+1} tends to zero]

$P-PU=DU$

$P-P(1+g)/(1+r)=D(1+g)/(1+r)$

$P(1+r)-P(1+g)= D(1+g) \quad P+Pr-P-Pg=D(1+g)$

$P(r-g)=D(1+g)$

$P=D(1+g)/(r-g)$

2. Growth and retention

$B_t=B_{t-1}+I-D$

$B_t=B_t-1+B_{t-1}ROEb$

$B_t/B_t-_1=1+ROE\ b$

$B_t/B_t-1-1=ROEb$

3. Equivalence of DDM and economic profit valuation models

$P_0=\Sigma\ D_t/(1+k)^t$

$B_t=B_{t-1}+E_t-D_t$

$E_t=D_t+B_t-B_{t-1}$

$X_t=E_t-k^*B_{t-1}$

$X_t=D_t+B_t-B_{t-1}-k^*B_{t-1}$

$D_t=X_t+(1+k)^*B_{t-1}-B_t$

$P_0=\Sigma\ [X_t+(1+k)^*B_{t-1}-B_t]/(1+k)^t$

$P_0=\Sigma\ X_t/(1+k)^t+\Sigma\ B_{t-1}/(1+k)^{t-1}-\Sigma\ B_t/(1+k)^t$

$P_0=\Sigma\ X_t/(1+k)^t+B_0-B_t/(1+k)^t$

[As t tends to infinity, $B_t/(1+k)^t$ tends to zero]

$P_0=B_0+\Sigma\ X_t/(1+k)^t$

4. Equivalence of dividend discount model and discounted cash flow model (where D is dividend, I is interest, k is cost of equity and r is cost of debt)

$V_F = FCF/(wacc-g)$

$V_F = (D+I-V_Dg)/(wacc-g)$

$V_F = (D+I-V_Dg)/[(kV_E/V_F+rV_D/V_F)-g]$

$D+I-V_Dg = V_F[(kV_E/V_F+rV_D/V_F)-g]$

$D+I-V_Dg = kV_E+rV_D-V_Fg$

$D+I-V_Dg = kV_E+rV_D-V_Eg-V_Dg$

$D = kV_E-V_Eg \quad (as\ I = rV_D)$

$D = V_E(k-g)$

$V_E = D/(k-g)$

5. Leveraged WACC formulae for different discounting of Tax Shelters

$V_F = V_A+I/(K_{TS}-g)tV_D$

$V_D = V_FW_D$

$V_F = V_A/[1-I/(K_{TS}-g)tW_D]$

$FCF/(WACC-g) = FCF/(K_A-g)/[1-I/(K_{TS}-g)tW_D]$

$WACC-g = (K_A-g)/[1-I/(K_{TS}-g)tW_D]$

$WACC = KA -(K_A-g)/(K_{TS}-g)ItW_D$

If $K_{TS}=K_A$

$WACC=K_A-ltW_D$

If $K_{TS}=I$

$WACC=K_A-(K_A-g)/(I-g)ltW_D$

6. Leveraged Beta formulae for different discounting of Tax Shelters

$V_F=V_A+V_{TS}$

$B_AV_A+B_{TS}V_{TS}=B_LV_E+B_DV_D$

$B_A(V_E+V_D-V_{TS})+B_{TS}V_{TS}=B_LV_E+B_DV_D$

$B_L=B_A(1+V_D/V_E-V_{TS}/V_E)+B_{TS}/V_E-B_DV_D/V_E$

$B_L=B_A(1+V_D/V_E)-B_DV_D/V_E-(B_A-B_{TS})V_{TS}/V_E$

$B_L=B_A(1+V_D/V_E)-B_DV_D/V_E-(B_A-B_{TS})[It/(K_{TS}-g)]V_D/V_E$

If $K_{TS}=K_A$

$B_L=B_A(1+V_D/V_E)-B_DV_D/V_E$

If $K_{TS}=I$ & $g=0$

$B_L=B_A[1+V_D/V_E(1-t)]-B_D(1-t)V_D/V_E$

7. Calculation of Fixed Asset Retirement under constant growth

$R=F/[1+(1+g)+(1+g)^2+...(1+g)^{n-1}]$

$F/R=1+(1+g)+(1+g)^2+...(1+g)^{n-1}$

$F/R(1+g)=(1+g)+(1+g)^2+(1+g)^3+...(1+g)^n$

$F/R-F/R(1+g)=1-(1+g)^n$

$-gF/R=[1-(1+g)^n]$

$R=-gF/[1-(1+g)^n]$

8. Dupont analysis

$R=P/CE=P/S*S/CE$

$CE=D+E$

$Y=RE+RD-ID$

$Y=RE+(R-I)*D$

$Y/E=R+(R-I)*D/E$

$r=R+(R-I)*D/E$

9. Economic profit terminal value

1. $P = D / (COE - g)$ Gordon growth

2. $g = ROE * RR$ Growth/retention

3. $P/B = (D/B) / (COE - g)$ From 1

4. $P/B = [ROE * (1 - RR)] / (COE - g)$ From 3

5. $P/B = (ROE - g) / (COE - g)$ From 2 and 4

If $g = 0$:

6. $P/B = ROE/COE$ From 3

7. $P = B * ROE / COE$ From 6

8. $P - B = B * ROE / COE - B$ From 7

9. $P - B = (B * ROE - B * COE) / COE$ From 8

10. $P - B = B * (ROE - COE) / COE$ From 9

11. $B_t - B_{t-1} = EPS_t * g_t / ROE_t$ From 2

12. $(P_t - P_{t-1}) - (B_t - B_{t-1}) = EPS_t \times g_t / ROE_t * (ROE - COE) / COE$ From 10 and 11

13. $PVGO = EPS_t \times g_t / ROE_t * (ROE - COE) / [COE * (COE - g)]$ From 1 and 12

Index

Milton Keynes UK
Ingram Content Group UK Ltd.
UKHW030633150224
437794UK00002B/41